BIG MEN FEAR ME

D1113801

BIG MEN FEAR ME

The Fast Life and Quick Death of Canada's Most Powerful Media Mogul

Mark Bourrie

BIBLIOASIS

Windsor, Ontario

Copyright © Mark Bourrie, 2022

All rights reserved. No part of this publication may be reproduced or transmitted in any form or by any means, electronic or mechanical, including photocopying, recording, or any information storage and retrieval system, without permission in writing from the publisher or a license from The Canadian Copyright Licensing Agency (Access Copyright). For an Access Copyright license visit www.accesscopyright.ca or call toll free to 1-800-893-5777.

FIRST EDITION

10 9 8 7 6 5 4 3 2 1

Library and Archives Canada Cataloguing in Publication

Title: Big men fear me : the fast life and quick death of Canada's most powerful media mogul / Mark Bourrie.
Names: Bourrie, Mark, 1957– author.
Identifiers: Canadiana (print) 2022027343X | Canadiana (ebook) 20220274193 | ISBN 9781771964937 (softcover) | ISBN 9781771964944 (ebook)
Subjects: LCSH: McCullagh, George, 1905–1952. | LCSH: Newspaper publishing—Canada—History. | LCSH: Publishers and publishing—Canada—Biography. | LCSH: Globe and mail—History. | LCGFT: Biographies.
Classification: LCC PN4913.M375 B68 2022 | DDC 070.5/722092—dc23

Copyedited by Linda Pruessen
Indexed by Allana Amlin
Cover and text designed by Ingrid Paulson

**Canada Council
for the Arts**

**Conseil des Arts
du Canada**
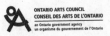
ONTARIO ARTS COUNCIL
CONSEIL DES ARTS DE L'ONTARIO
an Ontario government agency
un organisme du gouvernement de l'Ontario

Canada
ONTARIO | ONTARIO
CREATES | CRÉATIF

Published with the generous assistance of the Canada Council for the Arts, which last year invested $153 million to bring the arts to Canadians throughout the country, and the financial support of the Government of Canada. Biblioasis also acknowledges the support of the Ontario Arts Council (OAC), an agency of the Government of Ontario, which last year funded 1,709 individual artists and 1,078 organizations in 204 communities across Ontario, for a total of $52.1 million, and the contribution of the Government of Ontario through the Ontario Book Publishing Tax Credit and Ontario Creates.

The author acknowledges the support of the Ontario Arts Council's Recommender Grants program.

PRINTED AND BOUND IN CANADA

"There are newspaper publishers and editors in this country, apparently, who think that the freedom of the press was won for the sake of the press. Well, it wasn't. The freedom of the press was won for the sake of the people, and if the newspapers of this country are not prepared now to put aside party considerations and fight for that greater thing, the freedom of the individual, freedom for the ordinary man, then the day will come when the ordinary man will not fight for freedom of the press."

—GRATTAN O'LEARY, 1937

For Cam

CONTENTS

THE FORGOTTEN MAN

This is a book about a man who many people, including those at the centre of economic and political power, expected to be prime minister of Canada. Instead, he died mysteriously when he was just forty-seven years old. You've probably never heard of George McCullagh, because he's been deliberately erased from Canada's history. Toronto columnist Robert Fulford called his biography "one of the great unwritten books in Canadian history."[1] Well, here's his biography. It will be up to you to decide whether it's great.

So, who was George McCullagh and why should you care about him?

George McCullagh was a media rock star. He was the most powerful and dynamic man in Canadian publishing. He was also a giant in the nation's sports world—he was co-owner of the Toronto Maple Leafs and Toronto Argonauts, and had one of the best horse-race stables in Canada. McCullagh moved easily among the elites of the Western world and, though seen as a flawed man by those at the very top of Anglosphere governments, was feared and respected. A poor boy from London, Ontario, who dropped out of school in grade nine, McCullagh founded the *Globe and Mail* in the depth of the Great Depression, when he was just thirty-one years old. The *Globe* and the *Mail and Empire* had been around for decades before McCullagh came on the scene, but they were moribund newspapers that were dying of bad management. He hammered them together and made them the country's most powerful political newspaper. And he deliberately gave the paper its strange name because its initials were—still are—GM, the same as his own.

McCullagh worked his way up from nothing by hiking the backroads of rural Ontario selling newspapers during the terrible recession that followed the end of the First World War and the 1918 flu pandemic. While he rose from those dusty roads to a reporting job in the newsroom of the *Globe*, he dragged his own ball and chain. As a young man he was an alcoholic. Booze masked the fact that he was also bipolar, and that turned out to be the thing that stopped him from becoming a national politician. In the end, it was probably mental illness that killed him.

McCullagh, with the help of William Wright—Canada's richest man and a most bizarre multi-millionaire—became a force in national politics. He advocated for one-party government in Ottawa and at Queen's Park. And, for a while, he tried to convince Ontario's leaders to ditch democracy because partisanship got in the way of decision-making when Canada was struggling through an economic crisis. He used his media platform—his newspaper and airtime that he bought on radio stations across Canada—to start a national right-of-centre anti-democratic populist movement that peaked just before the Second World War. And when that war came, he fought news censorship, drove wedges that helped divide Canada when the country needed unity to fight Hitler, and helped make his best friend the premier of Ontario. When the war ended, he toured Europe and fired up hatred of the Soviets. Then he bought the Toronto *Telegram* and was the leader in Canada's greatest newspaper war.

McCullagh had a giant personality. Handsome, smart, funny, emotional, generous, and graced with tremendous social skills, he made friends among the elites of Canada, the United States, and Great Britain. He built an estate on the north end of Toronto that was home to some of Canada's best racehorses and show horses. But when things were going well, he would be struck down by depression and would sneak off to New York to see his psychiatrist. Dr. Robert Foster Kennedy was a man who believed mental illness was a mechanical and chemical problem, not something caused by spiritual or emotional distress. In those days, there was no mercy in Canadian society for anyone who needed psychiatric help, and McCullagh struggled alone, and in secret.

At the age of forty-seven, George McCullagh should have been making a move into national politics. The way was open for him to be leader of the federal Conservative Party when his friend George Drew was finished taking his turn. Instead, McCullagh died, almost certainly by suicide, after years of silent suffering and brutal psychiatric treatments. The stigma of his death is one of the reasons you've probably never heard of him. Soon after the massive crowds dispersed from his wake and his funeral, George McCullagh's name was removed from the masthead of the newspapers he owned. His picture came down from the wall of the *Globe and Mail*'s boardroom. Some years later, his widow, angry and bitter, burned all of his papers, leaving scorched earth for any biographer who tried to tell McCullagh's story.

The Canada of McCullagh's era has passed. Back then, Toronto was the second-largest city in Canada, a second-rate town in which "Britishness" was valued and a small Anglo-Protestant elite made the rules. It was a city of appalling class divides in which racial minorities, Jews, Roman Catholics, and anyone else who didn't meet the criteria for admission to the elites of Rosedale and Forest Hill were not true citizens. They were barred from the best jobs in the public and private sector, and their role was to work, serve, show up when Toronto's financial and political elite needed a crowd, and, otherwise, stay silent.

This version of Toronto is gone now, and frankly, it's not a huge loss. It's the Toronto where I was born, and it was the city where I had my first full-time newspaper job. Like McCullagh, I loved newspapers, and this is my gift back to an industry that made the first decades of my working life a delight. This is a love letter but also a kiss goodbye to an industry that is nearly gone. In the early 1980s, Canadians started turning away from newspapers. The decline started almost two decades before the advent of the internet. Now, Canadian newspapers are struggling. Canada's largest chain is owned by an American hedge fund, which has asset-stripped its newspapers to the point where their reporting staffs are no longer able to cover basic news in their communities. Many of their staff members are dedicated journalists who try to inform readers, but newspapers cannot cut their way to journalistic or financial success, no matter how deep those cuts may be. A supposedly temporary government bailout just papers over the systemic problems and delays the inevitable reckoning and restructuring. All of the rest of Canada's English-language dailies are privately held, and the hedge fund mentality of undercapitalization and poor local service afflicts most of those papers, too.

George McCullagh's Canada has also passed into history. It was a land where great veins of gold were waiting to be discovered by people willing to trudge through the boreal forests of Ontario in -45° weather, where a man with no education could become the most important publisher in Canada, where politicians had no problem inciting mobs in the country's arenas and city parks, rather than through Twitter and Facebook. It was also a country where a bright kid with unlimited ambition could decide to create a great corporation, find the capital to do it, and leave the country with a great media institution that continued to be relevant for fifty years after his death.

People who know about this project invariably ask me if there's some kind of moral to this story. I'd say there is. McCullagh's media power still exists, but not in newspapers. It lies in the hands of foreigners who, to be blunt, don't give a damn about Canada, other than ensuring our governments bail out these vulture corporations and turn a blind eye to their pillaging. McCullagh's first attempt at an open grab for political power also serves as a warning: Canada is still a country where populist anger lies just under the surface, and has erupted through the years as the United Farmers movement (which came to power in four provinces), Social Credit, the Co-operative Commonwealth Federation (CCF, forerunner of the NDP), the Reform Party, Alberta's United Conservative Party, the Fords in Ontario, and a string of nationalist regimes in Quebec. George McCullagh wanted to get rid of democracy—labelling it as "partisanship"—and this book shows how close he came to doing it. He didn't see one-party technocratic government under a strong leader (presumably him) as fascism. It was government-by-experts, rule-by-the-successful, or, more precisely, government by people like him. It doesn't seem to have occurred to McCullagh that people on the Left, in the union halls and in the farmers' movement, had a right to be heard. McCullagh was a sort of nice Canadian fascist, a technocrat who didn't see any need to work the angle of Christian white supremacy because that was already a given in Canada. Nor did he feel the need to whip up hatred, as people were already angry because their world had fallen apart in 1929, and they saw no simple solution and no obvious end to the crisis.

It's possible, even likely, that a more successful demagogue might come along, either from the streets or from within this country's political class. As problems become complex, the slick man with simple answers becomes very appealing. The selfishness that we have seen in the recent pandemic adds to my worry that someone may offer a set of undemocratic options that will appeal to a large swath of people.

I didn't plan to write a political manifesto, and this isn't one. I see no point in writing a book that doesn't tell a good story, or one that is not driven by fascinating characters. McCullagh is Gatsby, a Horatio Alger character, Gordon Gekko, Charles Foster Kane. Then there are his pals, the secondary characters: his best friend, George Drew, spent years hunting down and exposing the arms dealer who Ian Fleming used as his model for Ernst Stavro Blofeld in his James Bond novels, and became an advocate for veterans. Despite becoming premier of Ontario, he could never connect with the great mass of voters. McCullagh's financial backer, Bill Wright, wandered the bush of northern Ontario with pennies in his pocket until he lucked into one of the greatest gold strikes in history, and then did what he always wanted to do—hung out with horses rather than people.

McCullagh's enemies were just as fascinating. "Holy Joe" Atkinson was a scolding, arch-capitalist Marxist who ran the Toronto *Star* as a cash machine for social justice movements. He fought McCullagh daily, dragged him into court, and warned his readers that McCullagh was a point man for fascism in Canada. Holy Joe's last will and testament was thwarted by his much-younger enemies, led by McCullagh. Then there was William Lyon Mackenzie King, a disturbed, strange man who knew how to wheedle secrets out of McCullagh and would visit him in his Toronto hospital bed, hoping he'd find the *Globe and Mail* publisher dead or dying. And finally, frenemy Mitchell Hepburn, the oily populist premier, holed up in a suite of the King Edward Hotel with his hookers and goons, who ran Ontario for the highest bidder.

McCullagh's story straddles that part of the twentieth century when Canada became a nation. His Canada is not our Canada, but we can see how it became our version. His *Globe and Mail* looks like the newspaper of today, but that's just because of the logo, masthead, and type font. It's not George McCullagh's paper. The *Globe and Mail* of, say, 1950, dominated a very different media landscape. I am not always thrilled with the modern version, but its owners have every right to do what they can to keep the paper alive in a print media environment that is weighted against newspapers.

It's safe to say we'll never see another George McCullagh, at least in publishing. He was a man of his times. We should give a break to the people who want to build, rather than loot, institutions like news-papers—in print or online—because they have an important social value. But we must be ready to clip their wings when they try to use that media power to undermine democracy.

For those of us who live with bipolar disorder and depression, McCullagh is an inspiration. Although he could not, in the prejudiced world he lived in, speak openly about it and be an advocate, he did manage to fight hard against the black dog. In a better world, George McCullagh would have lived longer, been happier, and had the oppor-tunity to be honest about a condition that often struck him down. He was a man of his time, a human with strengths and faults, and that's what makes his life interesting. He was a flawed man, sometimes a good man, a person who loved his children, a man who loved his country. He was sometimes right, often wrong, but he was never uninteresting.

He deserves to have his story told.

1

THE HUSTLER

The summers of southwestern Ontario are so hot that the sun bakes crusts of pottery over the clay fields, with cracks so deep that a big man can shove his fingers into the earth and pull them out clean. In the late summer, the loud hum of cicadas fills the air, the big beetles calling their song of sex and death, leaving no place silent. The flat land between Lake Ontario, Lake Huron, Lake St. Clair, the Detroit River and Lake Erie is a land of mirages, of shimmering roads and fields. In summers and winters, storms brew on the lakes and move inland to pound the countryside. Some are as bad as hurricanes: the Great Storm of 1913 lasted five days. It sank most of the Great Lakes fleet, killed 250 sailors and created thousands of widows and orphans before burying the countryside under two metres of snow. Every few years, cyclones form on the big lakes, spawning tornadoes that sweep through farms and towns, leaving long streaks of damage as though some great finger has come down from the sky and smeared a line across the land.

Just after Labour Day of 1921, Canada was near the end of the economic depression that struck as the country struggled with a flu pandemic and the return of 500,000 Canadian soldiers from wartime service. A sixteen-year-old boy wandered the concessions and sideroads of Middlesex, Perth, Oxford and Huron counties, trapesing along dirt roads in the late-summer heat. He saw men, women and kids take off second hay crops and the fall wheat harvest as he shuffled past farms offering fresh eggs but "No Sunday Sales." This is good land, some of the best in Canada, but these farmers were poor. Most of the people living along these dirt roads were first- or second-generation Irish immigrants or newcomers from England who had come to Canada in the two decades before the war. The farmers and their sons had been the first to sign up in 1914. Most of the families on these back roads had lost a father or son or cousin in Flanders, and all the men who came back were damaged in some way.

Who was this gangly, handsome young man who made way when the farm carts came down the roads and who watched as the few trucks generated little comets of dust as they moved over the pitted dirt sideroads? It was Clement George McCullagh, travelling subscription seller for the Toronto *Globe*.

He did a lot of walking.

In most places in that part of the country, each concession road is a mile apart. Each sideroad, running at right angles to the concession roads on the old grid of rural Ontario, is also a mile from the next one. The roads frame a section of 640 acres. A typical farm was about a hundred acres, although some were as small as fifty, especially if the soil was good. That still made only six or seven farms on each square. His job was to go from house to house to house, trying to convince people to part with their money for a subscription to Canada's second-best newspaper. The *Globe* was Canada's great Liberal paper, solid and drab, as dry as the liquor prohibition tracts and church news that it ran on its editorial pages. There was no scandal or sin in its news columns, no racetrack results for gamblers, and, except for its wars on booze and vice, no great crusades like those pushed by its better-selling rival, the *Montreal Star*.

The *Globe* was Liberal in the politics of its times, but it was not liberal as we know liberalism now. Trade unions got no ink in its pages, except for criticism. Most social justice causes were left to the upstart Toronto *Star*, a paper that was scrambling to survive. Liberalism in 1921 was about the right of farmers and industrialists to do their work under the tutelage of market forces. That included the right to trade with anyone they liked, free of interference. In the first years of that century, liberals (and Liberals) supported free trade with the United States and wide-open immigration (of white people) to open the Prairies to farming and as a market for Ontario manufacturers. Quite often, they were just lukewarm in their support of British imperialism, though saying so was political heresy bordering on treason. Canada still saw itself as a British country, and "Britishness" was a synonym for fairness and gentility.

McCullagh was born in a very ordinary town to what looked, from a distance, to be a typical family. The timing of his birth on March 16, 1905, would shape his life and how he saw the world. Clement George McCullagh (who always used the name George) was born in a niche of time that made him too young to fight in the First World War and old enough to easily stay home during the Second. But it would be economic depression, not war, that would provide the opportunities and obstacles in his life. The first big downturn came in the years before the Great War, when McCullagh's father, a Protestant immigrant from Northern Ireland who was also named George, stumbled from job to job, dogged by his reputation as a union man and a troublemaker. These hard times would leave the family on the edge of destitution and show the boy the price of failure. The second, much bigger economic shock would strike just after the First World War and knock George out of high school at the age of fourteen. In those grim near-revolutionary postwar years, as strikers battled cops in the streets of Winnipeg and families went hungry in downtown Toronto, George would trudge those country roads, mile after mile in the heat and the rain and the snow, always thinking about ways to turn his little job with the *Globe* into a real opportunity. The third downturn, the Great Depression,[1] hit when he was at the age when most young men were settling into their life's work, getting married and having children. He reacted to this worst depression of all by making millions and becoming the most powerful newspaper publisher in the country. Shades of the economic downturn that flitted by in 1953 probably helped kill him.

McCullagh's hometown of London is a pleasant enough place today. A city of nearly half a million in its metro area, London is home to Western University, Fanshawe College, several research companies, a few corporate headquarters and some light industry. The town is comfortable and conservative, preppy, bland and smug. Its saving grace is its nearness to Detroit and Toronto, and to the beaches on the southeast shore of Lake Huron and the north shore of Lake Erie. People say it's a great place to raise kids because there are so few urban dangers. That middle-American normality seems to be a major draw to the people who have settled there. So is the security that comes from having a salaried job at the university, one of the insurance companies or at the several good hospitals in the city.

That part of Ontario wasn't always a nice place to live. In 1905, London was an industrial centre with about forty thousand people. The city was ugly, tough, and mostly slums. The small downtown was surrounded by factories making machinery, hosiery, bread, cigars and beer. In the early days, tourists were drawn to a sulphur spring that was supposed to burble water that cured them of various ailments. But London didn't become a spa town: someone bought the place and built a chemical factory on top of the spring.[2] Nearby, a factory turned out toilet seats. There was a meatpacking factory that killed five hundred hogs a day. Several brick-makers set up operations near McCullagh's childhood home, exploiting local clay to make the yellow bricks that were used everywhere in southwestern Ontario. Pioneer car-maker Sam McLaughlin, founder of the business that later became General Motors

(GMS)' Canadian operation, opened a factory and showroom in London when McCullagh was a small boy. London's downtown was full of bars and hotels made, like the rest of the city, from those yellow bricks.

Western University was just a small college on the edge of a backwater town. London was a community of brawlers, not scholars. McCullagh was born a quarter century after dress-wearing vigilantes just north of the town hacked up four members of the Donnelly family, and then walked a few miles through the snow and shot the fifth one in what was then called the Biddulph Feud. This was one of several ugly, murderous little wars between Irish-Canadian factions that seriously called into question the government's ability to maintain order on the back concessions of Huron and Middlesex counties. The public got little reassurance when all the murderers were set free by local jurors and police. In the early years of the twentieth century, when he was selling newspapers out in the townships, McCullagh almost certainly tried to sign some of the Donnelly killers and their friends to the *Globe*'s subscription list. Liberal-Conservative politics being a factor in the Biddulph Feud—the Donnellys and their few supporters being Liberals and the murderers Conservatives— McCullagh probably found that area challenging.[3]

In winters, the streets were often blocked with snow from Lake Huron squalls. When it melted, the Thames River usually flooded, pulling apart houses in the poorer parts of London and sometimes taking some Londoners with it.

The summers brought steaming days and nights that were so hot and humid that many people slept in their backyards. Most houses had no electricity. Electric fans were a luxury and air conditioning lay forty years in the future—or much farther, for people as poor as the McCullaghs. But modern appliances were coming. London was the home of Adam Beck, the almost-forgotten Canadian hero who realized all of Ontario could be powered by Niagara Falls. It was simple: take the province's industry, replace the steam engines that drove it with almost-free electricity, and Ontario could out-compete anyone. Ontarians would be able to have cheap power from a giant waterfall that belonged to the people, distributed by a provincial power company owned by everyone. People would get around on streetcars powered by this electricity. Radial rail—effectively, light-rail streetcars—would link the towns of the Toronto region. It seems so normal now, but in the early 1900s nothing was a given. Would privately owned power companies hold their customers to ransom? Would the power system be like the modern cellphone grid, where some places have good, reliable service and others don't?[4] And the modern analogy doesn't stop there. The automobile was the great tech breakthrough of its time. People started building cars everywhere, including just up the street from the McCullagh house. Would Ontario be the leader in the North American auto industry? Could Canada become self-sufficient in cars? Or would Detroit, just a couple of hours away by train, use its economies of scale to smother the Ontario manufacturers? Would Canada finally end up in the American economic orbit?

All that would be worked out in George McCullagh's lifetime. His hometown would influence the way he saw the world: it was simple, class-conscious, ambitious, insecure, out of the mainstream of politics and free of high culture. It was something to get away from, not aspire to.

In 1853, the Grand Trunk Railway built a line through the centre of London. The area north of the tracks held London's business district, farmers' market and its better neighbourhoods. Rich people—those who belonged to the city's hunt club so they could pretend to be English gentry—lived at the north end of the city, away from the factories. The south side of town was poor, with working-class people living in frame and yellow-brick row houses and making their livings from the factories along the railway line and in behind the main streets. McCullagh was born on the south side, the wrong side of the tracks. His family lived on Askin Street, southwest of London's downtown.

The street was dominated by the lovely Askin Street Methodist Church and a row of two-storey terrace houses. It was hardly a Dickensian slum, but it was not a prestigious address.

His father was a cabinetmaker, a trade that should have provided steady work as the city grew and fine houses went up along the river and east of the university lands. But the older George McCullagh couldn't hold a job. He was a complainer and a union agitator. And, partly because George McCullagh Jr. erased the story of his father from his own accounts of his life, George McCullagh Sr. becomes a mystery. He is a man so conspicuously invisible in his son's myth-making that his absence begs an explanation. The answer likely lies in the story of George Jr.'s mother, who we know much more about. While his father was radical and flaky, his mother—at least, according to her son—was a rock. But there's a bit more: she was den mother to two unstable men, each different in their own way. George Sr. was caught up in workers' rights fights and paid a price. And his son, George Jr., was an engine fuelled by ambition who saw the price his father paid—one that he was, as a boy, forced to pay, too—and decided he would rather be one of the bosses.

But, being one of the few Marxists in town, the elder George was as much of a risk-taker as his son. And the most interesting thing about George Sr. is the big black hole where he should be in this story. His son never mentioned him in anything he wrote, and talked about him just once in the many speeches he made. It's not because George Sr. was a nonentity. Far from it. George Jr. simply could not engage with his father's memory. Rather than be nothing, George Sr., invisible as he is, may well be the fuel that drives this story and the demon who consumed the son. He is a ghost, rarely mentioned but always there.

The capitalist son, not the radical father, was the true Londoner. London never was a union town, and, in 1905, it was the heart of Tory Ontario. The *London Free Press*, then—and now—the dominant newspaper in the city, had its headquarters on Richmond Street, the city's main north-south commercial avenue. The paper made no secret of its Toryism: Conservative politicians were welcome to speak freely from its second-floor window. The rival London *Advertiser* was open to new ideas, which would—after it was bought by social justice advocate and Toronto *Star* publisher Joe Atkinson—cause it to be rejected by readers and advertisers alike.[5] Union agitators were both brave and rare in London.

McCullagh's mother, Anne, was born in England in 1878 and gave birth to George at the age of twenty-seven. She was the main parental figure in his life, and those of his four sisters. She would stay at the centre of his world until her death in the spring of 1939, when her son was at the height of his financial and political power. When she gave birth to George, she was struggling to keep a household afloat in a dusty little southwestern Ontario town. As she lay on her death bed thirty-four years later, the Queen of England was saying prayers for her recovery.

The family always needed money because George Sr. was so often out of work. George Jr. was expected to do what he could, and began delivering the Toronto *Globe* when he was in elementary school. The *Globe*, founded by publisher-politician George Brown, prided itself as a national newspaper. It never lived up to that billing, but Brown had built a financially successful newspaper by tailoring his press runs to train schedules so that most people in Ontario got the paper on the day it was published. Brown's paper also provided the best financial news coverage in the country. Its Liberal, free-trade, free-enterprise editorial page reflected the values of many of the people living in southwestern Ontario, especially Irish Catholics who equated Toryism with the Loyal Orange Lodge, the powerful Protestant "fraternal" group that used its political clout and social connections to keep Catholics out of political office, the public service, the professions and most white-collar jobs.

George McCullagh was bright and had skipped a grade, but was not a great student. It would be foolish now to try to pin a label on the cause of his restlessness, but he was the kind of kid who simply did not have the patience to use education as a way of escaping poverty. Even if he had finished high school, there was no money to send him to university. He landed a part-time job driving a horse-drawn wagon, delivering meat for one of the city's butchers. It was the start of his love affair with horses. He hung on at school until the middle of grade nine, when his high school burned down. By then, the post–First World War depression, made more severe by the 1918 flu pandemic, was biting hard. Londoners, especially children, were dying in scores.

* * *

In a city like London, a big, bright kid, even a fourteen-year-old who'd just quit school, could land a job, despite the lousy economy. Even more surprising, he got one with a bank, although he quit a year later when the manager told him to work on New Year's Eve. Apparently, young George had plans for the evening.

Rather than working at a bank, George McCullagh wanted to be a *Globe* reporter. It's always been difficult to get hired as a reporter at a decent newspaper, but it's nearly impossible for a sixteen-year-old. Late in the summer of 1921, George went to Toronto to try and join the *Globe*. He carried a letter from his father, who knew A. Ross Malton, the paper's business manager. Executives at the paper were impressed by this attractive, bright, ambitious kid, but they weren't going to hire a teenage dropout from the boondocks to write for one of the country's premier political and financial papers. The *Globe* managers sloughed McCullagh off with a ticket to the Canadian National Exhibition and a pass for its rides. Then, when he came back to the newspaper office, they offered him work selling *Globe* subscriptions door to door and gave him a train ticket back to London.

Most people would have tried to get their old bank job back or set their sights on a smaller paper, like the *London Free Press*. But McCullagh didn't want to settle for a local reporting job. Instead, he took up the *Globe*'s offer and started selling newspaper subscriptions in the backwater towns and farm concessions of southwestern Ontario.

And could he sell. McCullagh's new boss told the teenager about the company's ten-dollar bonus to the salesman who sold the most subscriptions in a week. The regional manager said he would add five dollars of his own money if McCullagh won, and then sent the kid to Ripley, just inland from Kincardine. After changing trains a couple of times, McCullagh arrived at the village railway station next to a flour mill on Huron Street, just north of the town's main intersection. The leaves were just starting to change but the summer heat still hadn't broken.

McCullagh's challenge was to sell long-term newspaper mail subscriptions to the people of Ripley and the surrounding countryside. This was a farming community peopled by descendants of 109 impoverished Scots who'd immigrated to Canada in 1853 and settled on the frontier. Their community was connected to the outside world in 1873 when the Wellington, Grey and Bruce Railway built a line to Lake Huron. Ripley had a couple of grist mills, a lumber mill, a stockyard and a grain elevator. The teenager's job was to convince the local people that they needed to read the *Globe* to keep up on national issues. That meant the young man had to be able to talk politics with people of his parents' generation. There were important issues to master: liquor prohibition, electrification, the spread of communism from Russia, Canadian labour unrest blamed on communism, problems faced by returning veterans and the economic downturn that lingered in Canada.

McCullagh's timing was quite good. Current events mattered to people. Canada had never seen a more desperate time. Some sixty-seven thousand men had died in the First World War. More than 120,000 had been wounded, mostly by artillery fire. The 600,000 veterans who had been discharged from the army, navy and small air force were trying to readjust to civilian life during the worst pandemic in generations.

There were only about nine million people in the country, and more than one in five had either immigrated to Canada or been born in the country in the previous ten years. The Parliament Building burned down in 1916 and the House of Commons and Senate were meeting in a museum. (The dollar bills in circulation showed the Library of Parliament standing forlornly on the flattened ruins. It's probably the saddest and most defiant image ever printed on Canadian money.) Inflation was rampant. Thousands of people were out of work because wartime industries closed. The war had caused so much pain and social disruption and forced so many people—men and women—to rethink their ideas of safety and security. People wanted the war to mean something, and they wanted the new world that they believed they'd been promised. Their old world was gone, along with so many of their young men. And the tens of thousands of maimed men, people missing arms, legs, sometimes even faces, reminded everyone of the horror.

In those postwar flu pandemic years, Canada was polarized between the extreme right and extreme left, with new and powerful radicalism growing on both ends of the spectrum. Union activists and communists were firing up industrial workers. At the same time, the Ku Klux Klan was recruiting in parts of rural Canada. Immigrants, Black Canadians and Indigenous people were ground down by discrimination that often had the force of law behind it. Canada's old minorities, French Canadians who opposed the war and conscription (the drafting of men to fight overseas), still seethed from being ganged up upon by English-speaking Liberals and Tories who, they believed, had formed the wartime coalition government against them.

The wartime co-operation between many Liberal members of Parliament (MPs) and Sir Robert Borden's Conservative government was finished and a generational political change was underway. In 1920, Arthur Meighen took over the Conservative leadership. A few months later, he called an election. This was the first federal election in which all the women of Canada could vote. Sir Wilfrid Laurier, the

Liberal leader, had died in 1919, leaving his house and his party to an ambitious, strange young man, William Lyon Mackenzie King. The main party leaders were local boys: Meighen was from nearby Perth County; King was born and raised in Kitchener (called Berlin until 1916). The Progressives, led by Thomas Crerar, was a western party with some appeal to Ontario farmers. There was a strong "throw the bums out" wave sweeping the country. King won a majority in December 1921, and Meighen did not even keep his seat. The Conservatives placed third, behind Crerar's Progressives.[6]

In the early decades of the last century, farmers were the most radical people in the country, and there were enough of them to decide the outcomes of elections. Farm organizations across Canada that started as social clubs and mutual aid groups for rural women and men became politicized in the decades before the war. In 1914, farmer federations coalesced into the United Farmers of Ontario (UFO). Rather than just lobby governments for a fair deal for farmers, the UFO ran candidates, picking up its first seat in the Ontario legislature in a 1918 by-election on Manitoulin Island. In the 1919 provincial election, the UFO surprised everyone, including itself, by winning the most seats. The party had no leader. Its members met at Massey Hall in Toronto, right in the belly of the sin beast, to pick Ernest Drury, who didn't even have a seat in the legislature, to be premier.

These were not conservative, "get-government-off-our backs" anti-tax farmers. We would call them progressive populists, and many of them were sympathetic to the demands of urban industrial workers. Drury, a central Ontario farmer, cobbled together a coalition government with the Independent Labour Party, a Marxist group that promoted trade unions. The UFO government brought in sweeping welfare reforms. It established new forestry programs to replant the land in central Ontario that had been clear-cut for the lumber used to build North America's cities. It spent public money to turn old portage routes into highways and connected villages and farms to the electrical grid. Electric lights began replacing coal oil lamps in the houses along Ontario's farm roads. While being tight with government funds—UFO members of the legislature turned down raises and pensions—the activist government pumped money into agricultural and medical research, paying for the University of Toronto lab that gave the world insulin. The government enticed Theodore Loblaw to set up a chain of co-operative food stores. It brought in workers' compensation for people injured on the job. It established a minimum wage for working women. It also waged a brutal and sometimes bloody war on booze.

This was the height of the 1919 Red Scare, when Lenin and the Bolsheviks, along with Communists in Germany, were trying to spread communism around the world. Canadian soldiers were part of the Allied expedition intervening in the Russian Civil War, and capitalists everywhere were sure they were the next victims of Marxism. A general strike in Winnipeg shocked governments and industrialists, and kick-started labour agitation across the country. At the same time, the extreme right was on the move. In the early 1920s, the Ku Klux Klan oozed across the American border, and its appearance on the political scene was covered by the big newspapers. London was one of the Canadian strongholds of the Ku Klux Klan. Torchlight meetings and cross-burnings were big events in some of the communities west of the city.[7] There was only one way to keep up with all this change, and that was by reading newspapers.

* * *

McCullagh was able to sell a lot of newspapers. Sometimes he talked the locals out of their money by discussing politics. Other times, he bet farmers he could plow a straighter furrow than they could. McCullagh had a knack for horses. He couldn't afford one, but he knew what made a good horse. He watched them as he walked those country roads. He talked to farmers about them. By the time he was in his late teens, he was an expert.

By his own brains and hard work, McCullagh was able to defy the odds against a young stranger in a cheap suit selling a city newspaper to farmers in a backwater. That first week in Ripley, he'd learned something: the people who delivered the mail in town and along the concession roads earned a special commission from the newspaper company if they also delivered a *Globe*. It wasn't very much money, so few of them bothered to try to sell subscriptions. The eager teenager would make it worth their while to introduce him to the people along their route. Suddenly, the young stranger had a chance for a ride and a way to break the ice. At the end of his first week, he sent home sixty-seven dollars in commissions, the company's ten-dollar bonus and the five-dollar prize from the regional manager. (That pay had the buying power of at least $1,100 in today's money.) A year later, he had the manager's job.

After he was finished in Ripley, McCullagh began working the small towns and gravelled concession roads of Huron, Middlesex, Oxford, Perth, Waterloo, Elgin, Kent and Lambton counties, hunting down mailmen and chatting up farmers. He did this in the heat and the rain and the snow, which gave him a lot of time to think. At seventeen, while managing subscription salesmen and filling his own order books, he came up with the idea of the "Just Kids" Safety League, a sort of club that had just one requirement for joining: clipping a coupon from the *Globe* and sending it to the newspaper office. In return, kids got a membership card, some pamphlets on traffic and water safety, and a flier on the menace of addiction to comic strips. At a young age, McCullagh had realized the power of interactive marketing. People want to be engaged, to be part of something. Newspapers wanted the names of potential subscribers, which they collected from coupons sent by kids who'd bought the paper at newsstands. The idea was so brilliant that other papers quickly picked up on it. More than 300,000 children across North America signed up to safety leagues started by newspapers in Canada and the United States. McCullagh was able to hire other salesmen, among them a young Jewish man from Windsor named David Croll, whose political career would be, for a time, hobbled by an adult George McCullagh.[8]

On the verge of twenty, a superstar salesman as well as the southwestern Ontario regional circulation manager based in London, wunderkind McCullagh was sent across the rest of the province to sell subscriptions and advise the managers who used to be his bosses. He made a lot of money, but he wanted more than that. He wanted respect. He wanted the *Globe*'s managers to praise him, to feed his ego, to see that he had gone from being a tall, skinny teenager to a handsome, successful young man who made the paper a lot of money. Instead, McCullagh's first meeting with *Globe* owner and publisher William Gladstone Jaffray felt like a sucker punch, one he would remember for many years and would repay with interest.

McCullagh had just sold two hundred subscriptions in North Bay, Ontario. Jaffray called to say he wanted to see McCullagh in Toronto. During the six-hour train trip to Jaffray's office, McCullagh was ecstatic. Maybe he would get a raise. Or, even better, a desk in the newsroom. "I was called into Mr. Jaffray's office and went in with a light step," he said ten years later, "expecting a pat on the back and a $5 raise. Instead, I got a severe reprimand for a few indiscreet drinks I took in North Bay and a little poker I played on the train."[9]

Jaffray, McCullagh concluded, was an ingrate. Where was the future in an organization that was more concerned with an employee's private life than about making money and encouraging talent? McCullagh still wanted to be Canada's best sports reporter, preferably on the *Globe*. He probably could have landed a job on one of the southwestern Ontario dailies, good papers in their day, but he couldn't afford the pay cut. Still, he was able to talk his way into the press boxes of the London Gardens hockey rink and pretend to be a sportswriter for the *Globe*, and he filed long stories that were never used. From the box, he gave loud, unsolicited advice to coaches and players. Fairly quickly, he was tossed out by one of the local reporters. The teen then blew off steam by boxing, and he wore a crooked nose for the rest of his life because of it. He kept applying for other jobs at the *Globe*, but, as the months went by, it was clear he was far more valuable to the company as a subscription salesman. Finally, Wellington Jeffers, the financial wizard who edited the *Globe*'s business news pages, hired McCullagh as a cub reporter. He learned basic reporting on the police beat before being transferred to the financial news department. Jaffray opposed the move and, when he learned McCullagh's salary, he cut it in half. Jaffray would regret crossing George McCullagh. In fact, he would die wishing he'd never heard of the brilliant, ambitious young man who would later be so very, very cruel to him. Jeffers, on the other hand, had earned McCullagh's loyalty, which meant his job at the *Globe* was safe for years after McCullagh became a press lord.

2

NEWSIES AND GOLD

Meanwhile, in a far less settled part of Ontario, the men who were to shape McCullagh's life were carving out their own destinies. One was a prospector who loved horses more than people. The other was a miser who happened to be a social reformer.

William Wright was about the same age as McCullagh's parents. He was born poor in Lincolnshire, England, in 1876. Although Wright lacked McCullagh's natural gifts—he was small, homely, rather meek, and introverted—he did, like McCullagh, have a strong inner drive. McCullagh's was the need to prove his success by acquiring power. Wright's was horses. He loved horses much more than he loved money. That, however, did not stop him from making an awful lot of money.

After quitting primary school, Wright got a job as a butcher's apprentice. He didn't like the work, so, when he was old enough, he joined a British cavalry regiment and was shipped out to India. He stayed in the Hussars for eleven years, developing the camaraderie with horses that soldiers usually feel for each other. His unit was then deployed in

South Africa, where it was trapped in Ladysmith by besieging Boers—local farmers of Dutch descent—through the summer of 1899/1900.[1] The Boers were kind enough to fire a Christmas pudding in an empty artillery shell into the town with the message "compliments of the season," but it was a still an ugly fight. The Boers crushed two British expeditions that were sent to save Ladysmith. When the British garrison ran out of food for itself and the civilians in the town, Wright's officers—because he knew how to cut meat—put him to work killing and carving up the cavalry's horses. The work broke Wright's heart, and he promised himself he would make amends. The 118-day siege was broken when a relief column that included Winston Churchill cut through the Boer lines.

Wright went back to England after the war, but somehow got his hands on the deed to 160 acres of land in Ontario. There are different stories about how he got it. He either bought it from a Canadian soldier he met on a ship, from a cousin already in Canada, or was given it as settlement of a debt, but it doesn't matter. Wright now thought he had a farm for his horses. At about the same time, his sister, Frances, who was already living in Canada, married butcher-turned-prospector Ed Hargreaves. This gave Wright another reason to move to Canada, where he could graze his horses on lush grass and ride them alone across the countryside.

When Wright arrived in Ontario, he found he had been swindled. The land was in the Porcupine District of Ontario's Canadian Shield and clay belt country, and it was no place for horses. Grass is a rare commodity in that part of Canada, and what pastureland exists is under snow for seven or eight months of the year. Wright arrived in Canada with $1.25 in his pocket in 1905, visited his "farm," and then set out to make some money so he could buy some decent land for horses. He should have stuck around the area. The region, now part of the city of Timmins, Ontario, was one of the most gold-laden parts of the country.

Wright's first job in Canada was cutting hay on the Prairies for a farmer who was a veteran of the Klondike gold rush. It wasn't well-paying work, but at least there were horses. Wright was inspired by the farmer's stories and advice about prospecting, so he set out on his own, just as a new silver and gold rush began in Ontario. Prospectors were discovering northeastern Ontario's almost unbelievable wealth: just one mine, in Cobalt, Ontario, made more profits than the entire Klondike gold rush. And that was a silver mine, at a time when silver was worth a dollar an ounce. No one had found the gold motherlode yet, but it was there, thick veins of the stuff that were so rich you could see the metal braiding through quartzite. Wright was sure it existed, and that he could find it, even though he knew much more about horses than he did about geology. His brother-in-law, Ed Hargreaves, who was already prospecting in the bush, could help him out.

Wright was tough, but he was getting low on options. For a while, he had to get by on odd jobs, like painting the ore processing mill at the Mining Corporation of Canada's silver mine.[2] He learned how to live in the bush and studied up on hard rock geology, and how to stake a claim. Grubbing for gold was about the hardest work a person could choose. Prospectors tramped country filled with swamps, lugged their gear up granite hills, and dealt with the swarms of biting insects that began with blackflies in the spring and ended with deer flies in the late summer. The blackflies are the worst. They get in your eyes, ears, nose and mouth. There is no truly effective bug repellant now, and there wasn't in the early years of the nineteenth century. Prospectors, following local Cree survival techniques, smeared bear grease on themselves.

Wright couldn't afford to stay in the forest, even in the months when he could live comfortably in shacks that he built. Food, gear, bear grease (unless you have time to shoot and render down a bear) and claim registrations cost money. When they needed more cash, he and Hargreaves painted houses and did odd jobs to save for prospecting equipment and the hefty forty-dollar claim registration fees.

Wright had missed out on the Cobalt silver rush but there was a lot of Ontario that was his to discover. In 1907, Wright and Hargreaves hiked the wilderness in the Kirkland Lake area. One late fall day, while Hargreaves was in town picking up supplies, Wright scrambled over a hill, pulled back some moss and discovered an eight-foot-wide gold vein. White quartz along a geologic fault in pink feldspar shone with gold, and there seemed to be no end to it as Wright cleared away the overburden in the gathering dusk. This vein would become the Wright-Hargreaves mine, the first big strike of the Kirkland Lake gold field.

Wright wasn't the only prospector working the area. Harry Oakes, an American prospector who had struck out in Australia and the Klondike, had found his way to northern Ontario. He had theories about gold veins, which he shared with anyone who might lend him money. One of his ideas, which he insisted on believing despite all the evidence against it, was that most of the gold was in deposits under the lakes of the Canadian Shield.[3]

Roza Brown, a high-smelling woman who prospected, ran a local store, did men's laundry and grubstaked Oakes, turned out to be the muse of the Swastika gold field. "Gold has a mind of its own," she told Oakes. "Gold is a woman. All the gold in the world is waiting for just one thing, for the right man to find it. Maybe that's why I have never been able to get my hands on it."[4]

Some men were lucky and some were not: prospector J.E. Proulx camped right on top of the vein of gold that would become the Teck-Hughes mine and saw nothing. Oakes had better luck. He heard about some mining claims along Kirkland Lake that were about to expire in the early months of 1912. Oakes, broke and needing help, hooked up with the four legendary Tough brothers—George, Bob, Tom and Jack—and tried to talk them into snatching these claims in a night-time raid. They waited weeks in the shack town of Kirkland Lake, trying to keep their mouths shut, but on the night the claims lapsed, two Toughs could not live up to their name and dropped out. Oakes, wearing five layers of pants and a wad of shirts, set off with the remaining Toughs on a seven-mile walk through the bush in −45° degree cold. Fortunately, there was a full moon, its light reflecting on the twenty centimetres of snow on the ground. By the time they arrived at the prospect site, in Teck Township, the sun was lighting the eastern horizon.

As they worked, a fourth man emerged from the gloom. It was Bill Wright, still hunting after finding the Wright-Hargreaves motherlode. He had arrived on a freight train. Wright had also been waiting for the old claims to expire. Oakes and Wright met for the first time but knew each other by reputation. Some people might have become enemies in the circumstances, but Wright and Oakes began a friendship. The Tough-Oakes Mine that they found that morning made Harry Oakes a very wealthy man. Wright, whose toes were nearly frozen, went to work staking next to Oakes and Tough, claiming the land that became the Sylvanite Mine. It, too, would produce millions of dollars' worth of gold. Through the rest of the winter, Wright and Oakes staked claims around Kirkland Lake that made them billionaires in today's money. In all, there were eight big veins of gold. Just one trench along a surface vein pulled up 101 tons of gold-rich rock. The ore itself was worth $46,221, a fortune at the time.

Aside from their various gold strikes, the greatest excitement came on a late winter day when Oakes fell through the ice of Gull Lake. First, he became disorientated; then, almost instantly, he panicked when his head went under the water; then he flailed as he tried to claw his way out. Wright saw the accident and yanked Oakes from the icy water, and then helped him to shore as Oakes started to freeze to death. Wright built a big fire, stripped Oakes naked, or at least down to his long underwear, and watched as Oakes did a strange dance in front of the flames to stay warm while his clothes dried in the smoke. Oakes danced over gold-laden ground that would make him and Wright the richest men in Canada.[5] Through the Depression, Wright's annual income was $2 million when a person lucky enough to have a job would gladly work for two dollars a day and the president of the United States made $500 a week.

Oakes and Wright decided to cut up the Kirkland Lake gold field, with Oakes staking along the south shore of the lake and Wright's claims running into it. Wright made a big mistake on one of his claims, staking it at an angle to Oakes's and leaving a seven-acre triangle of land that held two-thirds of the gold in the ore body. It was, at the time, the richest strike in Canada, Another prospector, Athur Cockerman, found the mistake, staked the property and was bought out with $30,000 in cash and $50,000 worth of shares of Oakes's company, which Cockerman sold for two dollars a share.[6] The next summer, Oakes and his men found the Lake Shore Mine, with a vein of gold so rich that the rock contained nuggets. Oakes gave Wright 200,000 shares of Lake Shore for his claims along the side of the property. But both men struggled to hang on to their mines. Oakes was able to keep his because Wright helped him pay the small fee for claim registration. Wright and Oakes were rarities among prospectors: in those days, few people who found a vein of gold were able to raise the capital to open a mine. Most, like Ed Hargreaves, sold their claims to mining companies and died broke. But by peddling some stock and a few less-productive mining claims and finding what would be called "angel investors" today, both men were able to get their mines into production.[7] "I have never felt as sure of anything as I did of that mine," Wright said years later, when telling a newspaper reporter about those days of living in a tent, lying awake in −40° northern Ontario nights wondering where he'd get enough money to finance the mine and hold onto it. But he did keep it, partly by simply dynamiting that original seam and shipping the rock away to be smelted. When the cash came in, he sank a shaft and began collecting dividends from his own mine, as well as from Harry Oakes's company.[8]

William Wright was the angel investor who made McCullagh's media career possible. The former butcher and soldier was very good at finding veins of gold. (MUSEUM OF NORTHERN HISTORY, 983.1.47)

Wright kept looking for gold until it became ridiculous for a man that rich and busy with investments to go to the North and spend most of the year living in a shack. A picture of him in his thirties, likely taken just before the beginning of the First World War, shows a man comfortable in the bush. He's wearing a beat-up hat, jeans hiked up with suspenders, and a long-sleeved shirt to keep the swarms of bugs off his arms. He poses with one hand on an axe, the other on his hip, in front of a prospector's shack that's part log house, part tent.[9]

Wright, Hargreaves, Oakes, the Toughs, Roza Brown: these were all hard people willing to gamble their lives for a shot at a fortune. Long, depressing sub-zero winters didn't stop them, nor did the frequent fires that swept the gold camps and destroyed the shacks they used as homes and businesses. They handled explosives with little thought as to the consequences of a mistake. And, in their time, they became Canadian icons. People who would never travel north of Toronto bought stock as bets, putting their money on men, and on a surprisingly high number of determined women: some of the best prospectors, like Wilda

Brown (no relation to Roza) and Viola MacMillan, broke the gender rules of the time and found fabulous gold veins.

The selling of those dreams is part of the George McCullagh story. Years later, when Wright and Oakes were out of the bush and living in warm houses, counting their dividends, McCullagh would hustle gold stocks—the lottery tickets of the time—to people who had dimes and quarters to spare in the worst years of the Great Depression. For every fifty mining companies incorporated in Ontario between 1904 and 1933 (the peak years of the gold boom) just one dug a productive shaft.[10] But those numbers were still good enough to keep hope alive.

Wright found his mines just about the same time Canadians discovered the stock market. Joint stock companies had been around for about three centuries, and much of the country had once been owned by one of the oldest, the Hudson's Bay Company. Stocks, though, were traded only by the very rich, by bankers and corporate investors. When the Hudson's Bay Company was founded, investors were invited, not sought. The stock exchanges of the 1700s and early 1800s were trading places for bankers and rich merchants, not for people with a few extra dollars, guilders, francs and pounds. The retail stock dealer evolved along with a big consumer middle class in the late 1800s. At first, people could only buy blue-chip stocks like banks and railways, but it didn't take long for the wildly speculative penny stock trade to emerge.

From 1896 to 1913—almost coincidental with Wilfrid Laurier's Liberal administration—Canada went through the biggest sustained economic expansion in its history, partly fuelled by the big immigration wave from the United Kingdom that brought Wright to Canada. In those years, the Canadian economy grew by an average of 4.2 percent every year. Stock salesmen fanned out from Toronto, Montreal and Vancouver to tap into this new wealth. They showed up on the doorsteps of small businesses on main streets all over Canada with hefty rock samples in their hands. The savings of Canadians financed the opening of the mines, the building of ore processing plants, and the railways to connect all of that to the rest of the country. By the First World War, brokerage houses that would be known to later generations of Canadians, outfits like Dominion Securities and Wood Gundy, were already in business, along with many smaller shops.[11]

The first wave of penny stock issues gave their buyers tiny pieces of ownership in British Columbia's gold and silver mines. By 1900, that was shifting, as prospectors made big strikes in Ontario.[12] Timing is everything when it comes to making a fast fortune, whether in the Kirkland Lake goldfield or in the tech boom at the end of the last century. Wright was the right age, in great physical shape, unencumbered by children or career, open to new ideas, willing to take a risk, stubborn, and with a supportive group of friends. And he had the luck needed to put him over the top.

For the rest of his life, Wright never really believed he'd hit the bull's eye. He always kept his gear in spic-and-span condition, packed and ready to go in case he ever needed it or had to prove that he could do it again. His equipment was still neatly stacked when he died in 1951. Wright said to Oakes once: "Don't you worry sometimes, Harry, that this is all a dream, that it never really happened, that you will wake up one day and find yourself squatting over a tin plate of cold beans on some freezing scree in Alaska? I do."

"I don't," said Harry Oakes.[13]

* * *

Wright's next piece of luck was finding and hiring Albert Wende to manage Wright-Hargreaves. Wende had wealthy friends in the United States who were willing to help capitalize the mine through the risky early years. By the beginning of the First World War, the Wright-Hargreaves mine was in full production, with Wende in charge. Wright could have stayed home and ignored the war. He was thirty-eight years old and incredibly rich, but there were war horses to be tended to. Wende became owner of almost all of what had been Ed Hargreave's share of the mine and stayed behind while, in 1916, William Wright joined the 11th Hussars and became the richest, and one of the oldest, privates in the Canadian army. He spent most of the war in England, working as a driver. When he was briefly posted to France, he wasn't allowed near the front. Wright's heart was in the right place, but it wasn't much of an organ. Not only did he have a weak ticker, Wright was a wreck. He had scars all over his body, probably from his former military career and his prospecting. He'd had two bouts of influenza, one in 1917, and another during the big pandemic of 1918. Nephritis. Varicose veins. Scabies.

Still, the war was a break from living in the bush and worrying about gold. It didn't faze him when the Wright-Hargreaves vein seemed to peter out in 1917, and speculators short-sold the stock that was generated by Hargreaves's original share. (It was temporary. The vein thickened again and the short-sellers were burned badly when Wende, the manager, slowly bought their shares up for a song.) Wright ignored it all. Some eight million horses were killed or worked to death in and around the trenches during that war, and Wright had been given the chance to give good care to some of those that served.[14]

When the war ended, Wright came back to Canada, suffering from a hernia. He was discharged as medically unfit.[15] Still, despite all his health problems, the old warrior—weighing in at 130 pounds and standing five feet seven, had a good war.

When his business interests were settled after the war, Wright was able to hang onto a quarter of Wright-Hargreaves and 250,000 shares of Harry Oakes's Lake Shore Mine—where, on paper, he was listed as a vice-president. Wright was living with the Hargreaves in their home in Haileybury in 1922 when Ed Hargreaves's usual bad luck manifested itself in a fire that burned the town to the ground. He had already sold his Wright-Hargreaves stock for $3,000 and blown the money. The two Wrights and the man who'd been wrong moved to Barrie, into a weird, rambling house Wright named Statenborough. The Hargreaves worked as housekeepers while Wright hid inside.[16] The house, far back from Lake Simcoe, and away from Barrie's downtown, is big. That's about the best thing that can be said about it. It resembles a gigantic city duplex built at a right angle to the street, with no windows visible to passersby. The house was protected by a big yard covered with trees. It was not an inviting place, and Wright didn't want it to be. It was not meant to impress visitors because strangers were not welcome.

Prospecting opportunities seemed to be drying up. So, Wright plowed his money into the Brookdale standardbred and thoroughbred stables. Brookdale had been developed on the southwest edge of Barrie by the Dyment family, lumber barons who had bred winners—including four King's Plate champions—for two generations before going broke by making bad investments in the fledgling car industry.[17] As he eased into middle age, Wright became more isolated, travelling up to Kirkland Lake once a year to a Lake Shore Mine directors' meeting and, rarely, going to Toronto. His house began to fill with junk, his business affairs and tax records became a mess, and he was evolving into one of those men who, after years of being a bachelor, simply could not connect with other people.

He did connect with Barrie, though, and he became firmly Canadian. Sometimes, he'd go back to Lincolnshire to see family and old friends, but he'd get homesick for his horses and his house, and he'd cut short his visits. He didn't enjoy being around a lot of people, especially those who couldn't keep up with him in conversations about horses, gold prospecting or the First World War. He didn't want to engage in deep conversations with people who weren't his friends or members of his inner family circle. He kept to himself, wherever he was. Among the poor, that's a signal for potential interesting criminality. Among the rich, that made him "eccentric" and a "hermit."

Wright's days were split between hours at the barns and time at home, where he was often pestered by people arriving at his door with business proposals and hard-luck stories. And sometimes he gave these people help, which he usually regretted. Wright lived in fear of

William Wright's love of horses led to his friendship with George McCullagh. Wright is shown with two of his thoroughbreds at his farm near Barrie, Ontario. (TORONTO PUBLIC LIBRARY, TSPA_0090201F)

the moochers, the people who believed Wright's money could solve their problems. It wasn't too hard for these people to find out where Wright lived, but the Hargreaves were able to keep them away. When Wright went to Toronto on business, he made the Westminster Hotel his home, and the hustlers soon knew it. Once, a friend asked him to invest in some new venture. Wright took him to one of the Westminster's windows facing Jarvis Street and pointed over the city. "There's a lot of roofs over there," he said, pointing to the block of chimneys, "and I have enough second mortgages to cover them all."[18]

Then, one day, George McCullagh came knocking. It took a while for Bill Wright to answer, but his decision to open the door changed both their lives, along with the Canadian media landscape.

* * *

The second important actor in McCullagh's life was a very strange little man. Joseph Atkinson was forty years older than McCullagh and was eleven when William Wright was born. Atkinson's parents lived just outside the village of Newcastle, a community that is now on the edge of Toronto's sprawl but was, in December 1865, a self-contained village a half-hour train ride from the city. In the spring of 1866, when Atkinson was just six months old, his father, John Atkinson, was hit by a train as he staggered home after a night of boozing. Atkinson's mother, Hannah, was left with nothing but eight children to feed. She moved into town and opened a boarding house for workers at the Massey iron foundry, feeding and sheltering tough men. These boarders, immigrants from Britain, brought to the Atkinson dinner table stories of their battles with the factory bosses. Between listening to the complaints of these working men and seeing his mother struggle to feed and clothe her kids, young Joe developed a strong faith in God and a conviction that capitalism wasn't fair.

Hannah sent her children out to work as soon as they were big enough. Joe grew up counting every penny, and he would always be tight with a dollar. He had no real sense of fun as we'd know it: Joe spent his Sundays at the Methodist church, where he sang in the choir. Despite a stammer that he was able to overcome in his mid-twenties, Joe recited long passages of the Bible at morning services in the plain chapel of this rather dour faith. The minister paid him a few pennies to pump the church organ. There weren't many laughs in that childhood, and things didn't get better as time passed.

By the time Joe was fourteen, Hannah Atkinson, worn out from work, was dead. Although Joe was a keen, award-winning student, he had to drop out of high school to find full-time work to support his siblings, who were being raised by the oldest sister. By sixteen, he had a job in the post office but, because he was so tiny, he had to stand on a wooden box to see his customers. At eighteen, he started applying for jobs in banks, but before he found an opening, he took a job collecting delinquent accounts for the Port Hope *Times*. The only newspapers he'd ever read were the free copies of the Methodist weekly paper given out at his church. "I wanted to be a banker," Atkinson later said. "But six dollars a week was too good to turn down."[19]

The *Times* was on the edge of bankruptcy, partly because its advertisers were slow to pay their bills. Atkinson's arm-twisting of the merchants along Walton Street helped put the *Times* back on its feet but, after six years of working for the paper, Joe quit because his ingrate boss would not give him a dollar-a-week raise.

He soon found work on the Toronto *World*. This time, he was hired to write. After a few months of swallowing his own politics and writing editorials for that Conservative paper, Atkinson got a job on the Liberal *Globe* covering the Ontario legislature, following the spectacular career of premier Oliver Mowat, the great champion of provincial rights. Then he was assigned to the city beat, where he made his reputation writing human interest features—"sob stories" or "weepers" in the trade. He wrote his best stories after watching English fraudster Reginald Birchall hang in Woodstock. The sad, stressful assignment left a psychic scar, but his coverage of the murderer's last hours and execution put Atkinson into the front ranks of Canadian journalists. It also reinforced his belief that only God should have the power to decide whether men lived or died.

He stayed at the *Globe* for eight years, not making many friends except for William Lyon Mackenzie King, who joined the paper in 1893. The two men sometimes shared a desk, and they got along well because they were both quite strange. The year before King arrived on the paper, Atkinson married Elmina Elliott, a somewhat austere, liberal-minded journalist who wrote under the byline Madge Merton. (Women journalists in Canada almost always wrote under pen names in the nineteenth century to protect their privacy and avoid the stigma that came with paid employment.) Elmina also grew close to King and got to know his sisters. On the December 1921 day that King was sworn in as prime minister, Elmina placed flowers on the grave of King's sainted mother.

Elmina died in 1931, which made her much more interesting to King. She began to haunt his dreams, and it's clear that King's attachment to Joe had a lot to do with his necro-erotic feelings towards Elmina. He even sent a friend to Oakville to lay a wreath on Elmina's grave on the day that he was reappointed prime minister in 1935.[20] She became part of the pantheon of spirits who guided King's life and smoothed the way for him.[21] Atkinson likely knew of this obsession, but he does not appear to have taken advantage of it. He used his influence with King sparingly; for example, lobbying him for a comprehensive unemployment insurance program.[22] Holy Joe, as critics and staffers called him, put the *Toronto Star* at King's disposal when the strange little man was re-elected in 1935, but King, who was always tight with his own money, had no problem hitting up Holy Joe for a $1,000 donation the following year for a monument to his rebel grandpa William Lyon Mackenzie at Queen's Park.[23]

For two years, from 1897 to 1899, Atkinson was editor of the *Montreal Herald*. He returned to Ontario in 1899 to become publisher of the Toronto *Evening Star*, a floundering paper started by strikers at the Toronto *News*. The new paper was secretly backed by a syndicate put together by prime minister Wilfrid Laurier. It staggered through a series of owners and shed circulation for seven years. Atkinson took over the running of the newsroom and the business side of the paper, making a fortuitous deal with the owners that gave him a small salary but a steady stream of stock. Atkinson had to struggle against Sir William Mulock—a shareholder, Laurier government minister and mentor of Mackenzie King—who wanted to turn the *Star* into a dull Liberal Party rag. Atkinson was able to convince Laurier to rein Mulock in, and the *Star* began evolving into a great crusading metropolitan daily in the style of the Hearst and Pulitzer papers in the United States.

Atkinson built up the newsroom staff. He hired bright young graduates from the University of Toronto, bought big modern presses, redesigned the paper using large photos, half-tone engravings, and red ink on the front page. Atkinson also grafted it into the city's social conscience. It fought for social justice for the poor and advocated for women's rights. That didn't mean the paper would be considered progressive by today's standards. While it fought for the right of workers to unionize, and for Jews to be admitted to Canada from Nazi-controlled states, it was, at best, silent about discrimination against Indigenous people, Black Canadians and other racial minorities, including the often hard-pressed Chinese community. It gave no help at all to gays, lesbians, trans people or anyone else who didn't fit the gender norms of the time. It also had some strange views on the family, perhaps reflective of what went on in the Atkinson home. For instance, in 1938, the *Star* published an editorial advocating for a husband's supposed right to "spank" his wife:

"Husbands and wives in every part of the American continent and possibly throughout the world, have been intrigued by news from Winnipeg that a man in that city had been convicted for assault for spanking his wife and a year's sentence suspended over his head," a gobsmacked editorialist wrote. "The unfortunate husband may have been influenced by news reports to the effect that judges in other communities had commended he-men for administering chastisement that the court considered to be well-deserved. Everyone will agree that the uncertainty of justice towards such matters constitutes a grave domestic problem in the nine provinces of confederation that has its counterpart in other countries. Most decidedly, it is unfair that the authorities should leave husbands in doubt about the extent of their marital rights, privileges and responsibilities."[24]

The *Star* became a leader in attracting big display advertisements from new department stores downtown, and it worked hard to build circulation in the growing suburbs and in the cities along Toronto's borders, a strategy that is still the foundation of the *Star*'s business. At the same time, Atkinson built up his equity in the paper, buying out members of the original syndicate until only Mulock was left as a minor, if greatly enriched, shareholder. Atkinson had succeeded in leveraging his political alliances to create and gain control of a very powerful and profitable newspaper, and he was no longer a tool of the Liberals. He was a power in his own right. Supposedly, he was offered a Senate seat four times, and always said no.[25]

Holy Joe Atkinson used the paper to push his own religious and political agendas. A lifelong prohibitionist, Atkinson supported any politician who was serious about hobbling the liquor trade. Provincially, the Conservatives were usually the most adamant about closing saloons and banning booze. This put Atkinson in a political bind that was, in 1919, relieved by the election of the United Farmers of Ontario. While McCullagh was hiking the dirt roads of southwestern Ontario selling *Globe* subscriptions, Atkinson and UFO premier Ernest Drury were backing one of the strangest saloon-busters on the continent, Rev. Les Spracklin of Sandwich, Ontario, just south of Windsor.

The *Star* dispatched Roy Greenaway, its best reporter, to the Detroit River frontier to expose the rum-runners and their enablers and to hype the good works of saloon-busting vigilante Reverend Spracklin. The *Star* dubbed Spracklin the "Fighting Parson." Within days of Greenaway's first stories, Attorney General William Raney—who was another Atkinson friend—appointed Spracklin a provincial liquor law enforcer, independent of the local booze agents. Spracklin returned the favour by firing a bullet into the gut of saloon keeper Babe Trumble. The shooting spawned an inquest and a trial that showed both the sleaze along the Canadian side of the Detroit River and the over-the-top zeal of Spracklin and his men. Two of them would later be exposed as crooks who, when not blasting down the backroads of Ontario in hot cars to hunt smugglers, shook down bootleggers for protection money. A couple of years later, another of Spracklin's men went to jail for firing a gun through the wall of a Toronto duplex, accidentally killing a woman in the next house.

No paper in Canada was as determined as Atkinson's *Star* to cover this kind of story. While Holy Joe gradually lost the battle against the saloon and the bottle, his paper clawed its way through the overcrowded Toronto newspaper market and came to dominate it journalistically and commercially. In the first two decades of the twentieth century, the *Star* went from a dying paper with an empty newsroom to being home to Canada's most aggressive news team. Its sports reporters became legendary: Lou Marsh took over as sports editor when Bill and Foster Hewitt went to work for Maple Leaf Gardens. The paper also ran the best magazine in Canada, the *Star Weekly*, under Herbert Cranston, who joined the *Star* in 1904 as a kid reporter. Charles W. (C.W.) Jefferys was hired in 1900. Cranston commissioned Jefferys's first important historic drawing, of the death of Jean de Brébeuf, for a piece on Sainte-Marie among the Hurons.[26] Jefferys's historical drawings have been used in textbooks and commercial history books ever since.

Writer Joe Clark, who started at the *Star* in 1899, was "Atkinson's conscience." When Atkinson wasn't sure about what he should do with the paper, he would go into Clark's office and bounce ideas off his employee, who became the editorial page editor and first editor of the *Star Weekly* magazine.[27]

Under its second editor, Cranston, the *Star Weekly* gave contributors up to $100 for a piece. That was about what the best magazines in the country paid. (It was cut to fifty dollar during the Depression, a sum that was still decent money for the time.) By 1913, the *Star Weekly* was carrying colour comics, despite objections from Elmina Atkinson, who thought they were rude and distasteful. (She also successfully warded off an attempt to call the magazine the *Sunday Star*, since she found the idea of a Sunday paper to be quite repugnant.) By the end of the First World War, the *Star Weekly* was selling more than sixty-seven thousand copies a week. Later, the magazine would be killed, but the *Star Weekly* was the template for the *Saturday Star*, which, at its zenith just before the 1990 recession, sold more than a million copies a week.[28]

Readers loved the graphology column. They would send in handwriting samples, and an expert would analyze them. Eventually, the column took up an entire page and became so successful that the editors decided it had to be killed. They didn't have enough staff to handle the submissions. When the column was cancelled, there were still five thousand unopened letters. Cranston also bought articles from Nellie McClung and Emily Murphy. He serialized popular books and paid authors for the rights to print excerpts. Four of the Group of Seven (Franz Johnston, Arthur Lismer, Fred Varley and J.E.H. MacDonald) sold freelance illustration work to the *Star Weekly*.

Joe had been in the newspaper business for forty years when Elmina died, and he'd stay at it for almost two decades more. "Without a doubt, J.E. Atkinson lost his 'good angel' when his wife died, and the way was dreary for him afterwards," Cranston wrote in his memoirs. "He withdrew into himself, and became a lonely man in the newspaper household." Elmina had left her husband with several legacies, including his middle initial. The "J.E.A." at the end of his frightening office memos and on his business card included an *E* for Elmina. Holy Joe had no middle name.[29]

Cranston believed there were two separate Holy Joes fighting for control. "The first was a young, ambitious, hard-working and thrifty idealist.... The second J.E. Atkinson was the product of the *Star* skyscraper (which was finished in 1929). He created it and it possessed him. It became his master, a Frankenstein monster which demanded of him that he make the Star and his bank balance even bigger. With her companionship and the support of her idealism gone, the Chief gave his whole attention to amassing a great fortune."

Atkinson, unlike his competitors, plowed much of his profit back into the newsroom and bought the best technology to print his paper. The *Star*'s investigations into Canada's social problems were as good, or better, than any other journalism being published in North America at the time. If disaster struck anywhere in this country, a *Star* reporter—or, as likely, a team of them—would soon be on the scene. The paper hired the smartest, most talented journalists, people like Ernest Hemingway, who wrote features for the *Star* in Canada and Europe. Atkinson sent Gordon Sinclair and other correspondents on long assignments to the most exotic places on earth. The *Star*'s practice of throwing all its substantial resources at every big breaking news story in Ontario still makes the paper the best hard-news journal in the country.

Atkinson's strategy paid off. By the end of the 1920s, paperboys tossed the *Star* at just about every working-class and middle-class home in Toronto and surrounding towns, making it the leading newspaper in the city. The journalistic resources of the paper, combined with its huge circulation, made Joe Atkinson the most powerful publisher in the city. While other papers might be dominated by political parties, Joe Atkinson and the *Star* dominated politicians.

* * *

In the grim years of the Great Depression, these three weird men, McCullagh, Wright and Atkinson, would remake Canadian journalism entirely. Wright and McCullagh developed a partnership to create Canada's pre-eminent political newspaper. "Holy Joe" Atkinson built Canada's most successful metropolitan newspaper and helped make the Liberal Party the dominant national force in the twentieth century. With William Wright's money, McCullagh would fight Atkinson for every reader and every scrap of political power. The fight would continue through the Depression and the Second World War. And not even Atkinson's death would end it. In the end, Atkinson would be remembered and honoured. McCullagh would not.

3

GEORGE McCULLAGH'S TORONTO

The Toronto of the 1930s would be unrecognizable to people who know the modern city. Physically, the Toronto of a century ago has been erased or buried beneath the modern city. Only a few relics remain in the downtown core, and the swaths of housing built in Victorian and Edwardian times have changed, too. The culture of Toronto has also been overturned. Toronto used to be a town dominated by people from the British Isles. It was a place where rules against vice—everything from carrying an open bottle of liquor to opening a store on Sunday—were enforced with the law's full weight. Downtown Toronto was empty on weekends and at night. The city had very few restaurants. The best was on the top floor of the Eaton's department store, and it served English favourites, various types of roasted and boiled food. It was a city that stayed true to its roots: a settlement built in reaction to the American Revolution by people who deliberately, and sometimes at great cost, rejected the democratic and egalitarian ideas of the republic across the lake.

Toronto was founded in 1793, when Lieutenant-Governor John Graves Simcoe ordered British surveyors to lay out a street plan for a new town. The French had built a fort nearby decades earlier, and Indigenous settlements had come and gone over the centuries, but by the end of the 1700s no one was living there. The land belonged to the Mississaugas, and, in a council held on August 26, 1793, they asked Simcoe to build a town that would be a place where the First Nations could trade. It was certainly a "be careful what you wish for" moment.[1]

The first English and Scottish settlers were a tedious bunch. They came from the United States but they opposed everything about the new democracy. These refugees, many of them quite well-off and arriving with Black slaves, wanted to recreate pre-revolutionary America in this new province. They were, in politics and religion, reactionaries. And, having lost one country to the forces of change, they tried to make sure this new colony stayed true to their values. The people who ran Toronto demanded conformity and set up institutions of government, education and justice to protect their hold on power.

Toronto grew to become the country's leading town because of its location. When the Mississaugas and Simcoe agreed to create the settlement, Toronto Bay was at the south end of a canoe route up the Humber River to Lake Simcoe and Georgian Bay. The British soon laid out a road to Holland Landing, and eventually to Penetanguishene. Other roads cut into the wilderness of what's now southern Ontario brought business to Toronto (which was called York until 1834). A railway to Collingwood completed in 1854 strengthened the connection to the upper Great Lakes. Lines spread out to Detroit, Buffalo and Montreal, then across the country. The harbour, which is now buried under glass-fronted condominiums, was one of the busiest on the Great Lakes. (That harbour, which began at Front Street, was filled in decades ago.)

By the Depression, Toronto stretched up to Eglinton Avenue in the north, to the Humber River in the west, with footholds across the Don River in the east, and was separated from the lakeshore by factories, rail yards and grain elevators. Scarborough was a separate township where people farmed for a living. The Beaches was a cottage area, and Riverdale was a suburb. All the bedroom cities—Hamilton, Brampton, Newmarket, Oshawa—were towns of a few thousand people living an hour's drive from the fringe of the city. The Royal York Hotel, the tallest building in the British Empire, dominated the downtown skyline, until the old Bank of Commerce building surpassed it in 1931.

Having the tallest building in the British Empire gave the city, which has always been breathtakingly insecure about its place in the world, some bragging rights. Toronto was a British city. Its Britishness has long been erased and forgotten, but until the 1960s, it was an integral part of Toronto's identity. Politicians were judged by their loyalty to "British" values, and the rest of the people in town were slotted into social classes using British concepts of ethnicity: wealthy Protestant Anglicans, educated at private schools like Upper Canada College and Bishop Strachan School, were at the top; Scots and Ulster Protestant drones and their wives made up the bulk of the middle class; Roman Catholics, mostly Irish, but with a smattering of Italians and French Canadians, were at the bottom. People of colour, such as descendants of the slaves brought to the country in Toronto's early years and the few Black American underground railroad refugees who stayed on after the Civil War, did not rate at all. Nor did Chinese or Jews, who found many of the city's public spaces, as well as its university, law firms and its government jobs, off-limits.

It was usually impossible to break through Toronto's class barriers. Take the example of Horace "Lefty" Gwynne. Born in 1912, Lefty was a tiny but wiry man. He weighed only sixty-five pounds when he finished school at the end of grade eight. But Lefty had a lot of spunk, and he built himself up in his teenage years by working out at Stokley's

Gym. Lefty wanted to be a jockey, which would have been a decent job in that horse-mad city, but someone talked him into travelling to London, Ontario, and challenging for the Canadian amateur flyweight boxing championship. Lefty won those fights. He moved up a weight class and qualified for the 1932 Los Angeles Olympics, fighting as a bantamweight. Lefty went in as an underdog but left Los Angeles with a gold medal after knocking out German favourite Hans Ziglarski. He kept his amateur status for two more years so he could qualify for the 1934 British Empire Games, which were held in London, England. Lefty turned pro in 1935 and boxed for four more years as Canada's bantamweight champion.

Normally, that kind of success would make an athlete a local sports hero. After all, it would be another fifty years before a Canadian boxer had a serious shot at an Olympic gold medal, and it would come in Los Angeles in 1984, when a Soviet boycott thinned the competition.[2] But Lefty was a poor boy and an Irish Catholic. There would be no parade, no soft landing as a coach at a college, no easy white-collar career for a local hero. Lefty was given a job cleaning the Trinity Bellwoods recreation centre on Queen Street West, and few of the would-be athletes who went through that building over the next forty-five years had any inkling that the little guy with the mop had an Olympic gold medal in his china cabinet. Lefty left Toronto after he retired in the early 1980s because he couldn't afford to live in the city on his small pension, and settled in Midland, Ontario, where he died in 2001.

Lefty's story, except for his brush with athletic stardom, was typical of the lot of the city's Irish Catholics. Effectively blackballed from professional schools, elite social clubs, decent government jobs, managerial positions in the private sector, and politics, Toronto's Catholics had few opportunities and became victims of their own low expectations. The Loyal Orange Lodge, an anti-Catholic society so repugnant that it was banned in England, controlled the city government through the first half of the twentieth century. Orangemen dominated the police as well. Orangemen were officers in the city's militia units and prevented Catholics from enlisting. The Catholics tended to support the provincial and federal Liberals, not because the party had a soft spot for "RCs" but for the sake of Catholic schools. The Liberals were always willing to be a little more generous to them and hinted that the property taxes of Catholic businesses might be diverted from the public to the Catholic system. Someday. Later.

Still, until 1929, there were jobs for everyone. By the early 1900s, the city was one of North America's biggest meatpacking centres. The stench of giant industrialized slaughterhouses lingered over large parts of the city until the 1960s and can still be smelled in some neighbourhoods northwest of the downtown. When George McCullagh arrived in Toronto, its population was about 600,000. The city had become a manufacturing and financial centre that was self-supporting and, in many ways, disconnected from the rest of Canada. Like other cities, Toronto was a magnet for talent. Montreal, still the largest city in the country, was Canada's financial hub, but Toronto was catching up fast. Montreal was old money. Toronto was a place where an ambitious young man could make his fortune, if he fit in with the city's elite.

McCullagh, as a handsome descendant of Scots-Irish settlers, had only a small chance of breaking into Toronto society. His father's labour agitation was well-known in London, but not in Toronto. McCullagh wasn't Catholic and, best of all, he quickly made enough money to impress some of the social gatekeepers. And he was willing to spend it to buy his way in. He had absolutely no scruples about his social climbing. McCullagh wanted to know the right kind of people and to be their friend. His work life, at the *Globe* and on Bay Street, gave him access to Toronto's new rich, the men who made fast money financing the great gold boom in northern Ontario. McCullagh made these men, and their wives, the central players in his social life.

It helped that McCullagh had wit, a sense of humour, and the ability to tell great stories. People found him charming and smart. Many successful business people are sociopaths who can only pretend to be interested in other people. McCullagh was a man who had empathy, and understood human emotions because his own caused him so much pain. He was genuinely happy when his friends succeeded, and despite his sometimes crushing ego, he had no trouble spotting and fostering talent.

He was also, at heart, a shy man who preferred talking to small groups of people rather than lecturing a crowd. He had learned to respect working people as he hiked the flat country of southwestern Ontario, peddling newspaper subscriptions, even if he was determined not to be one of them. He seems to have been a good listener, and, in later years, that skill won him friends at the very top of the English-speaking world's political and business elites.[3]

* * *

The *Globe* job connected McCullagh with the men of Bay Street. At the time, the financial district was seething with speculation and hot money. This was the top of the Wall Street boom market of the Roaring Twenties. It was also the era when the big gold veins of northern Ontario were coming into peak production. As William Wright and Harry Oakes had learned, it took a lot of money to open a mine, and that capital came from big and small investors on Bay Street. The place was full of boiler rooms of people, at various levels of sleaze, peddling dreams.

For every Lake Shore Mine and Tough-Oakes, there were dozens of other small strikes that produced some gold. And there were many, many claims that had nothing at all. Companies were incorporated for all of them, and shares in these companies were sold to speculators all over the country. Before lotteries were legal, these shares were high-stakes gambling. People would sink their life savings into stories peddled by prospectors and stock hustlers. Stocks shot up even when the "mine" was nothing more than a few acres of staked land in the boreal forest. Writing boilerplate for new stock issues was almost as big, and as profitable, as mining. For every Wright and Oakes, for every Tough brother, there were dozens of mining millionaires in Toronto who had never been in the bush. McCullagh wrote about these men, got to know them as friends, learned how they operated, and sometimes bought into their stock fantasies.

Toronto might not have been cosmopolitan, but it was certainly more fun than London, Ontario, and the often-dry hick towns where McCullagh sold newspapers. McCullagh loved the racetrack and played the ponies with an eye for horses that set him apart from the other regulars. He did this despite his employer's insistence that gambling was a sin. William Jaffray hated it so much that he would not print anything in the *Globe* about horse racing. McCullagh also drank too much. But he didn't drink alone, and the Bay Street crowd loved its booze. There's no better friend than a drinking buddy, and McCullagh used booze to forge connections with the up-and-coming generation of Toronto leaders. He was an alcoholic before he turned twenty-five.

By then, the depression that had dogged him throughout his life must have been showing itself. Bipolar disorder tends to manifest when a person is in their mid-twenties, so it hit him when he was trudging those backwoods roads. Like most people who suffered from mental health challenges in those days—including the tens of thousands of veterans with post-traumatic stress disorder—McCullagh turned to booze. The sigma of mental illness was lethal to careers and social lives through most of the twentieth century. So McCullagh had to cope with it on his own. He couldn't seek help in Toronto, which treated its "manic depressives" by sending them to asylums. Private psychiatrists were rare in Toronto, and they probably would have done McCullagh more harm than good. Cognitive behavioural therapy hadn't been discovered. Nor had lithium drug therapy. People with bipolar disorder had to wait out the lows and hope that things wouldn't get too strange in the highs.

McCullagh hid his mental health problems through his life, and they appear to have been manageable in the first half of the 1930s. But as the decade went on, his mood swings became more extreme. Those who knew him well understood the pain he endured, while those on the fringe of his social circle and many of his political enemies thought he was just a troubled alcoholic. That reputation lasted long after he gave up booze.

All through his late teens and twenties, McCullagh had pushed himself hard and worked to impress others. If he had relationships with women during this time, they hadn't lasted. He had no one except his mother—living three hours away in London—who knew him well. He had no one close who could give him the grounding he would have needed. McCullagh, like any young man of his time, rammed down his feelings and kept going. Then he met Phyllis Laidlaw, a pretty young woman from Hamilton who seemed ready to buy into the McCullagh dream and was willing to share his night life and his mood swings. In return, she got an attractive and interesting man full of ambition.

Eventually, McCullagh was given the lofty title of assistant financial editor of the *Globe*, although the Jaffrays still believed his real value lay as a subscription salesman. In the spring of 1928, McCullagh was sent on a tour of Ontario to give lectures to new members of the "Just Kids" Safety Club. He started in eastern Ontario, organizing a meeting of six hundred adolescents in Gananoque, then a rally for a thousand children in Cobourg.[4] McCullagh had convinced school principals, town councils and local clergy to do the groundwork for these big events, where every member of the club got a membership card and a button.

Just as things got serious with Phyllis, the *Globe* job fell apart, and then the economy collapsed. McCullagh was never a good fit at the Jaffray family's paper, even when he was its best subscriptions salesman. The ugly meeting with Jaffray after his North Bay trip was the first sign of trouble. It was not the kind of place that welcomed playboys who were barely old enough to drink legally. By the spring of 1928, the Jaffrays had lost all love for McCullagh. He was called in by the publisher in the first week of June 1929 and fired, supposedly for smoking on the job. It was probably a mutual thing: the Jaffrays believed missionary work was the highest calling a man could achieve. To McCullagh, missionary likely had connotations that had little to do with travel to faraway places. McCullagh was a drunk on the staff of a newspaper owned by the country's second-most-vocal prohibitionist. (Holy Joe Atkinson being the first.) He was a hustler on a staff run by a man who inherited his job, in a newsroom of fussy old intellectuals. Both sides made the best of the situation: The *Globe* ran a short article saying McCullagh was joining an investment banking firm. There was a little party on the day he left, and people from all departments of the newspaper chipped in to buy him a set of golf clubs. "The next time I walk into this office, I'll own it," McCullagh half-joked as he walked out the door.[5]

He was twenty-four.

∗ ∗ ∗

McCullagh started at Harley, Milner (which soon became Milner, Ross & Co.)[6] and was named manager of the firm's stock exchange business. It might not have been the best time to become a stockbroker: the market crashed four months later. By then, McCullagh was Milner, Ross's floor manager on the Toronto Stock Exchange (TSE), so he was an eyewitness to the carnage. Most of his colleagues were wiped out, though the whiz kid was still standing. Industrial stocks had tanked, but the world still loved the gold and silver from northern Ontario, and stocks in those mines were McCullagh's specialty.

The near-collapse of capitalism was hardly enough to stop McCullagh's economic climb, but it did put a bit of a damper on his personal life. When the crash came, his confidence was shaken enough that he decided to postpone his marriage to Phyllis for a year. That was one of the few times he showed any fear. By 1931, the worst year of the

Depression, he was married and making big commissions selling and investing in mining and oil stocks. By early 1935, McCullagh was on the board of the Mining Corporation of Canada, one of the country's largest resource companies, and stayed there long after he became a newspaper publisher. He had left Milner, Ross to be the partner of Richard Barrett in the new firm Barrett, McCullagh. The Barretts had come into their fortune in a most peculiar way: the patriarch had answered an ad for lost heirs, found he was the closest living relative to someone he'd never heard of, and inherited several million dollars. Rather than stuff it into a bank account, the senior Barrett started a brokerage business and bought a seat on the Toronto Stock Exchange.

With Barrett money and McCullagh brains, Barrett, McCullagh became the fastest-growing firm on Bay Street. Its staff went from three brokers to forty in two months. The firm had offices in the Northern Ontario Building at 330 Bay Street, in the Sun Life building in downtown Hamilton, and agents across Ontario.

Most small investors and many of Canada's wealthiest people were wiped out by the crash and the Great Depression that followed it, but the gold mines of northern Ontario were still running, and the prospectors stayed in the field: gold was the big winner in the financial panic, rising from $20.67 an ounce in 1931 to $35 in 1934. And that was in deflated dollars. As gold went up, prices for just about everything, from land to cars to wages, went down. People were still putting what little savings they had into mining stocks. These penny stocks rarely paid off, but when they did, those who bought and held them made a lot of money.

There were big new gold strikes in the Red Lake area, at the other side of northern Ontario from Kirkland Lake. Mining stock hustlers pointed to Red Lake and insisted there were many more millions waiting for the penny stock investor who chose well. Some investors made their bets from advice in a booklet McCullagh published in 1936 that explained the geology of the gold fields and the skills used by prospectors.[7]

Phyllis McCullagh at a horse racing event. The McCullagh stables housed a collection of thoroughbreds that were raced and shown across eastern North America. (CITY OF TORONTO ARCHIVES, FONDS 1257, SERIES 1057, ITEM 3539)

The book was mostly nonsense that threw a few small hints to the suckers. Insiders like McCullagh could tell the difference between a real mine and a piece of moose pasture. Soon McCullagh's reputation as a rainmaker began to open doors. He joined the right clubs: the Granite Club and the Ontario Jockey Club, where he could engage with other people who shared his love of horses and mingle with people who showed up just because the Jockey Club attracted rich people. He had always been a social climber, but now, powerful men started coming to him. He was a millionaire before he turned thirty.[8]

McCullagh finally married Phyllis and settled into a new house in Toronto's up-and-coming Forest Hill neighbourhood. From the very beginning, though, George McCullagh's name was often preceded, in print, by the word *playboy*. Whether McCullagh started cheating on Phyllis right away or waited until he was bored with her, he certainly signalled his sexual availability. By the early 1940s, he was what we'd think of now as a serial sexual harasser and exploiter of the women who worked for him.

He also had a reputation as a hustler. His friend Allister Grosart, who had worked at the Toronto *Star* and went on to be a political operative and senator, remembered McCullagh and a friend of his, a man named Dawson, lurking around the financial district in the early months of his career, cadging ten-dollar loans that they'd promise to pay back at 100 percent interest by the end of the business day. Grosart was sure they'd take the money, rent a Cadillac and use it to impress a wealthy potential client, who would be conned into investing in some kind of sleazy stock scheme. Once, security investigators came after McCullagh and five of his friends. They flipped a coin to see who would take the rap. Dawson ended up the loser.[9]

A few years later, a man named Jefferies told Ontario Securities Commission chairman George Drew that McCullagh had worked with some of the biggest crooks on Bay Street, and he accused McCullagh of being the mastermind of a notorious scam involving South McKenzie Island Mines stock. South McKenzie Island was a garbage stock that was so worthless it was denied listing on the Winnipeg Stock Exchange curb exchange. But the Winnipeg brokerage firm of McKidd, Wither and Co. put its salesmen out onto the streets to peddle South McKenzie Island anyway. The firm set up a boiler room with long-distance phone lines to cold-call potential suckers across Canada. The backers of the scheme pulled in about $400,000. When the story hit the newspapers, the toothless Winnipeg Stock Exchange had to act. It fined McKidd $200.[10]

Jefferies also claimed McCullagh was hooked up with "Jake the Barber" Factor, one of the most notorious stock crooks in the world. Jake the Barber was the brother of makeup magnate Max Factor. He was connected to the mafia, and he lived one step ahead of the law, dodging cops and securities regulators in Europe before heading to the United States. Factor had fleeced royalty, rigged a table in Monte

Carlo's casino and broke its bank, and then had faked his own kidnapping in 1933 to escape extradition. (In 1962, he was finally ordered to be extradited, but was pardoned by President John Kennedy, despite the fact, or maybe because, he was now a front man for the mob in Las Vegas.)

Jefferies named three other scams McCullagh was supposedly involved in. One, a fraud involving Bidgood Mines, happened in 1927 when McCullagh was still writing for the *Globe*. Bidgood was being peddled by Solloway, Mills and Co., which was also secretly short-selling the stock. (Interestingly, Bidgood, near Kirkland Lake, turned out to be one of the few penny stock mines that had some gold in it.) The scammers had even swindled $750,000 from Bill Wright.

* * *

By the time McCullagh began his brokerage career, the Toronto exchange was a nest of thieves and scoundrels. Many of them were barely functioning alcoholics who pumped the value of penny stocks through scandal sheets like *Hush* and *Flash*, and tip sheets that they secretly controlled. Then they unloaded the stock on suckers who thought the value of the stocks would keep rising.

The Toronto Stock Exchange board of governors eventually caught on to some of McCullagh's schemes. In 1934, the TSE fined McCullagh $500 for playing fast and loose with something called Sakoose Gold Mines. The next year, regulators went after McCullagh twice more. He was nailed for being much too close to the promoters of the Natural Resources Company, which was another empty shell. A few months later, he was fined $100 for manipulating the share price of Bear Exploration and Radium. When the news of the fine came out, McCullagh phoned one of the exchange's floor governors, cursed the man out with a string of vile profanity and threatened him. The TSE made it clear to George McCullagh that he would be thrown out of the stock market if he ever did that again.[11]

In 1931, the Conservative provincial government tried to curb the worst abuses at the stock exchange by setting up a securities commission and hiring George Drew to run it. Drew had gone to all the right kind of schools, the ones McCullagh missed out on—Upper Canada College and the University of Toronto—before studying law. He was also an army officer who served with distinction in the First World War. Through his connections in the legal community, Drew had been appointed a master, a sort of minor judge who rules on legal issues before a case goes to trial. He had married Fiorenza Johnson, a glamourous opera singer who was daughter of the Metropolitan Opera's best tenor. Like McCullagh, Drew was handsome, charming and very smart. At first, the two men were at odds, but later they would team up to try to run the country.

McCullagh was in no danger of losing his business, no matter how many times he was gently slapped by regulators. There were always investors who believed maybe, just maybe, there would be another stock like Wright-Hargreaves or Lake Shore, or a winner like Temiskaming and Hudson Bay Mining, which went from eight cents to $300 in 1903.[12] But no casino ever went broke by paying too many winners, and no one was standing at King and Bay Streets in Toronto handing out dollar bills.

* * *

W.R.P. "Percy" Parker, another Mining Corporation board member, was one of those bright people who were taking over Bay Street. Parker was a corporate lawyer who had made millions speculating in oil and mining stocks. He was also a musician, bon vivant, social lion and a man who was good company. Parker was Toronto's most powerful backer of the federal and provincial Liberal Party. He was thirty-two years older than McCullagh, the author of two books on corporate law (including what was then the definitive text on corporate fraud) and one of the most well-connected men in Canada. He had gone to university with

Mackenzie King, along with men who were King's political opponents, Arthur Meighen and George Henry. The president of the University of Toronto was Parker's best friend, and they had known each other since college. His connections were just as strong overseas, especially among British and American investors. Parker made friends easily, and he was no snob. He liked interesting people, and they liked him.

McCullagh became Parker's protegé. Until then, the boy stockbroker had never shown any interest in politics. Sports was McCullagh's real love: he would, later in the decade, buy a piece of the company that owned the Toronto Maple Leafs and sit on the board of directors of Maple Leaf Gardens. He also became part-owner of the Toronto Argonauts football club and a generous donor to amateur sports teams across Ontario. But he did understand power—though, arguably, would never really comprehend how *political* power works—and he had an instinctive sense of where it was and how to court it. McCullagh and Parker co-founded the Centurion Club, which was a group of young, ambitious Liberals whose social haunts were around Bay Street. One night, Mitchell Hepburn, an onion farmer-turned member of Parliament from the back concessions of Elgin County, south of London, addressed one of their meetings. Hepburn was a troll-like demagogue-in-the-making, a greasy Donald Trump–like figure who was typical of the simplistic politicians who flourish in bad times. Hepburn knew talent when he saw it. He also understood the power of alliances, and soon became one of McCullagh's and Parker's drinking buddies. It's hard to see the attraction at first: Hepburn was an ugly, mean, whiny, oily man with tiny eyes, a round face and a dumpy body. McCullagh was tall, handsome, upbeat and slick. But they still had lots in common. McCullagh and Hepburn were from the same corner of the province, that flat, dusty country around London, and they understood, from close-up study, how the people on the farms and in the small towns saw the world. They knew what these people wanted to hear, and they had no qualms about telling them. Hepburn was smart enough to know when he was lying, but McCullagh was so self-absorbed and troubled that he likely believed his own guff. They were also young, successful alcoholics, something that forged a bond.

Being a provincial Liberal boss in early Depression-era Toronto was no great achievement in a city that was solidly Tory and Orange. Toronto Liberals of that age were outsiders: a mix of self-made men, Catholics, a few Jews, and some activist women (who were forced to stay behind the scenes). The younger ones were unfamiliar with power, but that was about to change.

A few months after that first meeting at the Centurion Club, Hepburn won the leadership of the Ontario Liberal Party with Parker's and McCullagh's help. It was a close-run race, but the leadership seemed like a worthless prize. Everyone expected the Tories, with their reputation for solid management and stable, predictable government, to keep Queen's Park for a while. But the mid-1930s were a time of sweeping generational change in Canada. McCullagh was the right age, and he'd taken the risk of hitching his political star to the Liberals when they were in Opposition in the Ontario legislature and the federal Parliament. It is much easier to sidle up to political leaders and top strategists when they are in the wilderness and hungry for support. Within a year or so of McCullagh's connecting with the Liberals, many of those players would be swept into power in Toronto and Ottawa, their phone numbers would be valuable, and their doors closed to ambitious strangers.

At the same time, dynamic and terrifying forces were at work in the rest of the world. Few people cared when Italy slipped into fascism in the early 1920s, but they took notice when Hitler came to power in Germany in 1933. Coincidentally, Franklin Roosevelt was sworn in a few weeks later as president of the United States. All over the world, hard times had left frightened and hungry people scrambling for solutions and looking for ways to make sense of the crisis. Throughout the authoritarian world, people supported murderous regimes because they seemed to guarantee survival. In the few surviving democracies, a lot of people thought Hitler, Mussolini and Stalin were on the right track.

The Ontario Liberals had a tough fight ahead of them. For a generation, they'd saddled themselves with unelectable leaders peddling unpopular policies. During the war, hatred of booze motivated Atkinson and other prohibitionists to support lawyer (and later judge) Newton Rowell, a die-hard "dry" who led the Ontario Liberal party from 1911 to 1917. Rowell turned out to be political poison, and was succeeded by a less dour man, Hartley Dewart, who was open to a compromise on booze. Dewart lost prohibitionist support to the United Farmers and was driven out of his job by Atkinson and the "drys." After the farmers' movement collapsed, the Tories returned to power on a pledge of allowing the sale of weak beer—Fergie's Foam—named after the leader of the Conservatives. It was just 4.4 percent alcohol, but it was strong enough to sink the Liberals, who were still under the bone-dry thumb of Holy Joe and his Social Gospel friends.

By 1930, the Liberals were a shadow: they hadn't been in power since 1905. In the last election, held in 1929, they'd won only 13 seats in the 112-seat legislature. The Tories won 90. (Independent members of provincial parliament [MPPs] and members of small parties, including the ashes of the UFO, won the rest.) The Liberal Party had become a club of ambitious, hopeful, outsider Toronto lawyers, with some meddling by federal Liberal cabinet ministers and senators. Joe Atkinson struggled to keep the party alive and dry, lobbying the federal party for an infusion of cash and for organizational help. No one seemed to care. In 1930, after losing eight elections under seven leaders, the Liberals held a leadership vote. Two former federal cabinet ministers, Peter Heenan and James Malcolm, wanted to run. So did Toronto lawyer Arthur Roebuck. Sydney Tweed, a member of the legislature, also campaigned. Some southwestern Ontario Liberals wanted a young outsider,

Paul Martin, but the hardest-working Liberal organizers backed Mitchell Hepburn, the first-term Liberal MP from Elgin West.

Hepburn made his first pitch to the Centurion Club at a meeting over Hunt's Store at the corner of Yonge and Bloor. Hepburn had something that no Liberal leader in Ontario of the past generation had: charisma in one-on-one meetings and the ability to whip up a crowd, even though his high-pitched voice was grating, especially when he became so worked up that it broke into a sort of shriek. Hepburn didn't have a speck of caution. He thrilled crowds with his violent denunciations of Tories. He didn't try to dodge the liquor issue. If a man wanted to drink, it was no one's business, he said. (If a woman wanted to drink, it was her husband's or father's business.) Put Prohibition aside, he told crowds, and fight the Conservatives on their economic record. That was a powerful message. This was the height of the Depression. Banks were seizing farms, and St. Lawrence Hall in Toronto was now a shelter for the homeless. No one knew how long the hard times would last, or how the Depression would end. (The last "Great Depression" had lingered from 1873 to 1896. Middle-aged people could still remember it.)

In a letter to Mackenzie King, Percy Parker described the impression Hepburn had made at the Centurion Club: "He created something akin to a sensation, and after the dinner was over, there were expressions that he was the man for Leader."[13] King, who only generated sensations of boredom when he spoke in public, should have been forewarned. Knowing the ambitious, sociopathic onion farmer as a member of his federal caucus and spooked by the idea of a Hepburn run, King did a very King thing and tried to bust up this phenomenon by talking Parker into running. It didn't work: Parker thought he was too old. King spent the rest of the undeclared campaign trying to sabotage Hepburn. Most, if not all, of King's machinations were reported to Hepburn, who had gained the momentum to win. While Hepburn was still running as a populist and an outsider, Parker was lining him up with Bay Street money.

All this attention thrilled Hepburn, who, beneath the bluster, was insecure and very susceptible to flattery. His own father, who had been a local candidate for the federal Liberals in the 1904 national election, had seen his political career smothered at birth when his Tory opponents had dragged him into court as a witness in a prostitution case. He had supposedly been seen in a whorehouse in the hamlet of Orwell.

The idea of an Ontario Liberal leader who every well-connected person in Toronto knew was a drunk, and who came with a fairly long list of other vices, mortified Atkinson, who worked with King to scuttle Hepburn's campaign. They eventually backed William Sinclair, the party's fifty-seven-year-old interim leader. It was a strange convention, which was held at the King Edward Hotel. Two candidates withdrew when their supporters nominated them, leaving Hepburn and Sinclair. Then Sinclair walked up to the podium. On the way from his seat to the stage, he looked over the crowd, felt the energy in the room and, to the horror of Atkinson, who sat at the press table, told the Liberal delegates it was time to step aside and let a new generation take over. Without a vote from the delegates, Mitchell Hepburn was now leader of the Ontario Liberals. He owed his election to people like George McCullagh and Percy Parker, and he would need them even more when it came time to pay for a provincial election campaign.

Holy Joe was willing to swallow his defeat and support Hepburn if it meant the Tories would finally lose power. He and McCullagh were on the same team, even though the anal little Toronto *Star* publisher wouldn't have been caught in the same room as the hard-drinking young stockbroker. Atkinson ordered some of his best reporters to leave the *Star* to work on the Liberal campaign. The Liberals picked up the salaries of Roy Greenaway and the other *Star* journalists who were lent to the Hepburn campaign, but they were still very much Holy Joe's men. Greenaway was put to work on political research, which he described as "digging up dirt," and writing speeches for Liberal members of the legislature during the run-up to the campaign. Greenaway got his hands on the "liquor toll gate letters," which showed that the managers of the provincial liquor agency took kickbacks from some of the distillers who wanted their products sold in government stores. Greenaway ended up buying some of these letters with his own money.[14]

McCullagh ponied up for the campaign and, like Parker, tapped his friends and clients for contributions. Hepburn was the kind of Liberal who could raise money on Bay Street. He ran what we'd see today as a conservative, populist campaign: he would reopen the beer parlours, slash government spending, sell the lieutenant-governor's mansion and auction off the government's fleet of limousines. He told farmers that he represented the poor people on the "back concessions." He told urban workers they were overtaxed and despised by the old Tory elite that ran the province. He was anti-union. He wanted Marxist professors out of the universities.

The parallels with modern populism didn't end there. Hepburn's own personal life couldn't bear any scrutiny. He was a pig when it came to women, an ugly drunk, and had no qualms about the people he hung around with. His behaviour would get worse and much more blatant as the years went by, and it would eventually kill Hepburn while he was still a young man.

4

OWNING
A PREMIER

In early September 1933, as the country went into its fourth year of the Great Depression, the leading thinkers of the federal Liberal Party gathered at the pretty little Lake Ontario town of Port Hope.[1] The Liberals had been thrown out of office in 1930, but they knew they had a shot at power in the election that had to be called soon. Famous and smart people were invited to talk about important domestic and international issues. The speeches and the conclusions were not that interesting, but the party gave the appearance of preparing its leaders to govern. Delegates at a round-table discussion on electoral reform heard about the success of compulsory voting in Australia and gave serious thought to proportional representation. Oliver Mowat Biggar, who had a perfect Liberal pedigree (he was the grandson of then-legendary, now forgotten Ontario premier Oliver Mowat[2]), pitched the idea of a mixed proportional-direct representation system. Other sessions debated issues that would be just as familiar to modern Canadians: the national debt, the country's relationship with the Americans, and the state of the economy.

But for this story, the issues were less important than the players. All the important people were at the Port Hope conference. All the movers and shakers who were friends of Mackenzie King. They were professors from McGill University and the University of Toronto, along with an academic from Beijing—a rather interesting choice considering King's ugly views on Asians[3]—and a smattering of British and American liberals. Each province sent a delegation, but there weren't any Hepburn followers. Mitch and his friends were not the right kind of people. They hadn't gone to prep schools like Upper Canada College and on to the University of Toronto, Queen's or McGill. Photos from the session invariably show white men in their fifties wearing tweed jackets in the late-summer heat, thoughtfully holding pipes. These were what historian Jack Granatstein labelled "The Ottawa Men," insiders who controlled government for three generations. They were, culturally, a world away from McCullagh. Sessions like the Port Hope conference were a reminder of who was *in* and who was *out*, politically and socially, in the incoming regime. King was a very skilled politician. Such a mediocre human being had to be. But he was also a snob, and his obvious contempt for Hepburn and his friends was to cause serious trouble for the Liberals and for Canada.

These tweedy Liberals came from money. People like Hepburn and McCullagh had to earn it, or get control of patronage so that cash flowed to them. McCullagh knew how Hepburn ticked, diagnosed his insecurities and understood that the onion farmer from the back concessions of Elgin wanted to be a much richer man. So McCullagh offered to handle Hepburn's investments. This was a savvy move for both men. McCullagh now had instant access to Hepburn, and Hepburn made a lot of money. McCullagh knew the rhythm of stock-pumping. He knew the stocks that were worth buying and keeping, and the ones that were short-term investments that needed to be sold before the suckers bolted. He and Hepburn were into Kerr-Addison at about fifteen cents a share before drilling results came back showing the company had found a big ore body and shares went to four dollars.

The engineer who had done the drilling at the Kerr-Addison strike had tipped McCullagh that the company's stock was a bargain. The same man told McCullagh of another prospect, Hislop, which was supposed to be just as good. McCullagh put his own money into that stock, and added some of the premier's. This mine came in, too.[4]

McCullagh made sure Hepburn's name was kept off the transactions, but the shares were Mitch's. The money that came from these investments paid for a lifestyle that started to resemble that of a gangster: a big suite at the King Edward Hotel, booze, women, and heavies who "assisted" the young Liberal leader.

Finally, in the spring of 1934, Mitch Hepburn got his shot at Tory premier George Henry. This was a time when people packed halls to hear campaign speeches. Hepburn made it worth their while. At one campaign stop, he climbed onto a pile of manure and apologized for speaking on the Tory platform. Everywhere he went, he accused the Tories of corruption. He and his campaign staff waved affidavits that, they said, proved Henry's government was crooked. Many of these charges were utterly bogus, but Henry didn't know how to fend them off before the next barrage of charges came in, and people were entertained and didn't care. Hepburn shredded his opponents with reckless accusations and with humour. His audience had been through the worst years of the Depression and there was no end in sight, and they wanted some rich guys to pay. The campaign became a sort of party, with Hepburn doing his stand-up comedy act in small towns across the province. The message was clear: Tory insiders were making millions off a province that was sinking into debt, while taxpayers were going broke. Hepburn promised to slash the cost of government by 50 percent. He'd get rid of all the board members and administrators who drew fat salaries and drove around the province in big cars. He'd fix Hydro, which was losing money on contracts that it had signed with private power corporations in Quebec and eastern Ontario.

Neil McKenty, a former radio journalist-turned-Jesuit scholar, wrote a stellar biography of Hepburn in 1967. McKenty describes the biggest Hepburn campaign rally of the election, which was not held in Toronto (where Parker was on the board of directors of the new Maple Leaf Gardens, which was bult by McCullagh's friend Conn Smythe) or Ottawa or even Hepburn's hometown of St. Thomas. It was in Midland, a south Georgian Bay community of just eight thousand people. The town council was bankrupt. The main industry, a shipyard that built Great Lakes freighters, was idle. Even the town's newspaper had gone broke.[5] Some five thousand men, women and children jammed into the town's hockey arena, with an overflow crowd of hundreds more outside. The brutal heat might have dissuaded some people from turning out to hear Hepburn, but those who did show up got one hell of a show.

Hepburn and his team blasted along the highways and dirt roads in a motorcade, down Midland's Yonge Street from Highway 27, the old Penetanguishene Road, through Little Lake Park and finally, very noisily, stopped at the arena entrance.

A bagpiper escorted Hepburn to the stage through waves of cheers, which rarely died out as he spoke. Hepburn wore a dazzling blue double-breasted suit. It was probably, in this world of poor workers and drab politicians, the flashiest piece of clothing anyone in Midland had ever seen. On stage, Hepburn's right arm flashed up into a wide wave and his face brightened with a big smile. "We want Mitch! We want Mitch!" the crowd shouted, and the candidate hadn't opened his mouth. When he did, his words were like wire whips, flaying the Tory Opposition.

He told Midlanders about "the malodorous record of Tory administration." Premier Henry's relief program was just make-work. "Where there are ditches on the highways, they're filling them in, and where there aren't ditches, they're digging them." (In fact, Henry had built the province's first four-lane highway, the Queen Elizabeth Way, from Toronto to Niagara. It was nowhere near Midland, so Hepburn could get away with misrepresenting it.) Then Hepburn began working a very cruel vein. Henry made the mistake of trying to match Hepburn's appeal to farmers by allowing himself to be costumed in old farmers' clothes, pretending to be a man of the soil. Henry did own more than four hundred acres of prime farmland on the edge of Toronto (which he would sell for millions of dollars in the 1950s) and had studied agriculture, but he'd spent his working life as a lawyer and everyone knew it. "They tell me 'Honest George' hasn't worn overalls since he gave up wearing three-cornered pants—diapers—sixty-five years ago."[6]

Hepburn heaped scorn on anyone who indulged in the trappings of power. In the Midland rally, as in many other speeches, he ripped into the province's lieutenant-governor, who, by constitutional convention, was prevented from fighting back. "There will be no more Lieutenant Governors in this province until we get out of the present period of Depression!" (This was a promise Hepburn could not keep, since only the British Parliament could change the Canadian constitution, which Hepburn certainly knew.) Then Hepburn—to more waves of "We Want Mitch!"—pledged, without any irony, to end the days of fat-cat cabinet ministers riding around Toronto in limousines. "If we are elected, we are going to line up all the limousines at Queen's Park and sell them to the highest bidder!" Premier Henry and the Tories could call him a communist. They could call him anything they wanted. But Hepburn had convinced the voters of Midland and those in farms and small towns across the province that he was their last real hope.[7]

The election was a rout. There wasn't a Conservative elected west of Toronto. And Liberals would hold many of those southwestern Ontario seats for the rest of the century, until another populist, Progressive Conservative "Common Sense Revolution" peddler Mike Harris, took them back. The Tories held a few seats in the Toronto area and their unassailable bloc in Orange eastern Ontario. Hepburn won sixty-six seats to Henry's seventeen. He now owned Ontario. And he was the most powerful Liberal in Canada. But there was one Liberal who was not pleased: Atkinson of the *Star*.

"The Chief (Atkinson), having closely investigated Hepburn, had changed his mind," senior reporter Greenaway wrote years later. "Senator Arthur Roebuck recently told me that the day after the election, Mr. Atkinson informed him: 'I don't like him. I don't like what he stands for, and I don't like the company he keeps.' If Mr. Atkinson could have heard the new premier state exuberantly as we [Greenaway and Hepburn] drove to Toronto (just after the election) that he was going to make the liquor interests pay entirely for future elections, he might have been even more confirmed in his decision."[8]

Mitch Hepburn was thirty-seven years old, eight years older than his friend George McCullagh. It was a sea change. A new generation of leaders was taking over, and McCullagh was right in the middle of it.

After trying so hard to get his message out, George Henry finally said something that would resonate: the people of Ontario "are in for interesting times."[9]

* * *

For the next two years, George McCullagh made money while his friend and drinking buddy Mitch Hepburn ran the province. McCullagh, partly because of his Liberal connections, his youth—he turned twenty-nine a few months before Hepburn was elected—and his personality, was asked to be on the boards of directors of several large and small corporations. He even took up liberal causes, joining the well-connected Canadians who helped spring model prisoner/reformed robber Norman "Red" Ryan from Kingston Penitentiary in 1935 and got him a show on news radio station CFRB, where he denounced the Depression-era crime wave in North America. (Ryan was shot by cops the following year while holding up a liquor store in Sarnia.)

Across the country, similar populist politicians were seizing power: Social Credit, a bizarre movement that combined Christian fundamentalism with demands for central banks to stimulate the economy through inflation, became the most powerful political movement in western Canada. "Bible Bill" Aberhart, elected premier of Alberta in 1935, made time in his busy schedule to go on the radio every Sunday morning to sermonize. (His "Back to the Bible" broadcasts long outlived him and were broadcast in rural Canada well into the 1980s.) A parallel movement, Christian socialism, fronted by J.S. Woodsworth, had co-opted the old Social Gospel movement and picked up some of the Prairie "progressives" along with non-Communist labour activists to emerge as the Co-operative Commonwealth Federation. Maurice Duplessis, who'd taken control of Quebec's Conservative Party in 1933, transformed it into the neo-fascist Union Nationale. Then, as attorney general, he sent his provincial police to crush those whom he considered communists—which was just about everyone who believed in democracy or criticized his government—and waged a dirty war on Jehovah's Witnesses. Canada was being pulled apart, splintering in the same way as Great Britain and parts of Europe.

Mackenzie King, re-elected in 1935 after five years in the wilderness, saw himself as the bulwark against extremism, much of which he rightly described as fascism. (Joe Atkinson went to Ottawa to help pick the cabinet. When Jaffray, the publisher of the *Globe*, showed up at King's house to give King his list of picks, the prime minister had to hide Holy Joe in the upstairs study. King's life often had the attributes of a 1960s TV sitcom.[10]) The stranger things became in provincial politics, the more King became a symbol of national unity and stability. And the more he became an immovable rock of centrist liberalism, the more of a target he became.

Meanwhile, Hepburn was doing what he said he'd do. He fired every provincial employee hired after October 1933. Every game warden in Ontario was pink-slipped. If people needed to hunt for food in these hard times, no one was going to stop them. Hepburn cut his own salary, a gesture that might have won less praise if the public knew of the windfalls he was making from McCullagh's management of his stock portfolio. Hepburn fired most of the board of Ontario Hydro, along with many of its managers. Ontario's tourism and trade office in London, England, got the chop. And the province pulled out of sponsorship of the Canadian National Exhibition. Hepburn even sent former premier George Henry a bill for $3,004 for repairs made to Henry's car by Ontario government mechanics.

He sold Chorley Park, the lieutenant-governor's mansion.[11] And, two months after the election, he kept his promise to sell the government's fleet of cars. An auction on the lawn of Queen's Park was impractical, so Hepburn booked Varsity Stadium at the University of Toronto. Eight thousand people turned out to watch the sale. They sat in the stands through the auctioning of forty-six cars before the big event: George Henry's Packard limousine was hoisted into the air and sold for $1,500. In all, the big sale netted the Government of Ontario $34,000. When a Liberal senator complained that the show was gaudy burlesque, Hepburn answered, "You can have too much dignity in government."[12]

Selling the lieutenant-governor's mansion and auctioning the limousines thrilled the unsophisticated. Dumping the game wardens was likely quite popular with impoverished people living in the boonies. These were the things that made the front page of the papers. At the same time, Hepburn was making institutional changes to the way the province was governed and entrenching machine politics into all aspects of regulation and decision-making. Firing George Drew and declawing the already toothless Ontario Securities Commission was one of those moves. McCullagh had a hand in that—Drew would eventually forgive him and become his best friend—and helped Hepburn cope with Drew's counterattack. Drew, who was as brilliant, charismatic and handsome as McCullagh, never, throughout his life, had qualms about turning policy disputes into personal feuds. He responded to the moves against him by accusing the attorney general, Arthur Roebuck, of shabby pre-crash dealings on the Toronto Stock Exchange. Then Drew went much farther. He dragged members of Roebuck's family into it. The ugly little fight generated at least one libel suit, but that didn't stop Hepburn from hiring Liberal lawyer John Godfrey to fill the job. Drew went on to write a series of anti-marijuana articles for *Maclean's* magazine as he waited for his shot at a political career. When it came, George McCullagh was at his side.

In early April, Latham Burns, one of Percy Parker's large circle of friends, died. Burns's funeral was held in miserable Toronto early spring weather, and Parker, who already had a bad cold, was asked to be a pallbearer. He could have begged off because of his illness, but Parker wasn't the kind of man who would let a friend down, even if that friend was in a casket, so he did the job. A few days later, his cold worsened and became pneumonia, and on April 21, 1936, he died too.

Parker's death left a huge hole in George McCullagh's life. It also shocked the country's political class. The prime minister was at the funeral, along with his nemesis, former prime minister Arthur Meighen. Hepburn and several former premiers, along with the entire cabinet, sat near the front of St. James Cathedral. Most members of the provincial legislature and Toronto-area members of Parliament showed up, and the rest of the church was packed with friends from Bay Street and the Ontario legal fraternity. The casket was surrounded by heaps of wreaths, some from mourners in London and New York. The list of people and organizations that sent flowers took up about ten inches of newspaper column space.[13]

Parker left behind a seat on the University of Toronto board of governors, which Hepburn gave to McCullagh. Today, there are a lot more universities and much bigger governing boards, so being on one is not a huge honour. In 1936, however, being appointed to the small board of the single university in Toronto was a big enough deal that the newspapers wrote about it. And the position was a huge door-opener for an ambitious young man who didn't even finish high school, let alone have a BA. Even McCullagh would admit he was no scholar: "I have just two hobbies: work and fishing," he told a reporter who called to ask him about the appointment.[14]

McCullagh realized the value of what, today, is a rather empty, unpaid bit of patronage. "I consider the honor most helpful to myself. I am proud to be associated with the truly great men on the board," he continued. He should have stopped there but, being McCullagh, he didn't. "I have great respect for the wisdom brought by grey hair," he added tactlessly.

Through the Depression, there were about eight thousand students at the University of Toronto. Most were men, from well-off families. The few women who studied there tended to gravitate to arts and to health-care training, studying nursing and occupational and physical therapy. Their numbers were rising: admissions to those women-dominated faculties doubled during the Depression.[15]

But the University of Toronto had serious problems. The post–First World War rise of the Left was reflected in the university's faculty, if not in its student body. In 1919, Professor R.M. MacIver attracted the wrath of corporate leaders with his book *Labour in a Changing World*, published during the Red Scare. In 1931, when the Toronto police banned a pacifist group called the Fellowship of Reconciliation, a petition signed by sixty-eight University of Toronto professors was circulated around the university.[16] At about the same time, the editor of the student paper, the *Varsity*, was suspended for a piece he wrote about "practical atheism" being prevalent on campus.

The board of governors didn't like all this controversy, but it kept coming. Anglican cleric Henry John Cody, president of the university, had been Parker's best friend, even though Cody was a Tory. Seeing the university as a potential enemy, Hepburn cut the province's grant in half, to just over $1 million. That caused the university to nearly double the annual tuition from $75 to $130. Faculty salaries were cut. The university's research budget was slashed from $80,000 to $29,000. The meagre scholarship fund was nowhere enough to help undergrad and graduate students, and some donors stipulated that scholarships only be given to white Protestant British subjects, which was fine with President Cody.[17]

This was a troubled organization, and, at first, McCullagh wasn't sure he wanted the job. Parker's death seems to have pushed McCullagh into a depression that he tried to soothe with more liquor. He knew his alcoholism was out of control and told his drinking buddy Hepburn how he worried that he wasn't up to the job, that a thirty-one-year-old drunk should not be on the university's board. Given time to think, McCullagh then decided he wanted the job so badly that he swore off booze. Later, when critics accused him of being a drunk, he made that pledge public. He wrote a piece describing how he'd "experienced great sorrow through drunkenness and witnessed the same pitiable misfortune for many of [my] generation."[18]

Privately, McCullagh even started helping other men give up liquor, sometimes becoming a pest among his friends. It's not clear whether McCullagh was always able to hold on to his sobriety, in the long run. Alcohol was still the only way open to him to deal with his lows. And it was the social lubricant that turned business associates into friends, or even into binge buddies who could be trusted with a man's dirty secrets. Booze was a question that dogged McCullagh all his life, perhaps because people saw his big mood swings and thought they had to be caused by some external thing. But it is safe to say that after 1935, McCullagh very much wanted to stay sober and was, at least, trying. Remaining sober would be difficult in the boozy world of Bay Street and Queen's Park, where "drys" were considered throwbacks to Prohibition and men who abstained were believed to be strange. People who quit weren't considered healed; they were believed to be so damaged that they couldn't socialize properly.

A seat on the University of Toronto's board moved McCullagh into a higher social class. It put him in the same room as ancient Sir William Mulock, ninety-three, the former Laurier cabinet minister and Ontario chief justice who had bankrolled the Toronto *Star* in its early years; Sir Joseph Flavelle, the seventy-eight-year-old entrepreneur who put the "hog" in "Hogtown" by opening a massive pork processing operation at the mouth of the Don River; Vincent Massey, scion of one of Canada's wealthiest families, who would later be the first Canadian-born governor general; future Supreme Court of Canada chief justice and Mackenzie King confidante Sir Lyman Duff; Newton Rowell, a well-connected Liberal who had just been appointed Ontario's chief justice; and two other judges. McCullagh was now connected to the inner core of Canada's legal and political establishment, especially the Liberal members of that elite.

McCullagh, with his connections to both old and new Toronto money, was a good catch for the university. Despite the controversies generated by some of its Marxist professors, most of the student body was pro-capitalist. He was a governor who was only a decade older than most of the students, a guy who had made it big in the teeth of economic events that had knocked most of the country onto its back.

There were some people in the university community who were appalled by the appointment. Cody took an immediate disliking to the high school dropout. Cody wrote in his diary that McCullagh talked for the first hour at his first board meeting about ways to make the meetings shorter, then wanted a say in everything that went on at the university.[19] That included meddling with tenured faculty. In 1937, after McCullagh founded the *Globe and Mail*, left-wing historian Frank Underhill complained in a Canadian Broadcasting Corporation (CBC) debate that he was now stuck with reading the opinions of gold-mining millionaires over breakfast. The *Globe and Mail* demanded his dismissal, and Cody went through the motions of calling him into his office, but Underhill, who would get into plenty of trouble at the university later, got off with a light warning.[20]

The announcement of McCullagh's appointment to the U of T board made the pages of the *Globe* and the *Star*. The latter could hardly be accused of overplaying the story. It gave the news four paragraphs on page six, quoting the government's press release: "Mr. McCullagh is recognized as one of the leaders among young men associated with the mining industry in Canada," it said blandly. A quote from Hepburn was tacked on. The appointment, he said, "was a gesture of recognition to the younger businessmen of the province, as well as the selection of a keen business mind and charming personality to the Board of Governors."[21] Another small story in the same newspaper reported on McCullagh's thrill at being appointed. He'd gone to work at his brokerage firm that day, and spent most of the time fielding phone calls and telegrams of congratulations. Parker's death had opened up this opportunity, but it also left McCullagh without an adult male authority figure and patron. McCullagh quickly found another one, and their partnership would change Canadian history.

5

MEETING
MR. WRIGHT

McCullagh was thrilled when the *Globe* ran a short editorial praising Mitchell Hepburn's government for putting McCullagh on the University of Toronto's board. Now it was obvious to the whole city that McCullagh's appointment was a big deal. It was one of the few times McCullagh had seen his name in the *Globe* when he hadn't needed to pay for an ad.[1] It seemed to be a signal from William Jaffray, the owner of the paper, that the boy he'd thrown out of the newsroom had made good. The editorial congratulating McCullagh was a small thing, but it made McCullagh think: If editors and publishers had the power to praise and belittle, to make and break careers, to create such intense feelings in the people they wrote about, why shouldn't he have it? The *Globe* was just a newspaper that had filled a bit of empty space with a minor news item, yet a few words on its editorial page had the power to change McCullagh's entire mood, to make him feel good about being George McCullagh. What if it was *his* editorial page?

For generations, newspapers had been small businesses. Printers, once they learned their trade, went off to start their own papers. Most towns had at least two newspapers, and some had half a dozen. The printing press was always being improved, so there were plenty of cheap used machines available in the United States that could be brought across the border. But in the late 1800s and through the early years of the new century, Canadians started to expect more from their newspaper than just a few pages of ads and some columns of old news and partisan opinion. This was especially true in cities, where competition had become fierce.

The market was oversaturated before the First World War, so there was an epidemic of newspaper fatalities in the first two decades of the twentieth century. Craft printers and politicians were driven out of the big markets, and outsiders with deep pockets started taking over newspapers for their value as investments.[2] This remaking of the market continued through the Roaring Twenties, and there were more newspaper closures during the Depression. Survivors were hungry for investment capital. Big-city papers now needed good presses, big staffs and downtown offices. The *Globe* could trade on its name, but it was becoming threadbare and worn, a throwback in a city with four big daily newspapers and scores of other news sheets and magazines. There was also labour trouble brewing: in the summer of 1936, journalists on the *Globe* and the *Mail and Empire* were trying to organize a union.[3]

But McCullagh could see the business potential of the paper. It probably still turned a profit, despite the Depression, and could make serious money when the economy was back on its feet. Since the *Globe* was a private company that didn't issue an annual report, he'd need to see the books to find out for sure. There was certainly more money to be made in the short term, just by accepting booze ads and running horse-race results. And that was before spending a dime to improve its stable of reporters and modernize its design to steal readers from the *Star*, the *Telegram* and the *Mail and Empire*. If it was going to be McCullagh's paper, it had to be the best, so he needed journalists who were better than the rest, and reporters who were willing to do more than just cover every religious revivalist who passed through Toronto. It needed a whole new vision of journalism. And presses. And building. And things to make it shine.

McCullagh knew the *Globe*'s weaknesses, but he also understood its strength, which would be forgotten by its bean-counting owners fifty years later: the paper got out to every farm and every backwater in Ontario—places like Ripley—and the *Globe* valued every one of its subscribers. McCullagh would make it indispensable to all the province's small-town store owners, building contractors, political activists, and country lawyers. It would not be, as it often is now, a trend-chaser appealing only to would-be sophisticates. McCullagh's *Globe* would provide the most incisive political news, the best coverage of business issues, and quick reporting of important legal cases. If something halfway important happened in Ontario, it would be mentioned in the *Globe*'s pages, in stories written by staffers and a network of freelancers.

There were obvious benefits to McCullagh, beyond the financial. Ownership of the *Globe* brought instant power and wide-open access to everyone else with power. The recent version of the *Globe*, something of a shadow of its glory years, had still given the senior member of the Jaffray clan the connections and clout to make him a senator. (Before becoming a newspaper publisher, he'd owned a chain of grocery stores.) Like the British newspaper proprietors, Canada's publishers were great and honoured men. One, Hugh Graham, who published the *Montreal Star*, had been raised to the British peerage as Lord Atholstan. That could happen to another great publisher. The wartime Nickle Resolution advising King George V to refrain from bestowing knighthoods and titles in Canada had been relaxed under R.B. Bennett's

government, and honours were flowing again.⁴ Sir George McCullagh
likely had a very nice ring to it.

This would be the first big step on the path to greatness. Everyone
told him he would be prime minister someday. Magazines even put it
in writing. Sure, there were moments of glumness, times when he felt
rage. But that was the price paid by great men like Abraham Lincoln,
William Pitt and Sir Isaac Newton. Winston Churchill spent most of his
working day drunk to keep his anxiety and depression at bay, and most
of the British political class covered for him. McCullagh had stopped
using booze to anaesthetize the black dog, and, so far, he was able to
keep his depression on a leash. If, and it seems likely, McCullagh was
bipolar, he was likely on a high through most of the Great Depression,
before hitting a low in the spring of 1939. He seemed to crash hardest
when he faced public humiliation, but life appeared to be going very
well in late 1935 and early 1936. He was married, with small children,
had lots of money and interesting friends, and, except for the death of
Percy Parker—which sent him into a brief tailspin that seems to have
ended with the University of Toronto job—no real setbacks.

McCullagh desperately wanted the *Globe*, and, judging from his
risk-taking, along with his indiscrete talk during and after the negotiations for the paper, he was on a manic swing. The paper was an
institution. It was high status. Controlling such a thing was beyond
the imagination of any thirty-one-year-old working-class man from
the bad side of London, Ontario.

Even though the *Globe* had been declining for some time, it was
still the most powerful paper west of Montreal. George Brown, a Scot
who arrived in Toronto in 1844 after a short stint in Boston, started
the *Globe* first as a weekly and, from 1853, published it as a daily newspaper. Brown, who created the *Globe* when he was just twenty-five
years old, was a quick adopter of technology. Railways were barely
getting started when he founded the *Globe*, but Brown could see them
coming. The paper went daily just as the network of new rail lines

spread out from Toronto to Georgian Bay, Montreal and the Detroit frontier. The rails that brought farmers' produce to cities could also carry newspapers out to the sticks and get news into the hands of those farmers on the same day that Toronto subscribers got their papers. The other newspaper publishers were using hand-cranked presses that were cast off by American printers, machines right out of the 1700s. Brown bought the newest steam-driven rotary presses. It was a big outlay, but the cost per newspaper was now much lower, and Brown's paper could be out of the newsroom, printed and loaded onto the trains while the competitors were still trying to set up their presses. Brown could print extras and special editions and flood the streets of Toronto in just a few hours. By wedding the best technology with an almost religious obsession with railway timetables, Brown had a truly national newspaper in the 1850s, when the nation of Canada spanned Quebec City to Windsor to Collingwood. Everyone bought the paper: politicians, businesspeople, farmers, merchants, tradesmen, professionals. It wasn't just entertainment. They needed the information Brown sold.

Brown knew he had something that gave him great political power. It may seem unseemly for newspaper proprietors to blatantly and publicly interfere in politics, but at the time of Confederation, every paper was financed by a political party, as in the case of the *Mail*, which was founded by Sir John A. Macdonald, and the *Star*, which would come on the scene forty years later. That paper, started by striking printers, was secretly financed by Liberals such as Wilfrid Laurier and William Mulock, who believed the 1890's version of the *Globe* had strayed from the Liberal flock. Almost every Father of Confederation had their own paper, or easy access to one.

Brown was editor of his paper from 1844 until 1880, when an angry ex-employee went into Brown's office and shot the still-young publisher at his desk. Although doctors expected him to live, the wound became infected, then gangrenous. He tried to work and ignore the pain, but he died seven weeks after the attack. He was just sixty-one years old and had expected to keep editing the paper into a long and comfortable retirement. There was no succession plan for the paper.

Brown's eldest son, George Mackenzie Brown, went to the United Kingdom, where he published Arthur Conan Doyle's Sherlock Holmes stories and sat in the British House of Commons. The paper passed through a series of owners, ending with the Jaffray family. Senator Robert Jaffray was symptomatic of Establishment Toronto: overcautious, intolerant, puritanical and arrogant. He was a true believer in the Social Gospel, the idea that morality—enforced by both church and state—would create a better man. This belief, embraced by people who would become the heroes of today's Left, generated some of the earliest Canadian feminist writings and campaigns. Its followers also embraced eugenics and supported laws against booze, drugs, Sunday shopping, gambling and other vices. The convergence of Christianity and early socialist concepts resulted in what we'd see as paradoxes— celebrated women's activist Emily Murphy's successful campaign for a federal marijuana ban, Tommy Douglas's MA thesis championing eugenics—but they made sense to the true believers. A better man was a better husband, a better worker, a man with a social conscience. When Jaffray died in 1914, his son William took over. But missionary work was William's real passion. He seemed stuck with a newspaper, but he found he could use it to spread his version of the Social Gospel, which was probably one of the reasons George McCullagh did not fit into his newsroom.

By the time the Depression started to bite, Toronto was something of a newspaper wasteland. There were plenty of publications, but none was particularly good. Alexander Brady, associate professor of political science at the University of Toronto, told a British audience in 1932:

> There is nothing very distinctive concerning Canadian newspapers. Those in the large cities tend to the American type, which is not without its representatives in England. They explore the

depths of sensationalism, relate in nauseating fullness the murders, robberies, suicides and other tragedies of the community; describe in many columns the stunt flights of aviators, and devote pages to baseball games and the life histories of Rugby stars; give a considerable amount of space to insipid or vulgar comic strips; and in general, convey the impression of being concerned more with startling and amusing than with instructing the public...

In Canada, as in other countries, emphasis upon the sensational set in during the Great War, and has continued ever since. However, it is fair to admit that the Canadian papers are more conservative, and have retained more conscience and sense of proportion in news than the average papers of the United States. They seek the sensational with less extravagance. They are content with smaller headlines, and on the whole are more sane in the apportionment of space to different items of news.

Attempts to start tabloid newspapers in the bigger cities had failed, Brady said, partly because Canadian cities were too small to support them, but mainly because these cities lacked "the large populations of illiterate immigrants to whom tabloids make their chief appeal in the American cities." (How illiterate people, immigrants or native-born, read these newspapers was left to the readers' imaginations. British people, literate or not, had no problems embracing London's tabloid press.)

Brady was almost certainly thinking of the Toronto *Star* when he wrote about sensationalist papers. The *Star* still reported suicides, especially high-rise jumpers. It was common to see a photo of a building illustrated with a dotted line showing the jumper's route downward, with an X on the sidewalk at the point of impact. It embraced every known social panic, including, in 1938, the scourge of marijuana. Almost all the stories were about raids on hemp growers and on

patches of wild hemp because real potheads were extremely rare, or
diabolically good at hiding. There were a few decent papers: the
Montreal Gazette, which was described as a Conservative Party organ
but played fair in its news pages, and the Liberal *Manitoba Free Press*,
then edited by the great John Wesley Dafoe. Brady said the *Globe* gave
"adequate space for world matters," which was faint praise, since foreign news from wire agencies is a cheap way to fill pages. The *Mail and
Empire* wasn't mentioned at all.[5]

This was a market that could use a little shaking up. And now,
because of the Depression, almost everything was on the market at
fire-sale prices.

* * *

McCullagh had made more than a million dollars, but he couldn't
afford to buy the *Globe* and rebuild it, so he went to see Bill Wright.

They had become a strange couple. Months before, McCullagh tried
to sell Wright some of his Red Lake gold mining stocks. Since the old
prospector rarely went to Toronto, McCullagh took the train to Barrie
in early 1935—months before the *Globe* plan started taking shape—and
arrived at Wright's door in a cab. Wright, holed up in Statenborough,
wouldn't see him. Too many con artists had come by and flim-flammed
him out of a few hundred dollars at a time. Some of them had even
dragged him into court. But Wright also knew his affairs were, literally,
a mess. His house was strewn with financial records. He hadn't filed
his income tax forms in years, and he had no idea how much he owed.
Wright didn't have much use for accountants and lawyers, but he
needed both very badly. When the taxman had come around to the
house the year before and tried to audit him, Wright became so angry
that he threatened to follow his friend Harry Oakes out of the country
and settle on the Channel Islands. (He was fortunate not to follow
through with that threat. In June 1940, German troops seized those
islands and all non-native islanders were transported to internment

camps in Germany. As for Harry, he was murdered in the Bahamas in July 1943. The sensational crime is still unsolved.[6])

McCullagh came back to Barrie a few weeks later. Somehow, through the half-opened door, Wright took a shine to the young hustler and let him in for ten minutes. McCullagh started talking very fast, but Wright wasn't buying what McCullagh was selling. Wright didn't need any more gold stocks. He knew no one would be able to beat his Kirkland Lake windfalls. "Even if it's all true, I don't want it. And besides I'm reading a good book," Wright said. Unlike so many suitors, McCullagh stopped talking, got out of the chair, said good night and left. It was the most impressive thing McCullagh did that day.[7]

McCullagh, Wright later said, was "the only promoter I met with the sense to take 'no' for an answer." For years, the constant door-knocking had been driving him up the wall: "More than 60 per cent of my time is taken up talking to people who want to sell me something," Wright said. "What I want is peace. I think I was happier when I had no money." But McCullagh was the one hustler who connected with Wright.

Wright wrote to Barrett, McCullagh to tell the firm he was hiring McCullagh to look after all his business affairs. These were quite substantial: Wright was earning $2 million a year in dividends, and, when he filed his income taxes, he owed more than any other Canadian. McCullagh went back to Barrie, boxed up Wright's papers, took them to Toronto and got to work. He organized Wright's financial life, likely saving him many thousands of dollars in taxes and penalties.

So how did McCullagh win Wright, and through him, access to one of Canada's greatest fortunes? Not by acting as his accountant. There were lots of those in Toronto, and McCullagh wasn't one of them. It all goes back to horses, those things Wright loved more than people. Horses, or at least the ability to plow straight furrows, helped McCullagh sell subscriptions on the back concessions of Huron, Middlesex and Oxford counties, and they were to be the bond between the unbreakable prospector and the handsome young stockbroker. They were also the playthings of Toronto's young rich, and McCullagh knew his ponies. Whether McCullagh was sly enough to talk about horses that first day, or stumbled on the connection later, we'll never know. But horse-love, more than anything else, fuelled the founding of the *Globe and Mail*.[8]

Wright trusted McCullagh with his money, and the cost of the *Globe* would hardly make a dent in Wright's vast and growing fortune. Wright would pay for both the *Globe* and the *Mail and Empire*. He would put up the money, some $1.3 million altogether, to make this new merged newspaper into a great daily, one of the best in the world. He'd even chip in extra money for a building to put them in. "We can't get far without a bundle of money," McCullagh said to Wright.[9] Once the details were worked out with Wright, McCullagh approached Robert Jaffray, sending a note of thanks for the board of governors editorial and asking for a meeting.

* * *

A few weeks later, McCullagh would tell the story: "In return, he invited me over to the *Globe* offices to chat with him. That was Tuesday, October 6. We reminisced over old times, recalling when I had served the *Globe* in many capacities, as carrier boy, subscription manager, special promotion agent, and lastly as assistant financial editor. The interview was most opportune. I do wish to be a constructive voice in the affairs of Canada, so I boldly suggested to Mr. Jaffray that if a controlling interest in the *Globe* could be acquired, at what I felt was a reasonable price, I would be an interested prospective purchaser."[10]

The two men spoke for a few hours, but Jaffray insisted the *Globe* was not for sale. McCullagh believed everything was for sale, if the price was right, and asked Jaffray to come up with a number. McCullagh gave Jaffray two business days to make the deal, knowing that a short deadline was much more likely to generate some action. Later that day and into the night, Jaffray had second thoughts about his refusal to sell the paper to the young man he'd once fired. He sent a note back to McCullagh saying they had a deal. And, a little more than two weeks after the little bit of flattery of McCullagh was published on the *Globe* editorial page, the two sides put their lawyers to work.[11]

At least, that was McCullagh's story. A rumour circulating in Toronto's power circles over the next few weeks credited Mitch Hepburn and his well-connected and deep-pocketed friend Frank O'Connor with brokering the deal for the *Globe* and later for the *Mail and Empire*. The rumour has the ring of truth, since Jaffray knew enough about McCullagh to be wary of the eager young man and his stock-peddling booze buddies.

An agreement on the price was reached on the Saturday afternoon, when Jaffray was squeezed against the deadline posed by next day's Sabbath, and was consummated at a *Globe* directors' meeting on the afternoon of October 14, 1936.[12]

This was a very sad meeting. Jaffray, McCullagh and their lawyers were in the room, which was decorated with pictures of George Brown, Senator Jaffray and Abraham Lincoln. Jaffray's wife and son were there, along with some of their relatives, and all of them were crying as the lawyers did their work. McCullagh looked at the pictures and praised the great men whose images hung on the walls, while watching the pathetic scene of the bawling Jaffrays. McCullagh knew Jaffray was making a deal that would screw the minority shareholders. That, McCullagh thought, wasn't very Christian of him.[13]

Before the deal was signed, Jaffray pleaded with McCullagh against publishing anything that would be used by people who gambled on horse races. McCullagh refused to make that promise. People, he said, bet the horses whether the newspapers published odds and race results or not. Jaffray then begged for a promise that the *Globe* would keep publishing fundamentalist editorials. McCullagh was ready for that one, too. The *Globe* would drop the holy-roller editorials, McCullagh said, but he had a promise that Bishop R.J. Renison of St. Paul's Anglican Church on Bloor Street would write a weekly column on the Saturday church page. Privately, McCullagh believed that no loving God could condemn a person to hell, no matter how badly they behaved, and he wasn't going to agree to publish sermons that preached damnation. But he agreed there would be no liquor ads. At least for now.[14]

Jaffray took a pen, wrote a note on a piece of paper, and passed it to McCullagh, who looked at it and read these words: "At 3:30 p.m. on Oct. 14, George McCullagh inherited a great trust." The terms of the deal were simple: for the bargain-basement price of $500,000, Wright bought six thousand shares in the *Globe*. Another three thousand shares were owned by outside interests, including 750 stored in the vault of the company that owned the *Mail and Empire*.

Later that day, McCullagh put out a statement that was supposed to ease Jaffray's mind and impress the public:

> In assuming control of the *Globe* as president and publisher, I am wholly mindful of the responsibilities involved and the opportunities offered. Its historical background, the outstanding position it has held for more than ninety years, its contribution to thought and action on all important public affairs, its vigorous support of popular rights, its uncompromising adherence to British ideals—such traditions have given the *Globe* a high place in the country's annals.
>
> I realize that it is a great trust and I appreciate my limitations. I hope to surround myself with able executives so that the *Globe* will be a constructive force in the affairs of Canada. It will be my aim to have this historic newspaper serve the Canadian people in accordance with the most worthy concepts of its past.[15]

McCullagh in the Globe office just after he bought the paper in 1936. (CITY OF TORONTO ARCHIVES, FONDS 1257, SERIES 1057, ITEM 3526)

For the first time since George Brown was gunned down, the *Globe* would have the capital to modernize and hire more journalists. "Its politics will be independent Liberal, supporting British democratic principles in the conduct of Canadian affairs. Reserving the right to commend or criticize from the standpoint of the country's interests. It will not be a party organ," he said. That last promise probably caused some eye-rolling among the people who knew how close McCullagh was to Mitch Hepburn.

McCullagh talked of his love of the newspaper business and his pride that he started out "as a youth selling the *Globe* on the back concessions." Now, he was returning after a seven-year absence "to devote my time to public service through the medium. My object will be to give readers of the Globe a virile, up-to-date newspaper."

William Jaffray also put out a press release in which his sadness and exhaustion were obvious. He had resigned himself to the idea that he and his paper didn't fit the times.

To relinquish the association long maintained and even the responsibilities which in recent years have been heavy, is not easy. Conviction that the *Globe* had a mission for service on behalf of the well-being of the people has compensated for the demands made on time and strength.

The responsibilities, the opportunities for service, and the satisfaction derived from their acceptance and fulfillment are now transferred to young and able hands...

It is difficult also to say farewell to a staff of loyal and energetic workers who exemplify the best in newspaper practice, who, individually and collectively, make duty and service their foremost consideration. My gratitude goes out to them for their devotion to the interests of the paper and its readers, and I bespeak their continued loyalty to my successor.

It's not difficult to imagine him sighing as he wrote the sentence commending his former employees to whatever fate George McCullagh had in store for them.[16] Jaffray had certainly turned the tables on the people who were trying to start a newsroom union. It's not clear when McCullagh found out about the union drive, but the insecurity that gripped the newsrooms of the *Globe* and, soon, the *Mail and Empire*, killed any momentum it had.[17]

∗ ∗ ∗

Within a few days, it became obvious that whatever kindness McCullagh felt for Jaffray had been purged, or that the pleasantries on the day of the sale were an act. Some two hundred of McCullagh's friends and cronies joined him at a dinner at Bay Street's National Club on the night of November 2. Premier Hepburn was there with all of his cabinet, along with Newton Rowell, the former Ontario Liberal leader who was now the province's chief justice. After promising to use his talents, Wright's money and the *Globe*'s influence to make Canada a better country, McCullagh tucked into a nice warm plate of revenge.

The *Globe*, now obedient to McCullagh, called the dinner "one of the more colourful and impressive ever held in Toronto." Everyone with power tried to get a seat. Important politicians, the country's top bankers, Toronto's industrialists, judges and senior lawyers, stockbrokers, mine owners, anyone with a lot of money, turned out to see McCullagh's triumph. Ian Mackenzie, Canada's defence minister, represented Mackenzie King's government. University of Toronto and National Club president Henry Cody was there with the members of the board of governors, and Sir William Mulock, the ninety-two-year-old former chief justice, former lieutenant-governor, and former cabinet minister in Sir Wilfrid Laurier's government, was master of ceremonies.

McCullagh walked into the big dining room of the National Club with his wife and little son George behind him and moved through the crowd to the head table while the guests cheered and gave him a standing ovation. After the introductions, McCullagh rose to speak. He knew his audience. The *Globe*, he said, would not sell itself to politicians, nor would its editorial page be offered up "on the altar of advertising." It would have biases. The *Globe* would be the champion of Canadian business. This made sense, McCullagh said, because, in the history of mining would also "be written the future history of Canada." It was all a bit confusing, but the people in the room got the point.

Then came the vengeance.

McCullagh cruelly described how he stripped old Jaffray of his power. The man was a fool who was stuck in the past century, and this was his undoing. "[G]entlemen, he had a principle, and as much as we may not agree with it, he stuck with it at the cost of his own pocketbook, in the face of the most adverse times in the history of newspaper work in Canada. Mr. Jaffray's attitude was really beautiful to behold.

"I had my good old red-haired lawyer Mat McIntosh with me and tears even came down that hardy Scot's cheeks. Here was a man relinquishing power that he had been born into, fully aware that he was being shorn of power and had to stand on his own feet." McCullagh told his audience about Jaffray's note transferring the responsibility for the *Globe* to him. It was the victory of the modern over the Victorian, of new money over old, of fun over Presbyterian morality. McCullagh was telling a sad story, but he did it with a smile.

Cody, who believed McCullagh was a blowhard, proposed a toast "to the Empire." Ian Mackenzie made a toast "to the press." People mingled for a while, and then went home to bed. Many of them were eager to see what would come off the *Globe's* presses on Monday.[18]

William Wright wasn't at the party. It wasn't his kind of place or his kind of people. Many of them would have pestered the old prospector to set them up, too. It was bad enough he was in Toronto at all.

* * *

On the Sunday night that the first edition of his paper came off the presses, William Wright was alone in a room at the Royal York Hotel. A Toronto *Star* reporter showed up at the door late in the evening. Wright let the writer in. Wearing short sleeves, and drinking cup after cup of weak tea, the new owner of the *Globe* sat down with the *Star* reporter and let the journalist scoop his own paper. It had been a busy day, but Wright was in an unusually chatty mood, telling the reporter, "I have been a prospector, mine owner, soldier and horseman but never have I aspired so high as to be a publisher." Wright said he didn't plan to interfere with McCullagh's running of the paper, but he knew of some big changes in the works. These almost certainly involved the coverage of horse racing. "But I will still be more interested in the Racing Form and the Breeding Journal than the ordinary daily newspapers. I intend to continue the breeding of racehorses at my home in Barrie." Ten mares and their foals were more than enough to keep him happy, Wright said.[19]

So the paper would have racing results. It would also have cigarette and booze ads. "I don't see any reason for refusing this advertising," he explained. "I smoke cigarettes myself." As for liquor, the subject that had vexed Jaffray and the *Globe* publisher's business rival, Holy Joe Atkinson, for so many years, Wright said, "I have no serious views" on it. There was one thing he thought the *Globe* lacked: the point of view of the prospectors and mine operators whose investments provided one of the few financial boosts to Canada during the Depression (and would continue to dominate market action on Bay Street for another forty years). "It was my interest in mining. My object in purchasing the *Globe* was not to make money out of it—at least that was not my main object. I thought I could do something for the country by making our mining industries better known. Anything that is advantageous to mining is advantageous to the country as a whole." When the reporter asked whether mines and miners were overtaxed, the man who bought the country's most influential political newspaper answered that he "wouldn't like to give any opinion on that."

Wright claimed to have no politics, which was absurd. It was true that he did not have a party affiliation, partly because there was no political party in Canada during the Great Depression that spoke loudly on behalf of multi-millionaires who did not like to pay income tax.[20] He also believed in as much freedom as possible for individual people. The paper's editorial policy would be independent, Wright said. The *Globe* would not dance to any politician's tune. It would act, not react. It would call the shots. It would flex its power as it saw fit.

Picking up on that thread, the reporter asked about Mitch Hepburn. Wright said he had never met him, which was an answer that dodged the question. But he went on to say that the provincial Liberals and their erratic, populist premier could not count on the *Globe*'s automatic support. "I intend to keep an independent political attitude. I will keep a free hand."

But the "hand" did not belong to Wright. He was simply the banker. This relationship never fell apart because neither man's interests clashed. McCullagh wanted power. Wright wanted to be safe from intruders. And they shared their love of Brookdale, Wright's stable full of horses at the edge of Barrie where McCullagh learned how to pick winners.

As the *Star* reporter and Wright wrapped up the interview, the first edition of the *Globe* arrived at the hotel room door. Wright left it there unread, said good night to the reporter and went to bed.

Reporters who collected quotes for the Monday papers found Jaffray at his home on the Saturday night that the deal closed.[21] Groggy when he answered the phone, Jaffray said the paper was now McCullagh's. There were no strings attached to the deal. He had let it go for a one-off cash payment and his publishing days were done. He resented being awakened from a good sleep "and now I'm going back to sleep to continue it."

McCullagh and Phyllis were wide awake at their Forest Hill home that Sunday night, bathing in the acclaim and attention that came with the purchase of the *Globe*. McCullagh had seen the first edition of his paper, and he was happy with it, though he did order his editors to change the article about his life. He wanted it rewritten to push a Horatio Alger rags-to-riches theme.[22]

Back home after seeing off the bulldog edition, McCullagh rattled on at length to the *Star* reporter, telling him that the *Globe* was about to become a "great metropolitan newspaper." There would be more money for news services, more journalists sent to the United States and Europe. The paper would be thicker, with the news section increasing from fourteen pages to eighteen right now, and plans to beef that up to twenty-four pages once more advertising money started rolling in. McCullagh promised to surround himself with the best news executives in the country and pay whatever it took to get them. The urge to buy the *Globe* had hit him ten years before, when he was a reporter. Now, he said, he was prepared to leave Bay Street and take a pay cut to oversee the transformation of the *Globe* into one of the world's great newspapers.

"I go back to newspaper work at a considerable financial sacrifice to myself, but that doesn't matter. There's a lot more in this world than the mere accumulation of money," he told the reporter, after complaining of tiredness from what must have been an exhausting day. "There is a romance in my dreaming of finance and return to my old love, newspaperdom. You are a newspaperman yourself, you will understand. It's in every newspaperman's mind. Once you have a taste, you want to go back. I always wanted to do something worthwhile with my life, something to help Canada. I made a material success of my life, but that didn't satisfy me. I was interested in politics, but I never wanted to be a politician. My new position offers me the kind of scope I wanted, to be a voice, a factor for good in Canada."

McCullagh said his version of the *Globe* would be "independently Liberal, reserving the right to criticize or commend, according to our best and unfettered judgment. It will in no sense be a party organ, in the sense of 'my party, right or wrong.'" McCullagh, not his rich friend Wright, would be calling the shots. "Although he is backing me financially, Mr. Wright will take no active role in the *Globe*. His financial strength is great and he is backing my energy and ability to make the *Globe* a greater voice for the good of Canada. I have full power of direction. The purchase has been made in my name."

There was no way he could lose. George McCullagh had never failed at anything. With cash to spend on the best executives and journalists, with job security for these people, many of whom had taken pay cuts and lived in the shadow of layoffs for the past six years, he would buy loyalty and productivity. "In addition, the very name of the *Globe* is a power in itself. Character and tradition are there, devotion to an ideal, more so than any other paper in Canada. It is not going to be run as a balance sheet paper. To provide our readers with the best news and feature coverage costs good money but we will spare no reasonable expense in gathering news for our paper."

McCullagh was right about the *Globe's* potential. In two days, he had sixty-three columns—more than six full pages—of ads that hadn't been in the *Globe* in two years. McCullagh wasn't above hustling ads himself. The *Financial Post* had bought a little ad on the *Globe's* financial page for years. McCullagh's people wanted the *Post* to pay a 25 percent premium for this prime space. Instead, the *Post's* publisher called McCullagh to remind him that the *Post's* little ad had often been the only one on the *Globe's* business page. McCullagh agreed that loyalty should be rewarded, and the *Post* got a break.[23]

When the first cigarette ad went through the stereotype machine, the apparatus jammed. McCullagh, who was standing nearby smoking a cigarette, remarked that the old anti-tobacco policy even permeated the *Globe's* machinery.

＊ ＊ ＊

Buying the *Globe* morphed McCullagh from the ranks of Mitch Hepburn's provincial political cronies to a national power broker. In England, ownership of an important paper almost automatically made a publisher a peer and a member of the House of Lords. Canada had no such tradition—some publishers were appointed to the Senate, but most weren't. Atkinson of the *Star* was offered a seat but couldn't be bothered to take it. Newspaper owners exercised real power already, without the risk of scrutiny.

During King's long term as prime minister, Ottawa was a place where, publicly, little happened. The country was governed through back channels that led to King's tiny office on the third floor of the yellow-brick house that he had inherited from Wilfrid Laurier. The old barn of a place, on a corner lot just east of the University of Ottawa, was stuffed with books and artifacts that King had pilfered in his years of travels: ancient furniture from England, Roman glass bottles given to him by John D. Rockefeller Jr. (who was one of King's wartime public relations clients), books, pictures of his mother and, of course, a crystal ball given to him by a rich woman who shared his interest in the occult.

The spiritualism seems strange today, but it was a normal pastime of upper-class and bourgeois people in the early years of the twentieth century. This was a time when many people were still mourning the young men killed in the First World War. King had lost two people he'd loved passionately: his mother and his friend Henry Harper, who had drowned in the Ottawa River while trying to save a girl who had fallen through the ice at a skating party. But, unlike most seances of the time, King's spirit chats were not just some late-night game-playing with friends. Spiritualism helped him cope with loneliness, and with a serious obsessive-compulsive disorder centred around the positioning of the hands of clocks. His diaries are laden with notes about the auspicious and inauspicious patterns of clock hands at the time that important events happened in his life.

King may have been half mad, but he knew potential when he saw it. On November 13, he wrote a letter to McCullagh praising the young publisher and telling him that, during his recent trip to Europe and the United States, the best news he'd received from Canada was of the sale of the *Globe*. It gave him "satisfaction and delight."

Finally, the *Globe* would return to the Liberal stable.

"In the seventeen or more years of the leadership of the Liberal Party, I have hoped and prayed that some day 'The Toronto Globe' might again become the exponent of Liberal principles and policies. I have never wished for 'The Globe's' return to the position of party organ, slavishly supporting Liberal Administrations either at Ottawa or Toronto, or the Liberal Party in office or Opposition. What I have longed for, above all else, has been that 'The Globe' might be the exponent of a true Liberalism at times such as these through which our country and the world is passing."

King wanted McCullagh to know that the old politician could take the odd hit. "I have never asked, nor have I ever expected, that any journal, however Liberal it might be, would necessarily endorse or approve either my individual views or those of the party or the government of which I have been the head. However, I have hoped that, through 'The Globe', enjoying as it has the reputation of being the leading Liberal journal in the province, Liberal principles and Liberal policies might be fully and fearlessly expounded, and that the government and the party, in its endeavor to make Liberal principles prevail in matters of government, might find 'The Globe' a strong ally, as 'The Globe' itself would find in the party and the government, in its efforts to further progress in accordance with Liberal views." King then asked McCullagh to come to Ottawa and stay at Laurier House.[24]

It was a remarkable letter, and it showed King's lack of self-awareness and failure to understand George McCullagh. A few days later, he followed it with another fawning letter, talking about how he "hoped and prayed" that someday the *Globe* "might again become the exponent of Liberal principles and policies." The day before, the *Globe* had mentioned that a new statue of King's grandfather, the rebel William Lyon Mackenzie, was approved for the Queen's Park lawn, and King had seen this story as a sign.[25]

Despite what he'd written to McCullagh, the prime minister could not take criticism. He was a spiteful man who had no use for inquisitive reporters and surrounded himself with pompous but pliable media stooges in the Parliamentary Press Gallery. King was adept at feeding his favourites enough information to keep them ahead of the rest of the pack, but most of King's important media contacts never questioned the honesty or sincerity of the prime minister and his government.

McCullagh had not bought the *Globe* to make it anyone else's mouthpiece. He certainly hadn't bought it for King, who had never done him any favours. He was unwilling to commit himself to being King's propagandist, but he did tell the prime minister that he'd like to bring his senior staffers to dinner at King's house. They'd set "somewhat of a precedent in journalism by cooperating with the government if I may, in working out some of their problems, rather than placing the government in a position to defend unwarranted criticism."[26]

It was a ridiculous thing to say. Was McCullagh telling King he'd face "unwarranted criticism" if he wasn't consulted? The pleasantries masked the fact that King was willing to give nothing to McCullagh except platitudes, and McCullagh was unwilling to share anything but boilerplate. Still, for a short time in the middle of the Great Depression, the owner of the most important newspaper west of Montreal was an ally and on good terms with both the premier of Ontario and the prime minister of Canada. George McCullagh had come a long way from hawking newspapers on those dusty back concessions.

Soon afterward, the new publisher sent King a four-line note thanking him for his praise and support, and said he'd visit Ottawa as soon as he was free. A week later, he bought the *Mail and Empire*, a Tory paper that could trace its lineage back to a cabal organized by Sir John A. Macdonald, Canada's first prime minister.

* * *

Meanwhile, McCullagh was turning the *Globe* into a much better paper. McCullagh's real attention was focused on the newsroom. The content and design of the paper had to quickly change, if people were to believe the things McCullagh was saying about making the tired old *Globe* into the best paper in Canada, and one of the great broadsheets of the world. Douglas Oliver, a well-connected political reporter based at Queen's Park, had been driven out years before. McCullagh hired him back. He also brought in Beatrice Sullivan, daughter of an Anglican bishop, as social columnist. For more than a decade, her "On Dit" social column had run in competing papers. McCullagh convinced Wellington Jeffers, who had been his mentor at the *Globe* and his entry into the business world, to leave the *Financial Post* and come back. A.A. McIntosh, a former editorial writer and lapsed schoolteacher, was made senior editor. J.V. McAree, who had spent fifty years covering politics, wrote a column that anchored the editorial page. But McCullagh had to face facts: the Jaffrays had let the *Globe* moulder through the Depression. The reporting staff was miserable. Two big pay cuts had hardly helped make the newsroom a happy place.

At least people such as Harry Anderson, the paper's editor, no longer had to sneak cigarettes and booze into his office, and didn't have to listen for warnings by Mary James, a reporter in the women's department, that Jaffray was coming. Female reporters, seen by women as social pariahs (for working) and by men as inferior, saw an immediate improvement in status. "Oh, it was a time when Mr. McCullagh came," James told Richard Doyle, who was her boss twenty-five years later. James escaped from the confines of the women's department and was allowed to write breaking news stories. Blanche Robbins was also sprung from the pink ghetto to write obituaries, a job that seems tedious, but, when done well, showcases the research skills and writing style of the author.[27]

McCullagh did inherit some great journalists when he bought the *Globe*, including the dashing twenty-five-year-old Oakley Dalgleish, an aristocratic-looking young man who wore a black patch to hide an eye that he'd lost to a reckless driver. While kicking around England he'd ditched his personal history, a sad story of growing up in the back end of Saskatchewan, where his father lost all the money that nine-year-old Oakley had been awarded for his injury. Now he was a man of the world. He would start to believe his own self-hype and develop into a first-rate snob as he rose through McCullagh's organization to eventually run the *Globe and Mail*, but that fall, he was one of the best reporters on the paper. He, like Judith Robinson, was also one of the few journalists in the English-speaking world who had Adolf Hitler figured out from the start.[28]

William Arthur Deacon, a lawyer who had been the *Globe*'s book reviewer for a decade, became Canada's first literary editor, beginning the *Globe and Mail*'s dominance of Canadian criticism that lasted until the second decade of the twenty-first century. Deacon was the driving force behind the Governor General's Awards for literature and the Stephen Leacock Medal for Humour.

McCullagh jazzed up the news and bought Walter Winchell's and Gracie Allen's columns (which he ran on the front page). He hired Allister Grosart to write a movie review column (the movies were reviewed only if a theatre or studio bought an ad). "He was a great, great man, in many ways, wild and crazy," Grosart told Peter Stursberg forty years later.[29]

McCullagh already had one problem simmering in his newsroom. Judith Robinson was thirty-eight when McCullagh bought the *Globe*. She'd been hired as a sports writer in 1928, the year before McCullagh had been kicked out of the newsroom. Robinson came from Toronto newspaper royalty: her father was John "Black Jack" Robinson, legendary editor of the Toronto *Telegram* who had died a decade before. She'd written opinion columns and news articles for four years, then left the paper to write freelance pieces from Europe for the then-handsome sum of six dollars apiece. By 1934, she was back at the *Globe*, first as editor of the Letters to the Editor page, but quickly emerging as the paper's best opinion columnist. She was older, likely considerably smarter, and much more female than McCullagh and most of the rest of the *Globe* staff. She was also a much better reporter.

Robinson was sensitive to the misery of the poor, likely partly because her own salary was so low. Under Jaffray, who had cut her pay, she wrote about the terrible effects of the Depression and supported President Franklin Roosevelt's New Deal along with the trade union movement that it fostered. Robinson had no problem injecting her own opinions into her pieces. In one column, she described the brawl between William Green of the American Federation of Labor (AFL) and John L. Lewis, president of the powerful United Mine Workers, who mined America's coal. Green, she wrote in 1936, was "well known in Toronto as in other labor centres. He is a dignified functionary who wears a dinner coat well. Alone, he would be as well-matched against John L. Lewis as a poached egg against a sledgehammer."[30] John L. Lewis, who had his eye on Canada's brutalized gold miners, was not the kind of man McCullagh wanted the *Globe* to praise.

But there wasn't much he could do about his star reporter. McCullagh knew the *Globe*'s readers loved Robinson's writing. He was willing to put up with her pro-union opinions as part of a political balancing act on the news pages, and so long as they didn't get in the way of his own pro-mining agenda. He also had no problem with what were called "sob stories" about the poor, if no fingers were pointed at the people who had real power in Ontario. Robinson raised money to build a homeless shelter in Toronto, and readers liked that. For three years, she and McCullagh worked together in relative peace. It probably helped that Robinson was much older and, in some ways, less attractive than the women McCullagh liked to chase. Eventually, they would clash. Robinson would be right, McCullagh would be wrong. And then Judith Robinson would come into her own, even when McCullagh set out to purge any John L. Lewis supporters from journalism and public life.

There was money to pay Robinson, along with the many reporters McCullagh started poaching from his competitors. And, most important, McCullagh's optimism was contagious. The browbeaten staff started to perk up.

Still, the *Mail and Empire*, the now-forgotten morning competitor, was the better paper. Its staff hadn't endured pay cuts. It sold more copies than the *Globe* every morning. Today, we have a hard time knowing how good it was, since printed copies are very rare. Almost everything, including its photo files, corporate records and bound issues, has been lost. But it seemed obvious to most people in Toronto that the *Globe* was the underdog in this fight. McCullagh knew it, too. But, unlike the owner of the *Mail and Empire*, George McCullagh could reach into a gold mine and take out what he needed.

6

THE *GLOBE* AND MAIL

The Depression's bread lines and bank collapses hadn't shaken Wright's and McCullagh's belief that there was money to be made through shrewd investments in the consumer economy. The two men deserve credit for their optimism, but the risk really belonged to McCullagh. He was rich, but didn't have the kind of fortune that could survive a string of bad investments. Bill Wright could walk away from his newspaper investment and not even notice the damage to his portfolio.

Izaak Walton Killam, the fedora-wearing Montreal-based owner of the *Mail and Empire*, decided after the *Globe* deal that he'd sell his newspaper, too. It wasn't a matter of economics: the *Mail and Empire* was making about $13,300 in profit in a typical month and Killam was almost as rich as Wright.[1]

Still, Killam wanted out. He was getting old, and he didn't need the aggravation of competing with the upstart young publisher and his deep-pocketed friend. Just as McCullagh was ramping up the *Globe* for a newspaper war, Killam called McCullagh, invited him to breakfast at the Royal York Hotel, and offered his paper. McCullagh offered $2.3 million for the *Mail* and its small stake in the *Globe*, which was enough to satisfy Killam. McCullagh called Wright and told him, "We're buying another paper." Wright asked, "Which one?" Before the *Mail and Empire* deal, Wright said it was time for the two millionaires to buy a weekly. Maybe, he joked, they could make an offer for *Hush*, a sleazy little scandal sheet that covered prostitution and pedophilia cases at Toronto courts, made up stories about movie starlets, gave hot tips on horse races, and reported on any freakish occurrences that happened in what was then one of the world's dullest cities. "It's a 'ell of a good paper," Wright said.[2] McCullagh gave it serious thought, but he knew he'd be finished in Toronto society if they bought *Hush*. So Wright agreed to buy into the *Mail and Empire* deal.

But Wright knew *Hush* would not impress his business community friends, nor would it come in handy if, say, the exploited miners of Ontario wanted to unionize, or some government came up with a policy that threatened the owners' profits. "My object in purchasing the *Globe*," Wright told *Mining World* magazine, "was not to make money out of it—at least, that was not my main object. I thought I could do something for the country by making our mining industries better known. Anything that is of advantage to mining is of advantage to the country as a whole."[3]

The *Mail*'s owner had never crossed McCullagh, so there would be no ceremonial stripping of his power, no gloating, no big victory banquet. The deal was announced to a surprised city on November 18, 1936.

Despite a proud Tory tradition going back to the paper's founder, Sir John A. Macdonald, Killam hadn't offered the *Mail and Empire* to any Conservatives, or even let them know that he was willing to sell. Tories were furious about that: the deal left just one trustworthy right-of-centre (by the reckoning of the times) newspaper in the city, the *Evening Telegram*. Members of the *Mail*'s editorial staff, who were much better-paid than their *Globe* colleagues, also saw the danger.

And they were right. At first, only five journalists would be kept. (Some were hired back later.) "We didn't blame McCullagh so much as Killam for selling such a prosperous paper," said Thelma Craig, one of the reporters who was temporarily let go.[4] And now Toronto was down to three daily newspapers. There would be just one morning paper: the *Globe and Mail*.

The *Kincardine News* called the deal a "menace to Protestantism and to clean, honest politics... Morally, we think he [Killam] had an obligation to the fair-minded Tories of this province to give them a chance to have continued the *Mail and Empire* influence for the benefit of Canada, leading Conservatives and the Conservative policy." The small-town paper said McCullagh was offering "fictitious independence for the purpose of holding Tory subscribers." McCullagh was just a front for Mitch Hepburn and his Catholic backers. They should have come out from the shadows, "but that has seldom been the way of supporters of the Roman Catholic church policy."[5]

The Toronto *Telegram* believed Hepburn had put the deal together to stifle critics of his Roman Catholic school funding plan, which seemed to be the biggest issue in the upcoming East Hastings provincial by-election. On the *Telegram*'s editorial page, Col. G.C. Porter wrote of the merger as though it had been arranged by organized crime: "(C)riticism in the morning field had to be stifled quickly if 'Mitch' and his handy men were to chloroform the voters of East Hastings in sufficient number to get by with the conspiracy. That was the reason why the plotters completed the job with such dispatch. The 'finger men' of the gang arranged for I.W. Killam to come down from Montreal on a Friday night. Over Sunday, the details of the job were completed."[6]

If McCullagh could retain all the subscribers of the Jaffray and Killam papers, he would be the most powerful newspaper proprietor west of Montreal. But if he could add to that base, he might become Canada's most important publisher. For the time being, that was the only thing that could satisfy the thirty-one-year-old financier. Then he could reach for political fame and power. But for now, financial and media influence—the ability to command the ear of the premier and the prime minister and to use the paper as a cudgel to force changes to national and local policy—was enough.

＊ ＊ ＊

Toronto's new morning paper was brave, bold and modern, and with a unique name. The new paper would be called the *Globe and Mail*, with the same initials as its owner: GM.

The *Globe and Mail* editors made sure the paper had reporters on the scene of any natural or man-made disaster in North America. The paper also had a small staff of city reporters who fought to keep up with rivals at the *Star* and the *Telegram*. Its reporters could never beat the clock. A morning paper like the *Globe and Mail* had a big disadvantage covering hard news, the stories about crimes and fires. Bad things tend to happen at night, and the *Globe* sent its first edition to press in the early evening. It had to have most of its copies printed and shipped in the middle of the night to be delivered to paperboys and shops before the city began to stir. The *Globe and Mail* could "replate," change the front page and a few inside pages for breaking news during its print run, but this was expensive and time-consuming. If something very big happened, the publisher could order an "Extra" to be printed, but these were rare. So morning papers like the *Globe and Mail*, the *Times of London* and the *New York Times* filled their pages with institutional news: politics, finance, court cases. It made them less interesting to most readers, but they covered things that wealthy, powerful people wanted to read about.

The class gulf between morning and afternoon papers was so wide that King George V's personal physician dispatched the dying king with a shot of morphine and cocaine at a time that was convenient for the journalists of the morning *Times* rather than the shabby afternoon London papers.[7]

The same schedule worked in favour of afternoon papers when they covered sports, though morning papers often held their front sports page for a midnight replate, to get scores and game highlights. The stockbrokers, lawyers, business owners and accountants who bought the *Globe and Mail* were as avid sports fans and bettors as their blue-collar neighbours.

In the early days, competition between the morning and afternoon papers was as much a matter of pride as it was a fight for ad dollars. Many retailers advertised in at least one morning and afternoon paper, and some families subscribed to every paper in the city. If something big was happening, newsstands would be busy all day as each edition of the morning and afternoon papers came out. It took more than market share to make the city's competing publishers into personal enemies. The jilted Tories at the *Telegram* may have been the most vocal critics of McCullagh's deals, but it was the rich leftist who ran the *Star* who would become McCullagh's obsession.

* * *

A great new newspaper had to have a true temple of journalism. And that was the second part of the announcement. Within a year, McCullagh told reporters, the *Globe and Mail* would be headquartered in one of North America's best newspaper buildings. Construction would soon begin at King and York Streets in the heart of Toronto's ten-block financial district. McCullagh needed a personal headquarters, a lair, a palace that would be a second home to him during the very long days he spent at the office. Bill Wright also wanted a safe, private space in the city during his infrequent trips to Toronto. The building wouldn't be taller than Atkinson's five-year-old Toronto *Star* skyscraper down the street, but McCullagh was working with architects to make sure it would be better.

For now, the "Globe-Mail," as McCullagh called it in those first days, until he became comfortable with the real name, would be

McCullagh meets a tradesman while touring the construction site of the new Globe and Mail headquarters in downtown Toronto. (CITY OF TORONTO ARCHIVES, FONDS 1266, ITEM 48069)

printed at the *Mail*'s building. McCullagh didn't expect many more layoffs, although the deal gave an excuse to get rid of some staff, including all of McCullagh's former colleagues in the *Globe*'s circulation department. They were fired on the day of the merger. The new publisher said the *Globe and Mail* would be carrying all the stories and features that readers of the old papers enjoyed. The paper would be "independent in politics" and "a constructive and helpful voice in the affairs of government," the young publisher said.[8] McCullagh planned to create a board of directors comprising leaders of the Canadian manufacturing, mining, financial and agricultural sectors. The board would be a sort of think tank, providing ideas that would show up on the editorial page. As the last edition of the *Mail* went to press, two printers played a tune on bagpipes. Toronto was still that kind of town.

On the *Globe and Mail*'s first front page, this promise appeared above McCullagh's name: "...Just and fair treatment for all parties in the discussion of political subjects will be sought. A newspaper which endeavors to serve faithfully must analyze party professions and performances and take a stand for good government. This announcement of policy for The Globe and Mail was made on Thursday: 'It will give general support to Governments in power, whether Conservative or Liberal, reserving, however, the fullest liberty to criticize any actions of any government which we do not consider to be in the public interest...'"[9]

The next day, the *Telegram* countered with an editorial headlined "Wealth May Buy Newspapers, It Cannot Buy Public Opinion." The author wrote: "For the first time since Confederation the Conservative party finds itself without the assistance of a provincial morning paper... The strangling of the *Mail*, the mouthpiece of the Conservative party in this province, was a ruthless abuse of the power of gold in an attempt to throttle public opinion.

"The public is not yet prepared to accept without questions the edicts of the young man who made a fortune in the stock market and who has just bought himself an expensive toy. Mr. McCullagh is in for a rude awakening if he thinks the tens of thousands of loyal Conservatives in this city and this province will submit to dictation from an organization that claims to be independent while shouting for Hepburn and Catholic schools... Notwithstanding the disappearance of the chief Conservative organ in this province, public opinion cannot be permanently smothered in gold."[10]

The *Globe and Mail* did publish letters challenging its editorial policies and chiding its publisher. One writer, "Debunker," who would have thrived in the age of Twitter, trolled McCullagh, writing, "Why not get out a special edition of your paper and tell everything that you want to about your glorious self, and work in all the family picture, etc. and get it over with? Then settle down and publish a morning paper. And this special need not cost you anything. Just think of all the paid-for advertisements of congratulations that would be taken by your admirers and friends from the Embassy down, and even some boys of the Golden north might take a page or so. Think this over, Puiltzer [*sic*]."

* * *

When he was on a high, as he certainly was in the fall of 1936 when he cobbled these deals together and started hiring architects for the new *Globe and Mail* headquarters, McCullagh was an optimist and believed the economy would come roaring back. This turned out to be a very profitable attitude. If nothing else had happened that fall, the purchase of the land for the new building would have been, by itself, a brilliant move.

Including the land—a corner lot in Toronto's financial district—Wright paid $1,600,000 for the most modern newspaper headquarters in the world. It had a state-of-the-art newsroom and page production facilities and presses. A wire machine, a sort of primitive fax, allowed its photographers to transmit pictures over the telephone lines. The photos may have lacked definition, but they allowed the *Globe and Mail* to scoop its competition on big stories, like the collapse of Niagara Falls' Honeymoon Bridge in January 1938.

The lobby of this news palace was designed to strike awe into visitors, whether they were advertisers, politicians or curious tourists. McCullagh commissioned six sculptures that represented the major industries of Canada. He had them installed over a revolving steel door that brought people into that lobby, which loomed almost two storeys and was finished in glazed tiles and with red sandstone brought from Indiana. These dazzling colours on the floor and walls were topped with a ceiling trimmed with gold leaf. But the real jaw-dropping space was off-limits to the public, unless they were invited. And anyone with any claim to power wanted to be. This little nirvana was the top floor, where McCullagh's modern office, panelled in walnut, adjoined an adjacent suite of rooms that had a squash court and a fantastic bathroom with walls lined in black and white French granite. There was a kitchen and bedroom. The ceiling was gold leaf. The light fixtures were trimmed with gold.

Many newsroom hacks never got to see it. When they did, they told their colleagues of its marvels. Tim Shea, a copy editor invited up to the suite by McCullagh, told his seatmate John Sweeney that the publisher's washroom, with its black and white marble and gold-plated plumbing "sure makes the old tool feel shabby."[11]

But people didn't have to go inside the William H. Wright Building to be dazzled. The exterior was a spectacular mix of limestone brought from Ohio and black granite from the Canadian Shield. A row of windows along York Street let people watch the next edition of the *Globe and Mail* being printed. People stood quietly as the big presses turned out the next edition of Canada's great new morning paper.[12]

It was all McCullagh's show. Wright had made the thing possible, but he was invisible, and that was how he liked it. A comic stripped that he loved, *Gals Aglee*, was the only thing he insisted be printed in every edition, and he'd call the newsroom if some fool left it out of the paper.[13] During the building's grand opening, which drew twenty-five thousand people to the *Globe and Mail* office on a spring Saturday, Wright poked his head into the newswire room and was told by a copy boy that "the public isn't allowed in here."[14] Rather than tell the kid that he paid for the place, Canada's richest man sheepishly withdrew his head from the doorway.

The visitors pawed through reporters' mail, looked through desk drawers, and took books from the library shelves until the paper's librarian locked the doors. They pecked at the new typewriters, gawked at barrels of ink, checked out the cafeteria. The people who worked for the paper were proud to explain their jobs to these tourists, who often came dragging small children. In the background, they could hear people making personal calls on the city desk phones. "You should see it, baby! I wouldn't mind working here, baby!" one caller was heard saying. The entire event was broadcast live on CFRB, the biggest radio station in the city. Everyone wanted to see McCullagh. They hunted him through the building, trying to find him in the crowd.

"(He) talked to me. He was so nice!" a visitor told the *Globe and Mail* reporter who was collecting anecdotes for that Monday's front-page lead story.[15]

* * *

The show went to London, Ontario, that year. McCullagh was guest of honour at a dinner held at the exclusive London Hunt Club. ("Exclusive" had real meaning in 1936. Jews and Catholics, Indigenous people, Black people and foreigners were kept out.)

All the business and political heavies of southwestern Ontario were there, along with top administrators and academics from the University of Western Ontario, who, presumably, did not see the irony of celebrating the successes of a grade-nine dropout. Two members of the Labatt family bought tickets. It was a bipartisan affair. Premier Mitch Hepburn did most of the hosting, and Tory leader Earl Rowe sat near the front. Almost everyone with political ambition was in the room. So were McCullagh's parents, and this was one of the very few times he acknowledged the existence of his father.

"I believe today the world is coming back to sanity, and I believe if we agree, Canada will benefit more than anyone else," Hepburn speached. "Our pioneers have left us a magnificent heritage in our free schools. William Lyon Mackenzie in 1837 won for us responsible government. Then with responsible government and free schools we should be able to face our problems with the leadership of that great institution, a free press. One has to endure the criticism of the press. It keeps governments in line. The press is a more important factor in our national lives than government. The press moulds public opinion. Governments have the responsibility of crystalizing that opinion. And so we have with us tonight a young man just 31 years old who has taken on a great responsibility."

Premier Mitchell Hepburn congratulates George McCullagh
at the London celebration of his new role as a media baron.
(CITY OF TORONTO ARCHIVES, FONDS 1266, ITEM 41753)

McCullagh was polite and tactful, saying his early days in London were his fondest memories, and that his chief delight still was to come back home and go out again with his father to his old boyhood haunts along the Coves. (These are little oxbow lakes along the Thames that were good places to hunt and fish.)

"The unselfish devotion of you, dad and mother, has been a great inspiration to me. And I only hope my career will vindicate your faith in me." He told Londoners the *Globe* would never be "sacrificed on the altar of advertising." It would always "continue to champion the best British ideals." He even promised that if Hepburn "sometime deserved it, he might expect to feel the fire of the *Globe*."[16]

* * *

Cub reporter Richard Doyle, an ambitious kid from Chatham, Ontario, met McCullagh soon after the creation of the *Globe and Mail*. Doyle would later edit the paper, and then go on to be a Canadian senator, but he was still in awe sixty years later. "This flashing-eyed man with the brooding good looks and the confidence that goes with power was thirty-one years old…McCullagh called himself 'just an ordinary man.' Yet there was something about him that led people to see him as a man above and beyond calamities. Fortune was fame. Better to whistle 'We're in the money,' than hum 'Brother can you spare a dime.' So look no further! Things were happening in Hog Town! Here was McCullagh, down on King Street, making no secret of his impatience with the way things were, not poring over philosophical conundrums as *Globe* editors had done before him, but simply insisting that things would have to change."

Doyle says the message was simple: "'I am offering no universal cure-all for this country's ills. I do not believe that any such quick and easy patent medicine exists. I believe only that these ills can and must be cured, and that the cure lies in our hands.'"

This was all vapid stuff. But it didn't matter in a city that was—and always seems to be—in dire need of someone to dazzle it. "Style—the man had style!" Doyle wrote in his memoirs. "Not to the manor born, he was the man who *built* manors."[17]

The *Globe and Mail* did become Canada's most dynamic newspaper. The paper was cobbled together just as the abdication crisis was playing out, and people in Toronto could read all about the sad love story of Edward VIII and Wallis Simpson. Readers in London and Manchester knew much less because the news of the crisis was self-censored by the British press. The *Globe and Mail* ran big stories about the Dionne quintuplets, fed the best stuff by Mitch Hepburn, who had seized the babies and turned them into a public relations and tourism prop. *Globe and Mail* reporters covered all the big stories, like the crash of the Hindenburg zeppelin in New Jersey and the coronation of George VI.

It sent reporters to cover big floods in the Mississippi Valley. It scooped other Toronto papers with pictures from the Japanese attack on the American gunboat *Panay* near Nanking in December 1937, an incident that could easily have caused war between those countries. When a natural gas explosion in New London, Texas, flattened a combined elementary and high school, killing more than three hundred students and teachers, the *Globe and Mail* was the first paper in Toronto with wire photos and had reporters on the scene very quickly.

When there was big news, the *Globe and Mail* was willing to spend the money to stop the presses, put on new plates with the updates, and fire them up again. With the paper's modern technology, photos and words from a big story could be on the streets of downtown Toronto in an hour.[18]

The newspaper had a company plane, mainly used by McCullagh to bring his friends from Hollywood and New York to Toronto. It was also, secretly, ferrying him to appointments with New York psychiatrist Robert Foster Kennedy, who had started aggressively treating McCullagh for his mood swings. When the plane wasn't meeting McCullagh's personal needs, it took reporters to isolated places in Canada to cover big stories.[19] The first *Globe and Mail* plane was a beautiful silver thing, a work of art itself. The plane, which was frequently written about and photographed by the paper's staff, inspired awe in everyone except the *Globe and Mail*'s competitors.

The paper's flashy, handsome young publisher was getting ink in big magazines. Writers couldn't say, as June Callwood would write later, that McCullagh "exuded sex."[20] It would be another couple of generations before magazine writers went that far. Still, *Saturday Night* magazine described him as an "Arrow-collar advertising man in the flesh: dark, crisp hair, of medium size but broad-shouldered with an athletic build. Readily, he smiles or jokes, glibly damns or consigns to hell what does not meet with his approval. But underneath this congenital [*sic*] exterior is an alert analytical mind—one that misses nothing, one that sizes up constantly and one that acts without hesitation."

That was nice, but it wasn't the big time. Real fame came when J.C. Furnas, a writer for the New York–based *Saturday Evening Post*, asked for an interview. The *Post* had the highest circulation of any magazine in the United States and a worldwide reach. Furnas relaxed in a chair in McCullagh's office and made himself comfortable, while his wife sat out of McCullagh's line of sight, taking notes. McCullagh laid it on thick, telling of his hard-luck childhood, and his rise through the newspaper business and onto Bay Street. When he built up Barrett, McCullagh into a forty-member gold-stock-trading outfit, "that was the time big men began to fear me."[21]

He talked of his great luck in meeting Mr. Wright. He explained how he'd bought the *Globe* and humiliated old Jaffray. How he'd bought the *Mail and Empire*. How he'd fought the unions. How he'd beaten his alcoholism. How he'd gone on the radio to save Ontario from socialism. Furnas claimed McCullagh could easily become prime minister of Canada, maybe even immediately, if he chose to.

The article that came out of the interview does not seem sarcastic, nor was there much in it that would be news to anyone who knew McCullagh or was a close reader of his paper. Mostly, it was a chronological account of a rather amazing life, with a chunk devoted to the extraordinary career of William Wright. Sure, McCullagh hammed it up for the portrait picture that ran on the first page. He's shown with one foot on a heating radiator, his left arm resting on a bent knee and his right fist dug into his hip. He looks so very young and serious, just a thirty-two-year-old kid newly arrived from the sticks, trying to look like a Bay Street player.

When the article came out on January 22, 1938, McCullagh loved it. That love soured a few days later when his friends began to make little digs about the piece, especially the claim that big men feared him.

Suddenly, people were laughing at him. From then on, McCullagh seized control of his own image-making and never gave another interview for a biographical article. It would be eleven years before an enterprising reporter took another shot at writing the story of George McCullagh.

* * *

In the fall of 1936, McCullagh started looking for big names for the newsroom of the merged paper. His first catch was John Bassett, son of a Quebec newspaper publisher. The senior Bassett, *Montreal Gazette* publisher Major John Bassett, had been one of the first important Canadian news executives to accept the unlettered upstart McCullagh into the fraternity of publishers. He'd even taken McCullagh to London to meet the Fleet Street barons, including Canadian-born Max Aitken (Lord Beaverbrook), the owner of the *Daily Express*, who became a friend of McCullagh's, and Lord Rothermere, owner of the *Daily Mail*. Major John was also a friend of the Duke of Windsor, which opened another set of doors in British society.[22]

John Bassett Jr., after years of grooming by his father and George McCullagh, would one day own the Toronto *Telegram* and start the first private television station in Toronto, CFTO. The younger Bassett was much like McCullagh: physically imposing, handsome, loud, opinionated and ambitious. Neither men was a snob, and the people who worked for them often came to adore them (or were quickly gone). And they both liked to ride horses. In fact, anyone at the *Globe and Mail* with office politics skills and a few dollars quickly bought a horse and brushed up on their equestrian skills. The fastest way to move up at the paper was to join Bassett, McCullagh and the rest of the clique of riders who rode together every Saturday morning and were quickly dubbed "McCullagh's Hussars."[23]

McCullagh tried to make life in the *Globe and Mail*'s hypercompetitive newsroom a little easier for Bassett: he pulled some of his reporters aside and told them to go easy on the kid. (Bassett was about eight years younger than his thirty-two-year-old boss). "His father's president of the *Montreal Gazette* and he's going to be publisher of *The Sherbrooke Record*, so see what you can do with him," McCullagh told his sub-editors. Journalists have never had a warm spot for rich kids who hang around for a few months playing reporter, but they soon liked Bassett. "He was just as charming, just as dominating in his personality and probably more handsome than the young Robert Redford," Royd Beamish, one of the reporters who worked at the *Globe and Mail* in the early years, told Bassett biographer Maggie Siggins.

And John Douglas MacFarlane, who would strike healthy doses of fear into his own reporters years later as editor of the *Telegram* and senior editor of the *Toronto Sun*, said Bassett "could charm the pants off almost anyone. He was a learner, he had what we call a capital L on his helmet. He was tall and attractive and he was not above letting people know who he was."[24]

Still, *Globe and Mail* reporters laughed out loud when Bassett, rushing to cover a big fire on the Toronto waterfront, ran into a glass wall in the newsroom and knocked himself out cold. And they rolled their eyes when Bassett, filing a "weeper" about a young man who lost his legs while trying to hop a freight train, told the rewrite desk to turn the material into a great piece "'cause it's going to carry my byline."[25]

Twentieth-century newsrooms were the last place to go for ego gratification. Competition between staffers was always very strong. Life in a newsroom only became tolerable if there was a belief among reporters and editors that the paper was doing its best to beat its competitors. Journalists tend to have a negative view of the world, and are harshest when judging their bosses and colleagues.

The *Globe and Mail* employed some of the best political reporters in the country, and those reporters knew McCullagh would stand behind their work. The publisher brushed off Mackenzie King when the prime minister wanted a newly posted *Globe and Mail* parliamentary reporter to be fired for asking tough questions. The young man hadn't realized how King had defanged the Parliamentary Press Gallery by handing out small tidbits of news. McCullagh also stood up to his friend and sometimes puppet, Mitch Hepburn, when the premier tried to push *Globe and Mail* staffers around. Ralph Hyman, one of the few *Mail and Empire* survivors in the newsroom, had the nerve to ask questions of Quebec premier Maurice Duplessis when the quasi-fascist premier was visiting Hepburn at the King Edward Hotel in downtown Toronto. Duplessis told Hyman that he didn't give interviews. Hyman persisted. Finally, Hepburn jumped in and said he didn't want Hyman's impertinence to reflect badly on the reporter's brother, who was a provincial bureaucrat. Hyman, distressed and enraged, went back to the *Globe and Mail* and told McCullagh about the threat.

"McCullagh picked up the phone, motioned me to stay where I was, and called the premier of Ontario. He gave him hell. The next day, nursing a very large hangover, Hepburn apologized."[26]

Clifford C. Wallace was another big name. He was hired from the *Edmonton Journal* after accepting a Pulitzer Prize on behalf of Alberta journalists who had fought the Social Credit government's press laws. Wallace, who turned out to be a newsroom tyrant, was fired after just three months at the paper. He and McCullagh had become friends, but the young publisher still had no qualms about sacking his famous editor when it became clear the newsroom staff wouldn't tolerate his bullying.[27]

Under the Jaffrays, the *Globe* had a policy prohibiting married couples from working at the paper. This rule survived the merger. When news reporters Iris Naish and Jack Fleming were on holidays in Alberta in the summer of 1937, they both stumbled into stories too good to ignore. Fleming filed a piece on the Social Credit government's new bank law, which obviously encroached on federal powers (along with containing aspects of Premier "Bible Bill" Aberhart's strange theories about banking). Naish lucked into an interview with former prime minister R.B. Bennett. Editors in Toronto did the math and realized the two reporters were a couple. (Their reporter colleagues had kept quiet about the fact that Naish and Fleming were secretly married.) Naish was fired immediately. But McCullagh, who was in the Bahamas when this small scandal broke, insisted the Naish be given her job back.

"This is *The Globe and Mail*, not *The Globe*," McCullagh shouted over the phone lines. "Jesus Christ. If they had been living in sin, you wouldn't have fired her." And Naish got a five-dollar raise. Her boss, Wilf Goodman, did it "just to fix those bastards" who had insisted on Naish's firing.[28]

Stories like that got around fast. They built the kind of loyalty McCullagh would need to win the wars he planned to fight.

* * *

Along with its solid news coverage, the paper gave space to McCullagh's sometimes bizarre interest and crusades. McCullagh adored Anglican bishop Robert John Renison, who he'd met years before through Percy Parker. He sent a memo to his staff saying they were to run a picture of the bishop any time that photographers found him doing anything photogenic.[29] Renison also had a weekly column, the last echo of the church chatter that had larded the pages of the *Globe* in the Jaffray years. Renison turned out to be a man with some taste for adventure, so he had himself transferred from his rich Toronto diocese—headquarters at St. James Cathedral, just down the street from the *Globe and Mail*—to the wilderness of Moosonee. There, he ran missions to the Cree, who lived in the Hudson Bay Lowlands and made up the great majority of his parishioners. The diocese operated three residential schools, at least one of which, St. John's in Chapleau, Ontario, had a graveyard in its schoolyard. In those years, the *Globe and Mail* wasn't interested in those kinds of facts. Renison went to the *Globe and Mail*'s newsroom to break the news to his friend that he was moving. He expected McCullagh to cancel their deal for his weekly column, but McCullagh told him to keep writing it.

Renison's column appeared on Wednesday's editorial page, below the fold, and was always illustrated by an uplifting pretty picture, things like dew-covered flowers. Renison was not a tiresome preacher in the Jaffray mode. He had grown up in the Canadian north after his parents immigrated to Canada from Ireland to be missionaries to the Cree. Renison studied at Wycliffe College, but, when he graduated, he was too young to be ordained. So he went to England, joined the Royal Inniskilling Fusiliers under a fake name, and was stuck in the army until his father paid twenty-one pounds to spring him. Renison learned Cree as a boy, and mastered the language as a young man. He translated religious prose and hymns into Cree and, later, Ojibway. In 1912, the Anglican Church had pulled him out of the north and sent him to a parish in Hamilton, probably seeing it as a promotion. Except for time overseas as a military chaplain during the First World War, Renison spent the next thirty years in the Toronto area, rising through the ranks to become a bishop, with responsibility for the most important church in the city.[30]

McCullagh was often chided for his obvious adoration of the Anglican bishop, but Renison must have been an interesting friend. He was as comfortable in the wilderness as he was in the social circles of Bay Street. McCullagh liked to get out into the woods to fish, but he rarely had the time for that, and if he had fantasies of proving his manhood in the Canadian forest, he was rarely able to act on them.

Renison seems to have been something of a spiritual advisor to McCullagh, and certainly knew of his mood swings. The title of Renison's biography, *One Day at a Time*, might explain the bond between the two men. It's one of the slogans of Alcoholics Anonymous.

* * *

Early in the 1937 provincial election campaign, the *Globe and Mail* carried an editorial saying Tory leader Earl Rowe was unfit to lead his party. To prove it, the paper would send a reporter on the hustings to bird-dog the Conservative leader across the province. This was something new: political campaigns weren't covered that way, and Rowe felt targeted. He lashed out by insinuating McCullagh was a drunk.

McCullagh responded with a letter printed in his own paper under the headline "Mr. Rowe Gets an Answer," written, anonymously, in the third person:

"Being a young man of thirty-two years of age, [McCullagh] may be called a product of the prohibition era, reaching the impressionable years of youth while prohibition legislation was operating. He was raised under the laws prohibiting the sale of liquor, designed chiefly to protect the youth of the province. Although it is unpleasant to admit, he experienced great sorrow through drunkenness and witnessed the same pitiable misfortune for many of his generation, but he is proud to say that a considerable time before he purchased these newspapers, he gave up alcohol in all its forms. In making this statement, the publisher has the full knowledge that his reputation and that of the paper will be subject to public judgment long after sidestepping politicians have ceased to be remembered."

He had quit when Hepburn put him on the board of the University of Toronto, and now, he said, Rowe had given him the opportunity to declare that liquor no longer had a part in his life. The *Globe and Mail* and its publisher would now, publicly, push the cause of temperance— but not prohibition. "Mature manhood" could decide whether to drink or not. But George McCullagh and his paper would be there to salvage those who slipped into addiction. "Consistent with this, the publisher has been able to help men regarded as chronic alcoholics or pathological drinkers." What was Rowe doing? He wasn't telling voters he believed booze was "the greatest scourge of mankind" and saying he'd wipe it out. Instead, Rowe was telling Ontario's big brewers "to lay it on the line in campaign funds."[31]

Booze, and accusations of alcoholism, would dog McCullagh for the rest of his life. Whenever his mental illness flared up, people assumed he had fallen off the wagon. But no one had proof. Unlike most men of his time, he was never drunk in public.[32] Some of his friends, who knew of McCullagh's highs and lows, thought the pain of the mood swings could have been relieved with a reasonable amount of alcohol. But his problems were more serious than that, and alcohol would have been a poor way to self-medicate. If he was a drinker, his depressions would have been much deeper and his death would have come even earlier.

7

POWER AND POLITICS

On November 17, 1936, McCullagh wrote to Mackenzie King to tell the prime minister about the deal for the *Globe*, but he didn't mention his play for the *Mail and Empire*. "I knew that you would be pleased that the Globe has been purchased by a person who is a firm believer in Liberal democratic principles," McCullagh told King. "Men in public life will always have a sympathetic voice in the Globe, believing as I do that their task is a most difficult one at the best of times, and that the press in the past has too often been willing to abuse and criticize without having well founded justification. I hope to set something of a precedent in journalism by cooperating with the government if I may, in working out some of their problems, rather than placing the government in a position to defend unwarranted criticism."[2]

In another letter to King, written three weeks later, McCullagh said he would try to be loyal to the federal and provincial Liberals, but sometimes the left-wing members of Hepburn's cabinets vexed him. "I am a great believer of Mr. Hepburn's sincerity, honesty and courage, but I must confess that some of the acts of the other members of his cabinet at times make me shudder, and though I do not intend to constructively criticize him during this critical by-election, I am afraid our paper will offend die-hard partisans when we, of necessity, must take under review some of the acts of his government."[3]

Yes, he would co-operate with King, but he did turn down the offer of a prime ministerial visit to the McCullagh home in Forest Hill. King liked to freeload off the rich and powerful. He usually stayed at Holy Joe Atkinson's house. (Joe's daughter, Ruth, would later describe her races with King to the Atkinsons' single bathroom.) King wrote McCullagh again when news of the *Mail's* purchase broke. The prime minister told McCullagh about the reaction in Ottawa: for a day or two, until the layoffs of *Mail and Empire* staff began, Conservatives in Ottawa were bragging that the Tory clique who wrote for the *Mail* would expunge or dilute the Liberal content of the *Globe*. King was thrilled that this wouldn't happen. He was also delighted by McCullagh's promises of discretion and deference. But, King said, the prime minister also needed to be discreet. There would be no public praise, no affirming pats on the head coming from Laurier House.[4]

King made it clear that McCullagh could come into the corridors of power, but it would have to be through the servants' entrance. Their friendship was supposed to stay secret. At the same time, King had no qualms about sticking his nose into McCullagh's business, writing to him in November to praise McCullagh for giving fired employees a month's severance and to lecture him on personal strengths and weaknesses after the *Globe* carried an editorial about the power of love and fear.

The prime minister also offered to carry some of the heavy burdens that poor young George was struggling with. There, King went too far. In an eight-line letter, McCullagh told the prime minister not to worry: "I would like to suggest, Sir, that it is by no means comparable to the task with which you are attempting to cope, in leading the Government of Canada through a period which to me appears as a very critical one."[5]

McCullagh could get by on his own, and if he needed fatherly advice, there was always his strange little prospector friend up north.

McCullagh was a good Liberal for a few months. The fawning, sometimes pathetic correspondence between the publisher and prime minister became an almost daily exchange of letters. Just after New Year's, McCullagh took the train to Ottawa to stay at Mackenzie King's house and meet top people in the government.

McCullagh and King appear to have had a real friendship in the first months of 1937, or at least as much of one as either man was capable of creating and maintaining. After the first blush of enthusiastic letters, McCullagh wrote to King from time to time, giving unsolicited advice on big national issues. A month after his first trip to Ottawa, McCullagh wrote a long letter warning King not to let Manitoba and Saskatchewan fall into bankruptcy. The credit of the entire country depended on a bailout of the two provinces, McCullagh said.

McCullagh's ambition didn't end with the ownership of the *Globe and Mail*, and Mackenzie King knew it. When the crisis came, it would test Canadian democracy. In a world of dictators and one-party states, where the Depression was being ruthlessly "solved" by Hitler, Mussolini, Stalin, the warlords of Japan and dozens of tinpot dictators who are now deservedly forgotten, Canada's survival as a democracy was not a sure bet.

But King saw McCullagh as the real threat. He knew McCullagh wanted power, and that owning a newspaper, even a good one with national pretensions, would not be enough. King believed the *Globe and Mail* was just one tool in McCullagh's belt.

"I fear it may become in time a big interest. Fascist organ, at a time when the real publication would be of great service from national point of view," he wrote to one of his friends.[6]

King was a politician who could never have made it to the top in this century. But he did have some superb, ingrained political skills. And here was one of them: he could read people. He knew McCullagh believed he was destined to lead.

* * *

McCullagh wanted to make a profit, but he wouldn't toady to advertisers any more than he would give in to meddling politicians. One business owner who complained about the *Globe and Mail* giving publicity to his competitor and threatened to pull his ads was told where to shove his complaints. McCullagh caught another unhappy advertiser in the paper's newsroom, berating an editor. The big man picked up his customer by his coat and trousers and tossed him out.[7]

Royd Beamish, one of McCullagh's editorial writers, said McCullagh often complained his reporters were writing propaganda instead of news.[8] At the same time, the kid publisher put his own thoughts all over the editorial page. It gave him a great sense of power, but it also opened McCullagh's ideas—many of which were half-baked when he slapped them down onto the page—to criticism from people who had a better grasp of politics and economics. McCullagh saw every attack on the *Globe and Mail* as an attack on himself. Often, he was right. People in the public eye—especially ones as abrasive and charismatic as McCullagh—need to be able to take criticism and counterpunches, and he just couldn't do that.

"George," one friend said, "is seven skins too thin."[9] He was sometimes Trumpian in his self-promotion. He called his creation of the *Globe and Mail* his "masterpiece." Time has shown that it was, indeed, a lasting and important newspaper, but men, even in the 1930s, didn't talk about themselves this way. "People think me high-handed and objectionable. I'll confirm it if they like," he told another interviewer. To an editor at one of his papers, he said, referring to himself in the third person, "Do you know anyone in Canada who's been attacked more than McCullagh?"[10] He might be able to dish it out while riding a high, but he never seems to have understood that he might get some of his own back. When he was feeling low, the criticism added to his misery.

He took solace from his staff. Some of the few women who worked in the newsroom thought McCullagh came on too strong. There were whispers that he had a thing for virgins.[11] But at least in the early years when his marriage was still solid and the McCullagh family was growing, he might have kept the sexual harassment at a level that didn't exceed clumsy flirting and sleazy innuendo.

The *Globe and Mail's* cafeteria became a kind of meeting place and lecture hall for McCullagh. He often went there when he was lonely and talked to anyone who might be having a coffee or eating lunch. He'd go on about politics, the business of running a paper, horses, an interesting homicide he'd read about, or, when he felt it was appropriate, the perils of booze—although he was not nearly as judgmental as the Jaffrays.

McCullagh wasn't the only *Globe and Mail* star who would hold court in that cafeteria. John Bassett, who mimicked McCullagh in so many ways, also used it. Jessie McTaggart, who was active in the newspaper union, had made friends with some Communists who were active in Toronto's labour scene. It's likely she wasn't a Communist, but she did like some of their ideas, like old age pensions and unemployment insurance.[12] For a while, she argued with Bassett; then she brought one of her Communist friends to the *Globe and Mail* cafeteria for what Bassett thought would be a thrashing. The battle lasted through an entire afternoon. The *Globe and Mail* was the kind of place where reporters were free to engage in a good intellectual brawl, once their stories were filed. People came and went during the four hours of sparring, and when it was all over, the Communist labour organizer and Bassett shook hands and had a good laugh at each other, though most of the people who'd watched the argument were sure that Bassett had lost it.[13]

∗ ∗ ∗

McCullagh created the *Globe and Mail* while Mitch Hepburn was facing a tough by-election test in the central Ontario riding of East Hastings. This was United Empire Loyalist country, a deep Tory-blue riding that ran from the shores of the Bay of Quinte north into the

Canadian Shield, deep into the Ozarks of Ontario. People there had every reason to vote against the status quo and to support a premier who offered simple populist solutions. The farmers at the south end, along Lake Ontario, could get almost nothing for their crops. Their land had become nearly worthless. Farms were being picked off by bailiffs working for banks that were, themselves, becoming shaky. Up in the Canadian Shield, the nearly empty northern part of the riding, mining and forestry jobs had dried up, and the people who still had jobs were blackmailed by their bosses into taking big wage cuts. Many of their employers were barely hanging on.

The local Tory MPP had died, and Hepburn, who planned to call the vote in the fall of 1936, saw this as an opportunity to show that his populism had changed the political dynamic of Ontario. He had a massive majority, and the seat wouldn't change the situation in the legislature, but Hepburn saw it as a referendum on his policies. Victory would prove that the poor farmers on the back concessions and the working men (and the few women left in the workforce) wanted Mitch's brand of change. This riding was in the core of old Ontario— people proud of their descent from opponents of the American Revolution were, six generations later, still suspicious of any novelty. McCullagh said Hepburn "seemed to think his own popularity was strong enough for anything."[14] It turned out he was wrong. People weren't stupid. After a couple of years of Hepburn's stunts, it was clear there was no difference between his brand of free enterprise and the pro-business policies of the Tories that he'd hounded from office.

In his first article in the premier edition of the *Globe and Mail*, McCullagh threw his support behind Hepburn, but with some caveats. There were "glaring weaknesses" in Mitch's cabinet. A "house cleaning" was needed. Hepburn was put on notice that McCullagh's support came at a price: a say in the make-up of the very top of the power structure at Queen's Park. McCullagh had nothing to say about the sad financial state of the people who would be casting ballots but, presumably, a dose of the publisher's wisdom would help the farmers, loggers and miners of eastern Ontario.

McCullagh wanted help for the rich. For instance, one of Hepburn's populist promises had to go. Hepburn planned to repudiate Hydro contracts that, he said, cheated the people of Ontario. These deals were between Ontario's public power utility and private electrical generating companies, mainly in the Ottawa Valley. When Hepburn tried to break these contracts, the power companies went to court and won. Hepburn's answer: pass a law to give him the authority to cancel the deals. His own advisors said the law would survive a court challenge, saying it was "bomb proof."[15]

Maybe it was, but the idea of governments legislating themselves out of responsibility to hold up their ends of contracts was appalling to McCullagh and his friends, who wondered whose business might be targeted next. After writing his editorial, McCullagh headed down to London to visit his parents. After a few hours with them, he drove to Hepburn's thousand-acre onion farm, Bannockburn, near St. Thomas. There, McCullagh shifted from being a publisher to acting as a lobbyist for the power companies. Attorney General Arthur Roebuck, the provincial minister who had quarterbacked the Liberal strategy, was a left-wing fanatic who had to go. (Most of Ontario's business, industrial and mine-owning elites were convinced Roebuck was an avowed Communist. Presumably, McCullagh held that view, too.[16]) Hepburn held his ground, so McCullagh went back to Toronto and blasted the premier in a *Globe and Mail* article headlined "The Price of Repudiation."

It was a vicious piece. Walking away from the contracts was not just contrary to centuries of common law, McCullagh wrote, it was a policy that undermined the "moral structure" of the people of the province. Hepburn would ruin Ontario's credit. People who had invested in insurance companies would be burned, since those companies had made heavy investments in power company bonds. McCullagh was alright with renegotiation of the contracts, but outright repudiation was symptomatic of a set of policies "setting up one class against another." He said it was part of Roebuck's secret, nefarious plan for class warfare.[17]

Hepburn answered with a press release issued under his name, but almost certainly written by Roebuck. It asked—and answered—the same questions about Bill Wright and George McCullagh that were being asked by everyone in the Canadian business and political classes:

> The cat is out of the bag.
>
> When one hears that a multi-millionaire [presumably Wright] has opened his money-bags to the extent of three and a half to four million dollars for fun, one is surprised and pleased. It is a pretty picture. Then when you learn that all this money is being used to purchase a great newspaper with a national circulation and historic prestige in order that the philanthropy of the millionaire might be used for the influencing of public opinion in the interest of humanity, rectitude, good government and everything else that is high-minded and noble, you pause and instinctively say, "What is the game?"
>
> Now we know...[18]

But Hepburn (or Roebuck) stopped short of naming McCullagh. Maybe the snark was directed at Wright—in which case, it might as well have been aimed at McCullagh. The young publisher had many issues, but his loyalty to Wright never wavered. In reputation, they were the same person. And Hepburn, who now realized what was happening, almost immediately began to defuse the little crisis. He started to publicly undermine his own attorney general. Within a few months, McCullagh and Hepburn would finish him off.

While the Hydro contracts case was grinding its way through the court system—it would eventually end up being decided by British law lords in the Privy Council—controversy opened on another front.

As rich people fought over the supposed sanctity of contracts, the poor voters of East Hastings, the press and the Tories were angrily debating the provincial funding of Roman Catholic schools. The riding was heavily Protestant in the populated south, and had a large minority of Irish Catholics and a smattering of French Catholics in the north. Catholic schools are a no-win issue that every Ontario premier avoids, if possible. Funding for Catholic schools is guaranteed by the British North America Act, which, in 1936, could only be amended by the British Parliament.

The issue went something like this: Say Mrs. Jones, a Catholic, owned a house in Deseronto, Ontario. It was an easy thing for her to have the education portion of her property taxes directed to the Catholic system. But what if she was part-owner of a small business, and her co-owners were Protestant? Where did the taxes go then? How much, if any, would be given to the Catholic schools? Taking this farther, say Mrs. Jones owned shares in a lumber company with a big mill on the edge of town. And lots of other Catholics did, too. Where would the mill taxes go? It was an important question to Catholics, who had to pay tuition for their last two years of high school. They believed they were forced to pay twice, that they subsidized Protestant public schools, and they were convinced their elementary schools were being shortchanged. But they, and any politicians who supported them, were up against the province's Protestant majority and its muscle, the Loyal Orange Lodge.

Toronto businessman Martin Quinn had created the Catholic Taxpayers' Association, and in the previous provincial election, it backed Hepburn. It had also managed to get one of its members elected mayor of Toronto, a remarkable victory in what some people called the Belfast of Canada. In February 1936, Hepburn paid the Catholics back with a new law that gave them a greater share of property taxes, with corporations being forced to ask the religion of their shareholders so they could divide their school levy along the religious lines of their owners. Percy Parker, McCullagh's mentor, had tried to warn Hepburn off, but the premier thought he had enough personal political clout to get the law through. Quinn wanted to make the East Hastings election his pulpit. He was backed by Frank O'Connor, a rich Catholic strategist of Hepburn's who came from the Hastings County village of Deseronto. East Hastings was a strange choice of battlefield for Catholic rights: from the Mohawks at Tyendinaga, on the shore of Lake Ontario, who did—and still do—have their own Orange Lodge (but couldn't vote), to the Madawaska Highlands, the Catholics were hard-pressed to find sympathy here. People in the riding mourned their old MPP, who had been a regional leader of the Loyal Orange Lodge. Opponents of government funding for separate schools flooded the riding with vile anti-Papist propaganda. Not only would the Protestants of East Hastings grind Hepburn, the Tories would use the by-election to prove the premier was in the thrall of Rome.

McCullagh didn't have any religious axe to grind. He simply believed Ontario didn't need Catholics and Protestants "fanning the flames of hatred, something which has no place in a God-fearing province such as ours."[19] But it was too late: in 1936, the biggest social cleavage in Canada did not divide social classes, people who spoke different languages or members of various races. The great split in mainstream Canadian society was on religious lines, between two groups of Christians. It's absurd now, but it wasn't during the Depression, or in the three decades after the Second World War.

This ugly by-election, with all its bigotry, played out during the abdication crisis, as Edward VIII agonized over whether his throne was worth the vapid companionship and supposedly interesting carnal delights of Wallis Simpson. In Ontario, the by-election was a bigger story: Hepburn moved almost all his cabinet—overwhelmingly Protestant, and not all enamoured with Hepburn's sop to the Catholics— to the riding. They set up shop in Belleville. Its most famous citizen, Mackenzie Bowell, a former prime minister and, at least as important to the locals, North American grand master of the Loyal Orange Lodge, was quietly mouldering in the town's best cemetery. Hepburn may not have realized his Catholic school policy was just as dead. Still, his ministers started fanning out to the riding's villages and hamlets, speaking anyplace where they could pull together a handful of voters.

This election was not simply about religion. It was about what was then called "race" by all the province's citizens, the vast majority of whom were white. Indigenous people and people of colour were invisible to this mainstream, and "race" talk wasn't about them. Irish Catholics and French Canadians were the main targets of the bigots. They weren't considered members of the same "race" as Anglo-Saxons, which, strangely, seemed to include Celtic people if they were Protestants. A National Film Board travelogue of 1941 summed up the attitude of the time, with the narrator saying about Ottawa, "French and English, Scottish and Irish have laboured together to build a city," and then going on to talk about "the French and English race."[20] French- and English-speaking people might—just might—tolerate each other in Ottawa, but the French language had been driven out of the school system twenty years earlier. Catholic schools survived but were starved of the money they needed for new buildings, books and trained teachers. Race in Ontario has always been a complicated thing, and Tory Ontario wanted to show that the French and the Irish, with their Roman religion, were at the bottom of the hierarchy.

Speaking in the hamlet of Plainfield, George Drew—who would later become McCullagh's best friend and political ally—showed just how ugly this thing was. "It is not unfair to remind the French that they are a defeated race and that their rights are only rights because of the tolerance of the English element, who, with all respect to the minority, must be regarded as the dominant race," Drew told his impoverished Protestant audience.

Rev. T.T. Shields, the bile-spewing pastor of Toronto's Jarvis Street Baptist Church, chased Hepburn through the riding, denouncing him for repealing most of Ontario's Prohibition laws and being a tool of the pope. At one rally, Reverend Shields shared his podium with Orangeman Cecil W. Armstrong, who wanted one school system "where the little red-headed micks and the Protestant pups alike can go." Earl Rowe, the leader of the Ontario Tories, stumped the riding. When his criticism of Hepburn started getting under the premier's skin, Liberal operatives leaked details of a car accident, during which Rowe had run over two little old ladies and nearly killed them. The Tories thought they'd covered it up, but the Liberals had just been waiting for the right time to use it.

The voters were willing to forgive Rowe, even if the elderly women he'd hit would not. The riding went Tory—Hepburn's belief in a Liberal victory had always been absurd—but the big margin of the win was a slap across the premier's face. Hepburn's prestige, and his reputation as a winner, had been hit hard. Hepburn soon put as much distance as he could between himself and his Catholic friends.[21]

* * *

Soon, Hepburn was in another mess. Franklin Roosevelt was re-elected president in November 1936. He had used big public works projects to try to revive the American economy. Roosevelt bent American rivers like the Tennessee to his will and built gigantic dams like Boulder Dam (renamed Hoover Dam in 1947) to generate the electricity that still powers Las Vegas. The St. Lawrence, which Roosevelt knew well, was his next target. Not only would the river be harnessed to generate power, its damming would also open the Great Lakes to ocean ships. To Americans, the project's value seemed obvious. To Canadians, who shared the river between Kingston and Cornwall, Ontario, the plan seemed threatening. Ontario had already suffered through a series of scandals over Hydro's purchase of power from companies in the Ottawa Valley and at Beauharnois, southwest of Montreal.

At the same time, an American pulp and paper company wanted to divert the north-flowing Ogoki River in northern Ontario through Long Lake and the Aguasabon River to generate power near what's now the town of Terrace Bay, Ontario. Water diversion into the Great Lakes—this time, from Hudson Bay to Lake Superior—required permission by Canada and the United States under the Boundary Waters Treaty of 1909.

Canada had good reason to be careful. The Long Lake-Ogoki plan would raise the level of the upper lakes, which was one of the American goals. The extra water would generate more power at Niagara Falls and allow bigger ships to get through shallow Lake St. Clair. But higher lake levels, which already fluctuated with some regularity, could cause trouble at harbours and marinas on both sides of the lakes. Some beaches would be lost, navigation charts would have to be remade, some wharfs might be submerged. There was also the risk of setting a precedent: allowing water to be channelled south from northern Ontario would likely open the door to a diversion through the Chicago River system to send water to the Mississippi. (Neither side seemed to understand the threat of introducing new species of marine life into the Great Lakes, which turned out to be the biggest ecological problem caused by the diversions and the construction of new ship canals.) Still, the idea of opening northern Ontario's forests to pulp and paper companies attracted by cheap power was intriguing to politicians and bureaucrats in Ottawa and Toronto.

The federal government was willing to buy into a big St. Lawrence River navigation and hydro project, as much to please the Roosevelt administration as to open ports like Toronto to ocean-going ships. King, however, didn't want to sink a lot of Canadian money into a project that might not make a profit for Canada. The Roosevelt administration wanted a greater share of the hydro power, including a promise that no generating stations would be built on the Canadian side of the St. Lawrence in the first six years of the new seaway. And

Roosevelt made it clear that the Lake Superior project wouldn't happen unless there was a deal for the St. Lawrence.

Ontario didn't need the electricity. It had more than it needed for its depressed manufacturing base, and enough for any economic revival. The Great Lakes shipping industry was doing as well as could be expected during the Depression and didn't want the competition from saltwater ships.[22]

Hepburn, however, liked the idea of a big hydro project north of Superior and sent two of his senior ministers to Ottawa to tell King that Ontario might go ahead with Long Lake-Ogoki, treaty or no treaty.

This is all complicated, and none of it would happen until most of the people involved at this particular moment had shuffled off the scene. The real result, for the George McCullagh story, is that in January 1937, Ontario's premier went on a week-long bender at the height of the negotiations and as his own party started tearing itself apart over what many of them—especially the lawyers in the Liberal caucus—saw as the sacredness of all contracts.

After spending Christmas with his family at his onion farm, Hepburn had gone back to his lair on the top of the King Eddy and started working the phones. But he brought with him a touch of bronchitis. He decided to self-medicate himself into a stupor. Hepburn's own doctor, backed by Ontario's health minister, handled the media while McCullagh hung around Hepburn's suite, pestering the premier and trying to sober him up. This bender was particularly hard on Hepburn. Doctors found Hepburn's blood pressure was much too high, his kidneys were failing, and his bronchitis was getting worse. Hepburn agreed to go south, to a friend's ranch near El Paso, Texas, though it's a mystery why the doctors thought less scrutiny and more access to booze and women was therapy. Whenever Hepburn travelled, his first visits were to bars and brothels. He could haunt those places in anonymity, something he couldn't do in Ontario. Hepburn was gone for a month, which is a very long time in politics.

But he wasn't free of McCullagh, who knew booze was the real problem. While Hepburn was still at the King Eddy, McCullagh warned the premier that liquor was ruining him, making him "prey to influences" that were beyond the understanding of the premier. Hepburn had fallen in with a "group of men who were wealthy but who liked drinking and that fast sort of life." They only wanted to be around Hepburn because he was premier, and they'd dump him in a heartbeat if voters sent him back to the St. Thomas onion farm. This was a "mistaken life," McCullagh told the premier. If Hepburn didn't give up on booze, McCullagh would give up on Hepburn.

The premier, hacking and wheezing while his mistress and body-guards sat idly in the suite, "took it very well," McCullagh would later say.[23] Hepburn might have been nodding his agreement, but the premier likely realized McCullagh would not abandon him, at least until something better came along. And there seemed to be nothing on the horizon.

At the beginning of the year, just before Hepburn went to Arizona, McCullagh slipped into Ottawa to visit the prime minister. King showed him a good time, introducing him to the capital's power-brokers and revealing to him the symbols and trappings of power. One evening, McCullagh and King sat down alone at Laurier House, where McCullagh told King every detail of the deals for the *Globe* and the *Mail and Empire*. King knew Jaffray and despised him, so McCullagh had a sympathetic listener. They agreed the former publisher of the *Globe* was a hypocrite who cheated his company's shareholders, including King's ancient mentor, old Sir William Mulock. He mistreated his employees and cut their pay. The *Globe* newsroom, where both men had worked (though a generation apart), had become a sweatshop where Jaffray's miserable employees clung to the jobs they hated because the Depression had left them with no other options. King was more interested in McCullagh's take on Hepburn: his drinking, his growing hatred of King, and, most important, any plans the populist premier might have for a run at the federal Liberal leadership. Later, the prime minister dictated page after page of the secrets given to him by the indiscrete young publisher into his diary.[24]

In return for those secrets, McCullagh got lectures. The prime minister pulled out a dry *Washington Post* editorial called "Ithuriel's Hour," about the Last Judgment, and read the whole thing to McCullagh. This, King said, was the sort of stuff that the *Globe and Mail* should be running. It was writing that showed great scholarship and great understanding. A newspaper like the *Globe and Mail* should serve the British Empire. In fact, King said, empire-boosting by a paper out in the colonies would do much more to preserve the Empire than any editorial in a London newspaper.

It must have been one hell of a night, these two odd men sitting in the Laurier House library, sipping some non-alcoholic drinks and talking of ways to make Canada a more important place in the British Empire.

The next morning, King got a call from Holy Joe, who was fishing for a grant for a Toronto doctor "on behalf of humanity."[25] Then, in the same breath, he asked for a radio station licence. The prime minister, still bathing in the glow of his new young friend, was irked by Atkinson's lobbying. It was the last straw, King thought. He told the *Star* publisher that the decision would be made by the federal broadcast commission, without the interference of the prime minister of Canada.

McCullagh returned to Toronto elated by the prime minister's hospitality and friendship. In the cold early January days, McCullagh held the whip with the Ontario cabinet while the premier was away, but the wheels were coming off Hepburn's populist movement. There was also some rebellion from inside the Liberal caucus about the *Globe and Mail*'s publisher. Rumours spread in January among Liberal backbenchers that McCullagh was a front man for power companies. Mitch had to send a message from Arizona: "I know positively that Mr. McCullagh has no connection whatsoever with the power interests. As far as our differences on the issue of power are concerned, they are just honest differences of opinion. We discussed the situation frankly and friendly, and finally agreed to disagree."[26]

But an absentee leader made a bad situation worse. The hydro deals did have a bad smell. And in another brewing scandal, the Liberals, supposedly there for the people, were letting the owners of Sault Ste. Marie's big Algoma steel mill dictate mining policy in the near-North.

At least there was some good news from McCullagh, who wrote a letter to Hepburn bragging about the money that he'd made for the premier. "There has not been a great deal doing since you left, excepting I have been watching your investments, and since you went away, I took you in as a partner with myself on a deal called Hyslop [*sic*] Gold Mines. We have purchased some shares at 11 cents per share with options...The shares are now 25 cents...We might make a real killing. Your name, of course, does not appear anywhere."[27]

Mitch, somewhat dried out, was back in Toronto by late February, and McCullagh did all he could to polish the premier's image. At the same time, he was supervising the construction of the *Globe and Mail's* news palace in the core of Toronto's financial district, handling Wright's affairs, looking for financial opportunities for Mitch, fending off King, running a newsroom and being a father. All of this was a heavy burden for a man barely into his thirties, and McCullagh sometimes cracked under the strain. He didn't get back on the bottle, or, if he relapsed, no one knew. But it was a tough winter, even with the high that came with testing his new political and journalistic power.

By February, McCullagh and Wright were exhausted. In less than six months, they had remade the Toronto and national newspaper market and invested more than $5 million Depression-era dollars— valued in today's money between $90 million and $1.1 billion, depending on how its buying power is measured—in an industry that most people thought was finished.[28] They headed south together for what McCullagh described as a much-needed vacation. Likely, they were on their way to the Bahamas to see Harry Oakes, who'd been living there as a tax fugitive since 1935.[29] Phyllis, who'd endured as much stress as her husband and his patron, was left behind with the kids. "I have just two hobbies, work and fishing," McCullagh had told a *Globe and Mail* reporter that fall. Now it was time to fish in shark-infested waters. Then they got back from Nassau, they would take on the American labour movement as it tried to creep across the Canadian border.

* * *

In early March, Hepburn brought in that great Canadian rarity, a balanced budget. Ontario was the first Canadian province to go into the black during the Depression. But another storm was brewing, one that would remake Ontario politics. After more than six years of hard times, workers in the United States had stopped waiting for "fundamentals" to improve. New streams of populism were building strength, from radio priest Charles Coughlin's bizarre mix of Catholicism and fascism—which was becoming less Catholic and more fascist as the months went by—to Marxist takeovers of what had once been employer-friendly unions. This campaign had some support from the Roosevelt administration. The president knew higher wages and consumer spending were the best way out of the Depression, and he had put many social justice advocates in key White House jobs. The new generation of union leaders was about to make big wins in the United States, and then head north.

By then, Hepburn had lost his populist touch. He'd gambled on what he saw as the fairness of the impoverished voters of East Hastings and he'd lost. And now, by repudiating the hydro contracts and making a law that lawyers claimed was a gross violation of property rights, Mitch had alienated rich people who, until then, might have seen his rural populism as quaint hucksterism by a man who would let them keep running the province. To the wealthy and their lawyers, cancelling contracts was a form of heresy and abomination that was far more radical than anything that happened during the Latin Mass.

Even McCullagh had doubts. But the *Globe and Mail* publisher still needed Hepburn. It was unlikely McCullagh could buy Earl Rowe, the Tory leader, and he'd already invested so much in Mitch. So how could the premier be rehabilitated? How could the onion farmer from St. Thomas, holed up in his suite at the King Eddy with his whores and drinking buddies, getting fatter and fatter on hotel food, be made more palatable to voters? Liberal leaders of the twentieth century rarely got a second term, and the smart money was betting against him.[30]

At the beginning of March, King was in Toronto to take the pulse of the city and to see how work was coming on the memorial to his grandfather, the rebel William Lyon Mackenzie. The centennial of Toronto's incorporation as a city had just passed and the hundredth anniversary of the Rebellion of 1837 was underway. King had a moment similar to McCullagh's 1936 visit to Jaffray, when the once-fired boy journalist had returned as a young man to buy the paper. King, too, was returning as the successful son. He stopped in at the *Globe* office to have a look around, then made his way to the *Mail* to see McCullagh (the new *Globe and Mail* building was still being finished). "I could not help thinking to myself how strange the change was that for a time I was a reporter on the 'Globe' and, later, reporter on the 'Mail and Empire'. I was now going into these buildings through the old doorways and staircases, and this time as Prime Minister of the country."

King and McCullagh had, according to King, "a pleasant talk." McCullagh told the prime minister that the *Globe and Mail* would still support Hepburn, but the premier had to tone down some of the populist stuff. King had mixed feelings about that. Then the two of them began to gossip, which was the part of the visit that King really liked. First, McCullagh told King that Hepburn was on the mend, and seemed to be beating his booze problem. (This was untrue. The premier still went on benders in his suite at the King Eddy. If King was skeptical, he didn't let on.) McCullagh offered up more juicy, original stuff. Jaffray had been in that day to do some paperwork related to the sale of the *Globe*, and he'd told McCullagh how he'd screwed the minority shareholders, including Sir William Mulock. "[Jaffray's] Christian principles did not go very far," King later told his diary. In return for this gossip, King showed McCullagh a personal letter that he'd just received from President Roosevelt. McCullagh was impressed. Then came King's gripes: a *Globe and Mail* reporter on Parliament Hill was too critical of the Liberals, and his pro-Opposition pieces were landing on the front page. McCullagh said he didn't think much of the man's work and would be getting rid of him soon.

Despite the supposed warmth of their friendship, King found time later that day to gossip about McCullagh to Atkinson. The *Star* publisher told King that McCullagh was lying when he said the *Globe and Mail* was selling well. In fact, it was the *Star* that had seen its sales jump after the merger.[31]

Within three weeks, the McCullagh-King relationship began to crumble. McCullagh let King know he thought it would be decent of King to find a good job for former prime minister R.B. Bennett, the Tory who King beat in 1935. Bennett was still leader of the official Opposition, but everyone expected him to quit soon. King was furious. "I told him I wd. not express an opinion one way or the other as I did not wish... to be getting rid of an adversary—the Globe is trying to be a dictator. McCullagh is just the instrument of Wright—they have dictated to Hepburn and they have bowed to his dictation on the [Roman Catholic] schools question."[32]

Whatever real friendship existed between the two men was about to be severely tested. King believed there was a place for labour unions. McCullagh thought unions were a threat to the economic and political status quo, far more dangerous than a few broken hydro contracts and a dispute over school taxes. Labour was on the march across non-fascist parts of Europe, was tearing Britain's political system apart, and had been waging a sporadic, bloody war in the United States.

Working men had been trying to organize unions long before the Great Depression, as McCullagh knew well. His father, that man he so rarely mentioned, had been an agitator, and young George, burdened with a spectacular Oedipus complex, had spent his life trying to be everything his father was not. Now, unions—especially those affiliated with the two-year-old Congress of Industrial Organizations (CIO) headed by John L. Lewis—were on the move. As the Depression waxed and waned, many more men and women on factory floors saw unions as the only way to protect themselves from more wage cuts and assembly line speed-ups. People like William Wright couldn't begin to imagine sitting down with union leaders to negotiate contracts for the miners who went a mile or more down into the unsafe shafts of northern Ontario. Income tax was bad enough.

Let the CIO into Ontario? No. Never.

The line had to be drawn at the Detroit River.

* * *

In the weeks after McCullagh moved from Bay Street to the publisher's office of the *Globe and Mail*, his new political opponents were digging up dirt on him. Drew found Jefferies, the crooked broker who said he'd planned scams with McCullagh. A memo written by Drew shows he certainly wanted to believe Jefferies, who, to a more objective reader, emerges from the page as something of a sleaze who is peddling a wild story to get help with his Securities and Exchange Commission case. Drew later became best friends with McCullagh, but he kept this memo all his life. A person who tried to erase George McCullagh from history after his death could have destroyed this memo. Instead, she allowed it to be sent to Canada's national archives after Drew's death.

8

SONS OF MITCHES

In the early 1930s, when McCullagh was still on Bay Street selling dreams of motherlodes and Mitch Hepburn was auctioning off the Ontario government's fleet of limos, the United Auto Workers (UAW) was an obscure union trying to get a foothold in Detroit and the auto cities nearby. It wasn't having much luck, despite Franklin Roosevelt's pro-union New Deal laws. The UAW's leaders were brave, tough men who had sweated for years on the lines. The women in their lives were just as brave. It was common for union leaders' phones to ring late at night, the muffled voice on the other end of the line making explicit death threats. Union leaders were gunned down through the windows of their homes and beaten by the car-makers' private goon-cops. The Detroit-based union was riddled with spies and paid informers. Its leaders were smart, dedicated and knew their opponents. By late 1936, they'd identified a choke point in General Motors' parts supply system: vital parts for all of GM's models were made in just two factories in

Flint, Michigan. Just before New Year's, workers occupied the two factories in the first UAW sit-down strike.

But GM would not fall easily. City and private police armed with heavy machine guns surrounded the two factories and tried to keep food out. After about two weeks, a police squad tried to storm the plant but were driven off by workers throwing punches, rocks and car parts. At the end of January, the strike started spreading to other GM plants. Enough time had passed for GM's management to realize it was unable to supply its dealers and was losing market share to its competitors: there was no solidarity among the automakers. General Motors caved to the UAW after forty-four days. The union, which had barely been on the political and business radar, was now the most dynamic labour organization in North America.

But there was no point bleeding in Flint and Detroit if one of the company's biggest plants was still unorganized. GM's big factory in Oshawa, Ontario, was not covered by the February deal. The UAW set out to fix that.

For a century, the Canadian labour movement had been a pale shadow of the US campaign for workers' rights. In small cities like the McCullagh hometown of London, activists like George McCullagh Sr. were blackballed. Workers at the Oshawa General Motors plant had tried to form a union in 1928. When they failed at that, they went on strike anyway. They lost. They went back to work angry and embittered, and they'd soon have more reason to want a union. In the United States, the automakers employed Pinkerton agents and other private spies to infiltrate their plants and ferret out union organizers. Canada's answer was something called Corporations Auxiliary, an employer-owned company that recruited spies for the shop floor. Workers had no legal protection from being fired for supporting or organizing unions. There was no seniority system. Every year, when the assembly lines were retooled for the next model year's cars, most hourly employees were laid off, and only the "loyal" ones were called back.[1]

The Depression made things even worse: GM cut wages of the thirty-seven hundred workers in its Oshawa plant five times between 1932 and 1937, and sped up the production line.

The idea of an autoworkers' union probably would have found a sympathetic ear with Mitch Hepburn in 1934, when he still believed his own populist bumpf. In his first year in power, Hepburn had brought in the province's first minimum wage law (although it only applied to men). But by the spring of 1937, Hepburn was McCullagh's creature, and McCullagh was deeply indebted to Bill Wright.

When the UAW showed itself in Oshawa, it became clear why William Wright had wanted to bankroll the creation of a powerful pro-business newspaper. In the United States, the United Mine Workers under John L. Lewis had emerged as the dominant union. Lewis was also head of the CIO, and it was Lewis, not the UAW's leaders, who negotiated the deal with General Motors that ended the Flint strike. Wright did not want Lewis's unions in his mines. McCullagh, smart enough not to need to be told, made Oshawa the test of strength of whether organized labour would get a foothold in Ontario. The *Globe and Mail*'s editorials identified the threat: "Along with the motor industry, steel plants, pulp and paper mills, the mines are in the [unions'] contemplated line of march."[2]

On April 8, just as the last snow was melting in Oshawa, the workers walked out. This was not an ordinary strike. It was, arguably, the second most important labour dispute in Canadian history. (First prize would have to go to the Winnipeg General Strike of 1919, when RCMP officers gunned down two strikers and union leaders were sent to prison.) This one drew worldwide attention: the *New York Times* kept a reporter in Oshawa through the strike, and ran some of its coverage on page one.

The Oshawa strike had political and journalistic consequences that last until this day. There would likely be no New Democratic

Party in Ontario without this strike. The strike was the reason for the final break between Mackenzie King and Mitchell Hepburn, something that made an opening for the Ontario Tories to eventually take power and rule the province for more than forty years. The strike also created a cloud over George McCullagh that he never saw, but that seriously affected the way Canada's political and media leaders saw him. The strike blew away the idea that McCullagh was a man of the people, something he'd try the rest of his life to fix. And the strike turned the already tough competition between McCullagh and Joe Atkinson into a hate-fuelled brawl that would keep going even after Holy Joe was dead.

The *Star* insisted the Oshawa strike, and other smaller walkouts across the country, weren't organized by communists. It was a claim echoed by smaller papers across the province, and all of them laid the blame on George McCullagh and the *Globe and Mail*.[3] But McCullagh was right when he said the UAW was infiltrated by communists: Hugh Thompson, the UAW's man in Oshawa, was a Red. Wyndham Mortimer, the UAW vice-president who had engineered the Flint sit-down strikes, was a communist, and communists had organized cells on the shop floor of GM's Oshawa plant.[4] And there were plenty of communists in Canada. The Workers Unity League, run by communists under the direction of Tom McEwen, had organized street demonstrations in some larger Ontario cities, including Toronto. McEwen, along with Communist[5] Party leader Tim Buck and seven others, were charged with sedition and sent to jail by the Tories early in the Depression. Back then, when Mitch was a novice MP, he'd said he sympathized with them but wasn't a Communist himself.[67]

At first, Hepburn tried reasoning with the company and the union. McCullagh was in some of those meetings.[8] It was clear, though, that there would be no deal without recognition of both the United Auto Workers and the Congress of International Organizations, a nonstarter for Hepburn and his puppet masters.

The second thing Hepburn did was call the cops. The Ontario Provincial Police (OPP) didn't exist, so Hepburn had to ask King for Mounties. The prime minister responded with one hundred, who arrived in Oshawa quite quickly. Ian Mackenzie, King's minister of defence and British Columbia lieutenant,[9] sat down with Hepburn and McCullagh and promised Ottawa's full support. McCullagh went back to his office and wrote this editorial, which appeared on the front page of the *Globe and* Mail the next day:

> If anything were needed to ensure the success of Premier Hepburn's campaign against the throttling of Canadian industry by the invasion of Lewisism and its handmaiden, communism, there can be misgivings no longer.
>
> The Federal Government is behind him 100 per cent.
>
> The message was brought from Ottawa by Hon. Ian Mackenzie, Minister of Defence. But, more significant, it was brought by a member of the Ottawa Cabinet who has a reputation as a radical, and who is perhaps the most uncompromising friend of organized labor in the Federal Ministry.
>
> This is the fortunate outcome of what appeared for a few days to be a conflict between the two Governments."[10]

Mackenzie denied there was a deal to bring in troops. Hepburn insisted there was.

"Yesterday in the presence of Bethune Smith, George McCullagh and myself, Mr. Mackenzie said that the entire resources of his department would be placed at our disposal," the premier told a Toronto *Star* reporter. "The offer was unsolicited. There is no need of Mr. Mackenzie trying to deny it. I didn't ask him for any federal assistance. The words were uttered voluntarily by him." If people didn't believe Hepburn, they could "check with Mr. Smith, Toronto lawyer, and Mr. McCullagh as to whether I am right or Mr. Mackenzie is right. The minister offered the entire resources of his department, militia and defence."[11]

No matter what Mackenzie had or had not said, only one opinion counted. The prime minister had the last say over emergency RCMP deployment. He kept his distance from Hepburn, and then yanked the rug out from under him. King told Hepburn that "under the existing circumstances having regard to our responsibilities in all parts of the Dominion it would not be advisable to withdraw a larger number of the members of the force [RCMP] from their present location." King's labour minister, Norman Rogers, sneered at the idea of Mounties and troops being used to break a legal, non-violent strike. "The right of association for legitimate purposes should be respected in the national interest and labour should not be denied the means of organizing for collective bargaining." Employers, he added, shouldn't attack the idea of government interference in the marketplace, and then, when things got tough, ask for cops and soldiers to work as taxpayer-funded strike-breakers.[12] All this controversy fired up King's paranoia, and he wrote in his diary about a Hepburn plot to use Oshawa as a way to drive him from office.[13] So Hepburn began recruiting goons.

He found them at a very strange place: the University of Toronto. The premier of Ontario personally swore in four hundred student strike-breakers.[14] The public—even people who didn't support the strike—dubbed these toughs "Hepburn's Hussars" and "Sons of Mitches." Even the governor of Michigan had never gone that far. That state's national guard was a trained, well-regulated militia, not a goon squad. Joe Atkinson stomped into the premier's office at Queen's Park and demanded Hepburn back down. The way the premier explained it to his friends, "He told me in the presence of one of my colleagues that, unless I supported his policy, he would harass me and attack me to the end of my public life. I had the privilege of telling him to get out."[15]

Readers of both the Toronto *Star* and the *Globe and Mail* must have thought there were two different General Motors strikes happening in the same city. The *Star* stressed the legality of the strike and the peaceful protests by GM workers. (The automaker retaliated by yanking its ads from the *Star*, but within two weeks its marketing staff and executives realized the car-maker couldn't afford to give up advertising in Canada's largest-circulation newspaper.)[16]

The *Globe and Mail* hyped the strike as the work of the CIO and John L. Lewis, who wanted a foot in the door so he could go on to unionize the real big game: Ontario's mines and forestry industry. The *Star* told its readers, "Premier Hepburn acted upon his large fund of inexperience in connection with trade unionism which was greatly augmented by his intimacy with the new publisher of *The Globe and Mail* who knows nothing of trade unionism but is deeply concerned with gold mining. These two young men have decided to run away with the province and establish control of it."[17]

Ralph Hyman was the unfortunate *Globe and Mail* reporter who was given the dangerous assignment of covering the strike. He was one of the best reporters on the paper, and his work was, mainly, quite fair. Hyman wandered around Oshawa interviewing strikers, GM executives and the mayor. At one spontaneous rally, the rank-and-file strikers were eager to lay a beating on Hyman, but a union leader climbed on top of a car and managed to talk them out of it. People like Hyman didn't deserve abuse. They were having a tough enough time just holding their jobs. At least one *Globe and Mail* reporter was ordered to rewrite a story because McCullagh told him "you couldn't have done a better job if you had been working for the CIO."[18] McCullagh might claim the paper had no sacred cows, but, at least when it came to unions, it had created a golden calf. The *Globe and Mail*'s publisher, like Atkinson at the *Star*, had moved into the newsroom and was deciding what went into the paper. Both men were speaking through their news columns, as well as their editorials.

The *Globe and Mail* couldn't intimidate the UAW, but its publisher and editors believed they could make and unmake local politicians.

The mayor of Oshawa, Alex Hall, was caught in McCullagh's cross-hairs. Mayor Hall tried to find some middle ground where he could save himself from the *Globe and Mail* and from Mitch Hepburn, and not be targeted by Joe Atkinson. In those days, Ontario mayors faced the voters once a year, and Hall was just weeks away from another election. He desperately tried to climb onto a fence: "At no time has my interest been anywhere but behind the people, the men and women of Oshawa," he bleated. "I don't say I'm behind the union. My only satis-faction in life is in doing something for other people. You know that I have no flourishing business, that money has never been my god."

But he did like to get elected, and, despite not saying he was behind the union, he couldn't pass up on the votes of almost four thousand strikers and the ballots of their wives and friends. Most were avid readers of Holy Joe's paper. Homer Martin, president of the UAW, went to Oshawa to be the headliner of a rally that drew five thousand people—the bulk of the city's voters.

The mayor could do simple math, and his final calculations showed he'd better start sounding like a union man if he wanted to keep his job. Hall worked up the nerve to challenge McCullagh and Hepburn's wilder claims: "The issue here is your right to join the union of your own choice. The history of the British Empire gives you that choice. I have more faith in the British constitution than in one who raises the bugaboo of Communism...I have seen no man-ifestation here of Communism. I see no reason to increase the police force here...It is the wonder of the world—not of Oshawa—how you [strikers] have conducted yourselves. I think there is no better argu-ment against Communism than law and order. I ask you to hold out four or five days longer and you will come out better than you ever were before."[19]

Rev. Arthur Eagle, minister at the Gerrard Street United Church and president of the Toronto unit of the Fellowship for a Christian Social Order, was not up for re-election, and he was willing to face

McCullagh head on. He would embrace atheistic Marxism, if need be. And he was willing to drop the F-word, even when pretending not to.

"The CIO and communism! John Lewis and communism! It would be just as unfair for me to say 'The Globe and Mail and fascism! George McCullagh and fascism! The Telegram and fascism!' It's not communism that will be the next thing we have to fear, but fascism," he hollered from a pulpit set up at a strike rally. "I'm a Christian minister but if you place before me one communist who does not believe in God but works for the things I believe to be the will of God and the things that Jesus Christ died for, and puts up with hardship, suffering and low pay to get them—and put opposite him the man who exploits and robs—then I'll take the communist. And I'll be in right good company, for I will be in the company of Jesus Christ, who said 'Woe unto the scribes and the Pharisees.'"[20]

It was clear McCullagh was the scribe, and Hepburn was the Pharisee. But neither man was willing to back down, despite Reverend Eagle's clear suggestion that, if they did give in, they would walk with Jesus. Rev. Dr. Salem Bland, a Marxist who wrote the Star's religion column, tried to put the lie to his name by taking the fight to the workers, whipping them up at a big Oshawa rally on April 14, as the strike reached its peak and thugs from the University of Toronto roamed the streets of the town, looking for any justification to crack some skulls.[21]

Bland made fun of the bogey of communism that Queen's Park was trying to use to scare the people of Ontario. He said McCullagh and Hepburn's talk of anarchy didn't scare him away from Oshawa. "One might feel a great deal of apprehension in coming down to Oshawa at this time," he said, the sarcasm clearly audible to his listeners. "There's no telling, if you came down here after dark, how many communists might be prowling around and other sinister things...

"The unknown perils of Oshawa, where it seems the welfare and liberty of Canada are just trembling on the verge. If we had not some loyal Mounties and provincial police around, who knows what might not happen? Canada might be taken by storm!

"The premier has listened to the voice of the tempter who said 'Kill the CIO in Oshawa. Don't let any plausible voice tell you how many more cents an hour you will get if you don't belong to the CIO. All those privileges might be withdrawn in a few months.'"[22]

McCullagh, the tempter, and Hepburn, who had been his creature throughout the strike, couldn't take criticism, and tallied up their serious political critics for future payback. Being mocked was something altogether worse. Bland's speech was printed verbatim in the *Star*, but if Hyman, the *Globe and Mail* man on the scene, submitted a story to McCullagh, it never saw the light of print.

And there was more. R.J. Irwin, high-profile minister at Toronto's Donlands United Church, stopped just short of calling Hepburn a fascist, but he compared "Hepburn's Hussars" to members of the Iron Heel, the government thugs in Jack London's 1910 dystopian novel that foresaw the totalitarian states that arose two decades later.[23]

The prime minister was saying pretty much the same thing. Confiding in his diary, King said Hepburn was wrong to equate the union drive with communism. "The truth of the matter is that he is in the hands of McCullagh of the Globe, and the Globe and McCullagh are in the hands of financial mining interests that want to crush the C.I.O and their organization in Canada. The situation as he has brought it into being has all the elements in it that are to be found in the present appalling situation in Spain. Hepburn has become a Fascist leader and has sought to have labour in its struggle against organized capital, put into the position of being under Communist direction and control. Action of this kind is little short of criminal... The Globe and Mail is just what I thought it would be at the time of the amalgamation, a big interest paper for the purpose of furthering material ends."[24]

All this criticism convinced the GM workers—and pretty much anyone else who followed the dispute—that Hepburn was the problem. The strikers wanted the premier, who'd been elected just three years previously as the working man's friend, to get out of the way and let GM and its employees settle the strike. Nearly three thousand strikers voted to endorse a union resolution condemning Hepburn for undermining his labour minister, David Croll, who, they said, "was successfully conducting negotiations, and immediately substituted compulsion for arbitration."[25] If Croll was to be kept out of the picture, the province should step aside and let the federal labour department organize new talks or arbitration.

Croll added to McCullagh and Hepburn's suspicions when he said the thugs sent from Toronto had to go. The Sons of Mitches were "entirely unnecessary in view of the discipline and peace which have marked this strike since its inception and can only be construed as a provocative measure," which only inflamed the situation, the union claimed, quite accurately.[26]

The union was right about what was happening at Queen's Park. Pushed by McCullagh, Hepburn shunted his labour minister aside and took over the government's strike strategy. Croll had wanted to recognize the UAW and send the strike to arbitration—hiring an independent, trusted, disinterested third party to come up with a deal to end the strike. Despite pressure from Atkinson, who, like McCullagh, was shuttling between his newsroom and Queen's Park, Hepburn scuttled that idea and Croll was out. The labour minister told reporters, "I would rather walk with the workers than ride with General Motors."[27]

Hepburn didn't care if he'd lost his best minister and made an enemy of the union movement. He wasn't playing to Oshawa, he was posing on the provincial and national stage. The people who owned Ontario didn't want unions in Ontario. Neither did the farmers and small business owners across the country.

At night, McCullagh and Hepburn spent hours conspiring in Hepburn's suite at the King Eddy, while Toronto *Star* reporters were often just a few floors away, eating in their favourite hangout, the hotel's basement restaurant. There was even a rumour, quite possibly true, that McCullagh was in the next room—Joe Atkinson said it was a washroom—when Hepburn demanded the resignations of David Croll and Arthur Roebuck.[28] The now-fired attorney general claimed his dismissal was payback for crossing McCullagh on the hydro bond issue. He hinted McCullagh had a lost a lot of money because of Roebuck's policies. McCullagh struck back in the pages of the *Globe and Mail*:

> Mr. Roebuck tells an untruth when he says I told him his speech cost me $10,000. Neither his speech nor the government's act of repudiation cost me one cent, as I never owned, nor do I now own, any of the bonds of the Quebec power companies.
>
> Mr. Roebuck argues that I made the price of *The Globe and Mail*'s support of the government his resignation from the Cabinet. This is also untrue, as I have never at any time made *The Globe and Mail*'s support contingent on whether Mr. Roebuck was in or out of the government. I did tell Mr. Hepburn on many occasions that, due to Mr. Roebuck's distorted views of right and wrong and his utter disrespect for the judiciary, he was an unfit man for the position of Attorney-General, and due to his lack of honor and principles in dealing with public questions, I regard him as a menace in public life.[29]

It only took a few minutes for Joe Atkinson to show up at the premier's office, and he was furious. He stormed in, slammed the door and screamed at Hepburn in front of several of his top ministers. The *Star* publisher's hollering could be heard down the halls of the legislature building. If, Atkinson said, Hepburn kept standing in the way of a fair deal for workers and insisted on purging his left-wing ministers, the *Star* would take Hepburn down. "He told me," Hepburn later said, "that unless I agreed with his policy on the c.i.o. he would persecute me and would attack me personally, and would not let up until he had driven me out of public life in this Province. I never thought anyone could have such a terrible temper," said Mr. Hepburn. "He said he was going to finish me."[30]

When a *Star* reporter asked whether McCullagh had become Hepburn's main advisor on the Oshawa strike, the premier said he and the young publisher were "co-operating in the fight," but Hepburn was deciding policy.[31] No one who closely followed Ontario politics believed that.

In fact, it was clear to anyone with even the roughest idea of what was happening that the Ontario government's policy was being set by the titans of Ontario's gold fields. Although the UAW hadn't yet taken up their Sudbury brothers' challenge to come north, Hepburn insisted he had "definite knowledge" that the CIO was infiltrating the gold fields.[32] The mine owners made their position clear: there would be no deal with any union, or anything that smelled like one. Jack Bickell was ready to shut down his big McIntyre Porcupine mine and starve its workers into submission at the first sight of trouble. J.R. Timmins, who ran Hollinger, was looking to crack some heads, assured by Hepburn of "ample protection" for any scabs that crossed a CIO picket line.[33] Bill Wright didn't have to make any threats. He had the *Globe and Mail* to make them for him.

Bickell, Timmins, McCullagh and Wright weren't paranoid. The mineworkers of northern Ontario worked in dangerous, soul-destroying conditions. They went down thousands of feet below the surface of the Canadian Shield without decent safety equipment. Death was part of the cost of doing business, and it was much cheaper to pay off some widows and orphans—and it was a very generous mine owner who would even do that—than to make the mines safe. After the wage cuts of the Depression, Ontario miners were quite open to the idea of unionization. By mid-April 1937, the fledgling miners and smelter workers' union in Sudbury was trying to entice the UAW to send organizers into the north.[34] At the same time, though, the UAW's leaders in Detroit decided they didn't want their American members to pay for a Canadian strike. The CIO might still have organizers in Oshawa, but it wasn't writing cheques either. The Oshawa union leadership knew they were running out of money, and had to make a deal.[35]

The Oshawa strike lasted fifteen days. Homer Martin, head of the UAW, had no idea that he was played by Joe Atkinson, who came up with the formula that settled the strike: there would be a deal with workers, but not—for now—with the UAW. After meeting with Atkinson, Martin went back to Detroit and sold the agreement to the UAW's executive board and to GM's managers.[36] Hepburn and GM saved face by claiming the UAW had been stopped: in the end, the collective agreement was signed by GM and "its employees of the company at Oshawa." Everyone in the plant knew the agreement had been negotiated by UAW officials. And, from then on, bargaining at GM's Oshawa plant would be done by the UAW, and, eventually, the Canadian Auto Workers. Publicly, McCullagh claimed the union had been broken. "The settlement was a permanent defeat for Lewisism and Communism in Canada," the *Globe and Mail* declared on its editorial page. Privately, McCullagh blamed Hepburn for caving to the union. Hepburn, unable to accept that blame, tried to transfer it to King.[37]

Unions weren't dead in Ontario. Industrial, transportation, forestry and mine unions would be important powerbrokers in Ontario until the 1980s. But McCullagh had purged Hepburn's cabinet of its left-wing: Roebuck and Croll were out. A year later, the Toronto *Star* carried a gigantic article, starting on the front page and running on two inside pages, detailing the way Roebuck and Croll had been fired, but by then no one cared.[38]

The strike turned organized labour against the Ontario Liberals, the *Globe and Mail* and most of the rest of the press. One of the paper's later, and perhaps greatest, editors, Richard Doyle, was just starting out at a small newspaper in Chatham when he was menaced at a CIO organizational meeting. "No Ontario newspaper lost as much credibility among working people as *The Globe and Mail* did," Doyle wrote in his memoirs.[39] Not only had the newspaper hammered the autoworkers in its editorials and opinion columns, but even Doyle, one of the staunchest defenders of the paper, had to admit that its anti-union bias was clear in its supposedly objective news coverage.

McCullagh and Hepburn came up with a plan that would fix everything. If politics was the problem, why not get rid of it? Why not make Ontario a one-party state?

9

THE COUP

It all seemed so sensible. If party politics stood in the way of getting things done, why not get rid of political parties? If there was an enemy at the gate—monolithic communism, masquerading as the United Auto Workers—why not put together a wartime coalition of the nation's business and political leaders?

All this, for a time, made sense to Ontario's leading politicians and many of the province's richest people. The idea of "national government" wasn't new. Before the 1935 federal election, business leaders like Sir Edward Beatty, president of the country's most powerful company, the Canadian Pacific Railway, had privately pushed for a peacetime coalition that could ram through legislation that no single political party would dare to impose. The United Kingdom had had such a government since 1931. But then-Opposition leader William Lyon Mackenzie King abhorred the idea, and it went dormant.[1]

In 1937, George McCullagh, with Beatty advising behind the scenes, talked Ontario premier Mitch Hepburn and Tory leader Earl Rowe into ridding Ontario of the nuisance of parliamentary democracy. Other provinces, such as Quebec and Alberta, had already elected quasi-fascist regimes that used brute force and lawyers to cripple their

Leader of the Ontario Conservative Party, Rowe was willing to join Hepburn in a coalition, leaving just one CCF member as the "opposition" in the Ontario legislature. (*GLOBE AND MAIL*)

opponents. But Ontario was the only province where political leaders actually made a deal to kill Westminster-style parliamentary democracy. McCullagh and supporters of his scheme wanted a regime that got rid of what the *Globe and Mail* sneeringly called "partisanship" but the rest of us would call "democratic debate."

What had scared McCullagh, Bay Street and the politicians of Ontario? It wasn't just the threat of unions. Their gold mines and stocks had come through the crash in good shape. The price of gold kept rising through the early years of the Depression, even as the purchasing power of fiat currency increased. In real terms, gold prices rose as the Depression worsened. By 1937, another gold stocks bubble had formed, and investors panicked. The fear started in Johannesburg and spread through the markets of Europe and North America. On April 9, Franklin Roosevelt calmed investors by denying he planned to cut the official price of gold. All this played out just before the General Motors strike.[2] They were afraid politicians would challenge their power over Bay Street and Queen's Park.

McCullagh convinced Hepburn that a coalition between the Liberals and Tories wouldn't just keep the unions out of Ontario mines, it might also shake Mackenzie King out of office. The premier was open to anything now. His determination to stop the UAW had been praised by many of the great newspapers of North America, including the *New York Times*. The Tory Opposition at Queen's Park couldn't find fault with the way Hepburn handled the Oshawa troubles, and were as convinced as he was that Oshawa was just the beginning of the Left's attack on the province's mines and industries.

Sometime in late April, at the invitation of George Drew, Hepburn and Tory leader Earl Rowe got together in a suite at the Royal York Hotel and cooked up a plan. If the Liberals, with their sixty-five seats, took in the Tories, who had seventeen members of the provincial parliament, there would be just four opposition members left in the legislature: one member of the Labour Party, one lone survivor of the United Farmers of Ontario, a single Co-operative Commonwealth Federation member, and an independent MPP. In reality, there would be no opposition.

The scheme becomes even more bizarre when the time frame is factored in. The last election had been in June 1934. Hepburn was three years into his term, and Ontario voters expected an election by the spring of 1938. This deal had a very short lifespan, unless the party leaders planned to keep it going through the next election. Would they have an election where voters would get to choose from two nominated candidates? Would the parties pretend to run against each other, and then come back and form another coalition? A week before the negotiations became public, Hepburn told the lieutenant-governor that he might ask for dissolution—not prorogation—of the legislature and a "union government." Hepburn would take four Tories into the cabinet. He'd fire natural resources minister Peter Heenan, a former union leader who McCullagh hated. Hepburn would even step aside and let Rowe be premier, if that's what it took to get the deal through.

And he'd make sure the Tories were well-financed for the next election, when (or if) it came.

On the Tory side, George Drew pushed for an agreement. He and McCullagh came up with this pitch to Hepburn and Rowe: if a coalition—call it a "union government" or a "national government"—was put together in Ontario, then Maurice Duplessis should have no problem organizing a similar coup against his own legislature. With the two big provinces governed without the annoyance of opposition political parties, Mackenzie King would have no choice but to follow, and, hopefully, finally step aside. McCullagh and Drew offered other shiny things to Hepburn and Rowe: reform of the bureaucracy and the remaking of Ontario Hydro, for starters.

On Saturday, May 1, the Toronto *Star* exposed the plot.

Atkinson, despite his own tyranny over his staff and his oddities, was a democrat, and he fought the idea with everything he had. First, he exposed the interests behind the plan, without going as far as naming names. They were, the *Star* said, "at least one prominent Conservative Toronto financier-industrialist and a small but powerful group of mine owners and executives from both political parties."[3]

The next day, Atkinson and the *Star* went much further. The paper ran an editorial called "The Coalition Against Labor." It warned Hepburn that the idea "is a blunder so fatal that only prompt recognition of the natural result can save him. It is easy to imagine from what politically amateurish source such a suggestion emanated. It is not so easy to see how an experienced politician came to accept it." The editorial writers understood Hepburn's ego, so the piece dripped with gentleness and kindness whenever advice was directed at the premier. Hepburn had strayed, but could be saved. He cared about workers. He had been misled into believing that this coup was necessary to save the province. But the *Star* piece ended with this punch: "Mr. Hepburn has shown on many past occasions a liberal mind. His only hope now is to get back to liberalism instead of playing into the hands of fascist advisors. And a coalition against Labor would be naked fascism; the same sort of thing that resulted in German and Italian dictatorships, but the kind of thing which would not be tolerated in Canada."

Nearby was a second article, a reprint of an editorial from the rather obscure *Lindsay Warder.* Its editors said all the things Atkinson's paper had tried to say in its main editorial, but there was no kindness towards the premier, nor was there any hiding of the names of the people behind the coalition plan. The Lindsay paper headlined its editorial "The Globe and Mail Communist Scare," and it called McCullagh out as the puppeteer who controlled the players in this bizarre scheme. McCullagh was Hepburn's "chief journalistic advisor and apologist" who had "developed all of a sudden an anti-Communist complex. He had swung so far to the left in the days gone by that he found that he didn't have very far to go to reach the extreme right." Together, the premier and the *Globe and Mail* publisher "commenced an anti-Communist drive. They developed an overnight realization there was a Communist menace which must be stamped out. Mr. Hepburn issued heroic statements to the press daily which were reviewed in glowing terms in the Globe and Mail." At the same time, everyone knew the commissioner of the Ontario Provincial Police, Col. Fred Fraser Hunter, was spending hours every day in the basement of the provincial parliament building "drilling his special army which was to quell any Communist-inspired uprising in Oshawa."

But, the Lindsay editor noted, there had been a problem with the plan. The Oshawa strike had been settled, "for the reason, we suspect, that there were no Communists among the Oshawa strikers...(I)t was clear to the fair-minded observer that they were actually taking no part whatsoever. After the strike was settled and people were able to view the situation in a common frame of mind the ridiculousness of the attempt of Mr. Hepburn and the Globe and Mail to connect it with the Communists became even more obvious."

Toronto Star cartoon from 1937, after McCullagh convinced the leaders of the ruling Ontario Liberals to join in a coalition with the Tory opposition.

And to make the point that Ontario was on the road to a one-party corporate-controlled state, the *Star* ran a cartoon on its editorial page showing Hepburn and the Tories on a pirate ship labelled "Ontario Liberal Govt Ship of State." "Liberalism" was portrayed as a sailor marooned in a dory. McCullagh, in a cook's hat, was poking his head out a porthole. And to make sure the reader knew what this was all about, the pirate captain flourished a sword with "FASCISM" written on it.[4]

So why weren't party politics killed in Ontario? Who saved Ontario from becoming a one-party state in the middle of the Great Depression? The saviour of provincial democracy—and maybe national democracy, if McCullagh, Drew, Hepburn and Duplessis had their way—is an unlikely character. He's a man who's pretty much forgotten in Canadian political history, mentioned from time to time because he held two of the shortest terms of any prime minister. Arthur Meighen might have been unlucky with voters, but, for a quarter century, he was one of the most influential people in Canadian politics. He was also one of the most feared. Meighen was big, he was smart, and he was tough. Rowe went to see him in Ottawa to tell him about Hepburn's amazing offer, expecting him to be dazzled. Meighen was anything but.

Former prime minister R.B. Bennett was still the leader of the federal Conservatives, though he was getting ready to leave Canada for good. The major Conservative actors in this strange drama showed up at the door of Bennett's suite in the Chateau Laurier hotel. Bennett's secretary, R.K. Finlayson, watched the action and leaked much of the story to his best friend, Norman Lambert, who happened to be chief organizer of the national Liberal Party.

Bennett seems to have been ready to support the plan. Meighen, the federal Tories' senior statesman, would not. Meighen's opposition was enough to kill it. And there was no appeal to the rest of the party. Its senior leaders were on a ship headed to England for the coronation of King George vi. (So was McCullagh, travelling from New York on another boat.)

The plotters of the failed coup searched for a way to spin it. Neither Hepburn nor Rowe, who both understood there would have to be an election in Ontario in the next year, wanted to be blamed for plotting to kill real representative government in Ontario. So they decided to blame the media. Not McCullagh, who had helped engineer the plot. They'd blame the *Star*. The story, the conspirators said, was fake news. Four days after the *Star* broke its accurate story about the plot, Hepburn told a rally of the Ontario Women's Liberal Association: "The only idea of a coalition I know of exists in the office of the president of the Toronto *Star*."[5] Rowe later said he'd rejected the idea at the first meeting in the Royal York, telling an interviewer in the 1970s that he answered Hepburn's offer by saying, "I'd rather rob a bank."[6]

The idea stayed alive for a few more weeks, even if Rowe did have cold feet after his Ottawa trip.[7] George Drew, still a powerful voice in the Conservative Party, was willing to join Hepburn's cabinet and bring much of the small Tory caucus with him. He didn't know Hepburn had made Drew's exclusion from cabinet one of the terms of the proposed deal. Through June 1937, Hepburn received reports from his provincial organizers that Liberals and Tories throughout the province wanted a merger. But Rowe just couldn't do it. "I refused," Rowe told fellow Tories at the Albany Club, "and pointed out it would be a gross betrayal of their confidence for me as their leader to end the Conservative Party that way." Rowe knew the stakes. What McCullagh and Drew wanted was not a coalition government. Drew told Rowe "the time had come to end the two-party system in Ontario." When Rowe refused to give in and denounced the plan in a speech in the small town of Arthur, Drew quit the Tory party. McCullagh lashed out through the *Globe and Mail*: "It is amazing that Honourable Earl Rowe finds anyone, except the Reds and the Pinks and others who thrive on discontent and agitation, to stay with him."[8]

The next year, Rowe would be out, even losing his bid for a seat at Queen's Park. (He'd go back to Ottawa, where he'd been an MP.) Drew would become leader of the Ontario Conservatives,[9] and the idea smouldered until the early years of the Second World War. McCullagh did keep pushing the issue with his friends and pestering King, which generated an entry in the prime minister's diary: "McCullagh's idea was that he could get millions from Americans and other capital invested into Canada if he could make clear that both political parties were united in suppressing the CIO and movements of the kind. He had gone to Hepburn... When Rowe turned the proposal down, McCullagh talked it anew with George Drew, and suggested to Hepburn uniting with him to form a sort of National Government again using the CIO as the excuse therefore... Hepburn gave McCullagh his assurances that everything would be worked out satisfactorily with

Drew, and [McCullagh] left for England himself [for the Coronation] with the understanding that when he returned, arrangements would be completed and an election brought on."[10]

There would be a provincial election. And there would be a real fight between independent political parties. *Coalition* became a dirty word in Canadian politics, and would remain so long after politicians and journalists forgot why.

∗ ∗ ∗

There's an adage in politics that you have to dance with the one who "brung ya," and McCullagh was stuck with Hepburn. It wasn't much fun. The spring brought the end of the legislature session. Under the stress of the General Motors strike (which Hepburn believed he'd won and McCullagh saw as a loss) and the failed coup against the political system, it's no surprise that Hepburn went on a bender. Journalists noticed Hepburn was AWOL through the first two weeks of June 1937.[11]

Maybe any premier deserved a rest after something as intense as the Oshawa strike, but Hepburn held six cabinet positions. And in those days, ministers were expected to actually run their departments. Drew was still in England after going to the coronation, on a tour that took him through the fascist states of Eastern Europe and to the Soviet Union.[12] McCullagh met Drew in England, and the publisher was due to arrive home around the middle of June. John Bassett was with McCullagh, and that sparked rumours that McCullagh, using more of Wright's money, was about to buy the *Montreal Gazette*. While the *Gazette* was still the junior paper in its home city—the *Montreal Star* was the bigger, better paper, and still the best paper in Canada—the thought of McCullagh controlling important papers in Canada's two largest cities must have caused some intense conversations between King and his dead mother.[13] Soon afterwards, rumours began spreading through the Canadian financial community that McCullagh was a front man for British publishers who wanted the *Montreal Star*.[14] These British press barons would use the *Star* to dictate federal policy, critics said.[15]

And there were more rumours going around Ottawa. Jimmy Gardiner, the Saskatchewan MP who was minister of agriculture in King's government, was said to be McCullagh, Hepburn and Duplessis's choice to replace King. Gardiner had been premier of Saskatchewan twice: for a short time in 1929, and again from June 1934 to November 1935. Gardiner was a tough man who had taken on the Ku Klux Klan in the 1920s. But when Gardiner went to Toronto on business that spring, Hepburn—who was, among so many other things, his own minister of agriculture—couldn't be bothered to sober up and leave St. Thomas to see him, and Gardiner, feeling snubbed, called the rumours "Tory propaganda."[16]

King went to England that summer. He happened to be on the same ship as N.L. Nathanson, head of the Famous Players movie theatre chain. Nathanson had given Hepburn important strategic advice in the 1934 election. Now he thought the premier was a menace to democracy.

Writing in his diary, King said Nathanson believed that "the greatest misfortune which has overtaken Canada was the purchase of the 'Globe and Mail' by Wright, and entrusting McCullagh with its management. McCullagh is wholly inexperienced, and his idea is to do away with party government altogether. Hepburn is lending himself to this idea and is really in alliance with Colonel Drew, the former aspirant for the Tory leadership, who is secretly working for the Globe. He said the methods Hepburn has taken to obtain money for his party would shame Tammany himself; that he, Nathanson knows the inside of the whole story. He says Hepburn is an alcoholic and in all probability will not last long. He thinks he will have a campaign in September, and that all he has been doing of late is toward that end."

Sir James Dunn, owner of Algoma Steel and a close friend of Lord Beaverbrook, chimed in to say McCullagh was too naive and inexperienced to pull off a major political coup, or to run the *Globe and Mail*.[17]

* * *

King would probably have been thrilled to learn that McCullagh was dealing with his own union troubles. The Newspaper Guild quietly organized a union at the *Globe and Mail* in the summer of 1937, just as McCullagh returned from England. The publisher moved between bouts of rage and self-pity. He ordered his editors to run an editorial claiming the union drive was an attack on freedom of the press, skipped important staff meetings and fired the lead organizer, reporter Harry Farmer. That firing was non-negotiable, McCullagh told his staff. They could organize a union and go strike forever, McCullagh warned, but Farmer would never be on the payroll again.

Firing Farmer was something the rest of the unions in Toronto would not forgive. Delegates to the city's labour council denounced the *Globe and Mail* as a "dirty rag." Maybe to show that the paper, which still had many working-class subscribers, was not entirely anti-labour, the *Globe and Mail* carried a sympathetic story about striking textile workers in Cornwall, Ontario. If that was supposed to cause some doubts among *Globe and Mail* haters in the labour movement, it was a failure. Activists denounced the paper's "crocodile tears." McCullagh countered by saying he wanted to see workers get a "square deal," but they'd have to stop listening to agitators from the American head offices of the AFL and the CIO. These organizers were "exploiting, and exploiting unmercifully," McCullagh said.

The Toronto Labour Council invited McCullagh to speak to its members, and the publisher was willing to do it, but Farmer's fate was sealed: McCullagh said he would never make a deal if rehiring the union organizer was one of the conditions. The labour council retaliated by rescinding its invitation.[18]

The news editor of the *Globe and Mail* posted a "loyalty petition" on the newsroom bulletin board and asked journalists to sign it. Very few did. At the same time, McCullagh said he really didn't care whether the newsroom was organized. Few people inside and outside the paper believed him. Fred Collins of the Upholstery Union rose in a labour council meeting, denounced the loyalty petition and tabled a resolution: "Whereas George McCullagh, publisher of the Globe and Mail, has stated to our committee that he is not against his editorial employees joining the Toronto Newspaper Guild if they desire, and whereas, as an attempt was made, if not by Mr. McCullagh himself, then by someone acting under his direct authority, to intimidate the members of the Globe and Mail editorial staff into signing the equivalent of a 'yellow dog contract,' be it therefore resolved that the Trades and Labor Council demand that Mr. C. George McCullagh communicate with this body by letter stating his position and policy in regards to the newspaper guild."[19]

McCullagh told anyone who would listen that he had told his editors not to discriminate against guild supporters. "But he added there was not a writer on the paper who was not getting wages in excess of the Guild schedule," reported the Toronto *Star*, which gleefully covered the dispute. It quoted Farmer describing how he'd made forty dollars a week at the *Globe* before the Depression. The Jaffrays had cut his salary to $28.50. When McCullagh took over, Farmer's pay was raised to thirty-five dollars a week.[20]

In the end, McCullagh had to make a deal. Because of the solidarity between newspaper unions, he couldn't stomp on the Newspaper Guild the way he'd pounded on Oshawa's autoworkers. Newspaper unions had a long tradition in Toronto. A paper couldn't get on the street unless the printers' union was satisfied. The Toronto Typographical Union, which set newspaper pages in type, was one of the city's oldest unions, and would hold publishers hostage until the Toronto *Star* broke its back in the 1960s. There would be a union in the newsroom of the *Globe and Mail*, or the printers would stop the presses.

* * *

There was a very good reason for McCullagh to settle with the union. At the height of the dispute, Mitch Hepburn called an election, and McCullagh couldn't give up his megaphone while that campaign was happening. McCullagh backed Hepburn through the provincial election in the fall of 1937, but also showed his anger over the collapse of the coalition. This is when the *Globe and Mail* publisher started seeing himself as a radio star. On October 2, McCullagh rented an hour of airtime on CFRB, Toronto's authoritative news voice, and on twenty other stations belonging to the CBC and private broadcasters across the province.

"Should we be thankful to any of the politicians of the day, be they Liberal, be they Conservative, be they federal or be they provincial?" the thirty-two-year-old publisher asked. "What are they handing down to us, the younger men, to carry on?" The answer, he said, was "a heavily mortgaged country.

"I am not as critical of the players as I am of the game," he added, but "because partisan politicians are playing the political game and governing to preserve the party at any cost, rather than serve the public's interest," the people were broke and the economy was a wreck. And some of those partisans had heaped abuse on him and his newspaper as part of their games. McCullagh said these attacks didn't trouble him, but it was obvious that they did.

McCullagh talked about "gun-toting" UAW organizers who didn't care who was premier of Ontario, as long as the head of Ontario's government was weak, and would cave to a sit-down strike. These organizers were "fresh from an orgy of lawlessness" in Flint and Detroit. Hepburn had been right when he refused to talk to them. "How in the name of common decency could he maintain his self-respect or the dignity of the office of Prime Minister [as Ontario premiers were sometimes pretentiously called at the time] if he had done otherwise?"

Some of it made no sense at all. What were listeners supposed to think when they heard McCullagh say, "The workingman's hope does not lie in vote-seeking politicians, but it lies in his ability to reveal the abuses before the great mass of public opinion and to this end I pledge my newspaper"? It was barely even a sentence. Were workingmen supposed to subscribe to the *Globe and Mail*? Do the work themselves? Expose abuses in the welcoming pages of the *Globe and Mail*?

In the radio speech, McCullagh repeated all the old shibboleths. No one should trust any federal or provincial politician, he said. The country and the province were "heavily mortgaged" and future generations would be saddled with the debt run up by spendthrift politicians.

And what did McCullagh get from his year of campaigning for better government? He and his paper had received hatred and abuse for their "independence and loyalty to British traditions." Politicians had smeared him with lies and innuendo.[21] But he managed to get by. (In fact, he spent the Sunday before the election at the Markham fall fair, where two of his horses won prizes.[22] Bill Wright liked that kind of thing.)

The radio speech was a maudlin show. McCullagh talked about his latest funk, how his wife had cheered him up by handing him a copy of the Henley poem "Invictus," which he read over the air. "I am the master of my fate; I am the captain of my soul..."

While McCullagh's radio talk was sappy, the coverage he received in his own paper was gag-inducing. Lorne McIntyre, one of the *Globe and Mail* staff reporters, sold whatever journalistic soul he may have had. The publisher had risen above the fray, McIntyre wrote in a front-page story, and had refused to take on the men who had insulted him and his paper.[23]

It's not clear what the speech did for Hepburn. He was always the front-runner in that campaign—the great mass of the public was still behind him after the Oshawa strike—but it had a profound effect on

McCullagh, who got two thousand letters and fourteen thousand phone calls, almost all of them congratulatory.

The next night, Conservative leader Earl Rowe started his speech at Massey Hall by saying his wife hadn't handed him any poetry before he went on stage. McCullagh, always thin-skinned, answered through the *Globe and Mail.* Rowe had stooped to a personal attack, "a sneering jibe at George McCullagh." Hepburn picked up his cue, speaking just hours before the polls opened: the Tory leader's speech had kicked off with "the entirely uncalled-for statements which Mr. Rowe made in regards to Mrs. McCullagh." Then the premier twisted the knife. "*I* don't fight women," he said.[24] Maybe the Ontario premier was a drunk who couldn't make it past a brothel. And maybe he surrounded himself with thugs and crooks. But in that one line, he nailed down the women's vote.

* * *

McCullagh was still pushing for his one-party province. On Monday, October 4—two days before the election—McCullagh had his editors run a front-page screed denouncing the very idea of the election itself, and claiming all the parties were soft on trade unions.

McCullagh's wisdom had beamed out on radio waves "to the cities and country homes, to the fertile farm areas of the south and the rich frontiers of the north." He had thrown down a gauntlet in the name of free and honest speech for the good of the working people of the province.

Presumably, no one could explain to McCullagh that this kind of pap was killing the credibility of the *Globe and Mail* and making the province's pre-eminent newspaper into a partisan rag.

On his editorial page, McCullagh had one of his writers ask why "the red-blooded British people of Ontario" were prepared "to condemn Premier Hepburn for what any true Britisher would have done when British laws and institutions were challenged by foreign racketeers? Are they prepared to endorse Mr. Rowe's condemnation of Mr. Hepburn's staunch British stand?"[25]

In response, Rowe went for the jugular. He was after Hepburn's enablers, as much he was running against the premier.

Through the campaign, Rowe attacked McCullagh as often as he pounded on Hepburn. Today, naming the publisher of the *Globe and Mail* would be an impressive trivia feat. In the spring of 1937, everyone in Ontario who had the slightest interest in politics knew who George McCullagh was. Rowe went into arenas and armouries in small-town Ontario to tell voters that the premier and the publisher were determined to destroy their rights. In Lindsay, a Tory fortress just up the highway from Oshawa, he reminded his listeners that the first man to join up in that town and go overseas to fight in the First World War was a union man. This would be very odd talk for a modern Progressive Conservative, and it was strange back then, too. Rowe, a horse breeder from Simcoe County, was no union man, but he played the cards that had been dealt him. Mitch Hepburn was a fake populist in thrall to Toronto money, Rowe said. And it was true. Since it was 1937, Rowe didn't go deeper and start talking about the whores and thugs in the premier's suite in the King Eddy, but some Liberals in the crowds likely were spreading stories about Hepburn's sleaze.

Rowe, on stage, did suggest McCullagh was a drunk. In a speech in the little town of Harrowsmith, inland from Kingston, Rowe called the *Globe and Mail* a mouthpiece for Hepburn, and then he started talking about booze: "I want to ask *The Globe and Mail* if it is going to stand by the traditions of the old *Globe*. Does the new paper endorse the out-of-control policies adopted by Mr. Hepburn? Does it endorse the opening of children's saloons in dives that were once taxicab offices and garages? Does it endorse the fact that 99 per cent of the liquor sold last year was sold without a record?

"After Oct. 6, I will abolish the out-of-control policies and clean up the abominable situation created by this Government."

The accusation that the *Globe and Mail* was pro-booze-for-children was so absurd that the paper put a story about the Harrowsmith speech on its front page.[26]

After the election, which Hepburn won in a landslide, Rowe broke the unwritten code of silence surrounding campaign contributions in Canada—one that survived for another seventy years, and lingers now—and said Hepburn should be investigated for taking dirty money. He wanted Hepburn to leave the Securities Act on the books so he could "show him where some of his millionaire broker friends have broken the law. We will show him where he gets millions to fight the election. We will show him who is the god of gold."[27]

After it was all over, McCullagh's faith in Hepburn was badly shaken. After all the talk, the GM workers in Oshawa had a collective agreement and American union organizers were still free to roam the cities and, even worse the wilderness of Ontario. McCullagh started taking a long, cold look at Hepburn's Tory competition.

Rowe, despite his fame as a harness racer, didn't seem to be the right guy to take on Hepburn, and his accusations about booze had stung McCullagh. A new man, in early middle age, handsome, charming and pliable, was emerging. George Drew, the scourge of reefer smokers, friend of power, natural citizen of Rosedale, had come up with a weak idea to build cheap houses, and had won a seat in Guelph as an independent Conservative. On December 8, 1938, Drew won the leadership of the Ontario Conservative Party. Drew...now there was someone with political legs. For a while, even Holy Joe liked him.

And radio. That was really something. McCullagh had discovered he liked being a radio star, and he wallowed in the praise he received from his listeners. Marshall McLuhan said newspapers are a cold medium. Radio is a hot one. McCullagh liked the heat.

10

RADIO KILLED THE NEWSPAPER STAR

In the run-up to the provincial election of 1937, McCullagh had written to his friend Eddie Wooliver that Mitch Hepburn "wasn't fit to be premier of a pub."[1] By the end of 1938, he was expressing his contempt for Hepburn and King in the pages of the *Globe and Mail*. Both leaders were, in a bizarre mix of metaphors, "hanging out their dirty linen and using it for a smokescreen."[2]

In January 1938, however, McCullagh was still willing to give King a chance. On his way to Montreal for a dinner with the president of the Canadian Pacific Railway (who had backed the one-party plan for Ontario), McCullagh stopped in to see the prime minister. It was one of those nights, just like the one exactly a year before, when McCullagh became completely relaxed at Laurier House, and his conversation was a train of indiscreet manic thought. A year before, King and McCullagh had spent a long evening trashing the Jaffrays while King pumped the young publisher for dirt on Hepburn. This time, the talk was all about Ontario's drunk, crazy premier. The prime minister had taken a year's abuse from this thirty-two-year-old, but he didn't mention any of it. King just sat back and listened.

McCullagh told the prime minister that when he'd returned home from England, he'd tried to shake some sense into Hepburn. He'd gone after the Ontario premier "so hard and partly lost his head, that Hepburn went to leave the room, but he went after him, and told him he would have to listen to what he had to say, and gave him his full opinion of him."

Two weeks later, King appointed a judge because McCullagh wanted it, but McCullagh was not a King insider and never would be.[3]

* * *

In 1938, the worst of the Depression was over, but there were still 471,000 Canadians on "relief." About half the people who were out of work in 1932 had found jobs by 1937. Even so, the unemployment rate, at 12.5 percent, was still five times higher than it was before the Crash.

An unemployment rate of almost 13 percent, in a world where decisive leaders like Hitler were bringing joblessness numbers back to pre-1929 levels, showed McCullagh that the country needed an unconventional, strong leader. He saw that man when he looked in the mirror. And he still believed a leader couldn't do his job unless there was an end to "partisanship." McCullagh decided he would tell this to the country, people would listen, and the noisy business of public debate—what he saw as partisan squabbling—would come to an end. If McCullagh gave any thought to the fate of a free press in this new political reality, he never shared it with anyone.

Professor Robert A. Brady, who watched the collapse of democracy in Europe during the Depression, defined fascism as "monopoly capitalism become conscious of its powers, the conditions of its survival, and mobilized to crush all opposition. It is capitalism mobilized to crush trade unions, to wipe out radical and liberal criticism, to promote, with the sum total of all its internal resources, economic advantages at home and abroad."⁴ McCullagh embodied "capitalism become conscious of its powers."

Lorne Morgan, writing in 1938, found that the fascist states—whether big ones like Germany and Italy or small ones like Hungary, Austria, Poland and Spain—had one thing in common: a leader who was held out as the embodiment of the nation. In the lead-up to their takeovers, Morgan noted, the dictators might have criticized the people who controlled the economy, but fascist leaders came to power when capitalists and demagogues realized their interests had meshed. Hitler and Mussolini recruited their followers by claiming to be socialists, but the elements in their movements that threatened established money were quickly and violently purged soon after they took power. All the cruel apparatus of police states was used against anyone who advocated trade unions or worker ownership of industry. The fascists did toss out a few bones, especially benefits for large families, and resorts that were affordable to working people. This made them popular, especially with women.

What was different in countries like Canada, Great Britain and the United States? Why were fascist politicians, especially at the national level, stopped dead?

First, because the democratic institutions in those countries—political parties, legislatures, the media, the courts, the public meetings that were such an important part of life in the early twentieth century—gave people an outlet for their anger and ideas. As well, there was nothing to be gained by Canadian, British and Americans using Nazi and fascist tactics of denouncing foreigners and picking fights with other nations. (In the United States, demagogues didn't have to whip up hatred for foreigners when Blacks and Mexicans were so conveniently at hand.) As Morgan says in his piece, which was published as McCullagh was launching his quasi-fascist Leadership League, Canada and the United States were *in* the world, but never saw themselves as part *of* it. They didn't fear any foreign armies. A sustained invasion of the United States was technically impossible, and any attack on Canada was seen in Washington as a threat to the United States. Canada was protected—free of charge— by the militaries of two great powers, the United States and Britain.

The standard of living in North America was already much higher than in Europe before the Depression, and stayed higher through the 1930s, even when so many people were jobless. But there was something else. The very system that had let George McCullagh rise from a newspaper salesman to a millionaire publisher worked against any possibility of fascism in Canada, and, to an extent, the United States: people believed the country was rich, and that a person who had the brains and the drive could tap into that wealth. If a kid who'd walked the back concessions selling newspapers could become a millionaire, so could you, or your son, or even your daughter. (That might not be true. It might have taken more than just pluck and luck to become George McCullagh. It always helps in Canada to have rich friends and mentors like Percy Parker.)

Still, Canadians were willing to listen to people who offered simple answers to complex problems. Ontario elected a right-of-centre populist government led by an alcoholic premier who was willing to let George McCullagh dictate policy. Mitch Hepburn agreed to kill parliamentary democracy in Ontario just so he could crush the unions and govern the way he liked. And, for a moment, so had the Conservative leader of the Opposition, Earl Rowe.[5] In Alberta, the provincial government went much farther. Premier Aberhart and his cabinet wanted to turn much of the business of government over to the Social Credit Board, a party committee that didn't need to worry about facing the electorate. They passed a law to muzzle and censor the press, requiring newspapers to print government press releases and official rebuttals to any news story.[6] In Quebec, Maurice Duplessis's fascist government outlawed any organization that the premier didn't like. He was especially cruel to Jehovah's Witnesses (as were the Nazis in Germany). Montreal's large Jewish community didn't fare too well

either: the government discriminated against them, and they were subjected to steady abuse in Quebec's Roman Catholic press. Mussolini was
a hero to the journalists at *L'Action Catholique*, and *Le Devoir* had a
sordid history of Jew-bashing. But, so far, mainstream Canadians were
willing to settle for fascism-lite, while wanting to keep what democratic
rights they had left. They might bellyache about hard times and target
the country's minorities for rough treatment, but they weren't ready to
break out the axe handles, pitchforks and torches. But that could change.

* * *

Radio was the new medium of the Depression. It was also, at that
point, the most powerful propaganda weapon on the planet.

The first commercial radio stations in North America went on the
air in 1920. Within five years, radio stations were broadcasting music,
news, drama and comedy. People enthusiastically embraced the new
medium, and its investors made fast fortunes. By the end of the 1920s,
most homes had a radio. Big chains like NBC, Mutual and CBS had
networks across the United States, and American stations used their
massive transmitters to broadcast into Canada.

The big commercial breakthrough in Canada came from hockey
broadcasts. Foster Hewitt of the Toronto *Star* was a pioneer, doing
play-by-play of Toronto Maple Leafs games from the Mutual Street
Arena (in what's now Ryerson University). Canadians listened to
American stations for everything else. The federal government didn't
seem to care: it collected licence fees and spent nothing on broadcasting. Churches followed the lead of the sports teams' owners by setting
up stations and organizing broadcasts. Fundamentalist Christians
and Jehovah's Witnesses led the way. They had stations in most of the
big cities. In Toronto, the Baptists, a more mainstream Christian
church, were broadcasting by the end of the 1920s. Then the churches
started fighting among themselves: the federal government got complaints about Jehovah's Witness broadcasts from mainstream Christian

ministers. That was to be expected, and Ottawa left the airwaves wide open. When, strapped for cash, the Jehovah's Witnesses started selling airtime to the Ku Klux Klan on some of their western Canadian stations, Ottawa started noticing.

At first, the fight was over censorship. Most federal politicians agreed on silencing the Klan, but what about the Witnesses? And if Ottawa went after them, what about the Loyal Orange Lodge, those fine upstanding people with their lock on Toronto's municipal government? They and the Klan were pretty much in agreement about Catholics, Jews and people of colour. What about union activists? Outright Communists? The government took the usual way out: it appointed a royal commission in the late 1920s. The King government seemed ready to start regulating and subsidizing Canadian broadcasting when it lost power in 1930.

As the Depression started to bite hard, most Canadians decided to simply stop paying their radio licence fee, which seems to have been collected on the honour system. A new Canadian Radio Broadcasting Commission was created by R.B. Bennett's Conservative government, and it did censor the Jehovah's Witnesses and the Klan, but broadcasting regulation still needed more work. King, re-elected in 1935, went farther, creating the Canadian Broadcasting Corporation, which not only ran a chain of stations but had the power to regulate all radio— public and private—in Canada.

Canada had its first taste of fake news during the 1935 election campaign. The Conservatives bought airtime on private stations for conversations with a "Mr. Sage," a small-town codger with a lot to say about politics. You didn't have to be profoundly stupid to believe Mr. Sage was a real person. In each piece, Mr. Sage gently set his young Liberal friend straight about several of the pressing issues of the day. The arguments and the delivery were convincing, so much so that the Liberals, who were on the verge of winning power, were enraged that the Canadian Radio Broadcasting Commission had allowed the Tories to set up a national network feed for these fake interviews. When they won power, the Liberals appointed a commission to get to the bottom of Mr. Sage and his national radio network.[7]

King's version of the CBC owned many radio stations, and it had regulatory power over the rest.[8] The CBC was given other important powers, too, some of them frightening. Its managers could let high-profile Canadians and political leaders give long "talks" across the entire national network. It could just as easily deny access to the network to controversial people and forbid them from broadcasting on private stations. This began the tradition of the CBC being accused of being a propaganda arm of whatever party was in power. In the early days, this criticism didn't just come from people who felt shunned or silenced by the CBC; it was also an accusation from private broadcasters regulated by the Crown corporation.[9]

In the early 1930s, populism was the hottest political movement in North America. Its simplistic messages were pushed over the radio waves by Canadian preacher Father Charles Coughlin, who broadcast across North America from Detroit and was the most powerful voice on the radio. Father Coughlin was a Basilian priest who was born in Hamilton, Ontario, in 1891. His career as a clergyman was uninspiring until the summer of 1926, when the Ku Klux Klan burned down his church in suburban Detroit. There wasn't enough support for Coughlin in Royal Oak, Michigan, to raise the money for a new church, so Coughlin took to the airwaves. He started sermonizing on WJR, a local station, and it turned out Father Coughlin had real skill as a showman. He also was a gifted marketer. By the end of the second year of the Depression, when McCullagh was hustling moose pasture stocks in Toronto, the Radio Priest had an America-wide network of seventeen CBS stations carrying the *Golden Hour of the Little Flower*.

The Radio Priest peddled a brand of populism that started off as progressive. But as the months went by, he became reactionary. Coughlin closed the ideological gap between himself and his former enemies, many of whom were now sending him dimes. Coughlin was so powerful and popular that, when he asked each of his listeners to send him a coin, there was an immediate shortage of pocket change across North America. At the height of his power, his stash of dimes, quarters and half-dollars was one of the world's largest silver hoards. Father Coughlin, master of the most ubiquitous medium on the continent, had name recognition everywhere in North America.

But Father Coughlin didn't just ask for donations. He sold stuff like tiny chrome crosses stamped with "Radio League of the Little Flower," accompanied by certificates saying these crosses had touched a piece of the True Cross. By 1933, he was taking in some $20,000 a week, mostly in dimes. It took 150 employees just to handle his mail and sort the money. Father Coughlin's church had been rebuilt. Its gigantic steeple supposedly resembled a giant farm silo. It was so big that there was room at the top for an office for the Radio Priest, and it was here that Father Coughlin drafted his sermons that were heard by some forty million Americans—about one-third of the people in the country— and many thousands of people in Canada who could pick up the Radio League from the high-wattage stations that carried it. His enemies called him "Silo Charlie," a name he hated.

The religious side of Coughlin's act would have been unimpressive to someone like McCullagh, whose faith was confined to Sunday mornings and a few lectures on temperance to people like Mitch Hepburn. Americans have always been suckers for religious hucksters, going back to the Salem Witch Trials. Where Father Coughlin becomes interesting is in his choice of message and his use of a privately owned, cobbled-together radio network that made him a model for other would-be demagogues, including George McCullagh.

Father Coughlin was so powerful that Franklin Roosevelt was afraid of him. The president threatened to expose Coughlin as one of the country's largest silver hoarders. Father Coughlin volleyed back by starting the National Union for Social Justice, which claimed 7,500,000 paid-up members (another template George McCullagh would use). Some of these social justice warriors took to the streets in gangs, looking for Jews. Others peddled copies of *Social Justice*, Coughlin's magazine. In 1935, the National Union for Social Justice published its manifesto for the next election cycle. It was, essentially, a fascist call to action. Coughlin went farther, starting, along with some non-clerical fanatics, a political party called "Union." They took on Roosevelt in 1936 and were badly beaten.[10]

Anything that worked that well in the United States was bound to be imitated in Canada. Coughlin's show could be picked up in most big cities north of the border, and politicians on both sides of the line tuned in to learn how to use this new medium. The opposition leaders in Alberta, whose farmers were impoverished by the collapse of beef prices, led the way.[11] Before and after he became Alberta's premier, William Aberhart, founder of Calgary's Prophetic Bible Institute, took to the airways to spread a gospel of hate. His message was a mix of Marxism and right-wing populism. He was against the "money barons" of Bay Street, but he had no time for democracy either. Social Credit was a movement founded by an Englishman, Maj. C.H. Douglas. Despite its wacky economic theories, it did offer a solution to the Depression: economic stimulus through inflation. But it had a nasty, anti-democratic edge that kept it from power everywhere except on the impoverished western fringe of Canada. Its simplistic, populist message got Aberhart elected, and Social Credit dominated provincial politics long after its members had abandoned their ludicrous monetary scheme.[12]

No mainstream Canadian politician could face down the populist storm by fighting back over the airwaves. Mackenzie King was annoying, pompous and pretentious on the radio. His extreme "Canadian Dainty" accent rattled most voters.[13] (McCullagh also affected this accent as the years went by, though never as strongly as King. In McCullagh's radio speeches of the late 1940s, "integrity" became "integritay" and consonants, especially *t*, were hit hard.) Hepburn sounded like a banshee when he took to the airwaves. All his power to whip up the yokels seem to disappear as soon as he got close to a microphone. McCullagh, not as skilled with words but with a voice that didn't grate, still sounded pretty good.

* * *

Holy Joe Atkinson was an early radio buff. He was one of the country's first ham radio operators before entertainment radio was a thing. Atkinson chatted on his wireless set years before commercial voice radio was rolled out in the United States in the fall of 1921. That year, the *Star* partnered with Canadian General Electric, which had a simple studio at its factory on Wallace Avenue, to broadcast the first Star Free Concert. The broadcast was picked up on wireless sets that were hooked up to outdoor loudspeakers in parts of the city. A one-hundred-watt transmitter was set up beside the orchestra in the Masonic Temple (the *Star*'s managing editor was chairman) and eleven hundred people crammed into the building to see the show. By the time of the broadcast, the *Star* had already locked up one of the country's first broadcast licences. About a thousand people heard the city's first commercial over-the-air broadcast on March 28, 1922, just six weeks after Guglielmo Marconi launched the first commercial station in Britain. After a couple of special concerts, the *Star* began sporadic daily broadcasting on April 10. Just over two months later, CFCA, the *Star*'s station, went on the air permanently. While the *Telegram* and the *Globe* were awarded licences, neither paper followed the *Star* into broadcasting. That turned out to be a mistake.

The *Star*'s radio offerings were grim fare: librarians reading kids' stories, *Star* reporters reading their stories over the air, and, of course, church services. Still, it was the only station that could be picked up in the city during daylight hours, so the *Star* had a lock on the new medium. It gained listeners in March 1923, when Foster Hewitt called the play-by-play on the first broadcast of a hockey game from the

Mutual Street Arena. This was a true Canadian historic moment. Hewitt had called AAA baseball, but his experiment that March night changed the entertainment patterns of Canadians, and changed hockey, too.

∗ ∗ ∗

In November 1937, the federal government tried to take control of electricity exports, and Hepburn was furious. McCullagh warned the premier to keep calm, to take some time to think about the consequences of breaking with King. Instead, Hepburn took the train to Ottawa, booked a room at the Chateau Laurier, and waited for the prime minister to come to him. King tried to be nice, but neither man was willing to give way, and Hepburn told King "this means an open break with your Government."[14]

What it really meant was that Hepburn and Duplessis, the two populists—King would call each of them fascists—who ran the governments of the economic engines and electrical powerhouse of the country were now at war with their prime minister. McCullagh wouldn't join an alliance with Duplessis. Just days after Hepburn's trip to Ottawa, the *Globe and Mail* ran an editorial headlined "MR. DUPLESSIS RUNS WILD" that McCullagh signed off on. Privately, McCullagh was saying the same thing. At a dinner at Rideau Hall in Ottawa, McCullagh told the prime minister, the governor general, and some visiting British aristocrats that Hepburn was "a little swine." According to King, McCullagh said the premier was a liar who had a swelled head and was "popped up with power." Hepburn thought he had won the election, but, "as a matter of fact, it was he, McCullagh, who had really won it, even if he said so himself."[15]

∗ ∗ ∗

McCullagh's attention was focused on building his new estate, which was taking shape on a hundred-acre property he found on Bayview Avenue in Thornhill. The mansion was rising about a kilometre north of Steeles Avenue, which was then a rural dirt road.

Sir William Mulock talked the prime minister into visiting McCullagh's home in July 1938. It was a twenty-minute drive from the edge of the city to this secluded spot. McCullagh asked King to be the first to sign the estate's guest book. King took a look around. He had to admit that the estate, with Bauhaus elements designed by Hans Bergström, was beautiful. McCullagh had left Forest Hill and built a huge wooden mansion, white with green shutters and surrounded by acres of terraced gardens. It was close to the Don River, and had a series of ponds that emptied into the creek below. The house was set far back from the road and secluded by big trees. The McCullaghs— there were three young children now—had given up the convenience of Forest Hill for a home that was part farm, part formal gardens. In return, they got privacy, easy access to their horses, and space for the children to play.

The house and grounds looked like a country club (and part of the property is now a golf course). There were stables along one side of the grounds for McCullagh's thoroughbreds and show-jumping horses. A tall north-facing portico framed the entrance to the two-and-a-half-storey mansion. Visitors approached on a driveway that dog-legged from Bayview Avenue and ended in a circle in front of the mansion. The house was huge, much more space than a family of five needed, even one with servants living on the attic floor. King took it all in and made some painful small talk to the McCullaghs, and to John and "Nannie" Bassett, who were visiting. John Bassett asked the prime minister to come to Montreal to visit the family paper, the *Gazette*. King said he'd be pleased to visit the newsroom to "straighten out" its political coverage. King meant what he said. He believed both publishers ran newspapers that had anti-King reporters covering Parliament Hill.

King was scandalized by this great show of new money. He wrote in his diary: "I was interested in seeing how these young men, each of them children of good luck and fortune, in their ways, were beginning to take on the manner and methods of wealthy social classes with their worship of false gods; of social recognition, in its different forms, quickly separating themselves in a class apart from the mass of ordinary men, from the lives of those of struggling kind of which only yesterday their lives were a part, aiming not for a greater liberty for the mass of men as the preservation of liberty for the privileged class. It went against my grain to make the call, and I did so because Mulock urged it very strongly; said that the Tories had been making very much of McCullagh, whom he regarded as vain and easily impressed."[16]

King was beginning to see the formation of a triumvirate of wealthy, handsome, charismatic, conservative young men who fully expected to run Canada through the mid-twentieth century. Eventually, they were at the centre of something called the Toronto Clique, a group of rich, attractive, ambitious people with a lock on Toronto media and the provincial government. In 1938, McCullagh's up-and-coming friends George Drew and John Bassett were showing their stuff to the world. Drew was touring the province, running to be leader of Ontario's provincial Conservative Party, a race he'd win in early December. During the often-ugly campaign, he bounced ideas off McCullagh.[17] Bassett, commuting between Montreal and Toronto, liked to speak in public, and was good at it. He hit the business lunch and service club circuit in Canada and the United States to make business connections and bathe in applause.[18]

McCullagh started thinking about creating his own political movement, one that was a real grass-roots operation. This was an age when people were willing to take to the streets, pony up their cash, and hold political meetings at their kitchen tables. Why couldn't Canada have a national movement that supported the political goals McCullagh cherished: the destruction of party politics, the shrinking of government, and rule by self-made businessmen? The movement would have the *Globe and Mail* as its big tent, and McCullagh would be the ringmaster. It would use the successful formula of the "Just Kids" Safety League that McCullagh had dreamed up on those southwestern Ontario back roads, except this time the coupon-clippers would be saving the country, not themselves. Father Coughlin had shown the way, with his radio speeches and his millions of followers mailing in dimes.

After spending some time in Ottawa seeing if the federal political scene was salvageable, McCullagh came up with the "Leadership League."[19] It's not clear if the *Globe and Mail* publisher thought it up as a single campaign, or if he was winging it as he went along. He certainly saw himself as the only serious anti-communist on the Canadian stage, with Drew as his apprentice. (Drew probably saw things quite differently.) Both men were after Communist Party leader Tim Buck, who fought back by denouncing McCullagh and his new buddy. McCullagh and Drew had been riding Buck, a key figure in the Communist International, since the 1937 Toronto municipal election, when Buck had shocked the city's business leaders by almost winning a seat on the Board of Control. Buck was a constant campaigner, speaking at union halls and leftist rallies across Canada, and, unlike today's Canadian Communist leaders, most people knew who he was.

"I could sue Col. George Drew for defamatory libel for calling me a gangster," Buck told a capacity audience at the Ukrainian Temple in Sudbury in the middle of January 1939. "All the attempts of *The Globe and Mail* and George McCullagh to besmear me and besmirch me are because I represent a growing idea in Canada," he said. "Col. Drew has given his ideals a new name. Why? Because he realizes that when 45,000 people in the city of Toronto are so determined they want a change that they vote for me despite the campaign of *The Globe and Mail*, then it's time that a new name be given to all that Col. Drew and McCullagh stand for. But it's still fascism. It is fascism in sheep's clothing."[20]

∗ ∗ ∗

McCullagh gently dipped his toe into the political waters. In early December 1938, he went on the air with Sir Edward Beatty, the president of the Canadian Pacific Railway, to raise money for Salvation

Army Christmas hampers. The public response had been positive.²¹ So in the new year, he mapped out a plan for a political campaign: five one-hour national radio broadcasts, one every week in January and early February. The title and theme of the series was *Marching on to What?* It's not clear what McCullagh expected to happen after that. He might not have given it much thought. He put *Globe and Mail* writers to work drafting the speeches and asked the CBC for airtime.

W. Gladstone Murray, general manager of the CBC, shut McCullagh down. When McCullagh was denied access to the national network for being too controversial, he tried to make a deal with a string of private stations across the country. The CBC used its regulatory power to block that, too.²²

Leonard Brockington, the chair of the CBC's board, later said he didn't know the details of McCullagh's case, but Murray would claim: "I did not do this without consulting the chairman of the board." Someone was lying, and this gave McCullagh an opening. He could show the CBC was dishonest, and that gave his claims of censorship much more credibility.²³

The CBC issued a ruling, which affected every radio network in Canada. It was obviously directed at McCullagh, one of the very few individuals who had the money and the desire to buy a big block of national airtime to express his own opinion. The CBC ruling said "(1) No individual may purchase any network to broadcast personal opinions." Nor could McCullagh do it through the *Globe and Mail*, since "(2) No profit-making corporation may purchase any network to broadcast opinions."

McCullagh wrote to Murray: "This ruling, I understand, would not apply if I was speaking as a representative of the Canadian Club, the CCF Party, or, in fact, the Communist party. In my opinion, this ruling is very unfair and greatly prejudices the right of free speech on a government-owned system of communication." He had a point there, too. McCullagh had every reason to take the new rules personally.²⁴

Father Charles Lanphier, radio director of Father Coughlin's Radio League of the Little Flower, threw another wrench into the works. He had been fighting with the Toronto *Star* for months over the *Star*'s favourable coverage of the leftist Republicans in Spain's brutal civil war. Father Lanphier had tried to start a Roman Catholic boycott of the *Star*. When that failed, he took to Canada's airwaves the day before Toronto's municipal election to denounce the *Star*'s support of two Communist candidates running for council. In his radio speech and at public meetings, he called on good Christians to murder Holy Joe Atkinson. On January 8, the CBC banned Father Lanphier from broadcasting in Canada. This over-the-top attack on Atkinson had the unanticipated consequence of forcing McCullagh to admit that the CBC was right to ban the incendiary priest.

"While we disagree with the Communistic principle systematically treated in *The Star*," the *Globe and Mail* editorialized, "and while we regard it as the more dangerous when they are subtly infiltrated into the public mind under the dignity of a metropolitan newspaper, we have nothing against Mr. Atkinson personally. We shall continue to use the influence of *The Globe and Mail* in full view of the public to combat these insidious doctrines, but we can't sympathize with Fr. Lanphier's threat against the paper..."[25]

On January 14, McCullagh's paper followed up with an editorial called "Canada's Air Fascism." The writer assured the *Globe and Mail*'s readers that this was a matter of principle, that they were not editorializing just "because the publisher of this paper and the paper itself are the victims." There was a "new weapon in government hands," radio censorship. "More than eighty years ago, John Stuart Mill had expressed the hope that the time had gone by 'when any defence would be necessary of the liberty of the press as one of the securities against corrupt or tyrannical government.' He hadn't anticipated the possibility of government domination of the very air itself."

Cutting McCullagh off from the main CBC network "was tyrannical interference with the people's right to use or not to use the institution they support." The government had tried to "shackle Mr. McCullagh and his paper. This was the sole purpose of the whole series of arbitrary acts.

"*The Globe and Mail* was paying for the time: Mr. McCullagh the spokesman. Since when has the ruling been made that a business corporation could not use the radio in Canada and engage anyone it wished to speak for it? The sham of the argument is self-evident. Mr. McCullagh's addresses are not libelous or seditious or in any manner destructive of our system of government. Neither are they of a partisan political nature. They are, in fact, the opposite."

The CBC—or the government, if one believed McCullagh and his friends—backed off on January 15, so McCullagh could turn down Fr. Coughlin's offer of his forty-six station network. McCullagh couldn't have the CBC network, but he was allowed to cobble together a national network of private stations.[26]

Now that he had the green light, McCullagh started promoting his radio shows. He even bought ads in the *Star* to get the message out. Holy Joe might've buried them in the back pages, but he still took McCullagh's money.[27]

* * *

There was a lot of wind in McCullagh's first national radio speech, and very little else. It sounded like a newspaper editorial read over the air, partly because it was written by people who wrote *Globe and Mail* commentary.

McCullagh's message is tediously familiar to anyone who has heard a speech at a Rotary Club: People needed to wake up. Governments had to stop spending money they didn't have. Political patronage had to end. Courageous, fearless men had to be given power so "sane fiscal policy could be established, business principles could be applied, efficient administration could be restored, and from the resultant return of prosperity thousands of now-jobless citizens could again enjoy some of life's amenities."

McCullagh told listeners: "I believe we can get better and more efficient government, and more prosperous times by an awakened people demanding the application of business principles to public affairs." There was no need for smart people in the halls of power. "We do not need great brilliancy in the administration of public affairs. We require rugged honesty, clear purpose, tireless energy and unswerving loyalty to principles that we, as citizens of average intelligence, can appraise fairly."[28]

The speech dragged on and on, through fourteen double-spaced pages of boilerplate and slogans. No one polled the audience to see if any listeners were still there at the end.

To be fair to McCullagh, he did have a point about the quality of political leadership in Canada. Up to McCullagh's time, Canada's prime ministers had been, with just a couple of exceptions, a sorry lot. The sitting prime minister, Mackenzie King, had been clinging to office for an entire generation, except for a few weeks in 1926 and the one-term Tory administration of R. B. Bennett at the beginning of the Depression. The Tories were stuck with policies—economic nationalism rather than free trade with the United States, high tariffs, frugality in a time of Depression—that were political poison.

And every Tory leader was hobbled by Quebec's hatred for the party. Writers have blamed Macdonald's hanging of Louis Riel for Quebec's detestation of Conservatives, but the Tory push for a national draft of young men to fight in the Great War caused as least as much hatred. The rest of the country was content with a federal government that, in a frightening world, was not radical, seemed professional, and didn't make things worse. That was all King could offer, and it fit the times. Luck like that is rare.

McCullagh, and anyone who knew King, saw a prime minister who was petty, bitter, out of touch, unimaginative and strange, though none of them knew how weird he truly was. Only a handful of his closest friends knew about his creepy spiritualism and superstition, his obsession with his mother before and after her death, and his odd belief that the position of the hands of clocks at the time of important events was significant. Smart men, even those who worked closest to him, despised King. They knew he was vindictive, superstitious, bigoted and grasping.[29] Norman Robertson, one of the country's great public servants, said at the time of King's death, "I never saw a touch of greatness in him." Jack Pickersgill, who had spent the late 1930s and most of the next decade at King's side, admitted later that "he felt no sorrow at King's death."[30]

King's friendship with Joe Atkinson, which went back fifty years to their time together as cub reporters on the *Globe*, was also a factor in King's success. McCullagh knew Atkinson and King spoke on the phone almost every day, and that King, a notorious cheapskate, stayed at Atkinson's house when he visited Toronto. He likely also knew Atkinson had turned down offers of a Senate seat. McCullagh's supporter Father Coughlin had condemned the *Star* as a Moscow-tainted publication. His opinion was shared by most of Canada's business leaders, and there was some truth to it. When a *Star* reporter was assigned to travel through Russia, Atkinson refused to run articles that were critical of Stalin's regime, while McCullagh was eager to print large anti-communist pieces filed from Russia by George Drew.[31]

McCullagh had lots to work with when he went after King and his overripe government. It really was time for a change, either through normal parliamentary elections, a coalition government or some other way to bring new blood and ideas to a sclerotic national capital. McCullagh might have even been a contender to replace King, despite being just thirty-three years old, but he lacked the knowledge of politics and policy to take a run at an old prime minister who was determined to hang on to power rather than face the horror of having the free time to stew in his own loneliness.

The Liberals were vulnerable on one front: King's government was lockstep with the appeasers in London and Paris. In a January cabinet meeting, King gave one of his rare talks about foreign policy issues. He named the main opponents of appeasement: "There will be an effort to stir up anti-Fascist feeling as there was anti-Communist feeling in the Ontario elections," King told his ministers. "The 'Globe' will be the main conspirator. McCullagh doubtless playing in with Drew, (Vincent) Massey and others. Meighen, in the Senate, attacking inadequacy of our contribution to defence while others in Quebec will exaggerate. McLaughlin, of the motor works, and Wright, of gold mine interests, will help to line up war veteran corps, etc."[32]

For all his faults, McCullagh was on solid moral ground when it came to the question of persecution of the Jews. His newspaper was sympathetic to Maurice Eisendrath, the rabbi at Holy Blossom Temple, who came home on Halloween night of 1937 to find funeral crepe and a swastika nailed to his front door. In the ugly provincial election campaign that had ended three weeks earlier, Eisendrath had warned Toronto's Jewish community and anyone else who would listen that fascism was on the rise. Not only did the *Globe and Mail* carry a new message from the rabbi about domestic fascism, but McCullagh also commissioned an investigation of the extreme right in Canada that discovered a web of fascist activists across Canada.[33]

The *Globe and Mail* was a constant critic of Hitler's oppression and Canada's weak response to it. McCullagh's friend Bishop Renison used his column to attack the Nazis. This was one issue where McCullagh and Atkinson were on the same page. On November 19, 1938, after the Nazis' "Kristallnacht" attacks on Germany's Jews, Canadian opponents of Hitler held a big rally at Maple Leaf Gardens that drew serious media heavies, including Atkinson, to the stage.[34] Through the spring and summer of 1939, the *Globe and Mail* was one of the papers that challenged King's cowardly policy on Jewish refugees, and the paper continued to attack Canada's closed-door policy during the war and in the postwar years.[35]

* * *

McCullagh's foreign policy speech should have been a watershed: there was so much for him and his ghostwriters John Bassett and sports editor M.T. Munns to work with.[36] But there simply wasn't a galvanizing message.

Faced with the thin arguments and lack of serious solutions offered by their boss, McCullagh's loyal journalists decided to please their publisher, rather than inform the *Globe and Mail's* readers. They decided to ignore McCullagh's failure to connect with his audience and, instead, focus on the CBC's censorship, writing page upon page of eye-splitting stories on the issue, with every tiny detail of the dispute.

Judith Robinson, the paper's best columnist, called the government's action tyrannical and unjust. She compared McCullagh's right to hire the radio stations of Canada for an hour to a poorer person's right to rent a hall to give a speech. McCullagh might be a rich man, and his purchase of radio airtime might have only been for himself, but he was still a freedom fighter. Any close examination of some decent history books would prove the righteousness of his case: "They show the whole of British history as a long series of struggles against injustice: struggles that didn't even get started until the injustices began to be felt on the upper income brackets. They show that every gain in the record of slow gains for freedom was won because oppressors went too far at last and tried to get away with oppressing the powerful as they had been oppressing the weak.... The theory that a wealthy man's wealth must bar him from the company of democrats is new. So is the theory that a wealthy man's wealth makes the wrong done him and free speech by irresponsible authority of no consequence to his fellow-citizens."[37]

The *Globe and Mail's* parliamentary bureau chimed in by hounding C.D. Howe, the cabinet minister in charge of the CBC.

All this coverage was driven home in an editorial called "The Free Speech Conspiracy." It described McCullagh's fight with the CBC and the federal government in excruciating detail before finally making its point: "The privilege of free speech denied the publisher of this paper applies to any individual as the Minister or the Government or the Broadcasting Corporation may decide. The ruling was trumped up to meet the wishes of the moment. Forget Mr. McCullagh. Remember the hard-won rights of British democracy now being destroyed."[38]

The fight between the publisher and the broadcaster/regulator was a big deal to journalists, especially those who hated the CBC, but it was hard for Depression-weary Canadians to sympathize. McCullagh could claim he was fighting this battle for everyone, but there were very few Canadians with the money and desire to rent the country's radio waves for an hour at a time.

While the fight over what McCullagh described as censorship continued, so did his radio speeches. On Sunday, January 29, people across Canada tuned in to hear the third in the series. The subject was unemployment, something that people really cared about. But, while McCullagh carried on about the virtues of thrift, optimism and the spirit of Horatio Alger, he had nothing new to offer the unemployed. Ending bilingualism in governments and converting Quebec to an English-speaking province for efficiency's sake was not an idea that would create jobs. McCullagh didn't come out in favour or against unemployment insurance or public works. In his world, the economic crisis could be solved by a change in attitude.

* * *

The next broadcast was focused on McCullagh's bizarre, unconstitutional plan to get rid of provincial governments. "The greatest public service Mr. Hepburn could do for Canada and something which would carry his name into history as a public benefactor would be for him to state publicly what we all know that our provincial governments are political misfits—luxuries we cannot afford—endless cause of disunity," McCullagh said in one of his usual run-on sentences. "If

Mr. Hepburn would state this, and pledge himself to end the provincial burden, he would carry us a long way toward the solvency and solutions we seek." The average annual income in Canada in 1937 was $438, of which, McCullagh said, $121.50 was paid to governments in various taxes. He continued:

> If we fulfill our function as vigilant citizens, pull in our belts and restrict our requests on governments for costly services, demanding a pay-as-you-go policy, we shall have something for our children and succeeding generations of which we can be rightly proud. The solution is not trick money schemes or dishonest debt repudiation. The solution is less government. Much less government.
>
> I am confident that if our tax bills were cut in half, the natural spending by the people of their own money would create sufficient industrial activity to take up the slack, and the accumulated effect would be the solution of our unemployment problem. Governments can provide certain pump-priming assistance in times of industrial inactivity but the ultimate basis for sound economy is activity backed by private enterprise and regulated by the law of supply and demand. I firmly believe when you realize fully that the power to tax is the power to destroy, you will demand better management of your government affairs, and thereby start us on the road to recovery.[39]

J.G. Ross, the Liberal MP for Moose Jaw, accused McCullagh of being a tool of Toronto men with $100 million. "If Mr. William Wright wants to be a sugar daddy for a political gigolo, that's Mr. Wright's affair." Another Liberal MP, R.J. Deachman, from the southwestern Ontario riding of Huron North, suggested McCullagh was hurting journalism. "If in the future the press is to develop to the stage where men who do not know its traditions, who have made their money in other fields of effort and who use the press for the accomplishment of their own purpose and, instead of presenting the views of the public present their own personal views on the editorial page, I fear that the boasted freedom of the press will to some extent cease, and some measure of restriction will eventually be adopted."[40]

Non-partisan listeners might have been bored, but some were inspired to write to McCullagh to praise his ideas and tell him to keep going. The next radio talk was directed at women and young people. In it, McCullagh urged women to become politically active and praised his mother, though the speech was hardly a rallying cry for feminist action: "If I have had any success of my life, let me honestly say that I owe it entirely to the unselfish devotion and burning ambition of a Christian mother who instilled in all her children a desire for learning and achieving, always holding up as examples men of success both in public life and the industry surrounding the community in which we lived." It ended with McCullagh saying, "Since next week brings the final talk, I would like you all to bring pencil and pad to the radio so you can join me in an experimental effort to see if we can assert our rights to govern and make democracy work."[41]

Feeling stung by political and media criticism of Wright and his money, McCullagh went off on a tangent in his fifth speech. The *Globe and Mail* and McCullagh's new political campaign were hardly about making money for Wright. Donations to McCullagh's new political organization weren't enough to cover the cost of his radio speeches, while The *Globe and Mail* earned a paltry $21,000 a year for Canada's richest man.

In the last speech, McCullagh said Canadians had allowed professional politicians to play with the complicated machinery of government "as if it were a child's steam engine. Our mistake has been allowing our servants to play with the machinery, not to work it.

"The remedy is with you. I propose that we form an association to be called the Leadership League. The membership is to be free of charge and open to all, the purpose is to help us all work together to continue and enlarge public affairs." Local groups could fight for tax cuts, job creation, and a clean-up of the system. But he wasn't advocating revolution.

"The old political tools are neither broken nor worn out, they are just dirty...Let's clean them up...Reshape the old parties...You cannot be a member of this League and put your party ahead of your country...If the [old parties] fail us...then will be the time to consider the formation of a new party. And if that time comes, I suggest a motto for the new party: A Plague on Both Your Houses!"[42]

Finally, the campaign had a name, and it had a strategy. All it needed was a leader.

* * *

McCullagh's closest aides later claimed there had never been a plan to start a political movement, and that McCullagh was inspired to do it because he had received so many letters, telegrams and phone calls of support.[43] It's hard to know if that's true. What was the point of the speeches if not to change the political landscape?

McCullagh, once seized of the Leadership League idea, threw his newspaper's resources into it, and added some of his own money. Top *Globe and Mail* journalists like John Bassett and some high-profile Leadership League supporters from outside the paper were sent off to speak to service clubs, ratepayer groups and business associations, mostly in the Toronto area. Warren Baldwin, a *Globe and Mail* parliamentary reporter, was put to work writing boilerplate copy to be printed in the paper and given away to people who wrote to the League.[44] So was Royd Beamish, another important *Globe and Mail* writer who was yanked away from his regular beat. "It was the sorriest job I ever had in my life," Beamish later wrote. "What I did was slant the news. When a

For Your Membership

THE LEADERSHIP LEAGUE
The Globe and Mail, Toronto, Ont.

I wish to join The Leadership League for the purpose of RESTORING DEMOCRACY, REDUC-ING TAXATION and PUTTING CANADIANS BACK TO WORK.

NAME ....
Please Print in Block Letters.

....
Street Address or Box Number.

....
Town.   Province.
One Cent Stamp on Unsealed Envelope.

THE LEADERSHIP LEAGUE
The Globe and Mail, Toronto, Ont.

I wish to join The Leadership League for the purpose of RESTORING DEMOCRACY, REDUC-ING TAXATION and PUTTING CANADIANS BACK TO WORK.

NAME ....
Please Print in Block Letters.

....
Street Address or Box Number.

....
Town.   Province.
One Cent Stamp on Unsealed Envelope.

For Your Member

(Address This Ballot to Your Local Federal Member.)

TO ....
HOUSE OF COMMONS, OTTAWA, ONT.
I am a voter in your constituency. I earnestly ask you to FORGET PARTY ADVANTAGE and CO-OPERATE FOR THE COMMON GOOD.

NAME ....
Please Print in Block Letters.

....
Street Address or Box Number.

....
Town.   Province.
Envelope does not require postage. Just address it to your Local Federal Member, House of Commons, Ottawa.

(Address This Ballot to Your Local Federal Member.)

TO ....
HOUSE OF COMMONS, OTTAWA, ONT.
I am a voter in your constituency. I earnestly ask you to FORGET PARTY ADVANTAGE and CO-OPERATE FOR THE COMMON GOOD.

NAME ....
Please Print in Block Letters.

....
Street Address or Box Number.

....
Town.   Province.
Envelope does not require postage. Just address it to your Local Federal Member, House of Commons, Ottawa.

The *Globe and Mail* ran full pages of Leadership League news, along with these coupons that readers could send to members of Parliament. The membership coupons sent to the *Globe and Mail* were an early system of consumer data collection.

story came over the teletype that had some slight anti-Liberal bias, I rewrote it to make that bias stronger. When Bassett or one of the others spoke, it was mandatory that the top writer cover it and God help him if he didn't gush."[45] A few months later, after the war broke out, reporters like Beamish and Baldwin would have other job options, but in the winter and spring of 1939, when the country was still locked in the Depression, they had little choice but to do their boss's bidding.

Much of their writing was centred on McCullagh's brilliance. A size-able amount focused on the failures of the people who ran the various levels of government, with special emphasis on Ottawa.

Starting on February 14—two days after the last radio speech—the *Globe and Mail* ran regular Leadership League features. The League articles and coupons took up full pages in the news pages of the first section of the paper, prime space that was normally given over to real

Leadership League Is Given Into Hands Of Canadian People

Great New Organization, 125,000 Strong, Formally Transferred to Citizens' Committee by Its Publisher-Founder Before Crowd of 10,000 Gathered in Rally at Maple Leaf Gardens

TRUST IS ACCEPTED BY HON. DR. BRUCE

The Leadership League—potentially powerful panacea for this country's present pressing problems—passed last night, for administrative purposes, into the hands of the Canadian people, in whose interests The Globe and Mail conceived and created it.

Out of its swaddling clothes—firm-footed and fearless, its young but lusty voice clamoring for deserved recognition at the nation's door—this great new organization, 125,000 members strong already, was formally transferred by its founder, the publisher of The Globe and Mail, to the very competent jurisdiction of a citizens' committee provisionally headed by Hon. Dr. Herbert A. Bruce, with Sir Frederick Banting, another outstanding public benefactor, vice-chairman and co-trustee.

The event was epochal. Its significance beggared description. Ten thousand, from every section of Ontario —of every creed and class and color, rich man, poor man, big man, and beggar—came to Maple Leaf Gardens to witness the auspicious affair; thousands bearing testimony by their presence and their attention to the work and worth of the League, holding high the torch of aggressiveness and action so effectively kindled by the publisher; thousands subscribing wholeheartedly to the League's stand that patronage and partisanship must end; that governments must work for the common good rather than for individual advantage and aggrandizement; and that Canada—to preserve democracy—must now and forever take her proper place within the Empire and speak in the forceful, fruitful language of any true whelp of the British lion.

HEART-STIRRING SCENE.

The setting was one of the most colorful in the history of a Toronto long accustomed to notable demonstrations. The press of humanity constituted one of the mightiest mass meetings ever held here. The purpose, as lofty and laudable as ever pronounced from pulpit or platform, rode

A clipping from the *Globe and Mail* puts the best face on the failure of the Leadership League to attract leadership talent and raise money. No one was sure what the league was for.

journalism. Each Leadership League page printed two coupons. One was a wallet-size membership card that could be clipped, filled in and saved. The second was a form note to send to the reader's member of Parliament. Membership cost nothing, and readers were reminded that mailing letters (or coupons) to MPs did not require a stamp. The coupon printed in the May 15 paper carried a fairly typical message: "I am a voter in your constituency. I earnestly ask you to FORGET PARTY ADVANTAGE and CO-OPERATE FOR THE COMMON GOOD." It was pure McCullagh, the same message he'd given Hepburn and Rowe two years before, when he tried to strong-arm the Ontario Liberals and Tories into a coalition government.

The Leadership League page also carried "Hansurdities," snippets of the more ridiculous debates in the House of Commons. *Globe and Mail* reporters on Parliament Hill, usually Warren Baldwin, collected MPs' drivel and petty sniping, recorded the amount of time wasted on each exchange, and calculated the wasted time as a percentage of Parliament's budget. One three-and-a-half-minute exchange between a CCF member and a Liberal backbencher was said to cost taxpayers $171, which was a decent monthly salary in 1939.[46]

The Leadership League was meant to be a grass roots organization—though, at least in its early weeks, it operated from an office in the newspaper's advertising office. And it got plenty of ideas from *Globe and Mail* readers who were sick of nine years of the Great Depression. They wrote to the paper to say the political system was broken—maybe not as broken as in the former democracies of Europe, but still obviously dysfunctional—and they believed this might be a good idea to remake Canadian politics.

Some agreed with McCullagh that the provincial governments should be eliminated or, at least, drastically scaled back. One *Globe and Mail* reader had the idea of replacing members of the provincial legislature with city mayors and county wardens. Others thought there were too many members of the House of Commons. Themes emerged as the Leadership League consumed page after page of *Globe and Mail* editorial space. There should be big reductions in the size of governments, if not the actual elimination of governments. There had to be tax cuts. Patronage had to end. Successful men, presumably business leaders, had to replace career politicians like Mackenzie King. Some policies, like the amalgamation of small-town and rural schoolboards into county boards, would happen a generation later. Other ideas were simply pipedreams.

On one Leadership League page, McCullagh's employees wrote:

> Count Your Problems
> GOVERNMENT—How to reduce it.
> TAXES—How to reduce them.
> PUBLIC DEBTS—How to reduce them.
> PATRONAGE—How to kill it.
> HOME OWNERSHIP—How to save it.
> FARMING—How to revive it.
> UNEMPLOYMENT—How to beat it.
> RAILWAYS—How to make them pay.
> RESOURCES—How to develop them.
> DEFENSE—How to speed it.
> FREEDOM—How to guard it.
> UNITY—How to get it.
> JOIN YOUR LEADERSHIP LEAGUE [47]

Those were all, in varying degrees, important national problems, and topics that were bound to inflame Leadership League page readers. These issues vexed Canada's political leadership for years, were constantly brought up in Parliament and in election speeches by politicians on all parts of the spectrum, and yet no one had found solutions. Simply listing them, discounting politicians' work on some of these almost-insolvable problems, and undermining the legitimate, elected political leadership of the country was a cheap and shallow way of tapping into the nation's anger. There was a real recklessness here. Delegitimizing elected representatives also drained away public support for democratic institutions. A natural thread of logic, one that was often picked up by Leadership League letter-writers and published in the *Globe and Mail*, was that democracy itself was not working, and that the answer to the country's problems could be simply solved by "leadership." Many Leadership League pages had a four-inch-by-two column box with a headline "What Parliament Has Done (As Condensed from Hansard)." The box had no text, just white space.

At the same time McCullagh's *Globe and Mail* writers were tub-thumping for leadership, they ran pithy quotes about the need to be vigilant for potential tyrants. One Leadership League page carried this quote from G.K. Chesteron's *Everlasting Man*: "A DESPOTISM may almost be defined as a tired democracy. As fatigue falls on a community, the citizens are less inclined for that eternal vigilance which has truly been called the price of liberty, and they prefer to arm only one single individual to watch the city while they sleep."[48] It's easy to see why Leadership League page readers would be confused. What was being sold here? Strong leadership? Enhanced democracy? If it was leadership, then who was to be the leader? And if it was democracy, how could it be made better by getting rid of provinces and their legislatures, and replacing the federal system with one-party government?

Joseph Haukbaum wrote from Vancouver to echo the pap that filled Leadership League pages: "George McCullagh has awakened the Canadian people and reminded them that they are responsible for the present drift. He has faith in our ability; he believes that when united we can solve our problems, and thousands of Canadians agree. I am convinced that in the very near future all Canadians will back him up. There is no problem too great, when a united nation earnestly and honestly cares to improve its welfare."[49]

People like G.G. Gordon of Toronto went after government waste: "I think you might follow up the adding of a woman employee to the Dominion Department of Agriculture—which means a cost of close to $4,000 a year. I think she is to tell the women of Canada how to cook vegetables, but this is only the first leg to another sub-department, which means putting up the taxation still further."

G. Ross of Regina, after demanding a complete overhaul of Canada's constitution, added, "I am convinced that what the people of Canada are waiting for is someone who is prepared to lead them out of the doubt and despair in which they find themselves." The editor added a note: "Does Mr. Ross mean lead or drive?" And that was the real question. Who would lead? There were a million ideas, but no one to carry them forward. It was the fatal flaw in the Leadership League. Everyone had ideas. Some of them were quite reasonable. But real change couldn't take place except through the national and provincial parliaments.

McCullagh and his followers, at the very least, underestimated the time and energy needed to organize a new political party, to take over an old one, or to develop a movement large enough to scare the existing politicians into making serious changes. And how far would the Leadership League go? Could it ever do enough to satisfy G.W. Anderson of Lanigan, Saskatchewan, whose note saying "Our farmers are in a hopeless condition. Thousands quietly hoping for war, would welcome rebellion, secession, or anything drastic, as a way of relief," was printed in the *Globe and Mail*?

The wording of Leadership League coupons was changed so readers would send a second flurry of mail to Parliament Hill. In the Monday, February 27, 1939, issue of the *Globe and Mail*, editors had written "Government's Only Income is Your Money." Leadership League coupons printed on the same page echoed those words. The February 23 Leadership League page carried a cartoon showing two boys marked Liberals and Conservatives fighting on a barrel labelled "patronage." A barrel of "pork" was next to them, and on the ground was a crying baby with CCF on his diaper, arms out in a plea to be picked up. A taxpayer who looks strangely like an older, bald Hitler (with toothbrush moustache) looks on sadly. A coupon on that page, which was addressed to the *Globe and Mail*, carried the text "I wish to join The Leadership League for the purpose of RESTORING DEMOCRACY, REDUCING TAXATION and PUTTING CANADIANS BACK TO WORK."

On February 28, the *Globe and Mail* started encouraging readers to form local Leadership League clubs. People interested in creating a league chapter were told to contact a local service club or church group and ask them to invite a league speaker. Most likely John Bassett, who was still a *Globe and Mail* reporter, Capt. Norman Rawson, who had run unsuccessfully for the provincial Tory leadership, or popular broadcaster John Collingwood Reade would show up. People seemed to like Bassett the most. Audiences found him to be very eloquent, with a good sense of humour and real zeal for McCullagh and his cause.[50]

After the league speaker spoke at a founding meeting, local Leadership League organizers were supposed to appoint a provisional governing committee that included at least one "business man, a representative of labour, a professional man, clergymen of various denominations and a prominent woman." These local committees were supposed to send delegates to a larger group that was to be set up in each federal riding, and both levels were supposed to be in close contact with the national organization. All this complicated organizing, which was similar to the structure of Russia's Soviet system, was explained in a kit that was mailed out by the *Globe and Mail*.[51]

More than forty Leadership League branches were started in cities and towns across the country, and the creation of each was covered as news. In its coverage of the creation of the branch in the backwater south Georgian Bay village of Coldwater, the person who wrote the *Globe and Mail* article editorialized that party hacks should not expect to be given important posts in the Leadership League: "Someone must serve in the rear-ranks. Why not ex-party stalwarts?"[52]

Once they had a strong local league, McCullagh's supporters could take control of mainstream party constituency associations, or just confront political candidates: "Party organizations choose candidates, therefore join party organizations, dominate them and demand the type of representation that will ensure your needs receiving consideration. The day when you will vote against the man promising you a post office for your town, knowing such a building is wasteful expenditure and vicious patronage, will be the day that Canada really can call herself great," Bassett told one group.[53]

For weeks, public support seemed to build, especially if a person read the *Globe and Mail* and no other newspaper. In fact, what McCullagh tapped into was the kind of anger and frustration that shows up these days on social media and in the comments under newspaper web page stories.

J.F. Ayrhart of Campbellville, Ontario, wrote directly to McCullagh: "Your paper's able leadership in tackling the major problems of the day—and your timely and pertinent remarks over the air, directly or indirectly—will be a benefit to Canadians, for which you will receive your just reward in the admiration of all young Canada. Continue to pioneer in the spirit of your paper's founder, George Brown. I am a young business man of 26, a local councilman and am prepared to give you every assistance in this quarter." So did Edison Hayman of McCullagh's home town of London: "I am confident that you will have the full support of all sane people of Canada who have been suffering through the years owing to the follies of our political parties. We are with you for good, sound and honest government for the people."

Other readers were left feeling there must be more. "I believe you are wasting time with both the old parties, and the majority of the people are only awaiting competent leadership for an independent party of some kind," F.C. Taylor, of Mount Dennis, Ontario, wrote.[54] And that was the rub. If the old parties were the problem, why not ignore them and start a new one? And, again, where was the leadership?

King couldn't cure the country's economic problems, but he did deflate McCullagh's criticism of the federal government's softness on Nazis. On March 30, King told a packed House of Commons that he rejected neutrality and isolationism, saying neutrality would give "aid and comfort to any country which may be inclined to aggressive action against the democratic peoples or against the United Kingdom specifically." But King insisted his government believed conscription "for overseas service would not be a necessary or an effective step." The following day, Neville Chamberlain laid out Britain's policy on Nazi aggression: there would be war if Hitler attacked Poland.[55] King, with his fond memories of Berlin, still had happy dreams about Hitler and Germany, but he kept them to himself and his diary.

* * *

Some fifty-four thousand Leadership League envelopes were delivered to members of Parliament in the first eleven business days of the league's first coupon campaign. About half of the league's members were women. Rural and small-town people were well-represented among members, but two-thirds came from Toronto.[56] Small-town papers also supported McCullagh's campaign. The Fort Erie *Times Review* took up McCullagh's campaign for business tax cuts, with the paper's editors making the case that overtaxed business owners could not afford to hire workers. Sales taxes should be cut too, so people could afford to spend more. Other newspaper writers were not so sure about McCullagh and his ideas. The author of the *Ottawa Citizen*'s long-running and dreadful "Own Diary of Our Own Pepys" believed "Mr. McCullagh wants a Leadership League which I fear will come to naught, for a condition of its existence is what Mr. McCullagh calls 'a vigilant and militant public' and there is no such thing. Some day the public will be heard from, but today it lacks commitment as a lamb." The Moose Jaw *Times-Herald*'s editors editorialized: "Mr. McCullagh knows that abolition of the provinces is impossible. But it is an idea that has some appeal to the unthinking, especially in Ontario, as a number of other things in his speeches do a large number of persons. They are a kind of sugar coating for something else."

Bigger papers were even less kind, and their editorial writers were able to cut through the fog and find the principles that were at stake.

The Toronto *Star*'s editors wrote of being startled by the intensity of McCullagh's attacks on the country's institutions and said the League was engaged "in a campaign which undermines the confidence of Canadians in democratic government." They deplored the populist overtones of the league and McCullagh's obsession with getting rid of the provinces: "It is mischievous nonsense, a proposal calculated to create further disunity in Canada, a Fascist proposal because it is admittedly bound up with a scheme for making the proposed all-controlling central parliament a one-party parliament. And such parliaments, with such powers, have been, in other countries, the first fruits of dictatorships."[57]

Editorial writers at the conservative Toronto *Telegram* were just as unkind, while the weekly magazine *Saturday Night* called the Leadership League "a newspaper stunt" and implied McCullagh was a bit dense. His idea that provincial governments were an unnecessary frill showed that "the story of Canada hasn't sunk very deeply into his consciousness." The *Hamilton Spectator* believed the Leadership League offered little but fear: "(I)t is dangerous for any group to condemn a structure in a time of unrestrained nervousness without boldly offering constructive alternatives on which the majority of citizens can pass judgment." Many newspaper editors outside Ontario believed the plan to get rid of provinces was simply a power grab by Toronto's business elite and the politicians who fronted for them.

The *Halifax Chronicle* warned that if McCullagh had his way, eventually the whole country would be governed "from a small office in the building of the Toronto Globe and Mail." British Columbia's premier, Duff Pattullo, who, in his own way, was at least as outrageous McCullagh—he'd threatened to unilaterally seize the Yukon Territory and annex it to his province—called McCullagh's campaign to get rid of provinces "nonsense." The *Vancouver Sun* echoed Pattullo's criticism of the Leadership League platform, saying what McCullagh really wanted was big cuts to farmers' subsidies, the cancellation of public works projects, and that the logical conclusion was "Canadian Fascism."[58]

* * *

Canada's prime minister agreed. At the end of February, he told the governor general, Lord Tweedsmuir, that McCullagh and John Bassett were trying to create a fascist movement to propel McCullagh into power. In turn, the publisher was a front for the country's financial elite: Colonel McLaughlin, the head of General Motors Canada; William Wright and his gold mining friends; Beatty of the Canadian Pacific Railway. Tweedsmuir, a man of some sophistication who was world-famous for his novels, published under his birth name, John Buchan—*The Thirty-Nine Steps*, a thriller set in the First World War, had been made into a movie by Alfred Hitchcock four years before—said he didn't think McCullagh had the brains to pull it off. But Tweedsmuir studied fascist propaganda techniques, and he saw that McCullagh was pushing some of the right buttons. "The idea of a leadership campaign was to get the young men associated with the word 'leader'—adopting the Duce, Fuhrer type in Europe," Tweedsmuir said.[59]

A week later, the prime minister was expanding on that idea to, of all people, the Japanese consul. King told the visiting diplomat that he believed the next election would be a referendum on democracy. McCullagh and his ilk were using the same methods as Hitler, Mussolini, and the now-forgotten second string of dictators in eastern Europe: whipping up dissatisfaction with the existing system of government; portraying parliaments and legislatures as too slow to get anything done; taking advantage of young people's idealism, offering them empty phrases and the easy solution of having a charismatic leader who could make fast decisions and end the gridlock.[60]

* * *

In the first ten days, 101,900 membership coupons were sent to the *Globe and Mail*. People called in to the radio stations that carried the five McCullagh speeches to ask for ballots and coupons. A Calgary radio station wrote to the *Globe and Mail* to ask for a thousand forms, and a station in Edmonton wanted 250. Stations in Sydney and Charlottetown needed two hundred. In one two-hour period on February 15, fifty people had called the *Globe and Mail* to get ballots.[61]

Some politicians were willing to consider some of the league's ideas and criticism, including the no-hope proposal to get rid of the provinces. Ontario's attorney general, Gordon Conant, who owed his job to McCullagh and who would be the next premier of the province, said he was willing to support the idea if someone could prove to him that it had some merit. "(C)ommon sense and determination can accomplish a great deal, and if our problems as a nation can better be solved by the abolition of any of our governments, then let us act accordingly...If the Toronto publisher succeeds in his agitation for the abolition of our legislatures, I may find myself among the unemployed. But I could not take any other position and be consistent, and if in the solution of this very serious problem I am eliminated, the interests of the nation must come first and the interests of the individuals must be secondary, and very secondary at that."[62]

Conant likely knew he could curry favour with McCullagh and the league with little risk. As a lawyer, he knew that there was no way the Canadian constitution would be changed by Britain's Parliament without the consent of the very provinces McCullagh was trying to kill.

Privately, Robert Manion, the Tory leader, twisted the knife in while summing up the Leadership League. "My own feeling is that there is far too much acceptance without question of suggestions made by George McCullagh who, after all, is only thirty-three and who has had no special experience except in making a bit of money."[63] Manion realized that 100,000 ballots, mailed for free, seemed like a lot of support, but there were four million voters in the country who hadn't leapt onto McCullagh's bandwagon. George Drew, the fastest-rising star in

Canada's conservative movement, thought differently. Although he did not embrace the Leadership League publicly, Drew carefully clipped its pages from the *Globe and Mail* and saved them in his files.[64]

* * *

McCullagh did attract some "names." Nobel Prize winner Dr. Frederick Banting, co-discoverer of insulin, was the country's best-known scientist. Banting was worried by Hitler. He was convinced the Third Reich would use bacteriological warfare against its enemies and believed Canada needed to keep on top of the Nazis. (Banting would go on to use his superb connections in the research community to kick-start secret Canadian germ-warfare research before his death in a plane crash in 1941.) Banting imagined and feared a war in which clouds of gas and viruses destroyed entire nations. The idea seems far-fetched now, but people like Banting had no reason to believe that the chemical warfare of the First World War would not be repeated and improved upon. If McCullagh was the man to replace the ridiculous, incompetent King and put some steel into the spine of Canada and her allies, so be it.[65] McCullagh also recruited a group of celebrities, including Arthur "Roy" Brown, credited by many as the man who shot down the Red Baron, and a few retired politicians. But the league was never able to attract an important incumbent politician.[66]

So what was the Leadership League? Was it a populist movement? A public search for common-sense solutions to political and economic problems? Or was it an attempt to generate a fascist movement in Canada, one that didn't call itself fascism and tried to incorporate Canadian middle-class "niceness"? Canadian media historian Douglas Fetherling called the Leadership League "at best anti-democratic and perhaps even fascistic in its sympathies."[67] That seems accurate.

* * *

After weeks of radio talks and a blizzard of coupons overwhelming the Parliament Hill post offices, it was time for the big show. McCullagh was about to find out if his supporters would do more than fill out forms and write short letters. The Saturday, March 11, 1939, *Globe and Mail* carried a full-page ad:

Get Your Tickets Now!
LEADERSHIP LEAGUE
Public Meeting Maple Leaf Gardens, Wed., March 15, 1939—8 p.m.
Doors open 7 p.m. Seats reserved until 7:45 p.m. only
Hon. Dr. Herbert A. Bruce
Sir Frederick Banting

Three days later, the Leadership League ran an ad in the Toronto *Star*. The paper buried it on page twenty-two. The text read: "Leadership League Holds Nation-Wide Mass Meeting by Radio... WEDNESDAY. Speakers George McCullagh, the Hon. Herbert A. Bruce, Captain Norman Rawson. (21 radio stations in Toronto, rural Ontario, Montreal, Calgary. Edmonton, Winnipeg and Vancouver)."

The meeting could have been an exciting rally. Instead, McCullagh chose to invite important and famous people who had never shown much interest or skill in talking to large groups. And rather than make it a big election campaign–style event, the main event would be the introduction of a "newly formed provisional advisory board which would take over the Leadership League from George McCullagh and The Globe and Mail." Banting, who hated newspaper journalists, would be on this committee.[68] So would Herbert Bruce, the retired lieutenant-governor of Ontario, and founder and owner of Toronto's Wellesley Hospital.[69] Maybe Bruce was the only person who could pass as a political actor who was willing to be on stage with McCullagh.

The crowd on the floor of Maple Leaf Gardens during the Leadership League rally, 1939. (CITY OF TORONTO ARCHIVES, FONDS 1266, ITEM 57322)

The publisher was going to speak, as was Capt. Norman Rawson, the Hamilton clergyman who'd run against George Drew for the provincial Tory leadership and placed fourth. There would be surprise guest speakers. And there would be music, too: the bagpipes of the 48th Highlanders, and the Lyric Male Choir. Real rousing stuff.

Admission was free. People just had to write to the *Globe and Mail* at the William H. Wright Building or call the newspaper switchboard to get tickets.

"Out of town members! Form Your Parties," the ads said. "Travel together, let's show our strength! The Most Important Meeting in a Generation!"

It was the most important meeting in a lifetime. But only for George McCullagh.

There were seats for twenty thousand people. Half that number showed up.

The pipers struck up "God Save the King" and the thin crowd sang along. Then the lights dimmed and the stage lit up, showing McCullagh,

William Wright (who was paying for the league, indirectly), Reverend Rawson, and Dr. Bruce. The latter two men walked up to the microphones. Rawson spoke first. Nothing, he charged, had been done by governments to help Canada's youth. The finest of Canada's manhood, he added, "was going to rot." That was just the start. The country itself was falling apart. "Well, I, for one," he stormed, "am not prepared to stand by idly and let that go on if I can do anything to stop it." "Me neither!" someone called out from the centre of the floor.

Rawson talked of the Nazi takeover of Czechoslovakia. "Here in Canada we are in a peculiarly vulnerable position. Why have we not been attacked before this? Has it been because of our navy and our army?" The preacher rattled off statistics about Canada's rank among the naval powers of the world, and the audience laughed louder. Canada, he said, was safe because England had been paying the shot.

Canada's politicians hadn't just failed the motherland. They had let Canada's young men waste away.

The handling of the unemployment problem in this country in the last nine years is a disgrace to a Christian people. Let me tell you, unless you liquidate this problem it will liquidate your Christian civilization. Do you know there are boys of 21 who are not wanted and have no place to go? A boy not long ago told me he prayed for war last fall so he would die decently and be buried near his two brothers who died in the last war. In 1914–18 we fought a war to make the world safe for democracy. Twenty-four years later, there are more nations under dictators than ever before.

Democracies do not crumble to the mere blast of some dictator's trumpet unless they have already been thoroughly undermined. The price of freedom is eternal vigilance. Let me tell any Ontario citizen who cites the type of freedom they see in Russia, Italy and Germany as one who knows these lands, loves their people, and despises their leaders, that there is more real freedom under the British flag tonight than under any dictatorship. I challenge you here tonight as a clergyman and an old soldier with the confidence of thousands of young people that we are not content to stand and let the young people of this country rot!

The audience erupted into cheers.

Then the minister did something quite priestly. He went through the ceremonial motions of handing the Leadership League over to the retired lieutenant-governor. And he did this on behalf of, and in the name of, George McCullagh.

Dr. Bruce took the microphone, and the quality of the speeches took a dive.

"I was born and brought up on one of these farms in this province, where I lived until college and professional work commenced. I never lost my love of the country and for the past twenty years have made farming part of my regular occupation," he said, referring to his horse stables on Bayview Avenue. "I can thus justly claim to be a Canadian with an intense love for my country, and I claim as well to be a Canadian who believes that Canada's membership in the British Commonwealth is of cardinal importance and unfading value. With such a background, I think you will understand why I am concerned about the future of this country."

Then he went on at length about the history of the national debt. It must have been riveting. Canadians were victims of "strangling taxes." Why was that? Because Canadians were paying for nine provinces and the federal government. What did people get for their money? Certainly not a strong army or navy. And, he reminded the crowd, Mitch Hepburn had turned down Bruce's plans for improving the housing of Toronto's poor. Mitch had also ignored Bruce's demands for tax cuts. His ideas had brought him scorn from the premier and the mayor of Toronto. He had thrown in with the Leadership League because, finally, people would listen.

Bruce might have won the crowd's attention with talk of tax cuts, but he certainly lost it when he rattled on, for a very long time, about the haggling in the 1860s over Confederation and the negotiation positions of the very many political leaders of that time. Bruce's point, which he arrived at after a five-minute verbal journey, was that the Fathers of Confederation wanted a strong central government and weak—or no—provinces.

Then he made a play for diversity. As well as British-born settlers and their descendants, "we have thousands of aliens who have sought asylum from the persecutions of their own country. They have chosen to come to us to live under the protection of the British flag and British institutions and to enjoy freedom of speech, of religious worship, and freedom of labour and enterprise within the law. We also have the descendants of a great French race, our French-Canadian compatriots, whose special rights under the B.N.A. Act this League will always respect, and, if necessary, help to preserve." Indigenous people and other non-Europeans stayed invisible to Bruce and everyone else involved in the Leadership League. So, it seems, did women.

We have on this platform tonight two men who I confidently believe history will record as having emerged at this time to help us in our great need. The first one is that modest little patriotic figure, Mr. William H. Wright, who, after many disappointments and long years of toil had the good fortune to discover a mine. His discovery resulted in the development of a whole territory, and in the birth of a town which now has a population of 20,000. He contributes to the government 20 cents out of every dollar he earns. Instead of hoarding his new-found wealth or spending it on luxuries for himself, he saw the opportunity of public service and purchased two newspapers. He did not do so to make money but to do something for Canada.

The other man is Mr. George McCullagh, whom I met for the first time at a banquet in his honour in 1936.[70] In his speech that night he amazed us all by unfolding to us his vision of rendering patriotic service to this Dominion through the medium of a great newspaper fortunately made available by Mr. Wright, who shares his vision.

Bruce had seen McCullagh in action, read his editorials and heard the radio speeches, "which have stirred this country as nothing else has in my memory."

Now Bruce held the stellar rank of chairman of the Provisional Advisory Committee for Canada.

Here's the way the *Globe and Mail* reported the wrap-up of Bruce's speech: "Against this significant background, the former lieutenant-governor of this British Province accepted in the dignified manner and eloquent language so characteristic of him the formidable trust bestowed on him by the directing head of Canada's National Newspaper."

Then Bruce introduced McCullagh as "a brave, inspired crusader and a great Canadian." The bagpipes blasted and the crowd was on its feet cheering as McCullagh got up from his chair and walked to the microphone. It was a make-or-break political moment. Opportunity was knocking. Was anyone home?

* * *

McCullagh started his speech by thanking Bruce and the other volunteers on the provisional committee, "thus showing their confidence in my immature judgment in trying to arouse my fellow-Canadians out of their lethargy and assert our right to govern. I trust over a period of time my actions will vindicate the confidence you have expressed in me.

"I am not here to entertain you but rather to give the reason and a frank discussion of how The Leadership League was created, how I believe it can become a force for good government, and I hope to infect you with some of the enthusiasm I have in the possibilities of The Leadership League." He had never thought, he said, the day would come "when I would see 10,000 people gathered together for a discussion of public affairs in which I would play a part (applause)."

Some might wonder why someone so young as himself should assume this responsibility, he said, but the answer seemed obvious: politicians who had come to power before and during the Great War had stuck around too long, and a new generation—what was left of the men who had gone overseas—had been shut out. It was time for the old generation to go. "I do represent the younger generation and I hope that I can inspire you to do something about the affairs of Canada rather than to sit back to sneer and criticize. There is a real job that can be done, and the only way we can preserve democratic principles is by the people themselves asserting their right to govern."

He was no Moses who could lead Canadians "out of the Egypt of their despair." And he was neither a fascist nor a man with ulterior motives. That out of the way, he gave a history of the Leadership League and started spelling out his answers. There were too many lawyers in Parliament and too few businessmen. (In fact, the prime minister was an academic and journalist, while the leader of the Opposition was a medical doctor, but lawyers have always been easy targets for demagogues.)

Business principles, McCullagh said, had to be applied to government or the country would get nowhere. Now McCullagh hit his stride, and his voice began to boom out. Canadians needed to be told of the stifling of "good, sound, honest business men—all too few in our public life today." He would tell them. He would go on a national speaking tour, first to the West, then to the Maritimes. Hopefully, Rawson and Bruce would come with him, and the Leadership Leaguers in western Canada would get busy drumming up crowds. It was clear

Rawson and Bruce hadn't been told about the tours. McCullagh seems to have thought it up while he spoke.

The league was now so big that it had to move out of the *Globe and Mail's* advertising department and into new offices in the Victory Building, on Richmond Street in downtown Toronto. Send your ballots there, he told the audience in the Gardens and the people listening on the radio. The more ballots that came in, the more the league would be a dominating force in Canadian politics.

McCullagh was really worked up now. He was sick of the lies that had been shouted at him, the claims that he was a fascist or a communist. He was "British to the core" and a true believer in democracy. "I know the system is expensive," he said, "but I wouldn't trade it for any other system in the world." He was no dictator. In fact, he'd stood up for rights of the Communist Party organ, the *Clarion*, even though it had printed lies about him every day. "'Parlour pinks'" were waging a relentless campaign of malignancy against William H. Wright. The little millionaire, with his war record and public service, could stand tall against the "claptrap Communist chieftains."

Looking over the crowd, he roared, "I say and I know you'll agree with me, that what this country needs is more Bill Wrights and fewer J.S. Woodsworths and Tim Bucks."

"Here, here," voices called. But this praise for the funny little mining magnate chain-smoking in a chair on the stage did not bring the crowd to its feet. McCullagh got a much better response when he talked of the need for a third party, which would certainly be formed if the two main national parties did not "quit passing the buck to each other." The crowd became even more fired up when he accused Mackenzie King of letting Britain down during the Munich Crisis the previous fall. "Let me say," he said, "God help this Canada of ours if England fails and falls in Europe!"

There was no heckling, but McCullagh failed to rock the hall. Even the *Globe and Mail's* fawning, anonymous reporter had to admit the crowd's outbursts were limited to polite applause and a smattering of foot-stomping when McCullagh mentioned Conservative heroes like Sir John A. Macdonald. The hall was silent when McCullagh talked of "the object lesson" of Hitler in Czechoslovakia.

Then it was over. Frederick Banting, the most famous person in the hall, never rose to speak. Neither did Red Baron–killer Roy Brown. The crowd filed out, unsatisfied.

* * *

The *Globe and Mail* covered the rally as though it was one of the greatest events in Canada's history. The Toronto *Star* didn't print a word.[71]

The *Globe and Mail* kept up its Leadership League coverage, publishing stories over the next few days about the farm debt crisis on the Prairies, and printing pithy quotes from people like Oliver Cromwell, who'd sent Charles I to the block in 1649. Senior reporters wrote about government waste, while others described the league's big new offices at 80 Richmond Street. There were suites for Reverend Rawson, Dr. Bruce and F.S.B. Howard, the general manager. They had a secretary to handle all those letters and ballots. Reporters wrote what their publisher wanted to read: "Late yesterday, League officials reported League activity at a higher level than ever, organization plans have been stimulated in many quarters as a result of the enthusiasm created by Wednesday's mass meeting." The league's secretary was getting "numberless calls" from people asking for organizational help.[72]

But nothing was happening in the heartland. The *Globe and Mail* had to scrape hard to find signs of life. All it could come up with were meetings in what was then the farm country of Scarborough, the little town of Burlington, and the one-store hamlet of Kinmount, up in the woods of Haliburton. The Leadership League, with no real platform and no serious leadership, was dying fast. McCullagh, though he was no politician, was not a stupid man, and he knew what was happening. He had put the word out to the people of Canada and to his rich friends that the league needed money. In return, he got $300. The whole exercise had cost more than $100,000 in printing, radio airtime and advertising, plus whatever the *Globe and Mail* had paid for staff writers and newsprint.

* * *

McCullagh's emotional and mental health, which had been on a high during his radio campaign, began sinking day after day as the Leadership League's failure became more obvious. Two weeks after the Maple Leaf Gardens rally, McCullagh was in Ottawa, testifying before the House of Commons's committee on radio and being bullied by King. The prime minister knew the *Globe and Mail* and McCullagh had been weakened by the league's failure. He got up in the House of Commons to denounce reports by one of the *Globe and Mail*'s Ottawa reporters, and then, in a late-night private meeting, twisted McCullagh's arm to fire the journalist. King switched the conversation to foreign policy, and made it clear to McCullagh that the young publisher simply didn't understand *realpolitik*: "I told him that the important thing was to have Canada kept united so that in the event of action being necessary, it could be taken effectively. That it would only help the enemy meanwhile to have a condition stirred up here in advance that would give the enemy reason to believe the Government could not bring the country in behind it, should it decide to do so. He seemed to see this for the first time. The truth is he is far too inexperienced...I had repeated what Laurier had said about 'when England was at war, Canada was at war and liable to be attacked.'...I never saw a more shilly-shally sort of responsibility than McCullagh and entourage seem to have."[73]

McCullagh and the CBC's management settled their differences and issued a press release that said exactly nothing about whatever deal they made.[74] A week later, McCullagh couldn't function at all, so he was packed onto a plane and flown to a sanitorium in California to recover from his breakdown out of the sight of Toronto gossips and his political enemies. This was the first time his mental health had deteriorated to the point where he had to be institutionalized. McCullagh's mood swings were getting worse, from the highs of the fall of 1935 to the lows of the early spring of 1939. McCullagh was still young, strong and capable of bouncing back. And he needed to recover. McCullagh would face devastating personal news within months, which would arrive at the same time as one of his greatest personal triumphs. And that was before war broke out at the end of the summer.

McCullagh's political ambitions ended, at least temporarily, when he had his April breakdown. The Leadership League was finally put out of its misery at the beginning of July, when there were no politicians in Parliament to mock its demise, and the country was distracted by the threat of war. The Toronto *Star* reported on the league's death, running the story on page three, under a picture of Rosie the Rogue Elephant, who'd attacked circus workers four times that year.

11

ARCHWORTH

McCullagh's stable had the best horses he could find. Many, of course, were bred by Wright at Brookedale in Barrie. McCullagh, who spent the then-fantastic sum of $30,000 collecting them, raced them throughout southern Ontario and showed them at fall fairs all over the province.[1] William Wright's stable bred King's Plate–winning thoroughbreds even before he'd bought the breeding operation, but it had also produced first-rate jumpers, hunters and standardbreds. In the summer of 1937, as McCullagh was still peddling the idea of ending party politics in Ontario, his horse Torqui won the feature stake at the Sutton Show. The *Globe and Mail's* equestrian sports reporter—very much a new position after the departure of the Jaffrays—described Torqui as a "gallant little brown mare" ridden by "Mrs. Ross Taylor." McCullagh was on the same horse circuit as some of Canada's richest, most powerful old-money bluebloods. Sutton might be an out-of-the-way town north of Toronto, but its show pulled in horses owned by some of Canada's richest people. In the jump-off, Torqui beat out a horse from the stables of the rich and powerful Sifton family.[2]

George McCullagh and his wife packed William Wright along with them when they went on the circuit. In 1938, the three of them went to Montreal for its annual horse show and stayed at the Ritz Carleton, though it's likely Wright had his own room.[3] In their early years, the McCullaghs stuck with show horses. Just Watch Me, ridden by Tommy Fields Jr., won the Handy Performance Class at the Toronto Horse Show in the spring of 1937, and the following fall placed second in show-jumping competitions in St. Catharines.[4]

All of this was reported in Canada's big newspapers. Canadians of the 1930s were still farmers or just a generation or two removed from the land. Horses were quite common on city streets, and Canadians were huge fans of equestrian events. Racing drew recreational and hard-core gamblers, but big crowds turned out for horse shows and jumping events where wagers were rare. The right kind of people sat in the expensive seats at these shows, and anyone with social aspirations showed up to be seen.

McCullagh pushed the horses as hard as he drove the people in his life. Glen Avon, a show jumper, worked so hard to win the 1938 Hunter Stake show-jumping competition at the Canadian National Exhibition that it dropped dead a few seconds after it left the field. Tommy Fields Sr., the groom who rode Glen Avon, said, "he wasn't an experienced horse. He broke it trying."[5] Archworth, McCullagh's best bet for the 1939 King's Plate, was also worked to the edge of death. McCullagh bought the horse from Wright for $500, and was determined to show he knew a bargain.[6] The rest of the racing industry had thought Archworth had no future. When McCullagh paid Wright $1,700 for Archworth's brother Archline (who was rated a much better horse), it made the papers. And, though $1,700 was more than many people made in a year, the price was considered low.[7]

But it would be the less expensive sibling that would make history. McCullagh's trainer, Mark Cowell, put Archworth through a regimen that was so brutal it drew attention from Ontario's tight little racing community. Even some newspaper reporters were shocked by the intensity of Archworth's workouts. Some claimed the horse was "over-trained" and would be a poor racer. They were wrong.[8]

In the fall of 1938, as McCullagh was mapping out his radio strategy, Archworth qualified to compete in "Mrs. Orpen's Cup and Saucer," making the cut out of seventy-seven horses from across the country.[9] That race, run in front of a crowd of ten thousand people, earned McCullagh a $6,100 purse, a very good return on investment. Writers described Archworth as "rangy and long-striding," and he easily beat the competition. Jockey Denny Birley quickly got Archworth clear of the gate and away from the knot of horses that formed up on the first turn. In the back stretch, Archworth was ahead by half a length. Jelwell, the three-to-five race favourite, was way back. Then Archworth opened a wider lead, and by the time he crossed the finish line, the race wasn't close. Phyllis McCullagh came forward to collect the golden trophy from Isabella Orpen, whose husband, Abe, had founded the Long Branch racetrack.[10]

Then Archworth won the Clarendon Stakes, making him one of the most-watched two-year-olds in Canada and the leading money-winner of that season. Archworth built a reputation among the betting crowd. He was a contender, according to Doug Eppes, the *Globe and Mail*'s horseracing writer, though he wasn't the overwhelming favour-ite for the 1939 King's Plate.[11] That's why McCullagh had his trainers work Archworth to exhaustion.

It was important for McCullagh to win the 80th King's Plate. For the first time, the King would be there to present the fifty guineas and $10,000 in cash—about $120,000 in today's money, but priceless in prestige and status, as well as future stud fees—to the winner. Because of the late spring, this would be a short training season, and in at least one trial, Archworth disappointed McCullagh and the people who followed racing. Some observers believed Archworth had faded since the autumn.

It's hard for modern Canadians and Americans to understand the importance of the 1939 royal tour. We're used to royalty travelling all over the world. If anything, Britain's (and Canada's) royal family is overexposed. Edward VII, George V and Edward VIII had travelled through Canada, and the troubled Edward VIII owned a ranch in Alberta that he'd bought when he was Prince of Wales. But these kings had visited long before they were on the throne. George VI was the first reigning monarch to visit Canada. And he, along with Queen Elizabeth, made the trip soon after Edward VIII had abdicated to marry Wallis Simpson. The monarchy was very much in the news, and people were still divided on the question of fair treatment for the now-exiled Duke of Windsor and his new wife.

In the fall of 1938, the world had been on the brink of war over Nazi expansion into Czechoslovakia. Britain's government was still trying to appease Hitler, but Prime Minister Neville Chamberlain also needed to strengthen support among his country's allies, just in case war came. The royal visit would firm up Canada's pro-Britain faction, which included McCullagh and his friends, and be a royal pep talk for Canadian nationalists, who counted Mackenzie King and his top advisors as members of the clique. The tour would take the King and Queen from Quebec City to Vancouver by train. Then they'd cross to the United States to try to win support among the American public and the Roosevelt administration, which would be asked to finance the war and supply the Allies with weapons. It was one of the most important royal tours in modern history. The British were desperate for it to succeed. In Canada and the United States, it was the biggest news story of the year, until war came that summer. It was also the biggest social event in Canada in the first half of the twentieth century, and everyone with financial and political clout wanted to be seen with Their Majesties.

The King and Queen arrived in Quebec City on May 17 on the Canadian Pacific ship RMS *Empress of Australia*. Three days later, they were in Ottawa, laying the cornerstone for the Supreme Court of Canada building and unveiling the new national war memorial. Mackenzie King, more of a social climber than a nationalist, clung to the King through the entire trip. The provincial premiers also glommed onto Their Majesties at every opportunity.

On the same Victoria Day weekend that the King was in Ottawa, George McCullagh got terrible news: his mother was dying of pneumonia.

McCullagh hurried back to London. Things were grim in his parents' house on Base Line Road. McCullagh's mother, who was only fifty-nine years old, had just a few hours to live. George stayed with her as the hours counted down to the King's Plate. On the morning of the race—Monday, May 22—Anne McCullagh told her son to go back to Toronto. He could not miss the King's Plate, especially since she expected Archworth to win. So George rushed back to the city, arriving in Toronto just as the race was about to begin.

The King and Queen arrived by limousine at the racetrack gate, near Queen Street and Woodbine Avenue. They transferred to a carriage, accompanied by footmen. McCullagh, late for their arrival, rushed from the train station to Woodbine. He hadn't brought formal wear with him to London, and there was no time to hunt some down. He did manage to find William Wright, and the two men watched the race together.

George vi, King of the United Kingdom of Great Britain and Northern Ireland and Emperor of India, stepped from the landau and raised his top hat to the crowd of fifty thousand. The Queen followed dressed all in blue, with a silver fox stole. In this most British of cities, the crowd was electrified. A military band struck up "God Save the King." The crowd followed with three rousing cheers while the King and Queen made their way to the royal box. People watched, enthralled. Those in the cheaper seats and standing on the field used periscopes to see the royal couple, neither of whom were very tall.

George VI and Elizabeth were in their element. The King might be a nervous, shy man, but he knew horses. He had to make small talk with Mackenzie King and Mitch Hepburn, but his eye was on the thoroughbreds that were paraded along the track. This was the first year that four-year-olds were not allowed to run in the King's Plate. (The other rules: the horses had to be foaled in Ontario and never raced outside Canada.)

The King spotted Archworth in the parade before the race and asked Hepburn about the horse's owner. The King had a good eye: this was a fine horse, and this was Archworth's greatest day. It's almost as though the horse knew how much this race meant to his owner. Archworth was edgy in the starting gate, which was not unexpected: he had a reputation as a hard horse to handle, and he had spent a lot of time in the paddock.

Archworth left the starting gate like a rocket, cleared the cluster of horses and got ahead of all of them. Within a few seconds, he was in front by two and a half lengths. He never lost that lead. He stretched it to five lengths by the half-mile point. In the front stretch, he lengthened the lead to ten lengths ahead of Sea General and Sky Runner. Archworth ran the mile and one furlong—a long distance in Canadian racing—in a respectable time of 1:54:20 It was about three seconds short of the track record, but more than enough to win this race. The King and Queen watched the entire race with binoculars, never taking their eyes off Archworth.

Archworth's jockey, Denny Birley, took his time getting back to the winner's enclosure. Then horse was calm, even though thousands cheered him and photographers' flashes went off near his eyes.

The King and Queen walked across the field to the steward's stand to present the gold cup and the purple and gold bag that held the prize money. A band played a happy martial air. McCullagh and Wright bickered, with the publisher insisting Archworth's breeder should collect the prize money.

McCullagh's horse Archworth won the King's Plate during the 1939 tour. McCullagh left the bedside of his dying mother to collect the prize from King George VI and Queen Elizabeth.
(CITY OF TORONTO ARCHIVES, FONDS 1257, SERIES 1057, ITEM 3536)

McCullagh walked up the carpeted stairs, nodded to the King and bowed low over the Queen's outstretched hand. People hurried across the infield to get a look. Some of the observers wore formal wear and clutched their top hats in their hands as they ran to get a good view.

The King said to McCullagh: "I congratulate you. You have a great thoroughbred there. Your horse is a real champion. He was never extended." He asked about Archworth's breeding, the cost of the horse and his racing history. The King laughed when McCullagh told him Archworth had cost a mere $500. McCullagh told the King that the sire was Worthmore and the dam Archipelago, from William Wright's stable.

The Queen added: "Never have I seen a horse go out and take such a long lead and hold it." Someone, probably Hepburn, had told the Queen that McCullagh's mother was very sick. She said she hoped

Anne McCullagh recovered, and, later that day, sent a personal message to the McCullagh home in London saying she prayed for a speedy recovery.

The King lifted the gold cup with his left hand and passed it to McCullagh. He bowed. Then the King picked up the bag full of guineas with his right hand and passed it to McCullagh, who bowed again. The two men shook hands again. Photographers and movie projectionists surrounded McCullagh as he walked away with the trophy in his left hand and his prize bag under his arm. The red carpet was rolled onto the track, the landau came back, and the royal couple left. The man whose horse came second in the King's Plate looked at McCullagh's travelling clothes and said sarcastically, "Nice suit." McCullagh answered, "You've got the suit and I've got the horse."[12]

Afterward, McCullagh praised William H. Wright, who had bred Archworth and whose stable was credited with the win. "It's a great day for me," said the thirty-four-year-old publisher, "but I am only the stuffed shirt who bought him for $500. My thrill is nothing at all compared to the joy in Bill Wright's heart. It's been a lifelong dream. When he came to this country from England he used to watch the races at Woodbine from a knothole in the fence. Standing there, he vowed that if he ever struck it rich, he would try to breed a winner of the Plate. The dream came true today. All the credit goes to Bill, to trainer Mark Cowell, and to jockey Denny Birley."[13]

Mackenzie King was disgusted by Archworth's win. So far, the royal tour had gone swimmingly—fawning journalists would craft it into one of Canada's greatest moments, an idyll in the last spring of peace—but here was McCullagh stealing the show. Evildoers had to be at work. The race must have been fixed. "I confess that when I heard that it was McCullagh's horse that won the King's Plate," King wrote, "I could not help feeling financial circumstances has accounted for it. Both Arnold [Heeney, King's principal secretary] and I had a feeling as though something had been done to ensure McCullagh winning."[14]

Despite the Queen's good wishes, Anne McCullagh did not recover. On May 25, three days after the King's Plate, she lost her fight with pneumonia. All four children and her husband were with her at the end. The newspaper death notice mentioned her four daughters and son by name. Her husband was also listed as one of the people Anne McCullagh left behind, but the obituary was more about her famous son than about the woman who died.

The *Globe and Mail* covered the death of George McCullagh's mother as though the sovereign had died. She got front-page treatment, and her famous son was comforted with a *Globe and Mail* editorial that noted "the tie was even greater than usually binds an affectionate and solicited parent and devoted son. Through all his life, Mr. McCullagh's mother has been his inspiring influence, advising him and encouraging him on to those accomplishments for which she recognized his talents."[15] The funeral, in Toronto, drew some of the most important people in Canada. Three former lieutenant-governors paid their respects, including the immortal Sir William Mulock. Dr. Bruce, still head of the Leadership League, wrote to former prime minister Sir Arthur Meighen to remind him to attend.[16] McCullagh was gradually morphing from a Hepburn Liberal into a Conservative, and this was no time for a snub from the latter party's senior statesman.

Bishop Renison conducted the service for the woman named in the program as "Mrs. George Henry McCullagh." The big story on the front page of the *Globe and Mail* described the service, which drew three hundred people—almost none of whom had ever met the deceased—as subdued and solemn. There was no eulogy, no singing, just the sound of an organ being played softly at the back of the chapel in a funeral home near the corner of Yonge Street and St. Clair Avenue. This was George McCullagh's show, and his father stood by as Anne McCullagh was taken to Mount Pleasant Cemetery. In any other family, the funeral would have been in London, where Anne's family and friends lived. Instead, the interment of Anne McCullagh bears a striking similarity to the funeral of a mafia don: more about the recognition of the power of the living than the memory of the dead.

Archworth's jockey was there.[17] So were the senior editors of the *Globe and Mail* and as many staff journalists as could be spared. Holy Joe Atkinson was near the front, sitting with his son and heir, Joe Jr., along with Charles Knowles, president of the Toronto *Telegram.* There were politicians in the crowd, including George Drew and representatives from the federal Conservative Party. Toronto's chief of police was among the mourners, as were several members of the city council. Bishop Renison read from scripture, and did not give a sermon. He also conducted the graveside service of committal. Here, family did dominate the proceedings, but, among the pallbearers was a strange little man chain-smoking cigarettes: William H. Wright.

As for Archworth, he won that year's Breeders' Stakes and Prince of Wales Stakes, but these would not make up Canada's Triple Crown until 1959. His next season was lacklustre, and as a five-year-old, he managed just one important win and two places. He retired to Wright's farm in Barrie with a respectable record of fifteen wins in forty-seven starts, and \$31,234 in prize money.[18] But on that May day, as McCullagh juggled his exaltation over Archworth's victory against the terror of the threat of losing his mother, the high-strung, long-legged horse earned all of his keep.[19]

12

GEORGE McCULLAGH AT WAR

McCullagh officially buried the putrefying corpse of the Leadership League in the heat of July 1939, just before leaving with Phyllis for New York and a crossing to England on the *Mauretania*.[1] He had no idea that Canada would be at war in two months. Canadians believed events overseas were moving fast, and that the dictatorships of Europe could drag the world into another global conflict. But there had been other trips to the brink, including the previous autumn, when Hitler had snatched Czechoslovakia, and there'd always been a deal. The independence of Poland was just another line in the sand.

When Hitler unleashed his army on the Poles and war came, George McCullagh and his Toronto Clique friends in the city's financial and sports elites had no doubts that Canada had to give as much support to Britain as possible. This was an opinion that was not shared across the country and on Parliament Hill. There's a myth that Canada came together against the common enemy of fascism. Reality

238 * BIG MEN FEAR ME

was much more complicated, and there were times when Canada's lack of unity risked knocking the country out of the war.

William Lyon Mackenzie King, who had dodged the First World War by moving to the United States to do public relations work for John D. Rockefeller Jr., was horrified with the idea of sending tens of thousands of Canadians to their deaths in trenches. And that was the kind of war most people expected: all the horrors of the last war, along with massive bomber attacks on cities, more effective poison gases, and, people like Frederick Banting believed, germ warfare.

Only a couple of MPs voted against the war resolution tabled in the House of Commons on September 7, but many Canadians were not willing to engage in a total war against Hitler. The Left was opposed to the war, though this changed after Hitler invaded the Soviet Union in June 1941. People on the Right were opposed as well, including many of Quebec's politicians and media leaders.

In the week between Britain's war declaration and Canada's, McCullagh wired King, telling the prime minister he was ready to visit Ottawa "at a moment's notice" to discuss the ways that McCullagh could influence public opinion.[2] McCullagh made a quick trip to London in the second week of the war to see Beaverbrook and Brendan Bracken, his news publisher friends. Both men were in key positions of power. Beaverbrook, who had headed Britain's successful anti-German propaganda campaign in the First World War, took charge of aircraft production in this one, while still running his newspapers. Bracken, the nerdy Irish founder of the *Financial Times*, engineered Churchill's takeover of the leadership of the Tory party in May 1940, and was rewarded with Beaverbrook's old job of minister of information. At the same time, Bracken became Churchill's right-hand man. When he spoke, it was with the authority of 10 Downing Street.

Both Beaverbrook and Bracken knew of McCullagh's struggles with depression. They almost certainly heard, through the Bassett family connection with Beaverbrook, that McCullagh had recently spent time in Manhattan being treated for the breakdown he suffered after the collapse of the Leadership League and the death of his mother. Still, McCullagh's connection to Bracken and his real friendship with Beaverbrook gave the Canadian publisher access to powerful British military and financial leaders who would otherwise have been out of reach to a Toronto-based Canadian, especially considering Churchill's contempt for Mackenzie King.

When he got back to Canada, McCullagh had a lot of advice for the prime minister, but now, after years of open and passive-aggressive fighting, King was no longer taking all his calls.[3] So McCullagh mobilized the *Globe and Mail* for war, started sharpening his own sword, and headed for Ottawa, uninvited. King finally opened his door to McCullagh, after he found a use for the thirty-four-year-old publisher: knifing Ian Mackenzie, Canada's defence minister. King wanted to replace Mackenzie with Norman Rogers, who had more fighting spirit. This would be an act of utter ingratitude and treachery by both men: Mackenzie had organized McCullagh's victory parties after he'd bought the newspapers, worked with McCullagh on the Oshawa strike, and taken the heat for King in the recent scandal over the purchase of Bren guns. Now, McCullagh was to push Mackenzie out of his job and, quite likely, his place in Canadian history.

They had a little chat, and King put his new stooge to work. "Past differences were past," King told his diary. "We went on to speak of it being pleasanter to be lending support to the government than to be 'manufacturing prejudice'. I thought that was a pretty significant admission of the role the *Globe* has been playing for some time past."[4]

The defence minister was shocked when the publisher of the *Globe and Mail* told him he was out. A promise of good publicity didn't soften the blow, especially since Charles "Chubby" Power, a notorious alcoholic, was to stay on as minister in charge of Canada's air force.[5] At least McCullagh kept the part of the bargain where he promised Mackenzie good press. By the third week of September, McCullagh had been on the phone to friends at the *Financial Post*, the *Winnipeg Free Press*, and *Maclean's* magazine to polish whatever was left of Mackenzie's reputation. Within days of this hatchet work, McCullagh realized he was being criticized by politicians and media people for betraying a friend. He asked King to set the record straight, but King edited his own memory to recast McCullagh as the villain. "Busy bodies usually get themselves in trouble," the prime minister told his diary.[6]

After the deed was done, McCullagh told King he wanted to be much more involved in the war effort. If King would let him, he'd leave the *Globe and Mail* to come to Ottawa to make propaganda broadcasts that would boost Canadian morale and bring the United States into the war. "He [McCullagh] said there were very few men who had a gift for radio speaking," King told his diary. "Roosevelt was one. That he, himself, was thought next to Roosevelt. He said he had received 80,000 letters at the time of his previous broadcast, all praising his work." None of this bragging helped McCullagh's case. King was determined to make sure that plan died fast. The prime minister had a serious fear of the emergence of a "Canadian Goebbels," a sociopath who was willing distort the truth and tell outright lies to accumulate power. It was only five months since the *Marching on to What?* broadcasts and the Leadership League. If McCullagh, in the mistaken belief that war had created a blank slate, had forgotten that spring's viciousness, his portly "friend" in Ottawa certainly had not.

McCullagh was sure that he had "tremendous influence" over young people. He was a young man himself, had made millions of dollars, won a powerful job, had a pretty wife and cute small children. McCullagh wanted to give back, and so he asked the prime minister if he could go overseas to work on propaganda to raise the morale of Canadian troops. King said there was no need for that. He could do enough by publishing and editing the *Globe and Mail*, and he could make broadcasts whenever he wanted.[7] They would, of course, be subject to censorship.

(This was definitely a gentle rejection of McCullagh. Three weeks later, King was on the phone to Joe Atkinson, asking the *Star* publisher to lend him Gregory Clark, the paper's best columnist, to help the prime minister write radio speeches. Atkinson agreed, as long as Clark had nothing to do with any of McCullagh's wartime radio shows.[8])

* * *

For a month at least, Canada's political and English-language media elites were united in the face of a common enemy.[9] The truce would not last much longer than that. As the leaves fell in October, so did the scales fall from McCullagh's eyes.

In late October, McCullagh told King that he was broadcasting later that week. The recording, on vinyl, had already been flown to England, where, supposedly, the British public was eager to be exposed to the wisdom of a thirty-four-year-old Canadian wunderkind. It was the first of a series of hour-long talks. "He was sure I would like them," King noted, with obvious skepticism.[10] When McCullagh went on the radio in November with the first of his wartime lecture-sermons, King was repelled. "I confess I felt incensed at his attack on the German people," King wrote. "It was a poor broadcast, school boy style of thing, evidently written for him by the one who writes his editorials. Certain to give rise to more complaints against the C.B.C."[11] McCullagh did call Germans "a murderous, war-mongering tribe" who were easily conned by tyrants. But at the same time, McCullagh condemned Hitler's anti-Semitism and the apparatus of the Nazi police state in clear, accurate and unequivocal words, and with far more force than King had ever had the courage to use.[12]

Nine days later, just after making a second anti-Nazi radio speech, McCullagh was in Ottawa for a dinner at the Belgian embassy, along with several cabinet ministers, senators, senior public servants and top-tier diplomats. Belgium was an important ally, and everyone expected this war's trench line to run through that country. As McCullagh ate, the leader of the Co-operative Commonwealth Federation complained to King about McCullagh's speeches. King quietly passed the gripes on to his secretary to take to the chairman of the board of the CBC, who had ultimate control over radio censorship.[13] King had shivved McCullagh again.

* * *

McCullagh was just thirty-four when the war broke out. He was the right age to be an officer, though he lacked the university degree or the level of militia training that would have fast-tracked him to a commission.[14] He believed he could not shirk what he saw was his duty. Friends like Conn Smythe, who McCullagh knew through horse racing and Maple Leaf Gardens, where McCullagh was on the board of directors, were signing up. William Wright had joined during the First World War, even though he was in his forties. So, despite the wrenching changes that were about to hit his paper, McCullagh, who was on a fast upswing in his mental health cycle, started to get his affairs in order and enlist. He'd join the air force, of course. It was the most glamorous arm of the services.

While McCullagh made plans to enlist, the federal government was rolling out a wartime censorship system that was partially based on the oppressive media control of the First World War, but had been tweaked to make it more palatable to journalists. King's government appointed the chief public relations officer of the Canadian National Railway, Walter Thompson, to run it. He'd made a lot of friends in the media on the boozy Royal Train journey across Canada and was the kind of back-slapping man who could connect with most of the journalists of his day.

This is where the architects of the system were clever: they didn't hire heavies to intimidate the press. Instead, they anointed senior, popular, respected journalists to police their former colleagues. Canadian media was, and still is, very respectful and deferential to

George McCullagh in his Royal Canadian Air Force uniform, Toronto, 1941.
The physical and emotional strain of military service cause McCullagh to
be invalided out of the air force. (CITY OF TORONTO ARCHIVES, FONDS 1257,
SERIES 1057, ITEM 3532)

those in the top tier of journalism. And it tends to be an industry of
social climbers.

Warren Baldwin, one of the Parliament Hill press censors, wrote
for the *Globe and Mail*'s Parliament Hill bureau before the war. More
importantly, he had worked directly with McCullagh as one of the
Leadership League's ghostwriters. Thompson, the chief censor,
assigned Baldwin the job of handling McCullagh's political writing.[15]
Bert Perry, the Toronto censor, was one of the city's best sports writers,
so McCullagh knew his work.

Press censors did not vet stories before they went into the papers.
Instead, with the power of the War Measures Act to back them up,
they sent out lists of rules that had to be followed. If journalists had
doubts, they could ask the censors for advice. Anything passed by the

censors was immune from prosecution, even if the journalist and the censors had let out information that helped the enemy.

At first, the *Globe and Mail* supported Thompson and the censorship system—although McCullagh and some other publishers did object to the hiring of Leonard Brockington, McCullagh's old enemy at the CBC, to lead the Bureau of Public Information, which was the government's propaganda arm.[16] King, already showing signs of stress, lashed out at that criticism, and relished the idea of censoring the *Globe and Mail*. "I have never had any help from the *Globe* worth mentioning, and by McCullagh, had his bitter opposition most of the way. Public opinion has now forced them to support me and the government they were doing their utmost to destroy," he told his diary. "I have had to wait a long time for this but it is an immense satisfaction to have this vindication of my whole attitude come at last. Of course, I am not sure that what is being professed today will not be discounted tomorrow...McCullagh took it for granted that different newspapers could do pretty much as they pleased in creating opinion which could favour or destroy a man."[17]

* * *

Canada's military couldn't do anything about the German invasion of Poland, since the country had no soldiers overseas, and our allies, France and England, didn't do much to slow the Nazis as they moved on Warsaw.[18] The real fighting was expected much later in the fall, or even in the spring of 1940, once Hitler was finished in the east.

Domestically, the country was going through wrenching changes as young men and women rushed to enlist, militia units were called up, factories were retooled and hiring, and ships were assembling in Halifax for convoys. Quebec went straight into an election and voters tossed out Maurice Duplessis, replacing him with a Liberal nonentity who was less likely to fight with Ottawa. (Duplessis's supporters, with good reason, blamed the CBC's radio censors for their defeat.)

The *Globe and Mail* supported the press and radio censors' decisions in that election, and even advocated for the suppression of US journalists who worked in Canada when publications like the *Saturday Evening Post* criticized the quality of the Canadian war effort.[19]

At the same time he wanted the *Post* banned at the border, McCullagh was receiving military secrets through back channels. In late November 1939, McCullagh's best friend, George Drew, who was now leader of the Ontario Tories and who had a superb network of military sources, was feeding the publisher information about Mackenzie King's lack of enthusiasm for the war. Early in the war, McCullagh and Drew were forming a two-man team that would seriously shake King's confidence, and, for a time, his grip on power.[20]

Rather than send many thousands of men overseas to be slaughtered in the trenches, King wanted Canada to fight with its wallet. Canada gave $1 billion directly to Britain. Officials in Ottawa organized a string of pilot training bases, often on land seized from First Nations, and hoped this contribution could offset Canada's stingy troop deployments. Drew warned McCullagh that King would ditch the training plan as soon as hostilities were over. He told the young publisher that American and many Canadian military thinkers believed Canada was doing a poor job calling up troops and organizing its first army units to be sent overseas. All of this was reflected in the *Globe and Mail's* news columns and editorials.

Though its newsroom was dominated by McCullagh's flunkies, the *Globe and Mail* found room to employ some of the toughest, most independent-minded journalists in Canada. Judith Robinson was not the kind of columnist to roll over for old-boy censors. Her Ottawa colleagues might be willing to defer to people like Warren Baldwin, but she certainly would not.[21] Robinson's first issue was the government's treatment of soldiers' dependents. She thought women and young children left behind deserved much more support than the government was willing to give. At first, the Toronto censors defended

Robinson's right to publish her opinion. That changed in early December 1939 when she submitted a column to the censors containing a paragraph with the words "Canadian boys are deserting from their units" and mentioning in passing that troops were "leaving for overseas." She had leaked the top-secret news of the departure of Canada's first contingent. These two sentences were cut. She then put them in the lead paragraph of the column that ran the next day. The censors saw them in the first edition, called the *Globe and Mail* newsroom, and had those words removed from the next edition before it went to press. This left Robinson and the censors ready for a fight, which came when she defended a Communist convicted and jailed under the War Measures Act. She had, one of the censors wrote, "made an extreme attack on constituted authority."[22]

Despite the skirmishes between Robinson and the censors, the *Globe and* Mail seemed to, at least philosophically, support the idea of wartime press censorship. In its December 11, 1939, editorial, "Newspapers and the War," the paper argued: "While the right to criticize is one of democracy's priceless privileges, self-imposed censorship in the name of patriotism is also a priceless privilege obtainable only in a democracy. Its free exercise is a more valuable demonstration than grudging concession to the censor's rules." The *Globe and Mail* believed Canada's newspapers should give the system a chance.[23] The next day, the paper changed its position, saying Canadian censorship rules had been found "stupid and irksome by journalists in Toronto and Ottawa, who have been forestalled by absurd and anomalous decisions. One cynic has defined a censor as a person who suppresses in Canada what the enemy already knows." Editors had been told overnight that material from a *New York Times* story on the Commonwealth Air Training Program could not be reprinted in the *Globe and Mail*. The ruling seemed absurd. Surely the Nazis read the *Times*. Canadians, the *Globe and Mail*'s editorial writers said, would not "stand for anything that smacks of the Gestapo in regard to national affairs and the conduct of the Dominion Government. What Canada expects is a military rather than a political censorship."[24]

But the next day, political columnist J.V. McAvee wrote under the column heading "Press Censorship in Capable Hands" that the censorship in the First World War had been much more oppressive and, "generally speaking, the censorship both here and in Great Britain, has one plain and necessary duty." McAvee argued that investigative journalism that helped improve the war effort should be tolerated, but "critics of avowed Communist tendencies can be viewed by the censors with less tolerance. The man who is against the prosecution of the war and tries to discourage recruitment is plainly in a different class from the man who favors the prosecution of the war and attacks what he considers government delays or blunders and indifference to the comfort and security of the soldiers."[25] In another piece, the *Globe and Mail* supported the federal government's prosecution of eight people in Montreal charged under the War Measures Act for distributing anti-war leaflets.[26]

These shifts in the paper's policies could have reflected McCullagh's own mood swings, the fact that McCullagh had been laid low by pneumonia for several weeks that fall, or they might have been generated by internal conflicts at the paper. But, at the very least, they show no one was really in charge. And things were about to get worse. It's hard to run a one-man shop when the man in charge is struggling to get out the door.

* * *

At the *Globe and Mail* newsroom, McCullagh was trying to deal with a staff screw-up that—if it ever got out to the *Star* or the *Telegram* or one of the scandal sheets like *Hush*—would have been a grotesque embarrassment to the publisher and the newspaper.

Lawrence Mason, a grandson of the man who had been mayor of Chicago during the Great Fire of 1871, was the *Globe and Mail*'s drama and music critic. Mason is one of the mid-century journalists who

puts the lie to the myth that early Canadian reporters were all unedu-
cated hacks. He had studied at Harvard and then at Yale, where he'd
earned his PhD in English literature. Mason did some scholarly editing before joining the *Globe* twelve years before McCullagh bought the
paper, had survived the merger, and was a *Globe and Mail* lifer. His
work appeared on Saturdays, taking up about a page under a standing
headline "Music in the Home—Concert—The Drama." Mason was one
of the most respected critics in North America, a writer whose work
generated thousands of subscribers to the paper. McCullagh was
proud to employ someone who was seen to be a scholar, an advocate
for Canadian artists, and who was so respected for being scrupulously
fair in his reviews.

Mason had just finished writing his page in December 1939 and
was settling into an evening in his apartment when he dropped dead.
McCullagh told senior editor Arthur Laidlaw to handle the funeral
arrangements and look after Mason's brother, who was coming in from
Chicago. Mason's funeral drew the elite of Toronto's newspaper
world—all the senior editors of the *Globe and Mail* and its competitors, including Holy Joe Atkinson. McCullagh's big floral wreath
dominated the altar. The service was lovely and went off without any
problems. But things went downhill after that.

Mason had asked to be cremated. That was unusual in Toronto in
those years, but the city did have a crematorium, and the critic was
properly disposed of. But Mason's brother choked on the cost of the
urn. He insisted he could get a much better one, at a more reasonable
price, in Chicago. The crematorium staff put the mortal remains of
Canada's best music and theatre critic into a small cardboard container, which was then dropped into a shoebox. Laidlaw took the
living Mason brother to Union Station and put him on the train. An
hour later, Laidlaw got a call from the surviving Mason. He'd lost his
brother. The shoebox containing the ashes of Lawrence Mason was
missing, probably lost somewhere in the Toronto train station. Laidlaw

took a cab back to Union Station. He searched the place and couldn't find the shoebox.

"There was nothing for it but to tell McCullagh," Laidlaw later told *Globe and Mail* editor Richard Doyle, who was working on a history of the paper. "Anyone who says McCullagh didn't have a temper should have seen him that day. He was appalled at what had befallen such a nice man and furious over what might happen if the story came out. 'I can see what the headline in *Hush* will say,' he shouted. 'You know what it will say, Laidlaw? It will say GLOBE CRITIC LOST IN A SHOE BOX! That's what it will say. And you will be out on the street, that's where you'll be!'"

Laidlaw fretted for several days, wondering if he would be tossed out of the *Globe and Mail*, but the editor was lucky: a railway porter had found the shoebox and turned it in to the station's baggage department, where it was retrieved by Laidlaw. He didn't know what to do with the box, so he put it in a locker at the station. No one was sure whether the critic could be mailed to the United States. It took nearly two weeks for Mason's brother to come back from Chicago to pick up the ashes, so each day Laidlaw or someone on his staff went down to the station to check that the shoebox was still there and put another dime in the locker.[27]

* * *

In December, McCullagh was back in Ottawa. King met McCullagh after a long cabinet meeting where ministers discussed the imminent sailing of the first Canadian contingent (whose departure had been leaked by Judith Robinson, to the horror of the military and the censors). King didn't mention McCullagh's latest series of speeches or the prime minister's involvement in having them investigated by the radio censors. McCullagh, who was very excited and chatty, had news: he planned to join the air force. For two years, he had been honorary wing commander of the Toronto-based 110th Squadron. McCullagh insisted he was sure about his decision. He'd told his wife and the minister of defence, but hadn't let his four sisters in on the plan.

McCullagh said he was tired of caring for his father and his sisters. Serving in the air force would give him a break from his past, time to think about what had happened in the last few years. He needed to do that. King said the decision was "a very gallant one" that would set an example to other young men.

As was usual in these sessions with King, McCullagh betrayed any loyalty he still felt to Hepburn, who was still premier of Ontario. Mitch couldn't be trusted. He wanted to set himself up as a fascist leader in Ontario. He had the mind of a dictator. He was ruthless to anyone who opposed him. King wondered why the *Globe and Mail* still sometimes supported Mitch, if he was so awful. McCullagh said the *Globe and Mail* always supported people who held high office, a claim that came as news to King. Whatever the case, King said, he was glad to have the paper onside. King told McCullagh he realized he had been criticized a lot by the press but had also had plenty of praise. McCullagh said he thought King got much more support than criticism. Even King's opponents, McCullagh said, believed the federal government was led by a man who was honest and capable. They might criticize some of his actions, but they had confidence in his leadership.

They found more common ground by cutting up Mitch again. McCullagh thought Hepburn planned to break from the Liberals and form his own party. He hoped he'd get support from the soldiers. This, McCullagh said, would be a misfortune for Liberalism. King spoke up, saying Mitch had seriously hurt the Liberals, and both men agreed that the Ontario premier was just using the party to serve his own personal ends.

As McCullagh left King's office, the prime minister told him he hoped God would protect him.[28]

A day later, McCullagh wrote to King thanking him for his "brotherly advice." McCullagh's "mind had been torn in conflict" over his idea of joining the air force. Once he'd decided to do it, "I do not think any-thing you said, Mr. Prime Minister, would have dissuaded me, but for you to have wholeheartedly agreed and to speak with such genuine feeling and sincerity, will always remain a cherished memory. It has also proven of inestimable value in the difficult discussion I had to undertake with my immediate family and Mr. Wright."[29] A few days later, McCullagh told his sisters and the staff of his newspaper. Newspaper "boys," many of them old, grown men, gathered at the College Theatre just before Christmas for an evening of skits. They praised their publisher and voted to send him a congratulatory mes-sage. McCullagh always had a soft spot for these people, and the *Globe and Mail* gave the story decent play.[30] On December 15, the newspa-pers announced McCullagh's enlistment.

This was all good news to the prime minister, who was determined to break up the "Toronto clique." Sending one of its members off to war—especially the immature amateur political animal who ran the *Globe and Mail*—seemed to be a good start. Christmas of 1939 would be a very happy time for King.

* * *

King was to soon learn that resistance to censorship was now ingrained in the *Globe and Mail*, whether McCullagh was calling the shots or not. McCullagh was in the air force on January 10, 1940, when Ontario Tory leader George Drew and Liberal premier Mitchell Hepburn formed an alliance to attack King's handling of the war. Drew wanted to say a lot about the details of the Canadian commitment to the Allies, so he went after the censorship system. Great Britain, he said, "does not feel constrained to criticize where it feels criticism is due."[31] The *Globe and Mail* carried a story featuring that quote, along with other stories attacking the way Ottawa was gearing up to fight.

A week later, Drew made similar charges in the Ontario legislature, denouncing "this disgraceful situation." Drew said the prime minister's "propaganda" speeches and the "half-hearted efforts" of the federal administration generally, had hurt Canada's war effort.[32] All of this criticism was given front-page treatment by the *Globe and Mail*. At the same time, McCullagh, who was about to be shipped out to the officers' training program at Kingston's Royal Military College, was sending word to the prime minister through C.D. Howe, King's most powerful minister, to "pay no attention to Hepburn; that he had killed himself." King should not call a federal election, McCullagh advised. King wrote in his diary that he had no confidence in the press and Parliament. He put his faith in the people, and he was prepared to ask them for a mandate. Hepburn and Drew had given him the excuse he needed.[33]

* * *

If the censors were wondering who was making decisions at the *Globe and Mail*, they were not alone. McCullagh, supposedly under the thumb of the air force, was still trying to dictate newspaper and political policy from Kingston. And that's as far as he got. Almost immediately, McCullagh regretted his decision and wanted out of the air force. His friend Dr. Bruce, the former Ontario lieutenant-governor who had backed the Leadership League, started working the phones. One of his first calls was to Lord Tweedsmuir, the governor general, who told Bruce that "the last thing he would ever care to do would be to interfere with a man's military obligations." Bruce also called King. "I [King] said it was extraordinary where there was wealth, men seemed to think it right to command the services of everyone."[34]

And while McCullagh was in the air force, he was being tempted with something that, for so many years, he'd been desperate to see. The Tories in Ottawa were willing to form a coalition government for the duration of the war, just as they had in the Great War, and as the political parties in the United Kingdom had done. Dr. Bruce wrote to McCullagh at the end of January to say Conservative leader Robert Manion would give McCullagh a federal cabinet post. At the very

least, Manion wanted some advice on how to make a national government work.[35]

But McCullagh was starting to break down mentally and physically
under the strain of trying to be the best in his officers training class while
also controlling Canada's premier political newspaper. This was his first
brush with a classroom since he'd dropped out of high school, and he'd
always carried some regret about his lack of academic success.

The military gave him a lot of leeway to keep in touch with his
senior executives and his powerful friends. The pneumonia that laid
him low in the fall of 1939 came back. McCullagh would not be a
candidate, and, before the federal election campaign ended, it wasn't
clear he'd even survive. Before the vote was held, McCullagh was
trucked off to the Toronto General Hospital. Other soldiers who got
sick were sent to the hospital, and then went back to their units when
they recovered. But not George McCullagh. It was clear to everyone
who knew him that he couldn't be a flier or administrative officer in
this war. And so, he was out for the duration.

* * *

The voters didn't care about McCullagh's defense of press freedom. By
the end of January, the *Globe and Mail* was almost alone in its demands
for uncensored journalism and liberty for candidates to state their
opinion in the press and on the radio. In an editorial entitled
"Democracy Under Test" published January 30, 1940, the paper's editors argued: "If censorship is imposed on speakers, there is no electoral
freedom; if it is relaxed, the war effort may suffer. Must democracy be
sacrificed in deciding which political party is to hold office in the coming five years?"[36]

The *Globe and Mail* also went back down the path that had been
such a dead end in the previous spring's Leadership League campaign:
attacking the CBC. Many, many political and media critics have gone
after the CBC in the decades since it was founded, but attacking the

Corp has never done them much good. The CBC of the 1930s and 1940s had a reputation as an authoritative, if somewhat flawed, news agency. A strong cohort of loyal listeners believed then, as they do today, that private radio stations could never match the CBC's quality. Fending off agenda-driven people like McCullagh added to the myth that the CBC was objective, or at least not in the thrall of the rich.

The *Globe and Mail* warned of "a radio Gestapo" of censors that was "an insult, not only to the candidates, but to the people who nominate them" and asked if "the Censorship Committee and the censors, and the government to which they are responsible, have a monopoly on loyalty and intelligence; if they are the only ones concerned with keeping useful information from the enemy and furthering the war effort, why an election at all? ... Why not go the full way with a dictatorship, as with a blacked-out Parliament, and have it over with?"[37]

* * *

As Canada moved toward war, McCullagh had abandoned Hepburn and found a new best friend in George Drew. Unlike the alcoholic, sex-addicted premier, this was a friend McCullagh could look up to and learn from. Here was a man of action. Drew was twenty when he signed up in 1914 to fight in the First World War. He was commissioned as a lieutenant and sent overseas. Two years later, he was wounded and invalided home, where he spent three years in bed. Drew eventually recovered enough to start studying for the bar exams, and he also kept his military ties, rising to the rank of lieutenant-colonel in the militia. This combination of war record, profession and age was political jet fuel. Add to it some impressive social skills and good looks, and George Drew had all the makings of success. In 1925, he was elected mayor of Guelph. Municipal politicians were elected every year in the early twentieth century. Rather than face the voters again, Drew served out his term and then moved to Toronto to be a master of the Supreme Court of Ontario, making him a sort of junior

judge who tried to simplify issues before they went to court. Drew
kept writing for *Maclean's* magazine, advocating for more money for
the military, blowing the whistle on shady arms contracts, and pushing for a ban on marijuana. He kept a toe in journalism through the
1930s, even after he had been made head of the Ontario Securities
Commission and when he was sitting in the Ontario legislature. By the
time the war broke out, he was ghostwriting military analysis for the
Globe and Mail.

It was obvious Drew would be the next premier of Ontario. Even
Hepburn seemed to know it. The two supposed political adversaries
tag-teamed to hurt Mackenzie King during the lulls between Hepburn's
binges in the King Eddy, waiting for the day when Hepburn would
shuffle off.

Drew was scheduled to make a major election speech in support
of the federal Conservatives on March 1. A.A. Fraser, the assistant radio
censor in charge of the Toronto district, went over Drew's speech with
the CBC's station manager in Toronto, and the manager made cuts.
Drew tipped off the *Globe and Mail*, which applied for, and was refused,
permission from the censors to print the material cut from Drew's
speech. An internal report by the censorship department called the
ruling against Drew "a foolish and futile attempt to prevent public
exposure of inconsistency in the censorship administration" and said
the *Globe and Mail's* subsequent trashing of the censors in the March
2 story was "inevitable."[38]

In the *Globe and Mail*, Drew charged the censorship system was
"nothing more than a political machine for preventing effective correction of Mr. King's misstatements." Hammering home his point,
Drew told the *Globe and Mail* that King, in a speech in Winnipeg,
"gave the number and types of aircraft, engines and weapons. When I
sought to give the correct figures, I was told that this was contrary to
the censorship regulations." He called the censors "political police"
and warned Canadians "that we are now living under the supervision

of a Canadian Gestapo whose duty it is to prevent just criticism of the Government reaching the ears of the public."[39]

The next day, Drew and the newspaper repeated the "Nazi" charge while speaking at a meeting of the West York Conservative riding association in New Toronto.[40] Drew accused King of establishing "a political censorship quite as effective as that imposed on Germany." Drew also read the parts of his radio speech that had been cut by the censors. He told the crowd that some Canadian soldiers were training with First World War weapons, while others had none at all. He also claimed—quite rightly—that the Canadian army had no decent tanks or fighter planes, its artillery had no modern field pieces and just four anti-aircraft guns, and one of its twelve-pounders was a relic from the Boer War.[41]

In his stump speech, the federal Tory leader took up the anti-censorship cause. King, Robert Manion told fourteen hundred members of the Conservative Business Men's Association in Toronto on March 2, was not content with "scuttling Parliament and threatening the existence of Canadian parliamentary institutions." He was now "attempting to gag free speech over the radio by a form of censorship which has reached ridiculous heights."[42] Two days later, Manion echoed Drew's accusation that the censorship system in Canada resembled the one established in Nazi Germany.[43]

Judith Robinson warned her readers on March 6 that "the war for liberty is only six months old, and already the system set up by the Federal Liberal Government can get away with freedom's murder." Robinson was angry that none of the major English-language papers in Canada had taken up the *Globe and Mail's* fight with the censors. "The sooner that great truth becomes plain to all newspaper publishers in this country the more freedom they are likely to salvage for themselves and others out of a Liberal Government's illiberal censorship system."[44]

Red Baron–killer Roy Brown, last seen sitting quietly on the Leadership League stage in Maple Leaf Gardens, made the front page of the *Globe and Mail* on March 12 when he charged King had lied about Canada's defence preparations, then banned all criticism of his government's war effort. "The very idea of Mr. King restricting you and me as to what we may say is embittering," he told an Ontario meeting held in support of Conservative candidates.[45]

The public didn't care. They expected news control during the war, and it was easy for the Liberals to convince them that criticism of the war effort was unpatriotic. Nor did they want a coalition government. The prime minister went into the campaign with no desire whatsoever to share power with the Conservatives, and no one, other than the Conservatives, wanted him to. He portrayed the Tories' "national government" idea as the brainchild of Drew, Hepburn, McCullagh and the *Globe and Mail*, and the rest of the Toronto Clique.[46] This cabal also wanted national conscription—to draft young men the way the European countries and the United States did. The country, especially Quebec, did not. They had seen how the issue had split the country in the previous war.

King wasn't too worried about what McCullagh, his rich friends and his staff thought. When the last big rally, held at Toronto Clique-owned Maple Leaf Gardens, was over, Toronto police escorted King's motorcade, which consisted of one car: Joe Atkinson's. The *Star* publisher and the prime minister sat in the back, reminiscing about their long friendship and King's dead parents.[47] That night, Atkinson showed the prime minister a picture of his wife, looking very sad as she lay dying. King made a special note of that.[48]

Just before the German army stormed into the Low Countries and France, King won a solid majority. In a sense, he had profited from the "Phony War" that lasted from the fall of 1939 to the invasion of France and the Low Countries in early May 1940, calling and winning an election at one of the very few times in the war when Canadians believed they could go on living normal lives. A few months after King's big win, when Germans were parading on the boulevards of

Paris and historic London was being bombed out, the war would seem much more real.

Tory leader Manion had lost his seat in Parliament and the Opposition was now rudderless. Ironically, Dr. Bruce was one of the few Conservatives who made it to Ottawa. Tories in his riding of Parkdale had wanted to give the nomination to McCullagh when he was still in the air force. McCullagh turned them down, so they settled for the doctor.[49]

* * *

As the war heated up with the German invasion of western Europe, so did McCullagh and *The Globe and Mail*'s battle with censorship. Judith Robinson infuriated the censors yet again when she wrote a column on May 11, 1940, using information leaked by the military to show that Canada's tight-fisted approach to the Commonwealth Air Training Program had produced only one hundred pilots, when it could have turned out five thousand. The *Globe and Mail* was getting leaks and counter-leaks out of Ottawa and from military bases across the country. Wartime unity was starting to show serious cracks.

* * *

McCullagh hadn't missed much when he was stuck in the air force. Now, back in Toronto, he was adjusting to life in a city disrupted by the war. The sports scene McCullagh loved was still running, but was more subdued. Archworth was racing, but not racking up the wins of the previous spring. McCullagh's sisters were spending more time at the Thornhill estate. In June, when McCullagh was better, Beverley Jean McCullagh, George's youngest sister, was married at McCullagh's house to Ralph Blackmore, a leading airman in the Royal Canadian Air Force (RCAF). The senior George McCullagh was, again, shunted aside as his rich young son took over the planning, but he was allowed to give the bride away. The *Globe and Mail* publisher invited his friend

Bishop Renison to officiate at the service, which was held in the mansion's drawing room. Blackmore's RCAF buddies held long white ribbons to form an aisle through the downstairs of McCullagh's house. The bride's table was in the white dining room covered with white chrysanthemums, and there was a tiered wedding cake topped with white begonia blossoms. After the ceremony, the couple drove to the Laurentians for their honeymoon.[50]

While the McCullaghs were celebrating a big society wedding, the world was crashing down. The Wehrmacht's tanks were chewing up the roads of France, heading for Paris. Ottawa was in a panic, which became almost intolerable when Norman Rogers, the defence minister, was killed in a plane crash in early June. King called Rupert Davies, the president of the Canadian Press wire service, into his office to talk strategy. King didn't want the press to panic, even though it was clear the Allies—including Canada—might have to ask Hitler for peace terms.

Air minister Chubby Power, who was at this meeting, suggested calling McCullagh. King was emphatic: McCullagh couldn't be trusted with secrets. King later confided to his diary. "I thought the fellow [McCullagh] was crazy. That the thing to do was to deal with him as we had begun to deal with Hepburn. Maintain our position." King went on to tell his paper therapist, "Among letters received today was one from McCullagh, of sympathy over Rogers' death and talking about the action of the *Globe and Mail* in being conscientious etc. He is part of the froth, if not the of the scum, of social life based on false standards of wealth."

King had also heard Hepburn had developed bronchitis that had worsened to pneumonia. "If so, it probably means the end of his earthly life." Hepburn's death "would be the best thing that could happen at this time." He would no longer be able to create panic and dissention, as he had been over the last few weeks. People would pretend to mourn for a while, but no one would really miss him.[51]

* * *

In February 1941, as Nazi planes bombed London, McCullagh's pneumonia returned, and he ended up back in Toronto General Hospital. For a while, he was listed in critical condition. The *Globe and Mail* published a daily bulletin, framed in heavy black lines, on its front page. Canada's prime minister, who was always keen to see a corpse in the making, visited him.

King arrived in Toronto on the evening of March 8 in his private railway car, a sumptuous travelling hotel suite. He woke up the next morning at Union Station, went to the dentist (who told him he needed to take much better care of his teeth), had himself driven to the house where he grew up, and went over to Queen's Park to see the monument to his grandfather. Then he stopped in at the hospital.

"McCullagh looks to me a pretty sick man," King told his diary that night. "He has had pneumonia and has lung trouble. I should not be surprised to see him develop tuberculosis which will carry him off in the end. He was, I think, surprised to see me and I was apparently the first to see him, since he was in for some days."

It was McCullagh who brought up the latest spat between the *Globe and Mail* and King's government. It wasn't personal, the thirty-five-year-old publisher said. He said he was as sincere as King, but they both had different views on how to fight the war. But King wasn't buying it. The newspaper's criticism of his government was based on false "facts," King said, and it was unfair.

King continued to be a lousy visitor. He mentioned the idea of national government and dismissed it, saying it was impossible to find new non-partisan leaders and to get them elected. They finally had a meeting of the minds when the conversation swung around—as it always did—to Mitch Hepburn.

"He talked very strongly against Hepburn," King reported. "Thought of him as a dangerous man, as one who might try, when I ceased to hold office, to get control and go to great lengths for the sake of power. Quite clearly, McCullagh sees him as a menace." Hepburn was into the fourth year of his term, but McCullagh was sure that the premier would wait until 1942 to call an election.[52] The prime minister thought McCullagh's analysis was nonsense. "The truth is there are a lot of amateurs at Queen's Park and in the Globe office. The latter really want to govern. Think they know as much about the country's needs as the people's representatives."

King then headed off to Joe Atkinson's house to report on his visit.[53]

A few weeks later, McCullagh left the hospital on his own two feet. From then on, however, McCullagh seemed frail. He caught every cold that was going around, and he had asthma.[54] He had always seemed much older than his age, and his life seemed to move at a different speed from those of ordinary people, maybe in dog years. In his youth, this resulted in fantastic achievements and praise as a *wunderkind*. As he neared middle age, however, the flip side of this reverse-Faustian bargain began to show.

* * *

In June 1941, the *Globe and Mail* ran a series called "War Problems Affecting Canada." The paper argued the supply of modern weapons could be greatly improved if procurement was taken out of the hands of the military and put into the hands of "manufacturers of great experience and energy."[55] The series was written anonymously, but senior military and political people believed George Drew was the author. The military's feedback (likely gathered by the Wartime Information Board, which did a lot of polling) was that the series had hurt them in Toronto and Hamilton. Gen. Harry Crerar, chief of the Defence Staff, told parliamentary journalist Grant Dexter of the *Winnipeg Free Press* that the criticism was destroying the morale of soldiers, leading them to believe "they belong to a second-rate show." It was hurting recruiting, and it was undermining the public morale. McCullagh had combined with the publishers of *Maclean's* and the *Financial Post* to fan discontent, mostly for political reasons: they wanted to undermine Defence Minister James Ralston and force him out.[56]

The army brass thought King and Ralston were spineless. The generals knew King had kept the military budget low through the Depression to make Canada's army and navy too weak to be of much use to its allies. After the fall of western Europe, the war had gone quiet again, except on the Atlantic, where U-boats hunted the convoys ferrying troops, food and weapons from Halifax to Britain. The war turned loud again at the end of June 1941, when Hitler invaded the Soviet Union. Suddenly, attitudes in Canada changed. Leftists who had either opposed participating in the war or declared themselves to be pacifists suddenly became hawks. The government had suppressed Communist publications. Now Communists were on our side.[57]

Eventually, the full Canadian army would have to face the Nazi legions. In Ottawa, the fight was over the size of that army. The general staff wanted to send eight divisions overseas. (Canadian divisions had about fifteen thousand men and required logistical support in Canada, England and behind the fighting lines.) King and the politicians wanted far fewer men to go overseas. In the late summer of 1941, McCullagh held a secret meeting with a senior officer of the general staff. The officer started the session by telling McCullagh that the *Globe and Mail* was wrong in describing Canada's land forces as "a bow and arrow army." The staff officer told McCullagh that the politicians wanted to equip just one armoured division. The generals wanted four. The officer pulled out secret plans for a new order of battle and showed them to the publisher.[58]

After this meeting, *Globe and Mail* criticism of the war effort shifted markedly: the paper had constantly criticized the military's mobilization efforts. Now the blame was placed squarely on the political side. Ralston knew about General Crerar's lobbying campaign for a bigger army. So did well-connected journalists on Parliament Hill, who kept the news from their readers. "The general staff, perhaps unconsciously, has declared war on the government. That is what it amounts to," Parliament Hill reporter Grant Dexter told the owner of the *Winnipeg Free Press*.[59]

The army's campaign against King began at another terrifying time in the war: the Wehrmacht was sweeping deep into Russia, heading for Moscow. Stalin didn't seem to be able to slow the invasion. In the West, Britain watched helplessly, with Churchill pinning his hopes on American intervention that, to President Franklin Roosevelt, was political poison.

Ralston believed army morale would plummet if he fired or side-lined General Crerar. Checkmate.

As the Germans drove deeper into Russia that fall, other media, including local radio stations, echoed the *Globe and Mail*'s criticism of the national war effort. Public opinion in Toronto began to shift towards conscription. In the fall of 1941, even Atkinson at the *Star* began to feel the heat, and was considering shifting the paper's policy. He sent an emissary to Ottawa in October to see what could be done to improve recruiting. Ralston told Atkinson's man that he did not want to enlist a large number of Canadian men if there was nowhere for them to fight. There was no point having thousands of fit young men in uniform bumming around the country when there was a shortage of industrial and farm workers.[60]

Winston Churchill quietly tipped off interim Canadian Tory leader Richard Hanson that he did not want Canada to split on the issue of conscription. Perhaps, the old bulldog suggested, there could be conscription in English Canada and some other kind of system in Quebec. This idea would not have gone over well in Canada, so Hanson never mentioned it. He did, however, start pulling his punches in the House of Commons.

George Drew, who had never kept anyone guessing about his opinion on conscription, saw this as an opening. Drew wanted the federal leadership, but wired-in political observers considered him a very long shot. For one thing, Drew was still relatively new in the job of Ontario Tory leader. He'd never fought an election against Hepburn, and one was coming fairly soon. Tory bagmen and party organizers knew of McCullagh's friendship with Drew and believed it was the reason the *Globe and Mail* had been gushing about him. Drew and his backers wanted to postpone the actual leadership vote for a couple of years while Drew built up a profile. McCullagh sent Bill Marchington, a reporter, to see Arthur Meighen and bring him into their plan of making him the temporary leader. Meighen told Marchington that he wanted nothing to do with the plan. He was too old to lead the opposition in the Commons. The work he as doing was already enough to keep him up all night. Judith Robinson, who was in Ottawa for a few days, told Grant Dexter, "Well, if the Tories are perfectly sure the party is dead, Arthur Meighen would make a splendid headstone."

In early November, McCullagh went to Ottawa to see if he could get the Tories to turn up the volume on conscription. When that didn't work, he started meeting Conservatives in his Chateau Laurier suite and pushing for Meighen's comeback. There was one serious problem. Most of the richest of Meighen's followers didn't care about military preparations and conscription. They wanted Meighen back in the leader's office because he was loudly opposed to price controls. McCullagh told a friend that he was ashamed to support Meighen on those grounds, but felt he had no choice. That got back to King, who told his secretary "to make a note of this conversation as being very significant."[61]

* * *

Socially, the McCullaghs were back after his stint in the air force and his long hospital stays. McCullagh had made many friends and useful contacts when he was at Trenton and Kingston. In early June 1941, McCullagh threw a garden party for his military buddies. It was a spectacular day, partly pomp—there was an air force honour guard and big Union Jacks—but also lots of fun. People arriving at the circular driveway were greeted by two signs, one with pictures of ponies and the other of children, warning guests to drive carefully.

Once inside, the air force trainees and officers could have all the ice cream they wanted. There was booze for those who were more inclined to adult vices. Some of the guests walked with their girlfriends through the terraced gardens, which were thick with pansies. They could watch the Dolphinets, a women's water dance team, in the estate's swimming pond. McCullagh booked an air force band that played patriotic music and swing tunes. Twice that afternoon, air force planes flew low over the estate. The McCullaghs had the pond area of Thornhill decorated with flowers, drummed up a large crowd of attractive women, and hired several fortune tellers to sit in front of crystal balls and tell the futures of the airmen. This might not seem like the most sensitive choice of attractions for young men heading to war, but they seemed to like it.[62]

* * *

In the fall of 1941, the prime minister began to see a way out of the storm clouds kicked up by an unhappy officer corps and their friends in the media. Near the middle of November 1941, in a comment that has intrigued historians, King told *Winnipeg Free Press* journalist Grant Dexter that he believed the Japanese would be at war with the Allies within a week or ten days. He said he expected Japanese raids on the Pacific coast of Canada. The Axis seemed to have military forces to spare: China was on the verge of collapse and Stalin was telling the British that they needed to open a second front in Western Europe immediately, start an all-out air war on Germany's homeland, and send the Soviets every piece of weaponry and food they could lay hands on, or he would have to sue for peace.[63]

Most Canadian leaders would have been flattened by this news. King wasn't. He saw that his route to survival lay through British

Columbia. War with Japan would allow him to redeploy many thousands of Canadian troops to the Pacific coast, out of harm's way.

In his record of the conversation, Dexter didn't say whether he asked about the Canadian garrison heading to Hong Kong.

On December 7, carrier-based Japanese planes bombed Pearl Harbor. At the same time, the Japanese army launched offensives across southeast Asia, including towards Hong Kong, where a Canadian contingent had arrived just a few weeks before. The Canadians, undertrained and poorly equipped, and their British and Indian allies made the Japanese pay heavily for the ground that they seized. Gen. John Lawson went down fighting, running from his surrounded headquarters with pistols blazing. The 1,975 soldiers of the Royal Rifles of Canada (a Montreal-based regiment) and the Winnipeg Grenadiers, supported by the Royal Canadian Corps of Signals, were pushed back from the mainland to Hong Kong Island. Grossly outnumbered, they tried to hold defensive lines stretched across the island, but had to give them up.

By December 20, the Japanese had reached the far side of the island and the defenders were split into two desperate groups. On Christmas Day, Hong Kong's governor surrendered the colony. The Canadian force had 290 officers and men killed and 493 wounded. As the Allied resistance collapsed, Japanese troops entered St. Stephen's College military hospital, murdered the doctors, raped the nurses, bayonetted seriously wounded Canadian and Indian troops in their beds, and tortured several Canadians to death. That was just the start of the nightmare. Before the war ended, 267 Canadian soldiers perished in Japanese captivity. They died of neglect or were worked to death. Many of the survivors were barely alive when they were rescued at the end of the summer of 1945. They would spend the rest of their often-shortened lives trying to get justice from the Japanese that had committed war crimes against them, and from the Canadian government, which found them to be an embarrassment.

13

WARS WITHIN A WAR

The expanded war left McCullagh with a depleted newsroom. More of his staff were joining the army: the war offered the kind of excitement that attracts young people to journalism. The *Globe and Mail* lost Ralph Allen, recently hired from the *Winnipeg Tribune*, who would later become famous as editor of *Maclean's*. When he signed up as a gunner for the Royal Artillery the day after Pearl Harbor, Allen wrote a glowing farewell column about McCullagh and his editors: "Never having owned a newspaper or even exercised authority over anyone in the business except an occasional office boy, we are in no position to say what makes a good employer and what does not. But if we are ever required to research the subject of human, sympathetic and generous bosses, we'll be able to fill the slate, from the top down, without going off these premises."[1]

In 1942, McCullagh had enough money to buy a controlling interest in the *Globe and Mail*, but William Wright stayed on as a shareholder with a big minority stake. McCullagh didn't change the name of the

Globe and Mail's downtown building. McCullagh might be the owner of the paper, but he would not cut the old prospector loose. Wright was still a father figure to McCullagh, and he was always welcome to stay in his namesake building.

In March 1942, the fight between McCullagh and his nemesis at the Toronto *Star*, Holy Joe Atkinson, turned very ugly. McCullagh believed, with some accuracy, that Atkinson was a hypocrite whose concern for working people ended on the sidewalk outside the *Star* building. The *Star* was—and would be for many years—a vicious workplace, where the paper's managers, according to one late-twentieth-century source, waged war on their own employees.

It was also arguable that Atkinson was just a mouthpiece for Mackenzie King. Everyone knew the two men had been friends for more than fifty years. Atkinson was also friends with some of the leading figures on the Canadian Left, people who would be denounced as communists during the postwar Red Scare. Toronto's business community believed Atkinson was a dangerous man, and not just because he'd pour out the contents of their liquor cabinets if he ever got the chance.

At the same time, Atkinson was convinced McCullagh and his rich, handsome playboy friends George Drew, Conn Smythe and John Bassett, were fascists. It wasn't an original idea. His friend, Mackenzie King, believed the same thing. So did many people on Parliament Hill.

The hatred between these two groups was fired up back in March 1941 with the publication of a *Globe and Mail* editorial headlined "From the Journalistic Gutter." It ran while McCullagh was still in the hospital with pneumonia, and came out the day after King dropped in at Toronto General to see if McCullagh was dying yet. The *Star*, according to McCullagh's editors, was "a slavish party organ with a reputation for violating every known code of journalistic ethics." The *Star* "colors its news to suit its aims" and was a "strange creature to pretend to principles of honest journalism.

"For months it has been trying to 'get' a provincial premier by methods no self-respecting journal would countenance. It puts on a face of sanctity, filling its columns with benevolent platitudes, and observes the opposite in practice. Fooling the public is its chief vocation, and full coffers are all it cares about. Does the *Star* think its racket pulls the wool over the eyes of thinking people? Honest journalism! It doesn't know the meaning of the words."

A few days before, the *Star* had denounced the *Globe and Mail* as a "rumour factory."

Atkinson sued. By the time the case got to court a year later, some other journalists thought the fight was ridiculous, and that both publishers were so blinded by hate that they were making fools of themselves and their newspapers. "Picture the situation," the little *Montreal Herald* asked its readers. "Here was a man with a skyscraper paper housed in a skyscraper building as a monument to his life's work. Joe Atkinson is getting along in years. He is the doyen of Toronto newspapermen. And here is the *Globe* with a mere boy at its head—George McCullagh is still the active captain of it—very pungently calling the *Star*'s ethics into question. Youth deriding age! It was too much."[2]

By now, Holy Joe had transferred some control of the *Star* to his son, Joe Jr. The younger Atkinson didn't want his father to sue, but the old man went ahead and claimed $100,000 for libel. Top *Star* reporter Roy Greenaway was assigned to help lawyer Alex Stark put together his case.

The trial started on April 8, 1942. Certainly, the *Star* had been defamed by the *Globe and Mail*'s harsh words. There was obvious malice involved, which made the defence more difficult. But Justice Keiller MacKay found there was a certain element of privilege—politically protected speech—involved. The question for the jurors was whether McCullagh and the *Globe and Mail* had gone too far when they said the *Star* was using "methods no self-respecting journal would countenance."

Holy Joe was the only witness. He was an honest man, and willing to admit one of the core *Globe and Mail* accusations: he was out to get Mitch Hepburn. He denied all the rest.

While McCullagh watched from the front row, the *Star*'s lawyer walked Holy Joe through each line of the *Globe and Mail*'s editorial. He read the line where the *Star* was accused of lecturing the *Globe and Mail*. Was that untrue? "Yes," Atkinson replied.

What about the accusation that the *Star* was "a slavish party organ?" Also untrue, Atkinson said. They kept going until they reached the line, "It puts on a face on sanctity, filling its column with benevolent platitudes, and observes the opposite in practice."

The lawyer asked if the claim was true.

Atkinson looked straight at the jury, cracked a small smile, and said, "The last part is untrue."[3]

In Ontario at that time, proving the truth of an accusation was one of the few ways to defend a libel suit. Libel was, and still is, what's called a "reverse onus" tort. That meant McCullagh, not Atkinson, was saddled with the burden of proof. The person who was defamed came into court with the assumption that the defamation was false and that damage had been caused. It was complex law, but it gave Atkinson a huge advantage.

Instead, the *Globe and Mail* chose a legal strategy that rarely worked in schoolyard fights, let alone in courtrooms. The lawyers for the paper said the *Star* had started the fight by calling the *Globe and Mail* a rumour factory.

Had it been a trial with just a judge hearing the case, McCullagh would almost certainly have lost. But this was a trial by jury—gentlemen of intelligence and education, according to the judge—and the defence worked.

It seems that the jury did not believe the case should have gone to trial. Both papers had the power to defend themselves on their own pages, and were giving as good as they got. And even the publishers didn't seem all that offended. The lawyer for the *Globe and Mail* pointed out to the jury: "As I look around the courtroom, I don't see Mr. Atkinson and Mr. McCullagh so annoyed with each other that they can't sit in chairs beside each other. I've seen that. Everything is going fine and we are having a splendid case. Good publicity."

Greenaway later wrote that the jury foreman winked at McCullagh when he announced the "not guilty" verdict. Harry Hindmarsh, Holy Joe's son-in-law and editor of the paper, was appalled, and he did something that was outrageous and illegal: he assigned Greenaway to track down, investigate and interview everyone on the jury. Greenaway came back convinced that the jury foreman, who had volunteered at the last minute when two other jurors were unavailable, was either biased or bought off. There was nothing the *Star* could do about it, but it deepened the hatred among the *Star*'s managers for McCullagh and anyone they saw as a Tory.[4]

McCullagh boasted privately, but he discreetly visited Atkinson to apologize. Holy Joe accepted McCullagh's excuse that he was in the hospital and not running the paper when the editorial was published. "A public affront requires more than a private apology," Atkinson replied, but McCullagh wouldn't do it.[5] It was an opportunity for the two men to try to patch things up, or to at least develop some civility. Instead, it set the stage for battles that were intensely personal, with much more serious stakes.

* * *

Mackenzie King believed some of McCullagh's journalists were as dangerous as their employer. The prime minister and his minister of justice, Louis St. Laurent, ordered the RCMP to investigate Judith Robinson and Oakley Dalgleish, who, alongside their *Globe and Mail* work, operated a weekly paper that was critical of the Canadian war effort. It's not clear what the cops were looking for or how deeply they dug into the lives of the two journalists. The story of the investigation of the two journalists was broken on March 12, 1942, by *Saturday Night*, a respected weekly where McCullagh had many friends.

Richard Hanson, the interim leader of the Tories, used his parliamentary immunity from censorship to rise in the House of Commons to ask St. Laurent if the story was true. The government had no business investigating "two journalists whose loyalty is unquestioned." Hanson accused King's government of targeting Robinson and Dalgleish to intimidate them and to scare smaller-fish journalists who criticized the war effort. St. Laurent said nothing that day, and gave a non-denial answer three days later.[6]

King was unrepentant. The two journalists worked for McCullagh, and King believed the publisher was part of a cabal that wanted to drive King from office and saddle the country with a "national government." To his confidantes and his diary, King named this clique's members: "Meighen, Drew, Hepburn, McCullagh, John Bassett and some others associated with them. Really a gangster gang with white collars...These men are merely a Nazi Fascist output with characteristics and methods comparable to those of Hitler and Goering and others."[7] And King was willing to use the power of the government of Canada to shut them down.

* * *

In the late fall of 1941, the Conservative caucus chose Sir Arthur Meighen to lead the party through the rest of the war. At first, Meighen wanted to keep his Senate seat and run the Opposition from there, but Canada had changed since the 1890s, when Mackenzie Bowell and John Abbott had led parties from the Red Chamber. In the third week of January, as the country was reeling from one disaster after another in the Pacific—the fall of Hong Kong, the collapse of the British fortress of Singapore, the invasion of the Philippines—Meighen resigned his Senate seat and filed papers to run in a by-election in the Toronto riding of York South. This gave the three Toronto dailies a chance to show their partisan fangs. The federal Liberals pretended to sit the election out in deference to Meighen's position as a party leader, but secretly funnelled money to the CCF candidate.

Early in the by-election campaign, everyone expected Meighen to win. By January 20, 1942, word was getting around Ottawa that the Tory leader was in trouble. King announced a national referendum on the divisive issue of conscription, stealing Meighen's best issue. Some Toronto Tories were telling McCullagh to claim victory when the referendum was announced and distance himself from the Meighen mess.[8]

McCullagh went to Ottawa to see if there was some way to save Meighen. He found hard feelings all over town. No one wanted to campaign, and donations dried up. In the Rideau Club washroom, McCullagh ran into Robert Manion, the former Tory leader who had lost his seat in the 1940 snap election. Manion, who had been a military surgeon in the First World War, was now working for King as director of the civilian air raid defence system. "How do you like working with these sons of bitches?" McCullagh asked. "Well," Manion said, "I find it not a bad change from the sons of bitches I was working with."[9]

On February 6, Meighen lost the York South by-election to CCF candidate Joseph Noseworthy. Meighen couldn't endure the humiliation of resigning from the Tory leadership less than two months after winning it, but he couldn't risk another by-election loss, either. He hung on through the year, more for appearances' sake than anything. Mitch Hepburn was the second loser. Toronto Liberals were now convinced he was finished.

* * *

In the early months of 1942, as the Meighen campaign began, Drew and McCullagh found a new crusade: the government's failure to properly equip the task force that was sent to defend Hong Kong against the Japanese. When "C" Force was deployed to the backwater Crown colony the previous November, it had seemed like a soft billet for well-connected officers. The British and Chinese assured Ottawa that the Canadians would be protected if the Japanese attacked, and few people had expected Emperor Hirohito to add Great Britain to his country's list of enemies. Japan seemed bogged down in its war against China and had been beaten by a Soviet army two and a half years before. There was no reason for it to take on the Western powers until the United States started imposing sanctions in late 1941. Yet Hong Kong had fallen. Details were scarce: families of the Canadian troops didn't know whether their loved ones were dead or in the hands of the Japanese, who had not signed the Geneva Convention.

The government tried to cover up the disaster. During the war, no one could challenge the King government's narrative. There were no survivors who had escaped the battle and could tell their story to the Canadian media, and the Japanese weren't talking. It's not clear how much Ottawa knew about the actual battle, where Canadians—poorly trained or not—had fought well and shown exceptional courage. But the military and the government knew they were open to criticism on two fronts: the failure to ship vehicles and other equipment along with the men; and the fact that the Royal Rifles of Canada got the exotic Asian posting because of social connections. One of its officers (now in captivity) was Frank Power, the son of the minister in charge of Canada's air force, Chubby Power.

And why hadn't King, with his belief that war with Japan was imminent in the fall of 1941, realized that Hong Kong was a trap? Was he more concerned with pleasing Churchill, who had asked for the Canadian troops, than with Canadian soldiers' lives?[10]

Sir Lyman Duff, chief justice of the Supreme Court of Canada who was also one of King's best friends, was appointed as a one-man royal commission to examine whether the troops sent to Hong Kong were adequately trained and equipped. King knew his man: at the beginning of the Second World War, Duff had burned many of the records of the 1917 conscription crisis, which were full of proof of favouritism and political manipulation.[11]

Duff's inquiry was held in a locked courtroom. The federal Conservatives managed to get standing in the hearing, and they appointed George Drew to be their unpaid counsel. Duff heard from most of the important people involved in Canada's decision to send soldiers to Hong Kong, but he made an order prohibiting leaks of testimony to the media. He also ordered Drew and other counsel to destroy all documents and notes in their possession once the hearings were over.

Drew, for all his faults, was a great choice of counsel. The generals took Drew seriously. He had a sterling record of service in the First World War, held the rank of colonel in the militia, and had been a member of the Conference of Defence Associations since it was founded in 1932. This organization, with its unassuming name, was a lobby group for senior military officers, with quiet backing of the country's arms industry.[12] Drew had joined the conference before his political career had taken off. Now he was very valuable to his friends in the military, and they were very useful to him. Through George Drew, McCullagh had access to the top soldiers in Canada, and they had the pages of the *Globe and Mail* at their disposal.

Drew knew how to get a story. He had bird-dogged Sir Basil Zaharoff, Ian Fleming's inspiration for SPECTRE leader Ernst Stavro Blofeld, since 1917, when Drew had seen British prime minister David Lloyd George scuttling into Zaharoff's suite in London's Carlton Hotel. It turned out Zaharoff was the major shareholder in the British arms maker Vickers, and with some digging, Drew found Zaharoff also owned a piece of Schneider-Creusot in France. Then Drew ferreted out the fact that Zaharoff also had a big stake in Germany's Krupp arms factory and the Škoda works in the Austrian Empire. So no matter who lost the war, Sir Basil Zaharoff was going to win. Drew was able to prove that one of Sir Basil's agents embedded in the 1927 Naval Disarmament talks had scuttled the chance of coming up with a treaty. In August 1931, *Maclean's* magazine published "Salesmen of Death"; it made Drew a star, especially among war vets who believed they had been pawns in a game played by international capitalists and stupid politicians. He became the go-to person for anyone in the military who had dirt to leak, and he got plenty of material showing how politicians and senior brass had blundered when they sent "C" Force to Asia.[13]

Despite Drew's efforts to ferret out the truth on the Hong Kong disaster, Duff did as King expected, finding the Canadian soldiers were properly equipped, trained and led when they were attacked on December 8, 1941.[14] Drew knew this was untrue.[15] Although he was a provincial opposition politician, Drew submitted a thirty-two-page letter to King criticizing in detail the conclusions of the Duff report. Copies were given to the Canadian Press and members of the Parliamentary Press Gallery. King met that day with Conservate House leader Hanson.[16] Hanson told the prime minister he did not agree with what Drew was doing. Hanson said he was being squeezed by McCullagh and the *Globe and Mail* for not demanding enough evidence of the fitness of the Hong Kong force, while the Toronto *Star* criticized him for asking for too much. Anything he did to stop the Ontario Tory leader was bound to cause a flare-up in the press.[17]

In fact, Drew was right. And the press knew it. The Drew letter was their route to being able to tell their readers the truth. Smart reporters like Grant Dexter believed the army was run by "incompetents" who had accumulated at national defence headquarters between the wars. He wrote to his boss, Victor Sifton: "On the one occasion when we had to organize an expeditionary force—Hong Kong—the General Staff, the Quartermaster General and the Adjutant General made a mess of it. The little junta here is saved by the fact that they operate at one remove from real war. They operate, really, as a forwarding agent for [General] McNaughton [then leader of the Canadian army assembling in England]and the British War Office. If we ever are invaded, it will be a disaster." Dexter could say this in a private memo to his boss, but he and his colleagues believed the public should also know, before worse things happened.[18]

The first Drew letter came out just as the Atkinson-McCullagh libel trial opened in Toronto, and just a couple of weeks before the country was to vote in a referendum on conscription.

King's first impulse was to sue Drew for libel.[19] Then he decided to use the threat of censorship and contempt of court citations to suppress Drew's letter.[20]

At 8 p.m. on July 16, 1942, the *Globe and Mail*'s first edition dated July 17 hit the streets carrying a story saying censors had suppressed the entire Drew letter and hinting that its contents were politically devastating. That day, McCullagh left for a fishing trip to ponder whether he was willing to risk jail by publishing the entire letter.[21] Telegraph censors intercepted messages between the *Globe and Mail*'s senior editors and their media colleagues in western Canada. It's possible that McCullagh's phones were tapped, too.[22] The *Globe and Mail*—joined, for once, by the *Ottawa Citizen*—lashed back with articles criticizing the censorship system and imploring other editors to join them in a fight against the suppression of Drew's analysis. The censors relented on the contents of a second Drew letter, except one paragraph that the censor believed drew on secret parts of the evidence given to the Duff inquiry.[23] At the same time, telegram censors were told to suppress any dispatches about the Drew letters from being sent to media in the United States.[24]

After three days in the northern Ontario wilderness, McCullagh and his managing editor, Bob Farquharson, were back in the Toronto office of the Directorate of Censorship asking if the press censors would pass Drew's first letter. Bert Perry, the former sportswriter who was the Toronto censor, said no. McCullagh wanted to know what was censorable in the Drew letter. Perry said he didn't know. When McCullagh asked what would happen if the *Globe and Mail* published the letter without censorship approval, Perry told him the newspaper was liable to be prosecuted under the Defense of Canada Regulations of the War Measures Act, and that McCullagh might go to jail. Perry wrote a memo to his boss saying he believed McCullagh was not afraid of being prosecuted.[25] For several days, Mackenzie King's government seriously faced the prospect of sending the publisher of the *Globe and Mail* to prison. In the end, McCullagh realized he couldn't endure jail and caved to the censors. His paper did everything it could to hint about the contents of Drew's first letter, but it was never published.[26]

The *Globe and Mail* published a round-up of critical editorials from across the country under the headline "Gagging Process of Censorship Draws Protest Across Canada."[27] The Toronto *Telegram*, in one of its few editorials on censorship, warned, "If the newspapers remain silent under the official ban on publication and fail to urge with all of the power at their command a full investigation by Parliament of all evidence they will go far to forfeit the trust of the public and to demonstrate that the boasted freedom of the press is a right to which they are not entitled." The *London Free Press*, a Conservative paper, supported the idea of wartime censorship but added "it is a dangerous infringement on the liberties for which we are fighting when censorship is used for other than its proper and legitimate purposes. Unfortunately, this is the impression which has been given in the present instance." A *Vancouver News-Herald* columnist said, "Colonel Drew's accusations are so astounding in many other respects that they demand complete publicity in parliament."[28]

While all of this was going on, Canadians were voting on whether young men should be drafted into the army. Canadians outside Quebec supported conscription. Francophone Quebecers were almost unanimously opposed. Mackenzie King was already paranoid on his best days. Now he had Drew and McCullagh harping about Hong Kong while his minister of defence, James Ralston, and the country's generals were pressing him to send out draft notices. In King's fevered mind, Ralston was planning to quit and run against him for the leadership.

Plugged-in Ottawa journalist Grant Dexter knew what King was thinking, so he met Ralston for lunch at the Rideau Club, which was across the street from Parliament Hill. Ralston said he had no plans to quit and he did not want to be prime minister, but he did believe he and King were irreconcilable on conscription. King had told Ralston that McCullagh of the *Globe and Mail*, John Bassett of the *Montreal Gazette*, and other Tory publisher-politicians were pushing the movement for conscription solely to take King down.

"Ralston said he regarded McCullagh of the Globe as so unreliable he could not be seen speaking to him except with others present, so that it could not be said he had any private conversation with him," Dexter told his boss in a memo he wrote later that day. "That he (McCullagh) was here the other day and he [Ralston] took care to talk to him while in the open, as he could not avoid him. As for Bassett, he was as corrupt as a man could be. Had no regard for anything and would have nothing to do with him."

In private, King ranted that Canada's conservative press lords "were anxious for titles." That, he believed, was one of the main reasons they wanted him out. The flow of knighthoods had stopped when King became prime minister after the First World War. Conservative prime minister R.B. Bennett had opened the taps during his one term in office, but King had closed them again. Yes, that was it, he thought: McCullagh, the Bassetts, the Southams...they wanted titles, "a certain precedence" over other people.[29]

Time was running out on the Hong Kong controversy. The failure of the Dieppe raid, a few weeks after Drew sent his second letter, took most of the oxygen out of the story. And, as far as the press, the public and the Opposition was concerned, no one could really say what happened in those awful days before Christmas.

In the fall of 1942, Drew and McCullagh took one last wartime shot. Drew, in the pages of the *Globe and Mail*, accused the government of tapping his phones and spying on him. The story didn't get any traction. But Drew, urged on by Hong Kong veterans and their families, kept at the issue for years, demanding to be allowed to publish his assessment of the cover-up. King blocked him long after the war was over. The Hong Kong survivors carried psychological scars and awful health problems that shortened their lives and kept them in pain. Their story should not have been suppressed to protect General Crerar's, King's and Duff's reputations.

In 1948, while Drew was running for the leadership of the federal Tories, Gen. Charles Foulkes, the chief of the general staff, ordered his officers to secretly analyze Duff's report. The military investigators found serious flaws in Duff's work, but concluded nothing could have saved the small Canadian force from the Japanese onslaught. The Chinese forces on the mainland were too weak to launch a counter-attack to relieve the besieged British, Indians and Canadians, while Britain's Pacific naval power had been crushed by the sinking of the battleship *Prince of Wales* and cruiser *Repulse* in the South China Sea two weeks before Hong Kong fell.

* * *

McCullagh's wartime machinations infuriated Mackenzie King. After the Hong Kong controversy died down the prime minister decided to destroy McCullagh by prying the *Globe and Mail* out of his hands. The way to do it, King believed, was by driving a wedge between McCullagh and William Wright. A man King describes as V. Bartram arrived in King's office in November 1942, claiming to be a friend of Wright's. Supposedly, they'd met during the Boer War. Bartram told King he had insider knowledge from Ed Hargreaves, Wright's brother-in-law, that the old prospector was fed up with McCullagh and would be glad to get the *Globe and Mail* off his hands. Wright supposedly said the paper had been losing money steadily, a claim that was absurd. Bartram also told King Wright was upset that McCullagh had built a house and manicured gardens that cost half a million dollars, the upkeep of which must be very great indeed.

"Hargreaves did not like the attitude of *The Globe and Mail* toward me," King confided to his diary. "He was 100% behind me and liked me personally and liked the policies of the government. If the right person was found to purchase the Globe and take the building, he [Wright] would be prepared to see that the interests of the Globe were parted with. Mr. Hargreaves said to Mr. Bartram that he was quite agreeable I should be given the further chance to suggest names of persons who might be ready to consider purchase."

They threw some names around, including McCullagh's old friend Sir Edward Beatty, president of the Canadian Pacific Railway. How about an American? "I said it would depend on who it was," King said. Bartram suggested Texas millionaire sportsman Col. Jim Flanagan. King said that would "suit me perfectly. While it is true he was an American, he was keeping a residence in Canada and I should welcome his getting control of the Globe."[30]

Five days later, Colonel Flanagan turned up in King's office. The prime minister told Flanagan to contact Hargreaves if he wanted to take a run at the paper. Flanagan said he would have done it if he were young, but, while he disliked McCullagh, he didn't want to engineer a hostile takeover.[31]

In December, King saw Bartram again, and, supposedly, he was there on behalf of Hargreaves. He wanted to know if King's political financers could buy the *Globe and Mail*. King said he didn't know who paid for his campaigns. That was party business and he kept out of it. King had friends who helped cover his own expenses, but they couldn't afford to buy the paper out from under McCullagh. They talked again about Beatty, but he was an old man and, besides, he was a friend of McCullagh's who had backed coalition governments and the Leadership League.

There is a strong element of nonsense to Bartram's negotiations. He insisted that Hargreaves was a wealthy man who opposed McCullagh on ideological grounds and had influence with Wright. Supposedly, Hargreaves complained about the vast amount of income tax that he paid, but otherwise he was happy with King's government.[32] But, in fact, Hargreaves was not a rich man: he had sold his shares in the Wright-Hargreaves mine at the very beginning, for just a few thousand dollars. He was living with Wright because he was married to Wright's sister. Maybe she would inherit the old bachelor's money someday, but Wright was still very much alive. Wright was still friends, almost family even, with McCullagh, who was a director of Wright-Hargreaves mine. And, according to McCullagh, Wright had sold the last of his share of the ownership of the *Globe and Mail* to McCullagh at about this time. Since the shares in the paper were privately held, the shifts in ownership are still murky, and it's possible that Wright was a minority shareholder who still owned the valuable King Street property but not the newspaper that was published there.

* * *

In the late fall of 1942, McCullagh gave up on the idea of "national government," at least temporarily. There were no backers among the people who had a serious shot at winning the Conservative leadership. King didn't want it, and the electorate would not get a chance to be heard on the issue until sometime in 1944 or 1945. John Wesley Dafoe, the legendary editor of the *Winnipeg Free Press*, a newspaper that dominated western Canada journalism, heard in November that McCullagh had stopped beating this dead horse. McCullagh called the *Free Press*'s owner, Victor Sifton, to talk about some issue affecting their industry.[33] The conversation shifted to politics, with McCullagh saying he'd heard that John Bracken, the populist former premier of Manitoba (who would be described as a Red Tory, if he were on the political scene today), wanted to be asked to be leader. He didn't want to have to run for it, though there would be a leadership convention.[34] McCullagh had some clout in the party: soon after Bracken got the leadership, he and another Tory money-man met Bracken to negotiate a trust fund that gave the new party leader some personal financial security.[35]

McCullagh tried to be king-maker and King-breaker. Despite the party's support for Bracken, he wanted Drew to get the Tory leadership some day. The position was bound to come open eventually. Bracken was the fourth new Tory leader since King won the 1935 election.

With Lord Beaverbrook's help, McCullagh managed to get permission for an extraordinary month-long trip in March 1943: from Toronto to England, Northern Ireland, north and central Africa, Trinidad and New York. Beaverbrook and McCullagh had developed a real friendship during the war, sharing gossip about the powerbrokers in London and Canada. Beaverbrook was often concerned about McCullagh's mental and physical health, which he realized was always on the verge of breaking down. (Beaverbrook often mentioned McCullagh's psychological problems when writing to other important people in the United Kingdom.) Still, Beaverbrook constantly urged McCullagh to visit England, with an open-ended offer of hospitality.

Accompanied by Beaverbrook, who published the *Daily Express* while working as the head of Britain's military aircraft construction program, McCullagh visited newspaper publishers on Fleet Street and toured bombed cities in England. He noticed how "the little people" had been able to make supportive communities in the ruins. McCullagh went to Aldershot to see some of the nearly 500,000 Canadian soldiers and tens of thousands of Royal Canadian Air Force personnel stationed in England. In North Africa, he managed to get close enough to the fighting front to talk to some of the three hundred Canadian soldiers attached to Field Marshal Montgomery's army as they fought Erwin Rommel's Afrika Korps.

Giving an interview in New York while heading back to Toronto, McCullagh said he was impressed by how much the British people loved Canadian servicemen. (In fact, it was complicated. The Brits found many Canadians to be ugly drunks, overly horny, annoying and rude, but both the Brits and the Canucks had something in common:

they secretly envied and quietly hated the Americans.) Despite his troubles with King, McCullagh said the Canadian government shouldn't be blamed for being left out of the fight for North Africa.[36] Monty's forces were enough to finish Rommel, and our soldiers would be needed when the Allies opened a second front in Europe. Whether McCullagh knew it or not, Canadians were already earmarked for the invasion of Sicily in three months.[37]

When Winston Churchill visited Washington in the spring of 1943, in the lead-up to the first Quebec Conference, McCullagh told Drew to contact Churchill and tell him to stop praising the King government's war work. "Now that you have this government over the barrel on their manpower and on their army establishment, and their sins are coming home to roost, it is not just that some statement by the Prime Minister of Britain should be used here to save the government's face," McCullagh told Drew.[38] The writing was clunky and the metaphors were mixed because McCullagh felt as though he was on the verge of another breakdown, and about to leave for New York again to see his psychiatrist before going to Washington.

He had access to many of America's top decision-makers, including Franklin Roosevelt, who received him at the White House for a visit McCullagh said "was largely social," but was likely an attempt to get Roosevelt fired up about Canadian conscription.[39]

* * *

McCullagh, who had supposedly been sober since 1935, had few outlets for the symptoms of his mental illness. His spring 1939 breakdown after the collapse of the Leadership League had been relatively short. He was back in Toronto and seemed to be in somewhat better shape by May, when he faced the two challenges of his mother's last illness and Archworth's run for the King's Plate. He may have had a collapse in the winter of 1941, and certainly his mental health had a severe setback when he suffered his physical and mental breakdown in February

1942. There may have been a serious mental health scare in the early winter of 1943, as well, though McCullagh seems to have been in good shape when he left for Europe in the early spring. These were the big events, but there were many days when he had trouble coping.

If McCullagh was, in fact, bipolar, the highs appear to have been outnumbered by the lows. He seems to have been soaring in the fall of 1936, when he bought the *Globe* and the *Mail and Empire*, and his behaviour in the late fall of 1939, when he impulsively joined the air force without telling most of his family, suggests there were serious ups as well as deep downs. It's difficult to know which episodes of ill health were physical and which were mental illness relapses. McCullagh certainly had problems with his breathing, and did have recurring pneumonia. It may have been a congenital issue—his mother died relatively young of that disease—and it may also have been caused by, or made worse by, McCullagh's smoking. He smoked cigarettes in his office and Cuban cigars when he went out to restaurants and sports events.

McCullagh was a patient of Dr. Robert Foster Kennedy, a leading expert on bipolar disorder who worked out of New York City's Bellevue Hospital. Kennedy was convinced that mental illness was a physical problem that could be corrected through shock treatments or lobotomy. He thought psychoanalysis was a waste of time.[40] While McCullagh's medical records are long gone, it's clear that he was subjected to electroconvulsive therapy that allowed him to bounce back fairly quickly. McCullagh had sought out the biggest name in American psychiatry. Kennedy was president of the Association for Research in Nervous and Mental Diseases in 1938 and president of the American Neurological Association in 1940. He was a medical professor at Cornell and one of the leading anti-Freud practitioners in America. Unlike most other psychiatrists, Dr. Kennedy saw no use in prying into McCullagh's sex life or his relationship with his parents.

Dr. Kennedy also fit into McCullagh's social world. He was tall, attractive, and gregarious. He'd wanted to be an actor, but chose medicine instead. After immigrating to the United States in the 1920s, Dr. Kennedy became a lion in New York's social scene. He made friends with powerful politicians, actors and celebrities, the same kind of people McCullagh wanted as his friends.

But the good doctor should have spent some time exploring McCullagh's family dynamics and his views about women.

McCullagh, whose personality demanded constant reaffirmation and success, lived in a time when women, especially young, single working women, were considered the property of the men who employed them. June Callwood, who joined the *Globe and Mail* in 1942 at the age of eighteen, quickly became a target. McCullagh pawed at her, chased her around the office, and made her life miserable. "The switchboard operator was a friend of mine," she said years later. "She'd tip me off. 'The publisher is looking for you.' And I'd go hide in the washroom."[41] McCullagh, she said, was after "virgins," and believed she was one. The sexual harassment likely stopped when Callwood married sportswriter Trent Frayne two years after she started at the *Globe and Mail*, but wartime brought many more young women into the newsroom, at least temporarily.[42] McCullagh also scandalized colleagues like John D. MacFarlane by swearing around women, something gentlemen didn't do. McCullagh had brought some women into the newsroom as colleagues, as well as potential sexual targets. He wasn't going to censor his language for them.[43]

Early in the war, he lost his best columnist. Judith Robinson, now almost forty-five and, seemingly, a *Globe and Mail* lifer, was even more extreme than her boss in her criticism of King's handling of the war. In 1941, she and Oakley Dalgleish had started a weekly paper to denounce what they saw as Canada's lame war effort. Some writers have said McCullagh fired her because of her advocacy for Canada's soldiers and veterans, but that doesn't seem likely. McCullagh was on the same wavelength. It appears she left the paper because of the breakdown of her relationship with McCullagh. At one point, McCullagh told her that he could call Franklin Roosevelt and convince him to join the war effort. "On whose side?" she supposedly answered. And that was the problem. Robinson saw the world from the left side of the spectrum, and believed McCullagh's support for the war effort hid his own dangerous authoritarian side.[44]

George H. McCullagh, the publisher's father, died in London, Ontario, on September 24, 1943.[45] That must have thrown McCullagh, who had worked so hard to make his father a nonentity. There was no big funeral in Toronto, no calling out of the country's elites to pay their respects. There was just a little service in London, Ontario. The mother of the publisher of the *Globe and Mail* might be buried among the powerful—including Mackenzie King's mother—at Mount Pleasant Cemetery in Toronto, but George Henry McCullagh was quickly hustled into the soil of Middlesex County, Ontario. There was no front-page coverage, and no prayers from the Queen.

* * *

In October 1942, Mitch Hepburn knew he was finished as premier. King had beaten him time and again: in 1940, when Hepburn's attempt to humiliate the prime minister ended with King winning a spectacular majority; and now, Meighen was losing his by-election despite Hepburn's endorsement. Ontario was overdue for an election and Mitch couldn't count on the support of any major newspaper in the province. His caucus was sick of the drunkenness and the philandering. So Hepburn quit. Or seemed to.

He installed his attorney general, Gordon Conant, as premier by convincing the lieutenant-governor to make the appointment. This was not Hepburn's decision to make. At the very least, Conant should have been chosen by Liberal members of the legislature, if not by a leadership convention. Many observers, including Liberals, believed the whole thing was a farce. Hepburn kept his jobs as provincial treasurer and leader of the Liberal Party. It took almost six months for the

Liberals to fix this situation by pushing Hepburn out of his last two jobs. Mitch sent a resignation telegram, the Liberals held a leadership race, and in May 1943, Harry Nixon was appointed premier.

Nixon was running out of time. He was a good man, but the provincial Liberal brand had become toxic. The question was whether the Conservatives, under McCullagh's best friend, George Drew, would win, or if the Co-operative Commonwealth Federation would take power.

As the Liberals scrambled to salvage the situation, an odd character named Iverach McDonald was touring Canada. Officially the military and diplomatic analyst for the London *Times*, McDonald was really an MI6 agent. During a tour of the United States and Canada in the first half of 1943, McDonald filed feature stories to the *Times* and confidential reports to Whitehall. His cover story was that he was on "a kind of travelling scholarship for the *Times*," but his MI6 assignment was to size up North American commitment to the war in Europe.

Drew met McDonald in Washington and sent the *Globe and Mail* publisher a note asking McCullagh to show McDonald around. He asked his friend to introduce the journalist-spy to opinion-makers and politicians in Canada. This did not go well. Two weeks later, McDonald, who had finished the Toronto leg of his trip and was now settled into Ottawa's Chateau Laurier hotel, wrote to Drew to warn him not to take McCullagh too seriously. The *Globe and Mail* publisher's opinions were, according to McDonald, who was recognized by many as the best military analyst in journalism, "specious."[46] But that was not enough to shake Drew off McCullagh. He desperately needed the publisher for the battle to come.

At the same time, McCullagh had the ear of the *Times*' real Ottawa correspondent. King believed J.A. Stevenson, long-time *Times* man on Parliament Hill, was one of his most dangerous enemies. Canada's telegraph tappers were reading all of Stevenson's cables to London and sending copies to the press censors, who kept a special file on the

Times writer. During the election campaign, Stevenson dictated a memo to George McCullagh about King's July 1937 trip to Berlin. King, Stevenson reminded McCullagh, had met with deputy führer Rudolph Hess, and dined with Luftwaffe commander Hermann Goering and gone with him to the opera. King, Stevenson said, had completely misjudged Hitler. (The world wouldn't know for another forty years, when King's diaries were finally released, that King's judgment was affected by a strange homoerotic fixation with Hitler.)

Stevenson refreshed McCullagh's memory of how King had told the Canadian people that Hitler's regime was just completing a "transition through which all countries are now passing in the readjustments which are being made to the existing social order." Germany, and the minor fascist states in central Europe that King had visited, did not want war and were, according to the man who was Canada's prime minister and foreign minister, "prepared to work out a solution to cooperate." Stevenson noted rather dryly that the German air force began bombing the airfields of Spain's left-wing Republic government just days after King's speech to Canadians. Six months later, Hitler marched into Austria.[47] Three years later, he would be the conqueror of France.[48] McCullagh gave copies of the memo to Drew, who put it away until he needed it. There was no need to play this card now: despite the brutal fight over Hong Kong and Drew's frequent criticism of King's wartime leadership, the prime minister would be sitting this provincial election out. There was no one who he wanted to win.

But Drew knew there were battles to come. Ontario might be the linchpin of Confederation, but to George Drew and his friends, Queen's Park was a stepping stone.[49]

* * *

The 1943 provincial election campaign was very, very ugly. Tory election managers W. Gladstone Murray,[50] Burdick Testrail and Montague "Bugsy" Sanderson ran what they called "Reliable Exterminators," named after Bugsy's pest control company. They were out to kill communists and socialists, so they went after the CCF. Polling was primitive at best, but it was obvious that the Liberals were due for a loss, and their donors knew it.[51] (They wouldn't hold power again for more than four decades.) Desperate to keep the Tories out, some Liberals and CCF activists worked together. Neither party had much money though, while the Tories had all they needed. And there were no spending limits in those days.

George McCullagh did his part by buying radio time across the province for a one-hour broadcast. In the speech, McCullagh said the provincial government was ignoring the "107 single unemployed men" who had been sleeping on newspapers in the streets of Toronto before the war and were now "locked in the comradeship of arms with their British and American allies on the plains of Sicily."

It was unclear how he'd come up with such a precise number of pre-war homeless men, but no matter. Homelessness, and whatever was happening to these men now, was the provincial and federal Liberals' fault. The Ontario Liberals might claim to care about the poor but "currently in this very city—the capital of the Province of Ontario—there is the most cold-hearted indifference toward hospital accommodations for those veterans of the last war, and those who have suffered misfortunes, including desperate wounds and nervous shock, in this war." The province was letting veterans down by building a wing on their decrepit Christie Street Hospital, "located in a noisy factory district of Toronto, though there has been strong objection from veterans' and women's organizations."[52]

McCullagh might've been talking sanely about the First World War vets, but whenever he tried to link Harry Nixon's Ontario Liberals with the Mackenzie King Liberals in Ottawa, the talk became strange. McCullagh, with all seriousness, accused King of trying to create a one-party state. And said the prime minister was in the thrall of Quebec. King's "deferential reference" to French Canada, he said, was a threat to national unity, while Quebec was a demographic threat to Canada's Britishness. McCullagh believed that if they kept up their volume of baby-making,[53] French Canadians would outnumber those of British origin by 1971. There would be what Quebec nationalists called "the revenge of the cradle." McCullagh asked his listeners why Quebec felt it needed revenge.

The publisher went on, working his way through a thick catalogue of grievances and accusations about the prime minister. King had stacked the 1942 conscription referendum to please Quebec. Holding the referendum was a cowardly act. It was a waste of money that exposed the "racial" cleavages in the country. Before the war, King and his colleagues in Ottawa had shown themselves to be anti-British, puppets of Quebec's anti-Anglo francophones.[54] Despite Ontario voting 83 percent in favour of conscription, King had "bowed to the minority" and had drafted very few men. He'd also promised not to send any of the conscripts overseas.

The next night, McCullagh was on the air again, this time saying Ontario needed George Drew and his Conservatives as an "unbreakable bulwark" against King's treachery and Ottawa's all-consuming bureaucracy.

Whether you were a veteran, a working man, or a misunderstood mining magnate, you shared the misery of being governed by rapacious fools: "The hand of the tax-gatherer reaches deep into the pockets of everyone, of workers in every walk of life. Billions of dollars are spent at Ottawa without the effective supervision of Parliament which has been reduced by a servile, top-heavy majority to little more than a cypher. Officials with absolute power spring up like mushrooms to regulate the coming and going of every man in the operation of his business, his work, his farm—and every woman, too, even into the operation of her household."

The British, as usual, had found the answer. Winston Churchill's government, made up of MPs from all the major parties, had protected

British citizens from such a fate: "because the government there is held together only by the emergency of war, and because it is composed of men who have different points of view on almost every subject except the conduct of the war. They will not tolerate an attempt by any group to put itself in a position of permanent advantage."[55]

Earlier that evening, Drew had also used a province-wide radio network to make a pitch to voters. King listened to and was impressed by Drew's delivery. But the speech had a "jingo appeal," the prime minister wrote in his diary. McCullagh got harsher treatment: "His whole speech was stirring up prejudice against the French and, for the most part, making an attack on the Federal government and myself in particular; bringing in a reference to the plebiscite etc. All claimed to be catering Quebec. It seemed to me that McCullagh's voice indicated shaken internal condition. I was, on the whole, pleased that he had come out as he did, for it made clear he is supporting Drew and voting for him, which means the Globe has Tory influence in provincial politics...I hope our people will now make clear that the Globe and Mail is just a Tory organ, both federally and provincially. Nixon has done the right thing in opposing McCullagh and he will win large support in doing so."[56]

King sent federal MPs and some of his Ontario ministers onto the campaign trail. G.G. McGeer, the Liberal MP for Vancouver, told people at a Liberal rally in Aurora (then a small village a half-hour's drive from the edge of the city) that Drew was just a "selfish" puppet of McCullagh, who wanted to become the dictator of Canada:

(I)t is on the record that George McCullagh, whose paper supported the ill-conceived National Conservative Party in 1940 when it was not only hopelessly defeated, but destroyed, is now asking the electors of the Province of Ontario to place their provincial government in the hands of Col. Drew, the self-styled military expert, who has never been right, and who has always been wrong.

Public men of the McCullagh and Drew type always calculate that the public's short memory is always the politician's long
suit. But surely the people of Ontario have not soon forgotten
George McCullagh's ill-starred 'Leaderless League.' Fortunately
for Canada, it died a-borning. This weird political adventure
was conjured up by McCullagh, and had it been accepted it
would have been the first step toward a national dictatorship,
no doubt with McCullagh in the driver's seat and Bay Street and
St. James Street in control. Hitler was a good salesman, and he
sold himself to the German people. McCullagh, while a good
salesman, has failed to sell himself to the people of Canada. His
technique is not nearly as clever as Hitler's.[57]

While the Liberals and Tories clawed at each other, the CCF was
working the doorsteps and labour halls. They were the real threat to
the status quo in this election, and they almost won it. On election
night, McCullagh, Drew and King finally realized what had happened.
Drew's Progressive Conservatives had thirty-eight seats in the ninety-
seat legislature. The CCF had thirty-four. The Liberals, who went into
the campaign with sixty-three seats, lost all but fifteen of them. There
were two Communists (calling themselves the Labour-Progressive
Party). And there was Mitch Hepburn, who'd left the Liberals when he
was pushed out of his last cabinet post and was sitting as a Liberal
Independent. Drew had the shakiest of minorities, and his government could only survive if it had the support of the Liberals.

Some of McCullagh's old Liberal friends blamed the *Globe and
Mail* publisher for driving centrists and left-of-centre votes to the
CCF,[58] but McCullagh's campaign probably just pushed a few more voters to the obvious conclusion: Mitch Hepburn was the wrong person
to lead Ontario in wartime. He was unstable, reckless and, at the same
time, stale. His party, whether it kept him around or not, also deserved
to be punished, and it would stay in the political wilderness until 1985.

* * *

According to two great Toronto *Star* journalists, Val Sears and Roy Greenaway, Drew effectively shut the *Star* out of all official Queen's Park interviews and tried to make it impossible for Atkinson's reporters at Queen's Park to cover the Ontario government. Drew had made that decision before the election. When Greenaway went to the Conservative victory party on the night of the election, Drew took him aside, accepted the reporter's offer of a handshake, and told him that, while he liked Greenaway as a person, no *Star* reporter would have access to his office.[59] Almost all of Drew's ministers fell into line, but Tom Kennedy, Drew's agriculture minister (and Drew's successor as premier), fed Greenaway stories and became his mentor. Still, the usual flow of news from cabinet ministers, backbenchers and bureaucrats dried up almost instantly. *Star* reporters even had trouble getting basic information on crimes from the Ontario Provincial Police.

Rather than change its tone, the *Star* dug in and waged a decades-long fight to get the Ontario Conservatives out of power. It took forty-two years.

Queen's Park was open for business to McCullagh and his staff. But the flow of information went both ways. Drew fed the *Globe and Mail* stories that pushed the Tory agenda of wartime conscription while McCullagh sent Drew drafts of *Globe and Mail* editorials. Together, backed by friends at the very top of the Canadian military and by people like Toronto Maple Leafs owner Conn Smythe, who was still in the army overseas, these two men coordinated the main English-Canadian opposition to King's handling of the war.[60] (An almost mirror situation existed in Quebec with Maurice Duplessis, still in Opposition, in a symbiotic relationship with nationalist papers like *Le Devoir*.)

In one editorial vetted by Drew, McCullagh's editorial writers were commenting on the hostile reaction to the disbanding of three Canadian divisions, even though they were just military units on paper. The *Globe and Mail* said: "Unless the Minister of Defence announces that his first statement was wrong and that Canada is not, in fact, reducing its fighting strength by three combat divisions, then there will be serious and continuing misunderstanding of our course in the United States... The plain unvarnished truth is that this was a fake set up from the very beginning to give some appearance of usefulness to more than sixty thousand men who could not be moved into any field of battle where the enemy could be fought because of the cowardice of the government in dealing with military manpower."[61]

King's government was "misleading our British partners and the Allied Nations as to what was taking place."

It was tough talk in a country that was supposedly rallying around the flag, engaged in a life-and-death struggle for freedom. People in Ontario, who, the year before, had voted strongly in favour of a military draft, could see that King's government was dragging its heels, that King was willing to spend money, build a navy, and do anything but send men overseas to die. And the great crisis of the war was yet to come. In the summer of 1943, most of the Canadians who would be killed in the Second World War were still alive.

But the relationship between Drew and McCullagh wasn't just professional. The two men, along with John Bassett, were still the triumvirate at the core of the Toronto Clique. Drew and McCullagh often wrote to each other, especially when they were travelling. The wives of the three men were also close friends.

In the fall of 1943, McCullagh managed to get to England to visit some of his contacts in the British government—including Beaverbrook and Bracken—and the city's business community. McCullagh offered Beaverbrook advice on a second front in Europe, and for the Churchill government's postwar policies.[62] Beaverbrook let McCullagh stay in his country home and introduced him to Fleet Street's most powerful publishers.

Bassett went on a tour of western Canada. Bassett was the most personable of the three men, and he had friends across the country who would be useful when the clique made their move for national power. Drew was in Montreal, looking for support from the Anglo-Quebec business community, which was still a powerful force in the country. He wanted to fight the Quebec government's plan to keep wages down, which, Drew believed, was a blatant attempt to steal Ontario's wartime manufacturing jobs. That must have been a tough sell on Montreal's St. James Street. Drew also made connections with service clubs, which he hoped to harness to his campaign for conscription. He was leaving soon for London and planned to stay at the Savoy Hotel in Westminster.

"I am more convinced than ever that there is a tremendous job to be done over there, particularly in establishing some effective basis of contact with the troops themselves," Drew wrote to McCullagh. It didn't seem to dawn on the two men that campaigning for conscription among Canadian troops deployed in Britain in wartime was wrong, even if—and it's a pretty big if—it was legal.

Drew praised McCullagh for attracting James Henry Gundy, partner in Wood Gundy, to their clique "because he has done a decent job both there [Montreal] and in Toronto which I am convinced no one else could have done" to help build up Bracken, for which the Tory leader could thank McCullagh "almost entirely."[63]

Everyone at the *Globe and Mail* knew McCullagh and Drew were feeding each other. So did most other people in Toronto's journalism community. At the end of 1943, the country's press censors tried to make use of this connection. They wanted to shut down the pro-fascist *Le Devoir* for the duration, but King and his Quebec ministers opposed the idea of shuttering Quebec's most important political newspaper. Censor Lew Gordon tried to turn up the heat on *Le Devoir* by writing a memo to McCullagh about an inflammatory article written by *Le Devoir*'s blatantly pro-Vichy Ottawa correspondent Léopold Richer. Gordon, knowing his audience, suggested McCullagh pass the article on to Drew.[64]

14

SENDING ZOMBIES TO WAR

George Brown founded the *Globe* in 1844. George McCullagh celebrated its centennial in a very different world. Brown had built his career with railway timetables, and become one of the most powerful politicians in Canada. McCullagh had taken to the air in radio broadcasts and launched a failed political movement. He had built his political apparatus around another man: George Drew. He'd also ignored Brown's profit obsession by chucking out columns of wartime ads to make room for stories in his slimmed-down newspaper, which had been reduced in size because of wartime newsprint rationing.

In March, McCullagh threw a big banquet in the Crystal Ballroom of the King Edward Hotel. About eight hundred people, newspaper staff, friends and supporters filled the place and watched Phyllis blow out the candles on a giant birthday cake. The paper's staff had collected money to buy the publisher and his wife a silver tray. In return, employees who'd been with the papers for twenty-five years got a pin and a twenty-five-dollar war bond.[1]

There was no escaping the war. Many of the paper's best reporters weren't at the party because they were fighting or reporting from Italy, or waiting in England for the invasion of northern Europe. The National Resources Mobilization Act, passed at the beginning of the war, allowed the government to draft men into the army, but a clause in the law prohibited the draftees from being sent overseas. The April 27, 1942, referendum had allowed Canadians to decide whether to strip out that part of the law. Quebec voted overwhelmingly—72.9 percent— to keep draftees in Canada. People in the other eight provinces cast their ballots in favour of drafting fighting-age men and sending them overseas. In Ontario, 82.3 percent of voters supported full conscription and overseas deployment. This was political dynamite that, if detonated, could take down King's government.

King struggled against the generals who wanted to use this power. Backbenchers and some ministers were either pro-conscription or were well aware that their constituents supported a draft. King, himself a pacifist, saw things from a national and an international perspective: the fate of the Allies did not hinge on the size of the Canadian contingent, but Canada's unity during and after the war was truly at stake. King did what he did best: he stalled. He played passive-aggressive games, hoping that the Nazis would collapse while Canadians bickered. The last thing he wanted was Quebec mothers getting telegrams saying their drafted boys were buried in an overseas grave. He promised another plebiscite before sending drafted men overseas.

James Ralston, the First World War veteran who was King's defence minister, resigned. King refused to accept the resignation, but he kept the letter in his desk drawer.

The 1942 plebiscite on conscription calmed the issue for more than a year. Canadian men kept volunteering and being shipped to England, where they settled into a routine of training for the invasion of Europe. In 1943, some of these soldiers left for Sicily, but there was still no shortage of Canadian soldiers. Someday, there would be a lunge across the English Channel, and the military knew that the fighting units would be stretched thin. But that was in the future. Meanwhile, eighty thousand men had been drafted and were being trained in Canada. People in the army started calling them Zombies, and the public picked up on the term.

The 1942 conscription referendum gave the prime minister the power to send the Zombies to overseas fighting fronts. Mackenzie King hoped he would never have to put drafted soldiers in harm's way. The brief and feeble Japanese threat to the West Coast allowed King to send thousands of these men, wearing Canadian army uniforms, to British Columbia. They guarded the big munitions depots at Prince Rupert, where supplies were sent to Americans fighting in the south and central Pacific. They even ran an armoured train between Terrace, BC, and the coast to guard that important rail line. The greater the level of public fear in British Columbia, the more Zombies were needed. This fear was also turned against the Japanese-Canadians living on the West Coast, making them victims of racism as well as King's military policy.

In 1943, when the Japanese grabbed two of the islands off Alaska, Zombies were among the five thousand Allied soldiers sent to liberate Kiska. They were willing to fight, but the Japanese had already pulled their garrison out. But since they had been forced into the army, the soldiers had been treated like dirt by civilians and volunteer soldiers, maligned in the press and used as political pawns. Their morale sank as the war went on.

The French-English split in Canada was brilliantly reflected in the politics of the Zombies themselves. Many were from Quebec, and almost all of them, whatever part of Canada they were from, had their own reasons for not enlisting voluntarily. Some were pacifists. Some were farm boys who believed they were needed at home. A fair number were industrial workers who were radical unionists. Many were Quebec francophones who had grown up listening to stories of how the English in Canada had tried to use conscription to force their fathers and older brothers to fight a European war that was none of Quebec's business.[2]

Sometimes, the split between Quebec and English Canada broke through to the surface. In the spring of 1944, the Toronto Maple Leafs faced the Montreal Canadiens in the National Hockey League semifinals. The Leafs went into the series with a .500 win/loss average. The Canadiens' record was .830. McCullagh, as a minority shareholder in the Leafs, went to the Leafs' home games in the series and travelled on the road with the team. There were only two home games, and Toronto lost them both. The second home game was a 4–1 thumping, but the real humiliation came when the Habs finished them off at the Forum in five games with an 11–0 win. Toronto fans took their resentment out on Quebecois, saying the best Leaf players were overseas, while the Canadiens still had most of theirs.[3]

Between the end of the series and the beginning of May, McCullagh used his pull in Washington to get a pass to fly to England to see Lord Beaverbrook. He wanted to take the measure of the morale of senior Canadian military officers and the British ruling class and to visit some of England's best racehorse stables. King was furious that McCullagh was in London at all, let alone while King was in the British capital for meetings in the lead-up to D-Day.

Ten weeks after the blow-out in the Forum and just over a month after McCullagh arrived in England, Canadians were on Juno Beach in Normandy. Now Canada's fighting men were bleeding and dying on two fronts, Normandy and Italy. The Allies expected a fast break-out into the open countryside of France. Instead, they found themselves bogged down in ancient cities and hedged fields where the Germans fought desperately to drive them back into the sea.

* * *

Canadians had been bloodied in Sicily and Italy before D-Day, but were able to replace the casualties with more volunteers. In Normandy,

Canada's army—by far the biggest all-volunteer force in the campaign[4]—had higher casualty rates than the German army on the Russian front. The bleeding continued as the Canadians closed the Falaise Gap in Normandy and headed northeast across the old battlefields of the First World War and into Belgium. Now the army needed men to fill the gaps in the line. There was some dispute in the army itself as to whether the Zombies should be fed piecemeal into depleted units or go into the lines in their own regiments, but something had to be done. Clerks and cooks in volunteer units had been strong-armed into joining front-line units, and there was nothing left at the bottom of the barrel.

The Opposition saw this as an opportunity. King would either be forced to send the Zombies, now numbering eighty thousand to Europe—and lose support in Quebec—or he would keep them in Canada and lose the rest of the country. King's strategy was to run the clock, hoping the Germans would sue for peace in the fall of 1944.[5]

By that fall, the leaders of the pro-conscription forces had jelled: George McCullagh, owner of the most important political newspaper in Canada; Ontario premier George Drew, who had no qualms about politicking among soldiers and their families in wartime; and Maj. Conn Smythe, owner of the Toronto Maple Leafs, and just back in Canada after being wounded in action at Caen in Normandy.

Smythe was still technically a serving officer in the Canadian army. Drew had visited Smythe in England just after he was wounded. Now, from his hospital bed at Chorley Park—the old lieutenant-governor's mansion, closed by Mitch Hepburn back in the day and turned into a recovery centre for officers[6]—Smythe worked with Drew and McCullagh to fill the pages of the *Globe and Mail* with stories saying Canada's military could no longer do its part. In fact, McCullagh was Smythe's first visitor in Toronto.

Two days after the end of the Second Quebec Conference, just after Franklin Roosevelt and Winston Churchill went back to their home capitals, Smythe issued a long press release about the manpower crisis

McCullagh, with Toronto Maple Leafs owner Conn Smythe at his right, at a horse race, spring 1945. Smythe and McCullagh's fight for a military draft shook Mackenzie King's government and split the country. (CITY OF TORONTO ARCHIVES, FONDS 1257, SERIES 1057, ITEM 3533)

faced by the Canadian army. It said the government was sending "green, inexperience and poorly-trained reinforcements" against the Germans when thousands of "well-trained" conscripts remained in Canada. Smythe was echoing complaints made by commanders in the field, who said the army was sending almost-untrained men scraped up from rear-echelon jobs into battle to be slaughtered by elite Nazi troops.[7]

Defence Minister Ralston, shaken by the press release and the storm it created, went to Italy and northwest Europe to see for himself.

Ralston was overseas as the Canadians finished clearing the Scheldt Estuary, opening the great port of Antwerp to Allied shipping. He sent a telegram to King saying the Zombies had to be sent overseas. There was to be a lull in the Canadian campaign in the Low Countries that would be ideal for revitalizing the regiments that had been bled white. Ralston thought wounded Canadians were being forced out of hospitals and sent back to the front lines far too quickly. He believed what the generals told him: that the Zombies were a valuable pool of trained infantrymen. What the generals didn't tell the minister was that they'd screwed up the training program. They'd put far too much emphasis on organizing and training rear-echelon men and women, and not enough effort into making men ready for front-line fighting. There were 150,000 volunteer soldiers in England and Canada who just didn't know what to do when they came up against the Wehrmacht.

* * *

McCullagh's paper openly campaigned for the deployment of the conscripts. Much of the journalism is jingoistic, and some of it is flat out anti–French Canadian and anti-Catholic. Religion—the split in Canada between Protestant and Catholic Christians—was still one of the main fault lines in Canadian society. Some readers of the *Globe and Mail* thought its publisher was not going far enough in his Catholic-shaming and Protestant-boosting. One subscriber, J.J. Ridley, of London, Ontario, was angry about a slight criticism of the Rev. Dr. T.T. Shields, head of the fundamentalist breakaway Baptist sect headquartered in Toronto's Jarvis Street Baptist Church (and last seen in this narrative denouncing GM strikers in Oshawa). Shields was a fire-breathing old-time Gospel radio preacher with a large following in the Ontario boondocks and among the less-bright urbanites of the province. This included Mr. Ridley. Shield's theology could be summed up in his quote "Modernism is not Christianity diluted, it is Christianity denied, it is not a modification of the New Testament religion, it is absolutely unchristian from top to bottom."

Ridley said he regretted having such a poor grasp of English that he could not commit the full extent of his indignation onto paper:

> Dr Shields is absolutely the best informed man on his subject on the North American continent, you (even you) dare not meet him in debate, and you can not produce a man even the great Catholic divines among the hierarchy who dare face him. But the

last and smallest thing you have done is condemn him in your paper; without telling the public your reason why. The fact is you are not man enough, not British enough, to let the public judge; but inflict your omnipotent judgment on your readers.

I could write on; but suffice it to say that the stock of The Globe and Mail has sunken many points in the City of London, where the papists are eating the city up. Personally, I refuse to patronize it at all. I would rather give the mail boy a dime to pass on. May I say before closing that it was the Protestants, not the Catholics who elected Drew and between him and you, I doubt he could go to the country and win a seat.[8]

McCullagh read the letter and had a copy made for George Drew. He dispatched it to the premier's office at Queen's Park as evidence that something was brewing in the hinterland.[9] Canada had been able to cope with its air force and navy losses, with the casualties in Sicily and Italy, with the mobilization of hundreds of thousands of young men and women, with rationing, wage controls, and the opening of the workforce to women. It could handle the increase in family breakdowns, juvenile delinquency, sexually transmitted diseases, and all the rest of the social upheavals. But once the hard fighting started in northern Europe and men started to die in large numbers, the country began to come apart.

It seemed like a good time for McCullagh to get out of Toronto for a while. He and Drew went to the expensive, exclusive Griffith Island fishing and hunting club in Georgian Bay, off the Bruce Peninsula town of Wiarton. It was a great place to be alone. The club's gorgeous clubhouse, its private forest stocked with pheasants, and its trails through forests and along the shore were all out of sight of voters and newspaper readers. The place even had a private turf airstrip, so the two friends could quickly get back and forth to the city. McCullagh enjoyed the privacy of the twenty-three hundred acres of mature forest and open land owned by the private club. Despite the short, gloomy late-fall days, the controversy that menaced the federal government and the demands of running the paper, McCullagh decided to stay on, alone, while Drew went back to work. When the premier was getting ready to leave, he found himself short of cash, so he borrowed twenty dollars from the publisher of the *Globe and Mail.*[10]

Things weren't so relaxed and congenial for the prime minister of Canada. On October 25, just over a month after Churchill and Roosevelt left Quebec and Smythe had distributed his press release, King faced his cabinet in a brutal meeting on conscription, with each minister getting up and stating his case. Ralston reminded the prime minister that he'd seen many wounded soldiers forced to return to the front before they were healed. The minister believed he would be blamed if the army did not get enough reinforcements. The Quebec ministers, led by Chubby Power, weren't prepared to budge. King threatened to resign and hand the government to Ralston, who could face Parliament and the country with his plan for conscript deployment. In the end, no one went through with their threats, but nothing was settled, either. One of the ministers leaked the details to Grant Dexter. "[W]hat he [Ralston] disliked most of all was the fact that McCullagh, Drew and Connie Smythe—that group would have the satisfaction of saying 'I told you so' if we were to run short of reinforcements. He did not see how he could remain in Government unless we could be sure of reinforcements."[11]

A week later, after a steady pounding in the *Globe and Mail* and most of the other newspapers outside Quebec, Ralston was out, but he stood up in the House of Commons and refused to take King's government down with him. King replaced Ralston with retired general Andrew McNaughton, who did not have a seat in Parliament. King also offered to send sixteen thousand conscripts overseas, but it wasn't enough for the generals. By the end of the year, they were threatening to quit en masse. Zombies revolted in the big base in Terrace, BC. The mutiny spread to camps across the country, and at New Year's, hundreds of draftees deserted from billets in London, Ontario, after they realized they were about to be shipped overseas.

Nearly half of the military-aged men in Ontario and the Maritimes had joined up without waiting to be drafted. Many of the rest were either physically unfit, or were married men with children. In Quebec, only 23 percent of military-age men had joined, and most of these were anglophones from Montreal and the Eastern Townships. The Conservatives, their friends in the army and most of the press in English Canada insisted Quebec's men were the last untapped pool of potential soldiers in Canada.

King wanted news of all this censored, and he blamed his ministers for not clamping down on the press.[12] But there was no way to keep these facts from the public. People living near army camps knew what was going on, and so did tens of thousands of people in the military. Ottawa was a small town then, just as it is now, and there were very few secrets, so the political reporters knew there was a serious crisis. The censorship system had shown, through the years, that there were no serious consequences for important publishers who pushed the rules to the edge of breaking.

In January, the *Globe and Mail* breached censorship by printing an editorial that reported on the London mass-desertion. At the same time, news of the conscript revolt in Terrace, BC, was showing up in the media. So far, the protests had been peaceful, but this changed when a soldier shot a conscript dead in New Brunswick during a draftee protest. This was a crisis that threatened Canada's ability to fulfill its commitment to the Allies, and was a serious blemish to the reputation of the government of Canada at a time when the Allies were so very close to finishing Hitler.

By late January, after the setbacks of Operation Market Garden and the Battle of the Bulge, the Allies had a real shot at finishing Germany. The Canadians were pushing hard into the Netherlands and needed replacement troops to take the place of the soldiers lost between Normandy and the flooded polder country where Canadians were now up against Wehrmacht units that were under orders from Hitler to fight to the death. Now, even opinion-makers like Holy Joe wanted the Zombies sent to Europe.[13]

But by February, the Russians were pushing three big armies towards Berlin. There was talk of a Nazi last stand in the Alps, but Hitler was finished. The army could have rounded up every conscript in Canada that winter and sent them to Holland, but that couldn't change anything. The time for planning and organizing Canada's war effort in Europe had long passed. The army was scapegoating conscripts, pacifists and slackers for decisions about troop training that its own leadership had made years before. Later that spring, McNaughton lost a tough by-election fight in the central Ontario riding of North Grey. King had lost two defence ministers, but his government had survived.

In the end, 12,908 conscripts were sent overseas and 2,463 made it to the fighting front before the Germans sued for peace.[14] It was a miniscule number, considering that a million men and women, out of a population of eleven million, had voluntarily put on a uniform. Whether it was the work of the spirits or just plain good fortune, King and Canada came out of the war looking like winners to Canadians, while McCullagh and Drew seemed to deflate and disparage the war effort. If McCullagh hadn't had bad luck in politics, he would have had no luck at all.

∗ ∗ ∗

Once the conscription crisis died down and the Red Army was busy probing the suburbs of Berlin, McCullagh's attention turned to the Maple Leafs and to local politics. In March, the Leafs paid the Canadians back for their 1944 humiliation, winning the Stanley Cup semifinal in six games. The Leafs had a spectacular final series against the Detroit Red Wings. They lost the first three games before making a four-game comeback and winning the series on the road. As a major shareholder, McCullagh had good seats at Maple Leaf Gardens and travelled with the Leafs on their three trips to Detroit. ·

Politics was as interesting and rewarding as the playoffs. On March 23, Drew's government lost a non-confidence vote on its Throne Speech. The premier called an election for June 24, making it a very long campaign. It was a fortuitous time for Drew: the vote would be held as the province basked in the joy and relief of victory over Hitler. Berlin fell to the Soviets and what was left of the Nazi state surrendered halfway through the campaign.

But Mitch Hepburn was also back, and he had Drew in his sights. The former premier could still draw big crowds for nasty attacks on the Conservative premier, whom he called "arrogant." Giving Drew a majority would mean turning the clock back to the darkest days of the Depression. "We are going to live in this country as neighbours despite the Drews and the McCullaghs. If you want the seat of government transferred from Queen's Park to the editorial offices of the Globe and Mail, then vote for the Tories. George Drew is nothing more than the Charlie McCarthy of George McCullagh."[15] Most people would not have the gall to do such an extreme rewrite of their own history, but Mitch was never a man of scruples.

At the same time, the two Communists elected to the legislature in 1943 were using their party status to get air time to attack McCullagh, whom A.A. MacLeod, leader of the two-man caucus, called "Canada's boy wonder." McCullagh, the Communist leader said, couldn't "make up his mind about what brand of hypocrisy would be best calculated to delude the people of Ontario into keeping his protégé, George Drew, in office."[16]

On the night of May 23, Toronto *Star* reporter Roy Greenaway got a call at home from CCF leader Ted Jolliffe, who had a bombshell accusation. Jolliffe, who was working with CBC journalist Lister Sinclair on a speech that he'd make in a few days, told Greenaway that Drew had created a secret "Gestapo" to spy on CCF politicians and labour leaders. Information gathered by these spies was shared with McCullagh, among others. A man named Osborne-Dempster, codenamed D208, ran the operation. According to Jolliffe's source, at least four OPP undercover cops were assigned to it.

Later that night, Jolliffe met Greenaway at the *Star*'s office and gave him copies of reports stolen from the "Special Force" files by an OPP officer who had scruples about this type of black ops. Atkinson was told about the accusations. The publisher backed Jolliffe, telling the *Star* editorial writers to run an editorial on the front page every day for the rest of the campaign. In one of them, the *Star* compared Drew to Hitler.

As soon as McCullagh heard the accusations, he went to Drew's house to plot strategy. The two men decided to deny that they or anyone in the Tory party had been fed information by the Ontario Provincial Police. The next day, McCullagh called Jolliffe's office to demand a meeting. A secretary said the CCF leader wouldn't be available all afternoon, so McCullagh went to Queen's Park to confront him. Jolliffe didn't show up, so, after almost an hour of waiting in a hallway, McCullagh left.

McCullagh hit back at Jolliffe in a CBC broadcast that aired across the province on May 31, 1945. He accused Jolliffe of lying about the alleged spying, but then he went much farther. He accused the CCF leader of betraying his law clients. In 1941, according to McCullagh, Jolliffe represented journalists at the Canadian Press wire service who were trying to organize a union. McCullagh, who was on the Canadian Press board of directors, had opposed the workers' demands for better wages and the recognition of their union. McCullagh strongly implied Jolliffe had sold out the union in return for a deal on wages and working conditions.[17]

As for Drew, the premier would admit the CCF and labour leaders had been spied on by a couple of OPP undercover cops. But Drew said he hadn't known about it. The cops, supposedly acting without orders and working on their own time, claimed to be looking for communists. Drew appointed Justice LeBel to investigate. That was enough to kill the scandal. It also ruined the CCF's campaign. They went from official Opposition to third-party status. The day after the election, Drew's lawyers filed a statement of claim against the *Star* for $100,000. All the stories and editorials, according to the claim, were libelous.[18] It took two years for the lawsuit to be dismissed, which meant it hung over old Joe Atkinson, now nearly deaf but still very much in charge of the *Star*, for most of the rest of his life.[19]

But was Jolliffe right? Certainly, members of the OPP did spy on trade union activists and members of the CCF. Drew's own papers on the affair are in Library and Archives Canada. For forty years, historians have been trying to see these records. Some of Drew's papers are available, and his correspondence with McCullagh has been used in this book. But Drew's files on this affair were sealed by his children until after their deaths. In 1981, a journalist asked Drew's widow if she would allow access. She said it was not her decision to make. As for McCullagh's role in this scandal, his papers were destroyed years ago.

The reports written by "D208" that were leaked to Jolliffe show the OPP had gained solid knowledge of the CCF and its leaders, including David Lewis, who would go on to lead the federal party during the 1960s. (His son Stephen would become provincial NDP leader and bring the party back as official Opposition in 1975.) But they also contain wild charges that the provincial party was financed by communists. The cops believed the CCF wanted to nationalize the banks and the country's industries, and collectivize Canada's farms. These were absurd claims. So the question remains: Was Ontario's provincial police force used as a political weapon by the province's premier? The answer seems to be "likely," though perhaps the operation did little more than reinforce the stereotypes and hatred that McCullagh and Drew already had.[20]

* * *

The last full year of the war had a strange ending for McCullagh and the *Globe and Mail*. In the run-up to that year's municipal election, Montague "Bugsy" Sanderson, the owner of Reliable Exterminators—which was also the name he and his Conservative friends used for their anti-socialism campaign—bought an ad in the paper denouncing sixteen CCF candidates who planned to run for Toronto city council. Several CCF candidates had been elected to city council in the 1943 municipal election, and there was a strong fear in the business community that the party could win a majority in 1944. Sanderson, who seems to have fronted for a group of anti-CCFers, called the leftist candidates communists, and the CCFers sued.

A jury was picked after Christmas 1945. The trial became a deep dive into the beliefs and political actions of the CCF men. Most of them likely were not communists, but they had worked on campaigns with members of the Communist Party and had done more benign things, like help organize May Day celebrations. The plaintiffs had another big obstacle: the judge ruled that the ad was protected by some privilege, since it dealt with election issues and candidates for office. The CCFers couldn't prove malice, which would trump that privilege. Nor could they show that their reputations in the community had suffered. Several had won their seats, and those who had lost couldn't prove that Sanderson and the *Globe and Mail* were responsible. Yes, the *Globe and Mail*'s lawyer said, there were mistakes of fact and outright lies in the advertisement, but who could say whether they had been made maliciously, or had diminished the community's respect for these admitted leftists?

The politicians said Sanderson's claim that they were members of the Communist Party, or kept common cause with them, was too much of a whopper to be protected by privilege. The Communist Party was still illegal under the War Measures Act. There was no public interest in hearing lies about these candidates, especially when those falsehoods were accusations of criminal behaviour.

In the end, the jury threw out the claims of fourteen of the CCF candidates. The two who "won" were awarded the sum of one cent. They may have been right in law, but the members of the jury believed their reputations were worthless.[21]

* * *

A few weeks before the war in Europe ended, Drew got his hands on a copy of *Canadian Affairs*, a special publication for the Canadian Armed Forces. He wrote to McCullagh to complain that Canadian troops were being fed leftist propaganda.

"If you will look at Page 4," Drew told McCullagh, "you will find a statement in regard to the income of young people in Canada which is wholly inconsistent with the facts as they are today. In my opinion, this is very destructive material to be given to the troops in discussion groups, particularly when such statements may be repeated to the people in Britain or elsewhere in subsequent conversations by these young men."[22]

On the day of the Ontario election, King was gossiping with the governor general about how the vote would go, and about a visit from England by former prime minister R.B. Bennett "and what he might be able indirectly to do to destroy me. McCullagh was the one around whom others were focused in Canada."[23]

The *Globe and Mail* was an important platform that King and any other national politician could not ignore. Through the 1945 federal election, held just weeks after Drew won his majority in Ontario, McCullagh used his paper, and yet another series of radio speeches, to go after King and the socialists. When King worked on his final national radio election speech, he wrote a passage calling out McCullagh by name, but he decided to take it out. It might have seemed ungentlemanly.[24]

Drew had made a trip to western Canada in the late spring, probing to see if it was time to take a run at the federal Progressive Conservative leadership. Pundits believed he did more harm to the Toronto Clique than good. In fact, *Winnipeg Free Press* parliamentary correspondent Grant Dexter believed Drew's campaigning in the months leading up to the election solidified, rather than weakened, the federal leadership of former Manitoba premier John Bracken.[25] Yet, in the end, Bracken joined that long list of Tory contenders who King managed to keep out of the history books.

In King's mind, McCullagh was Canada's great villain, and Drew was just his puppet. In 1947, the Niagara Parks Commission installed a carillon, a musical instrument made of bells. Mackenzie King had a thing about bells, and had written a book called *The Message of the Carillon*. King had made a speech at the dedication of the Peace Tower carillon in 1927 that equated carillons with national unity. King had even travelled to England to see the forging of the bells that were installed on Parliament Hill. But when the Rainbow Carillon Tower was unveiled in spring of 1947, King was horrified to find his name left off the bells, which were dedicated to the Canadian and American war efforts. They were inscribed: "to our wartime leaders," naming Churchill and Roosevelt. The prime minister believed it was all McCullagh's fault. The Niagara Parks commissioners were old Hepburn loyalists. McCullagh had pulled their strings, and Drew had done nothing to stop him. For days, King had some of the government's most senior public servants and cabinet ministers investigating this snub. Supposedly, he even considered resigning over it. "I begin now to see the significance of the vision which I had yesterday and recorded at the time," he wrote in his diary. "Warning in the nature of danger."[26]

15

THE GREAT TORONTO NEWSPAPER WAR

Just a few weeks after the 1945 federal election, Igor Gouzenko, a clerk at the Soviet embassy in Ottawa, stuck a military-issue pistol in his belt, scooped up as many incriminating documents as he could find and fled into the late-summer night. He tried to see Mackenzie King, who lived just down the street from the embassy. Turned away from Laurier House, he went to RCMP headquarters, but the cops at the front desk didn't believe his story. Then he tried the *Ottawa Journal* newspaper office, but none of the journalists could be bothered to talk to him. It was now very late at night. Gouzenko went back to his apartment at Somerset and Percy Streets and watched from the park across the street as Soviet secret agents, waving flashlights, searched his home. Someone called the city police, and the Russians left. The next day, Gouzenko was able to get the ear of someone in the RCMP Security Service, who took Gouzenko and his wife to a safe house. The Cold War was on.

Gouzenko has sometimes been portrayed as a lowly clerk, but he was, in fact, the person responsible for handling the Soviet embassy's secret codes. His job was to translate reports into those encryptions and send them to Moscow. That meant he read everything that went back to Russia, including much of the data from Canadian and American scientists who, for ideological reasons or money, betrayed the secrets of the atomic bomb.

The RCMP quietly briefed Canada's allies and went to work arresting espionage suspects, picking up thirty-nine people. They were taken to the RCMP barracks on the edge of town and subjected to sleep deprivation to make them talk. Most did. The same thing was happening in the United States and Great Britain. But it took months for the story to come out.

McCullagh, laid low again with exhaustion, went alone to Glitter Bay, in Barbados, just as the Gouzenko spy affair was about to blow wide open. Phyllis stayed home, and she and her friends—"the girls"—held a party in the Thornhill mansion.

Drew fed McCullagh the latest gossip from back home. On February 15, Drew was in Ottawa for a meeting of the Co-ordinating Committee of the Federal-Provincial conference. It was likely as boring as it sounds, so Drew wrote McCullagh a fifteen-hundred-word letter full of speculation that was bound to agitate McCullagh.[1]

Drew believed King was on the way out, Liberal organizers were in open revolt, and that ministers at the meeting—members of King's so-called Brain Trust—were jockeying. Defence minister Brooke Claxton kept putting himself forward as a contender but was not getting much support from the other ministers. Drew believed King wanted the conference to fail and break up early, though Drew did not know why.

Perhaps, Drew gossiped, it was because news was leaking that ss general Kurt Meyer, condemned for ordering the murder of Canadian troops captured by his 12th ss Panzer Division Hitlerjugend in Normandy, may have been illegally convicted by a tribunal established by an order passed by cabinet under the War Measures Act. The law had a maximum prison penalty of five years and, Drew wrote, "my informant suggests that because of this it was found necessary to commute Meyer's sentence and because of this [Major General Christopher] Vokes (who granted Meyer's appeal of his death sentence) was simply called upon to be the goat for the government." Drew told McCullagh not to share that gossip, since the Tories wanted to surprise King's government with a question on the order paper.

"It is the only reasonable explanation I have heard for what happened. After all, if Meyer was guilty at all he should have been shot and if he was not guilty they have no right to hold him."[2]

Drew, who'd just returned from the same resort before heading to the conference, wrote to McCullagh again on February 19, with news of the Gouzenko affair, which had come out just as the conference was winding down. "These past few days have been exciting here," Drew wrote, "though there is little positive news beyond the fact that a number of people have been detained." It was not even certain that any of them were under actual arrest, in the strict meaning of that word.

"Perhaps the most interesting single sidelight of the present situation is to be found in the antics of the *Star*. They have gone farther out on the limb than anyone in imputing widespread espionage tied in with local organization, and [the paper's] articles from Ottawa have not hesitated to go all out in attributing the widest activities to the Russian embassy."[3]

Though the premier had kept Atkinson's paper frozen out at Queen's Park, Drew did have sources who told the premier that Joe Atkinson was troubled by the spy revelations. Margaret Gould, who was Atkinson's sounding board and mentor on social issues, seemed compromised. Gould was a friend of Atkinson's who had been a Toronto social worker and executive secretary of the Child Welfare Association starting in 1929. She was accused of being a communist by the *Catholic Register* in 1936 after writing a series of articles for the *Star* following a trip to the Soviet Union, just before Drew visited the same region and filed to the *Globe and Mail*. Atkinson hired her full-time in 1937, but their relationship seems to have been more student-teacher than employer-employee, with Gould as the teacher. Drew's sources said Holy Joe was worried about how she "may have been leading him."

Drew's take, which he explained to McCullagh, was that Washington and London knew the Soviets had run an espionage operation out of their Ottawa embassy, focused on stealing the engineering secrets of the atomic bomb project. Rather than confront Stalin directly, they chose to use the Gouzenko revelations as cover for exposing what they already knew. Canada, Drew told McCullagh, was seen by both big Allied powers as the place to let the world know about the Soviet operation: inconsequential, and immune from Soviet retribution since there were so few high-stakes relationships between the two countries. The British and Americans still had to face the Soviets in Berlin and occupied Germany, and leaking their material through Gouzenko made it look as if they were being forced to act.[4]

King, Drew believed, would never have stuck his neck out on Gouzenko's claim of espionage rings out of the Soviet embassy unless the intelligence was rock-solid. It all seemed so obvious to Drew now: through the war, the Soviet embassy had been a nest of spies, and probably still was.

"You may remember the very handsome Russian Colonel who was introduced to the Ontario Legislature a year ago at the request of Mr. [Alexander] MacLeod [a Communist who sat in the legislature as a "Labour Progressive"]. You will recall that Mitch was all set to give a very glowing introduction if I had not forestalled him. This Colonel is one of those who suddenly disappeared...He certainly had all the qualifications of the fiction spy. Agnes McPhail has not been the same since she laid eyes on him."

Drew believed the split between the wartime allies over the espionage crisis would not lead to war because, he claimed, Russia had no real air force. The Russian land mass would be helpless against the mechanized armies of the United States.[5]

The newsy two-thousand-word letter ends with: "Now that you are really away, make sure that you have enough rest this time. A few days one way or the other won't matter and I have a feeling that it is going to be extremely important that you are in good shape in the months ahead."

It must have been hard for a publisher who loved a good read to sit quietly on a beach while the biggest story of the postwar world was breaking back home.

* * *

Once back in Canada, McCullagh started looking for another Archworth. He often made trips to Barrie to look over Wright's new colts, and in October 1945, he paid Wright $4,000 for a dark chestnut colt named Tularch. The Toronto *Star* carried a brief story on the sale, its horse-racing writer saying the payment—enough to buy a decent house at the time—"is like taking it from one pocket to another." But it would be a couple of years before McCullagh had a King's Plate contender.

In August 1947, McCullagh was at the posh fishing resort of Camp Chimo, in eastern Ontario's Temagami country, with his three young children. Phyllis McCullagh and Fiorenza Drew were having a great time at McCullagh's estate.[6] This was one of many trips that McCullagh took without his wife. It seems that the marriage was under strain, with Phyllis spending most of her time with her friends and volunteering for a handful of charities. Still, life went on in Thornhill, and the McCullagh family seemed to make things work. Their social life, which seemed to usually include the Drews and the Bassetts, continued to be very busy.

In November 1947, McCullagh's friend Lord Beaverbrook flew to Toronto to join McCullagh at the University of Toronto, where they were given honorary doctorates, along with Helen Rogers Reid, publisher of

Phyllis McCullagh (left) and two of her friends at the McCullagh estate in Thornhill.
(CITY OF TORONTO ARCHIVES, FONDS 1257, SERIES 1057, ITEM 3540)

the *New York Herald Tribune*.[7] Afterwards, Beaverbrook and McCullagh flew to New Brunswick together in McCullagh's Grumman Mallard, a gorgeous airplane that could land on the water or on an airstrip.

"Where could you match this country?" Beaverbrook asked McCullagh as the two men looked out the windows at the forests, lakes and the rolling Appalachian Mountains. Beaverbrook said he loved this part of Canada, that it was his home. McCullagh, who felt a strong connection to the wilds of northern Ontario, suggested Beaverbrook see more of McCullagh's province. While Beaverbrook saw himself as a New Brunswicker, McCullagh reminded the British baron that he'd actually been born in Maple, just north of Toronto.[8]

Meanwhile, Drew was laying the groundwork for a run at the prime minister's job. Among his strategies, Drew hoped to dredge up the wartime Hong Kong cover-up and use it against the Liberals. At the beginning of 1948, he wrote a thousand-word letter to McCullagh, telling the *Globe and Mail* publisher what the series of stories should say. Drew had even designed the pages and written headlines.[9]

It was clear to everyone, except maybe to the man himself, that the King era was coming to an end. The Toronto Clique had to go national: Toronto wasn't big enough to contain the egos of Drew and his friends. There were rumours that King was finally going to leave after he broke Sir Robert Walpole's record as longest-serving prime minister of a Westminster democracy. Maybe no one else was keeping track, but King was: Walpole served 7,620 days, and King was closing in. King retired on November 15, 1948, with almost two hundred days more than the much-forgotten eighteenth-century British prime minister.[10]

* * *

McCullagh hadn't tried to expand his newspaper empire since 1938, when he tried to buy the *Montreal Star*, but he was cooking up a plan to expand his media power. If he pulled it off, McCullagh (and Drew) would have control of every paper in Toronto, except for Atkinson's *Star*.

John Ross Robertson, founder of the Toronto *Telegram*, died in May 1918. Robertson left his paper to a trust, with most of the *Telegram*'s profits going to the Hospital for Sick Children. In the summer of 1947, Robertson's widow died. The trustees now had the power to put the paper on the market, with the proceeds from the sale going to the hospital.[11] As Mackenzie King was shuffling off the stage, McCullagh, with some dread, bought the *Telegram*. These were not the heady days of 1935, when a more reckless George McCullagh had strong-armed Jaffray and Killam into selling their papers, McCullagh was racked with insecurity: right to the last minute, he believed the *Telegram* deal would fall through. He even bet the *Globe and Mail*'s press foreman that someone else would snatch the *Telegram* out from under him. McCullagh wanted to bid on the *Telegram* secretly, but

This *Financial Post* cartoon shows the Toronto *Telegram*, the old, grey afternoon conservative paper, being dragged into McCullagh's media harem.

when Bill Aiken, Lord Beaverbrook's nephew, protested, the trustees of Robertson's will opened the bidding to the public. By then, McCullagh had offered $3.6 million.[12] Again, it was Wright's money, handled through a special trust.

McCullagh opened negotiations for the *Telegram* the same way he'd bought the *Globe* and the *Mail and Empire*. He sent a friendly note through *Telegram* executives to the administrators of the trust, feeling them out about selling the paper. McCullagh knew—possibly through Drew—that the Hospital for Sick Children wanted to build a new twenty-three-storey tower and hadn't been able to raise the $20 million needed for construction.

The Robertson trustees wanted $7 million. At that stage in the talks, other bids were still in play, including one from *Telegram* employees. Financier E.P. Taylor also considered a bid, in partnership with CKEY radio station owner Jack Kent Cooke.[13] Charles Knowles, who handled the negotiations for the trust, was willing to settle for $5 million. Roy Thomson, founder of the multi-billion-dollar Thomson

Reuters media empire, lowballed with a bid said to be for $2 million. Aiken's bid was just below McCullagh's $3.9 million offer. But McCullagh had to agree to publish the *Telegram* as a separate newspaper, operating from its own building, and he could never merge it with the *Globe and Mail*.[14]

McCullagh kept getting cold feet. He told the Toronto *Star* he'd withdrawn his bid,[15] which might have been true when he said it, but there was definitely a McCullagh bid on the table in the final hours of the process. As the clock ran down, McCullagh spent the last night seething, conjuring up his old hatreds of Atkinson and the *Star* and fuelling his insatiable competitiveness. At the last minute, he slipped in a bid that was higher than Aiken's. He also trumped an offer from a brokerage firm that was probably representing a Conservative senator, F.K. Morrow, who, himself, was almost certainly a stalking horse for the Conservative Party or its chief financial backers.

Now McCullagh was competing against himself, owning two papers in Toronto. It seems crazy now, but in 1948 Toronto, a metropolitan area one-sixth the size of the modern city, there was a market for both, and the giant Toronto *Star* as well. McCullagh's papers sold more than the entire Southam newspaper chain, which had papers in most of the rest of the country's major cities.[16] Still, the *Star* outsold them all, even if the Southam, *Globe* and *Telegram* circulation was combined. The *Star*'s daily circulation was 365,000 copies (and, in terms of print sales, about three times what the *Star* sells today).

The day after the deal closed, McCullagh called a meeting of the *Telegram* staff in the paper's ancient newsroom. "The outstanding thing that brought me into the evening newspaper field was to knock off the Star," McCullagh said. "The Star has done enough to the profession of journalism that we ought to go in and teach it a lesson...I'm going to knock that fucking rag off its pedestal."[17]

McCullagh was much less combative in the signed editorial that he ran on the front page of the December 1 edition:

I realize, too, that it is a great trust, and I recognize my limitations. I hope to surround myself with able executives and ask you to believe in my sincerity of purpose. It has been stated that the Telegram will be independent in politics. This requires explanation for the sake of clear understanding. Political independence is open to several possible interpretations. There is so-called independence that evades responsibility, lest offence be given. There is the kind that is better described as indifference.

The Telegram would not be worthy of itself or of public confidence if it permitted a neutral or indifferent attitude to interfere with public duty. It will seek to give fair treatment to all parties in the discussion of public issues. But a newspaper, like the public, has a right to free expression. This, the Telegram will exercise, without subservience to any party, commenting or criticizing in accordance with the interests of the community and the nation, as it sees them. Inspired by an uncompromising adherence to the highest ideals of British democratic practice, the newspaper will be vigorous in support of those basic principles—individual liberty, racial and religious tolerance.[18]

But McCullagh was not well. Just after buying the *Telegram*, he headed for Montreal on business McCullagh was frail, exhausted and had started suffering from nosebleeds, so he took his doctor with him. It was a sign of things to come.

One of his first calls was to John Bassett, who'd been his protegé a decade ago. Bassett had bought the *Sherbrooke Record* in the Eastern Townships of Quebec.[19] Bassett was offered the job of advertising sales manager, but McCullagh made it clear that he'd have most of the power of a publisher. According to Bassett biographer Maggie Siggins, who did long interviews with Bassett in the 1970s, McCullagh asked, "When can you come?" Bassett replied, "Is tomorrow too soon?" He meant it.

Within a couple of days, he was in Toronto, and Bassett would stay with the *Telegram* until the day in 1971 when he shut the paper down. "I really thought we could catch the *Star*," Bassett told Siggins. "But the Tely was a mess. I had no idea before I came how bad it was. And McCullagh had no idea what he bought. The circulation manager wouldn't even give me the circulation figures. The whole thing was a façade."[20]

For fifteen years, the *Star* had been outselling the *Telegram*. When he started planning the takeover, McCullagh was sure he could restore the *Telegram*'s dominance. It was only after the deal was done that McCullagh learned his new paper was barely in the game. It sold 200,000 papers a day, just half of what the *Star* was printing.

The *Telegram* building, on tiny Melinda Street, just around the corner from the *Globe and Mail*'s headquarters, was the opposite of McCullagh's King Street news palace. Press operators toiled in three dungeon-like sub-basements. The newsroom and business offices were dumps. An iron spiral staircase rose from the grubby little lobby to the dirty newsroom.[21]

The newsroom was a great firetrap right out of a Hollywood movie. Ancient desks were piled high with a mix of notebooks, official papers and trash, and many of the drawers had liquor bottles stashed in them. Not much light came though the filthy windows. The place was very noisy, with the clanking of manual typewriters, ticker tape machines, newswire printers and the vacuum tube system that carried reporters' stories to the typesetting room.

In fact, McCullagh had been hornswoggled. He was really buying little but the paper's name and its real estate—though that piece of property was a good investment. John Bassett, who would eventually own it, said years later, "If George McCullagh hadn't bought the *Telegram* in '48 and if we hadn't bought it in '52...if anybody of the other bidders in '48 had bought the *Telegram*, in my view, there would have been no *Telegram* in '52. It was just a façade, really. It had been ruined over the long years from the death of John Ross Robertson..."[22]

The *Telegram's* employees could barely get a paper out the door, and what was printed was decades behind the times. The ancient machines in its Dickensian subterranean pressroom couldn't print colour, which meant the weekend *Star* would always have better comics. This was a big thing in the 1950s. Nor could these presses print a large paper. The most they could handle was forty-eight pages. That ruled out a fat weekend paper to compete with the *Star Weekly*.[23]

The trustees of the Robertson estate had refused the capital investments that were needed to keep the *Telegram* competitive, and had hired poor managers to handle the day-to-day operations of the different departments of the newspaper. By the end of the 1940s, despite McCullagh's pep talks, the *Star* was far ahead in the lucrative classified advertising business. People bought these expensive little pieces of newspaper real estate to advertise jobs they wanted to fill or apartments they had for rent. Torontonians looking for a home or a job bought the paper to see these ads, so the paper profited twice from every ad it sold. The *Telegram* called itself "The Paper with the Want Ads," but by the third year of McCullagh's ownership, the *Star* was outselling both his papers combined.[24]

It would be hard for any publisher to convince the staff of a paper like the *Telegram* that they could win a fight with the *Star*. The *Star* was rich. It might be a horrible place to work—editor Harry Hindmarsh seems to have taken special delight in firing people at Christmas—but it paid well and gave its best reporters some fantastic assignments. The *Star's* real edge came from its ability to deploy a small army of journalists to any big story.

McCullagh knew he had to rebuild the *Telegram*. There were great reporters on the paper, but there was no money to support them, and they needed better leadership. Fortunately, McCullagh, unlike his counterpart at the *Star*, could spot and keep executive talent.

∗ ∗ ∗

McCullagh had two challenges: keeping his newsroom staffs from being spread too thin and maintaining his own health. He was still dealing with his highs and lows; he was often exhausted because he pushed himself too hard; his lungs were always a problem; and now he had given himself a second full-time job. Fortunately, men like John Bassett, John D. MacFarlane and Oakley Dalgleish were maturing into solid managers.

Loyal *Globe and Mail* and *Telegram* journalists fought proxy wars on McCullagh's behalf. Jim Coleman, one of the country's best sports-writers, wrote a mocking column when Andy Lytle,[25] the sports editor of the *Star*, suggested McCullagh used his influence with the provincial government to get a tax cut on horse-race betting. True, Coleman wrote, McCullagh was a member of the Horsemen's Benevolent Association, which wanted the tax break. But, the columnist claimed, McCullagh had never been anything more than a member of a delegation representing horsemen, racetracks and breeders, and he'd never interfered personally. "If the provincial government has come to any conclusion in the matter, it is without any newspaper proddings."

Coleman tried to buttress that denial with a direct attack on Lytle's credibility. Lytle, according to Coleman, had tried to imply McCullagh was the man behind the city's AAA-league baseball team, the Maple Leafs. That, the *Globe and Mail* sportswriter wrote, with his tongue firmly in his cheek, was actionable, considering the "lamentable career of the Maple Leafs."

"We don't know a lot about Mr. McCullagh, except that he has not yet hit us with a horse whip," Coleman wrote about his boss. "He's a guy who seems to have toughened himself to criticism and flattery. We would suggest that flattery is the harder to withstand. The only time this staff had any trouble with him was last week when two Boston players referred to him on the same day as 'handsome' and 'scholarly.'"

But McCullagh was no scholar. McCullagh could use his fists and his muscles when he thought he needed to. Coleman told his readers that McCullagh was sitting beside the New York Rangers bench in Maple Leaf Gardens one night when Leafs defenceman Gus "Old Hardrocks" Mortson came close enough that the benched Rangers were able to swing at him with their sticks. McCullagh grabbed Bill Juzda, the nearest Ranger player in uniform. The two men struggled back and forth for several minutes while officials and ushers attempted to restore order. People close to the action believed they could see McCullagh snarling threats into Juzda's ear as they wrestled and rocked in each other's big arms.[26] After the game, people went up to McCullagh to congratulate him on his wrestling. Box seat holders shook his hand and slapped him on the back. But two weeks later, sportswriters learned the "threats" McCullagh whispered were actually the words "For Gawd's sake, Bill you're standing on my feet." And his shoes had the skate cuts to prove it.[27]

The journalists believed they knew their boss, and that he had their back. Unlike later managers of Toronto newsrooms, McCullagh did not try to put distance between his employees and himself. He may have had a very elegant, private space at the top of the Wright Building, but when he was lonely—which seems to have been his normal state on most weeknights—he haunted the *Globe and Mail*'s cafeteria rather than go home to his wife and kids in Thornhill. For many staffers, these cafeteria sessions were a valued perk of the job. McCullagh would come into the cafeteria after the first edition was off to conduct small seminars over coffee. Sometimes, he'd lurk and listen to people talking at different tables, trying to find the best argument to jump into. He knew just about everyone on staff by their first name, and he knew their problems. If one of them was bereaved, they got a handwritten sympathy letter from the publisher. If an employee or spouse couldn't cover a medical bill, McCullagh might pay it from his own chequebook. He once set up one of his male reporters—and most of the journalists he hired were male—with a pretty blonde *Globe* secretary, giving the couple fifty dollars for a night on the town.[28]

He had time to troll the newsroom and the cafeteria because Harry Kimber, his loyal general manager, was making the hundreds of little decisions that a newspaper publisher had to handle every day. McCullagh bought The Globe and Mail Park at Port Dover—an old cottage court—had the old shacks torn down and built nice new cottages that *Globe and Mail* employees could use if they didn't have the money to own a vacation home.[29] McCullagh didn't let social norms prevent him from employing colourful characters, either. Bobbie Rosenfeld, a Barrie, Ontario, native who won gold at the 1928 Amsterdam Olympics, was one of the *Globe and Mail's* most important sportswriters. She was utterly irreverent. Richard Doyle tells of one of McCullagh's cafeteria talks, where he told journalists, "It doesn't take much to make a good reporter." Rosenfeld shot back, "I've been trying to make one for years and haven't managed it yet." What people didn't say was that the reporters that Rosenfeld wanted to make were women. Her lesbianism was open and accepted in the *Globe and Mail* newsroom.[30]

Yes, George McCullagh could be moody, annoying, opinionated and ruthless, but no one—not even his enemies—called him treacherous. He earned the loyalty of the people in his organization. If they couldn't tolerate his politics, or wanted a different boss, they were free to leave. *Globe and Mail* journalists were usually welcome on other papers.

* * *

To beef up the *Telegram's* newsroom and prepare it for the coming newspaper war, McCullagh sent for John D. MacFarlane from the *Globe and Mail* newsroom. MacFarlane was one of the toughest journalists in the country. During the war, he'd been promoted to major while in his late twenties and appointed editor of the *Maple Leaf*, the Canadian army's newspaper for soldiers, but he was fired just after the war for fighting back against censorship. He'd printed an accurate story, airing soldiers' complaints about the point system that was used to determine when Canadians deployed in Europe were to be sent home. MacFarlane had worked for the Toronto *Star* before the war, but McCullagh offered him a better deal in 1946, and MacFarlane became one of the most feared and respected city editors in Toronto history. Now, still in his thirties, he was to lead the *Telegram* into a newspaper war that he believed he could win. "McCullagh had taken a fancy to me at the Globe," Val Sears recalls MacFarlane saying. "He felt I was putting some sparkle and life into the Globe, and the Tely was much in need of a similar approach. I agreed to go if he would make me city editor and pay me as managing editor. He said okay, so I went."[31] MacFarlane came to adore McCullagh, and was willing, along with Bassett, to take up the slack when McCullagh disappeared for weeks at a time.[32]

A man as ferocious and competitive as MacFarlane could not run a newsroom on his own. There had to be a "good cop" to MacFarlane's "bad cop," and McCullagh discovered he got one when he bought the *Telegram*. Managing editor Bert Buckland was a bear of a man who inspired devotion from his staff. He had a strong conscience and firm ethics, and he was the voice of common sense when members of his staff became giddy and senseless in the newspaper war that was to come. McCullagh wisely kept Buckland on, including him in the McCullagh-Bassett-MacFarlane management team that was going to dust off the *Telegram* and make it battle-ready.[33]

But McCullagh's purchase of the *Telegram* wasn't just about making money or the satisfaction of winning a newspaper war. The *Telegram* deal was about power. No one could doubt he was the most powerful Tory in Ontario, with, possibly, the exception of the premier. One worried Conservative told a *Time* magazine reporter: "It's going to be awfully tough on anyone who breaks with George McCullagh."[34]

The new *Telegram* came out swinging. "We are not hampered in this effort by having to hew to the Communist line—or any other line.

In this we are unique in the Toronto evening field," McCullagh wrote in a front-page editorial. Subscribing to the new, soon-to-be-improved *Tely* "is the best way for you to join the crusade to protect our way of life and improve it. Keep Canada free of subversive influences."[35]

The *Star* hit back the next day: "The lady, it seems, is changing her old ways along with her old dress. Going to be independent she says... Out of courtesy we'll have to take her word for it just at the moment. All the same we'll be surprised if her feet stray very far from that old Gold Dust Trail."[36]

* * *

McCullagh didn't get the kind of congratulations that came to him when he bought the *Globe* thirteen years earlier. There was no big dinner with Ontario's power elite, no offer of a spare bedroom at King's mansion in Ottawa, nor a meeting with the cabinet. Those days were long gone. But McCullagh did get a congratulatory call from Henry Luce, the owner of *Time* and *Life* magazines. Instead of thanking the powerful American publisher, McCullagh told him, in blunt and unpleasant terms, what he thought of *Time*'s Canadian coverage.[37]

Soon afterwards, McCullagh was interviewed by a reporter for *Time*, who wanted to write a news story about the purchase of the *Telegram* and McCullagh's efforts to make it a better paper. McCullagh might have believed the Luce publications' Canadian coverage was trash, but he couldn't resist the platform offered by one of the most powerful magazines in the world. The *Time* journalist, unlike his Canadian colleagues, was not afraid to ask McCullagh tough questions. Why had McCullagh added only 21,697 subscribers to the *Globe and Mail* since 1936, even though he and Wright had sunk so much money into a new building and hired so many new reporters? Even the sad-sack *Telegram*, which everyone in the industry believed had been neglected by its owners, had increased its circulation by 42,290, while the *Star*, during the same period, had gained 121,059 subscribers.

McCullagh didn't have much of an answer: "The smart talk will soon be about the waning *Star*." He did promise to get the *Telegram* out of its rut though. "'The Globe & Mail will be the pattern, particularly in such things as...racial and religious prejudice.'"

Time reported McCullagh saying *Star* editor (and Joe Atkinson son-in-law) Harry Hindmarsh was "so ugly that if he ever bit himself, he'd get hydrophobia [rabies]."[38]

John Bassett was floored when he saw the *Time* article. It seems Bassett, who would become the managing mind of the *Telegram*, knew McCullagh's business better than he did. The managers of the *Star* had the power to kill the *Telegram* any time they wanted to. Bassett later told writer Maggie Siggins: "I went up to George's farm that night and he said, 'Have you seen Time today?' I said 'Oh, yes, I've seen it.'

"'That was a great crack you made. But do you know what I'd do tomorrow if I was Harry Hindmarsh? I'd put the *Tely* out of business. Don't you know that during the war, in order to conserve manpower, the *Star* and the *Tely* had carrier boys carrying both papers. Every boy that carries the *Star* carries the *Tely*. What do you think would happen next Monday if Hindmarsh said to his circulation manager: No kid carrying the *Star* and the *Star Weekly* can carry the *Tely*. He could take his choice. You'd have no carrier boys.'

"George went white," Bassett told Siggins. "He was shocked. Then he said, look, I tell you what you do. You make an appointment with Hindmarsh, be very polite, call him sir and all that....speak about your father...ease the situation...tell him maybe we ought to separate the carriers now."

Just as he'd been unable to make a real apology to Holy Joe before the wartime lawsuit, McCullagh didn't have the courage to smooth things over with the terrifying Harry Hindmarsh, who, after Atkinson's death, was running the business side of the *Star* while editing the paper. He sent Bassett, who very carefully and politely apologized to Hindmarsh and made excuses for McCullagh. The *Star* did not play its trump card, probably because the city's business community and Toronto's major advertisers would have considered it to be rough play. Hindmarsh gave Bassett and McCullagh time to build up their own network of newspaper carriers.[39]

Many observers would have seen Hindmarsh's mercy as out of character. He was loathed by most people who knew him, and almost everyone who worked with him or for him. He had been driving talent out of the newsroom for years, starting the long tradition of a snake-pit work environment at that paper. McCullagh often gave *Star* refugees new homes at the *Globe* and the *Telegram*, bases from which to wage their own wars on their former tormenter. Every Christmas, twelve of those ex-*Star* employees wrote Hindmarsh a Merry Christmas telegram. But they sent it collect.[40]

* * *

While McCullagh was taking control of the *Telegram*, his best friend was taking a run at the national Progressive Conservative leadership. George Drew had lost his seat in the previous Ontario provincial election, but Drew had used Queen's Park as a stepping stone anyway. John Bracken, ill and frustrated, had given up the leadership, and everyone expected the leadership convention, held in Ottawa on October 2, 1948, to be a coronation. It helped that Fiorenza Drew was bilingual (unlike her husband) and was able to charm the Quebec delegates.

Prairie lawyer John Diefenbaker, who saw himself as a natural leader, and his eager campaign workers hadn't got the message that Drew had the convention sewn up. Toronto lawyer David Walker was part of Diefenbaker's inner circle. Walker thought Drew was a snob, a man who didn't listen, and made for lousy company. Walker said Drew had a gift for public speaking, but was another loser in a string of Tory leaders who had flamed out since the Tories lost power in 1935. Walker managed to get a Diefenbaker partisan into one of Drew's strategy sessions. McCullagh, who was there, later found out about this.

"They got a little vicious, George [Drew's] crowd headed by McCullagh of the Globe and Mail," Walker said years later in an interview with journalist Peter Stursberg. The Drew camp thought Dief's team "were vipers and no good people and it got pretty rough."

Drew's people phoned up Dief delegates to tell them they were missing out on the chance to support a winning team. Dief's camp spread the word that Drew had been booed at a meeting of French-Canadian delegates. Drew won by a wide margin. Dief would have to wait until next time.

Soon after the convention, the *Globe and Mail* ran an editorial accusing Walker of running a discreditable campaign and demanding he be run out of the party. Walker was sure McCullagh wrote it. One of Walker's friends sent him a cheque for $1,000 to sue the paper for libel, but former Ontario premier Howard Ferguson and Canon Henry Cody of the University of Toronto talked him out of it. "I never forgave this guy for that," Walker said thirty years later.

Walker invited McCullagh to speak to the Lawyers Club. The publisher was thrilled. "He was flattered to think that I after that dirty editorial would invite him. I was trying to turn the other cheek you see, I wanted to cut his damn throat."

But McCullagh cancelled. Walker and most of the rest of the Tories heard he'd been sent to a rehab clinic to recover from alcoholism. The episode speaks to the way McCullagh hid his mental illness behind the rumours of alcoholism, despite chafing at the idea that people thought he was a drunk. Walker said he heard McCullagh "went a little whacky, you know, you knew he was whacky for a while there, so he didn't turn up." During the interview, Stursberg asked Walker, who was then a senator, if McCullagh had a nervous breakdown.

"Yes, he was in bad shape...Everything he did was fiercely done, fierce in his endeavours and he was a terrible person to have against you."

In fact, McCullagh was hiding in an apartment he kept in Manhattan and spending two months in intensive therapy with Dr. Kennedy.

McCullagh's career could survive the stigma of alcoholism, but mental illness was still something that had to be kept hidden.[41]

* * *

A few months after McCullagh bought the *Telegram*, he got a call from a young writer at *Maclean's*. Pierre Berton was, like McCullagh, a prodigy: at twenty-one, he'd been made city editor of the *Vancouver News-Herald*. He'd already earned a bachelor's degree in history and had been the star of the University of British Columbia's college paper. Berton joined the army and spent the last years of the Second World War in Canada, then had another starring stint in Vancouver, at the *Sun*. He ability to write long, interesting features caught the attention of editors of *Maclean's*, and they talked the twenty-eight-year-old into moving to Toronto. Soon afterwards, he met George McCullagh at the publisher's office in the *Globe and Mail* building. And that would change his life.

"Don't take your coat off. You're not staying," McCullagh told him. "I'm not giving interviews after that last piece, which was highly unethical!" McCullagh was afraid of magazine writers, fearing he'd regret letting them into his life. Twice, with writers from *Time* and *Saturday Evening Post*, he thought he'd had good interviews, only to have the stories blow up in his face.

But Berton did stay. He could see that the publisher, who Berton described as "tall and handsome in a raw-boned, blue-eyed sort of way," the "Boy Wonder of Canadian journalism," had mixed feelings, and might, at some level, want to take another shot at an article that portrayed him the way he saw himself.

Berton said he wanted to write a *Maclean's* piece about a man who came from nothing, defied Canada's stifling class system and become the most powerful newspaper owner in Canada. In the late 1940s, magazines were at the peak of their power. Everyone read them. They attracted the best writers in journalism. And *Maclean's*, a large, fat magazine that ran stories that went on for page after page, was the best magazine in the country. Only the *Star Weekly*, which would never run a word about George McCullagh, came close to *Maclean's* quality and prestige. So McCullagh tried a saw-off: he'd let Berton into his life and sit for interviews if Berton showed him the article before it ran. McCullagh knew better. He was asking Berton to break a basic rule of North American journalism, and trying to co-opt the young writer into agreeing to a deal that no serious journalist would ever agree to. It was a bargain that any *Globe and Mail* and *Telegram* reporter would have been fired for making, and they both knew it.

Berton said that was a non-starter.

"We'll see about that," McCullagh said, picking up the phone. "Get me [editor Arthur] Irwin at *Maclean's*."

Irwin, the best Canadian magazine editor of his generation, was soon on the line. He wouldn't show the story to McCullagh, but he was willing to let a third-party fact-check it.

"Who are you suggesting?" McCullagh asked.

Irwin suggested *Globe and Mail* managing editor Bob Farquharson, who was a long-time friend. "Not him!" McCullagh answered. Then McCullagh suggested editorial page editor Oakley Dalgleish. That was fine with Irwin, but now Berton balked. "How can Dalgleish check the facts when he doesn't know all the facts about you?"

McCullagh had a solution for that: "He'll check them with me."

Berton knew Dalgleish was McCullagh's protegé and that if he gave Dalgleish control, Berton was really handing McCullagh a veto. Berton wouldn't accept the offer.

"Then you're on your own," McCullagh said. The publisher was willing to give Berton free rein in the newsrooms of the *Globe and Mail* and the *Telegram*. Berton spent three weeks hanging around the newsrooms and digging through the *Globe and Mail* clipping library. He came out of it with a story that was probably the best profile written of McCullagh during the publisher's lifetime. It ended with a prediction and a question; "What's next for him? Probably a national weekly paper to fight the mighty *Star Weekly*. At forty-three, his story is only half-told." When it ran in January 1949, McCullagh sent Berton a handwritten note of congratulations.

McCullagh's opposition to the article had created a challenge that Berton was forced to meet. Toronto's financial community was small, insular and closed to the media. The city's power brokers and many readers saw journalists as poorly paid working-class people who were, at best, good for publicizing a stock issue or floating a political trial balloon. They weren't capable of explaining nuance or thinking for themselves. Berton put the lie to that: by investigating a hostile subject who had the power to push back, he had gone farther than he ever would have if McCullagh had been co-operative.

The McCullagh feature was a turning point for Berton, who realized that shoe leather is journalism's best fuel. Rather than court the powerful for access, he would do his best work digging for facts and piecing together anecdotes. Later, reclusive powerful men like industrialist E.P. Taylor would cringe when they heard that Berton was bird-dogging them, and would come out of the shadows to offer interviews to try to control the narrative. Berton would use these new investigative skills to write books that tackled social issues and common scams. He then began researching the in-depth histories for which he's remembered.[42]

16

FIGHTING HOLY JOE'S GHOST

On Saturday, May 8, 1948, Holy Joe Atkinson, that strange mixture of social justice advocate and soul-crushing capitalist, died quietly at his home. He'd been in failing health for about a month, and his family and friends knew the end was coming. Atkinson's last letter was from Mackenzie King, who was still hanging onto power in Ottawa. It was a heartfelt message of friendship, describing their days as desk-mates at the *Globe* and their long alliance to build a liberal Canada.

The next edition of the *Star* came out on the afternoon of Monday, May 10. It carried the news of Atkinson's death. It also dropped the shocking fact that Atkinson's 16,570 shares of Toronto *Star* stock—out of twenty thousand—had been left to the Atkinson Charitable Foundation. Atkinson's two children and Pate Mulock, grandson of Sir William Mulock, owned the rest. The younger Atkinsons had promised that, on their deaths, their shares would also go to the foundation.

Atkinson had several reasons for doing this. He didn't want anyone to accumulate the power that he'd held. He didn't want the paper to be sold and fall into the hands of someone like McCullagh, who'd bend it to their own ideology. And he wanted a legacy, a steady flow of money to Ontario charities and social justice causes. Atkinson truly believed the *Star* had been given to him to enable good deeds. Its columns exposed social problems and offered solutions. Its opinion writers advocated political and economic reforms. Much of the big profits made by the paper went to good causes. There was no other paper like it in Canada. There still isn't. Atkinson, through his will, hoped to control its ideology and profits from the grave.

Mackenzie King, his old friend, had braced for Atkinson's death but was still saddened by it. "The more one looked at his life, the more one is impressed with the help he has been to his fellow men and how marvelous his attachment to causes related to human brotherhood," King wrote in his diary.[1] The prime minister went to the funeral and stared down into the open coffin of his friend and McCullagh's nemesis. "Mr. Atkinson's face looked as though he had been through some pain. There was a sensitive expression in it as though he had suffered; a fine determination. Great strength; also great peace. The face of a man who looked the world in the face. Certainly, as he lay there, he looked triumphant in death."[2]

George McCullagh and George Drew were determined that Holy Joe would not be a winner in the hereafter.

There were a few problems with Atkinson's plan. First, the *Star* had always advocated hefty estate taxes, and the Atkinson Foundation would have been able to dodge them if the will was solid. The *Star* shares would be transferred from Holy Joe's estate to a foundation, denying the province a windfall that the government and legislature could spend as it pleased, on social programs or anything else. (To be fair, Atkinson did follow the paper's editorial policy that heirs should not be handed unearned fortunes. The Atkinson children had, as far as the newspaper was concerned, been left out of the will, though they did get money from his personal savings.)

The second issue was the foundation itself. Was it really a charity, or was it Atkinson's private wealth being spent, untaxed, on his pet political and social issues? In 1948, charitable donations got a 50 percent tax writeoff. The drafters of this will expected this bequest to dodge all estate taxes, giving a dead Atkinson a bigger tax break than he would have received if he'd given the *Star* to the foundation when he was alive. Atkinson and his lawyers had gone to Ottawa to ask King to make sure the laws lined up with this plan. The prime minister, who had known about the idea since April 1943, promised to make changes that might be needed, but took his time.[3] Atkinson died before King got around to creating the loophole Atkinson needed.

The will also had an escape clause: if, for some reason, the transfer of ownership to the Atkinson Charitable Foundation was blocked by the provincial government, the trustees of the estate could put the *Star* and its real estate up for sale and give the proceeds to the kind of organizations that Atkinson had supported.

John Ross Robertson had made a similar play in 1918, when he'd left the *Telegram* to the Hospital for Sick Children. This had put the paper in the control of trustees of an organization that saw it as something as a cash cow. They had no interest in running a brave newspaper, just a profitable one. (This was also a problem the *Star* faced in 1948.) The *Telegram* bequest, made through a complicated trust, held up for more than thirty years, until George McCullagh succeeded in prying it out of the hospital's hands.

McCullagh had no hard feelings against Robertson. But he despised Holy Joe. And the feeling was mutual. From the grave, Atkinson wanted to ensure McCullagh never got control of the *Star*. Years before, he'd told a *Star* reporter who was researching Atkinson for a pre-written obituary, "I am fixing things so nobody could destroy my paper."[4]

Joseph Atkinson Jr. was, within days of his father's death, made chairman of the *Star*'s board of directors and president of the Atkinson

Charitable Foundation. The trustees stopped work on a new building for the *Star Weekly*. With money in the bank to pay for the best lawyers in the country, the trustees of Atkinson's legacy braced themselves for the assault they knew was coming.

* * *

During the municipal election campaign of 1948, both of McCullagh's Toronto papers blasted the *Star*. One front-page editorial carried in the *Telegram* and the *Globe and Mail* accused the *Star* of "lying, dishonesty and trickery." Another editorial, titled "Don't be a Dope," was directed at the city's voters. The *Star*, it said, was "joining hands with the Communists" and asked voters, "are you going to be a dupe of this dishonest paper?" In reply, the *Star* kept referring to the *Telegram* and the *Globe and Mail* as "the gold-dust twins."[5] They knew McCullagh chaffed at the idea that he was simply a pawn of Bill Wright, and that he never would have succeeded without the old prospector's grub stake.

The election became a referendum on whether Ontario would stick with its annual municipal elections (supported by the *Star*) or go with a two-year term for mayors and councillors (McCullagh's choice). Voters chose candidates who wanted to stick with the old system. "Those who watched from a distance the campaign of vituperation McCullagh's newspapers unleashed upon the Toronto *Star*...will feel some satisfaction at the outcome," the *Ottawa Citizen* commented.[6]

Within six months, the *Telegram*'s circulation had risen from 200,000 to 260,000. MacFarlane had whipped—the more accurate word might be terrorized—the newsroom into shape. Fawning stories on the Loyal Orange Lodge were gone. If McCullagh's efforts resulted in anything good, the list of accomplishments would have to begin with driving a spike into the heart of that colonial holdover. Columns that had carried news of the celebration of the Glorious Twelfth of July and the annual Orange parade were now full of crime news. The *Telegram* and the *Star* covered every major crime in the city, and made stars out of criminals. Bank robbers, especially the Boyd Gang, who started their crime spree the next year, got big headlines on the front page. The *Telegram* scooped the *Star* by landing an interview with gang leader Edwin Boyd's wife while the robbers were still on the lam. Then they hammered the *Star* again by getting an exclusive interview with Boyd after he was caught.[7]

But there was more than one way to catch a star, whether or not it was falling. Just after the municipal election, rumours started circulating in Toronto's business community that big political news was coming about Holy Joe's still-unpublished will.

* * *

The first fight came over the valuation of the company for tax purposes. The trustees gave a figure of $8.76 million. McCullagh and other critics of the Atkinson legacy plan said the number was absurd. A few months after Holy Joe died, McCullagh paid just under $4 million for the moribund *Telegram*, and it was, by far, the junior afternoon paper. The *Star's* circulation, and rate and column inches of advertising, dwarfed the *Telegram's*. And the *Star's* real estate was much better property than its afternoon rival's. The trustees had undervalued the *Star*.

George Drew, now leader of the federal Progressive Conservatives, had turned over the premiership of Ontario to caretaker Tom Kennedy while the provincial Tories held their leadership race. But Drew and his former finance minister, Leslie Frost, were very much in charge. Drew and McCullagh were still close friends, and *Globe and Mail* editor Dalgleish was tight with Frost. Word got around that McCullagh and his allies were going to "fix the Star."[8] A little newspaper in Brockville put that rumour into print. The trustees of the *Star* also heard the story.

It took nearly a year, but the rumour became fact on March 25, 1949, when the Charitable Gifts Act was given first reading in the Ontario legislature. Furious opposition MPs and journalists claimed

McCullagh had pushed the law through and had even dispatched his lawyer, John Tory, to draft the legislation.[9] There could be no doubt that the proposed law's sole purpose was to thwart Joe Atkinson's will. Frost justified the law by saying companies owned by charities couldn't serve two masters: the employees and managers of the company and the interests of the charity. That was a weak argument, and no conservative would have cared if this conflict existed. The business would rise or fall based on the quality of its management and the effects of external market forces. Frost had a second argument that was much stronger: the tax breaks given to charities made them unfair competitors against other companies that paid taxes. McCullagh's *Globe and Mail* picked up on that, asking whether the trustees of some unnamed business left to some unnamed charity might run the business into the ground and not take a profit, just to undercut their competition.

The *Globe and Mail* drew on someone's legal training to come up with an argument for the law and against Holy Joe's will. The paper ran an editorial saying the will violated the ancient rule against perpetuities, which prevents property owners from using trusts to control their assets long after they're dead. The editorial claimed there was case law showing that wills like Holy Joe's could be declared void for being contrary to the public interest. The *Globe and Mail's* editorial writer claimed to agree with the idea that a millionaire could leave his assets to charity, but argued that he had to do it in a way that was open to public scrutiny. Or he could simply make donations that would be 100 percent tax-free. The Atkinson Charitable Foundation was to be privately run. The people would not know if the federal and provincial governments were getting their fair share of *Star* profits from the foundation. The new bill, according to McCullagh's paper, would put the *Star's* shares into the hands of the charities themselves. They could collect *Star* dividends or sell the shares.[10]

Two days later, the *Globe and Mail* was much meaner. In an editorial titled "Pay Up and Shut Up," which does not seem to have been written by someone with the deft hand and skilled logical mind of a lawyer, the paper said:

> Through Communists and Socialist stooges in Labor circles, it [the *Star*]has sought to enlist public sympathy for itself by suggesting that the act is the result of connivance by the publisher of The Globe and Mail. Putting words in the parrots' mouths, it sets forth the proposition that the act had no other purpose than to force the sale of the Star. With this, of course, was coupled to the suggestion that in this way Mr. McCullagh hopes to gain control of that newspaper.
>
> Both are pure melodrama. Both are easily answered. Mr. McCullagh can have no interest whatsoever in seeing the Star passing from the control of the incompetents now guiding it to a new and able management. As for any desire to own it, in his own words, "I would not pay a plugged nickel for that contaminated sheet, now or ever…"
>
> The trustees can pay the succession duties, keep control of the newspaper and continue to "disseminate" the founder's "doctrines and beliefs."
>
> We would suggest they pay up and shut up.[11]

Both papers ran editorial cartoons that were as ugly and mean-spirited as their print criticism. The fight was brutal, often drifting into overkill. It's unclear if the people of Toronto and the rest of Ontario cared about the will of an old millionaire, but the newspapers certainly did, and they expended acres of forests on the topic.

A front-page editorial in the March 29, 1949, *Star* called the province's interference with Atkinson's will a "violation of sacred rights."

"Never before have the rights of free people been so seriously challenged by an act of a British legislative body," the editors said without irony. This was the first of a series of editorials that the *Star* ran on its front page, each becoming nastier as the bill came closer to passing. The *Windsor Daily Star* and the *Ottawa Citizen*, both controlled by the Southam family, opposed the bill. The *Financial Post*, hardly a communist parrot, warned that the bill might force the University of Toronto to sell Connaught Laboratories, founded after the university patented insulin. Smaller papers, many of them long-time Tory backers but run by independent publishers who wanted their wills respected, backed the *Star*. Most media that backed the *Star* were opposed to the retroactive aspect of the bill, the fact that the provincial government had waited until Holy Joe was dead and his will was read to make changes that were, according to Premier Kennedy, necessary and overdue.

The opposition parties, backed by the *Star* itself, called out the law for what it was: harassment of a newspaper that was a constant critic of the Ontario Tory government. It's clear that Frost, Drew and McCullagh didn't expect the *Star* to go out of business, but they did believe the trustees would be forced to sell the company. There were no other left-of-centre capitalists lurking in Toronto, and whoever bought the paper—maybe even McCullagh—would certainly yank it to the right. The *Windsor Star* spelled it out in an editorial: "The Toronto Star always has upheld the interests of the minorities, of the poor, the unfortunate and the downtrodden. Never has it presumed to speak for special interests. If it is to be sold, it will be sold to someone with a lot of money…The lower income people in the Toronto area might end up without any newspaper to speak on their behalf."[12]

CCF leader Ted Jolliffe tried to block the bill with a filibuster speech in the legislature. This was a lost cause. It's almost impossible to stop a bill from passing when there's a majority government. The *Globe and Mail* took no pity on the exhausted leader of the CFF, accusing him of trying to curry favour for his party with the *Star*. The *Star* carried pictures of MPPS holding big handfuls of mail or, apparently, fielding phone calls from constituents who were angry about the plan.[13] The CCF, normally in favour of taxing private wealth, especially estates, opposed the Charitable Gifts Act. Agnes Macphail, one of the party's most famous MPs, suggested a five-year moratorium on the law to allow the province to see the charitable foundation at work and determine whether the claims made about it were grounded in reality.[14]

Even Frost was willing to admit that Atkinson's bequest was crafted in a way to protect the *Star*'s traditional editorial slant. The will, Frost told the legislature, "was drawn up to continue promotion of the doctrines and belief of the owner. Charity was secondary."[15]

But some Tories choked on the idea of using a law to thwart a person's will, no matter the politics involved. Anyone who believed in property rights would agree that a person should be able to pass their wealth—either taxed or not—on to their designated heirs, who could be their children or a charitable trust. This seemed like government overreach, motivated by spite. And, to make it worse, the law was retroactive: what had been completely legal when Atkinson and his lawyers drafted the will was now to be illegal. Opposition to the bill stiffened across the province. Charities and labour unions opposed it. So did lawyers and trust companies in downtown Toronto, who drafted and executed wills. And very wealthy people were wary of government action that encroached on their power over their fortunes.

Everyone blamed McCullagh. In one editorial, the *Star* called the Charitable Gifts Act: "This adopted child of his [Frost] whose parentage is undisclosed." The *Globe and Mail* feigned innocence while delivering editorial backhands to the *Star*'s trustees

The *Ottawa Journal* was one of the publications that called McCullagh out by name: "The fact that Mr. George McCullagh...a close personal and political friend of Mr. Drew is the *Star*'s sole daily newspaper competitor gives a sinister aspect to the whole measure... If the *Star* is forced to sell it may, of course, be picked up by moneyed interests in sympathy with the Tories."[16]

The Ontario government came back with two important amendments. The first gave the trustees seven years to find a buyer for the

Star. The second change was much more important: it allowed the trustees of the paper to buy the business themselves. In the end, that's what happened. The issue of the *Star's* ownership dragged on for ten years, ending when no one really cared anymore.[17]

If the attack on the *Star* and the Atkinson legacy was supposed to humble the paper, the move backfired. The trustees, free of any restraint from Holy Joe and enraged by what they saw as dirty dealing by their competitor McCullagh and his Tory pals, turned the newsroom loose. The newspaper war had been intense since McCullagh bought the *Telegram.* Now it became outrageous.

As for McCullagh, the war against Holy Joe's ghost cost him most of his influence at Queen's Park. Leslie Frost, who became premier during the fight over the *Star's* fate, was a far different man than George Drew. He was a shrewd, simple but effective small-town politician with no national ambitions. And he realized in 1949 that George McCullagh was more trouble than he was worth.

* * *

Dazzled by the *Telegram's* big circulation leap, McCullagh decided to cash in by raising the price of the paper from three cents to a nickel. MacFarlane, who had done so much to increase the *Tely's* numbers, knew what would happen. The *Tely* wasn't that good of a paper. The *Star* was still bigger and was all the newspaper any afternoon reader really needed. So, with two comparable newspapers published at the same time in the same city, sitting side by side on the shelf of a newsstand, why would readers pay more? It turned out they wouldn't. Within a few weeks, the *Telegram* lost all the readers it had gained since McCullagh bought it.[18] McCullagh wouldn't have made such a rookie error in the 1930s, but by the time he bought the *Telegram*, he was in a steep decline.

McCullagh was just forty-three, but friends thought he was starting to look much older. At that age, many executives are just starting to come into their own. It is a prime time of life to go into politics. But

McCullagh seemed to be past all that. His staff could see he was obviously a sick man. He rarely got a decent night's sleep. He seemed to catch every flu that went around. McCullagh never shook the asthma that had set in after his 1942 pneumonia bout. And almost every cold progressed to a new case of pneumonia. John Bassett and his wife often travelled with McCullagh to New York on the *Globe and Mail*'s company plane.[19] The Bassetts would go out on the town while McCullagh had long sessions with his psychiatrist, Dr. Kennedy. Most people who knew McCullagh realized he had problems. He was still entertaining rich, famous guests at Thornhill—royalty like the Duke of Kent and movie stars, mostly—and he was a fixture at hockey games and boxing matches, but the glow was fading fast.

When there weren't house guests, McCullagh's mansion was just another farmhouse on the edge of town, though it was bigger and better than most. Ann McCullagh Hogarth, the last survivor of the little family that lived in that mansion, said the place might seem glamorous to adults, but it was just an ordinary home to her. The house was isolated, at the end of what was then a dirt road, and "a lonely place for a kid to grow up."[20]

Her father, on his good days, took them to hockey games, and loved to perform for the kids, "telling stories and reading poetry aloud. He'd tear up and cry out loud at some sad poetry." The kids loved him and enjoyed living with him. To them, he was a kind, sweet, emotional man.[21]

"Living at Bayview seemed completely normal to me. I wished I lived in the city, so I got around by bus," Ann said. She said her father warned her against becoming a snob: "He was very strict about the way we treated people." He provided the example that he wanted the children to follow. "My dad knew all the names of the old guys selling papers downtown. We would come out of Maple Leaf Gardens after a hockey game and he would greet the guys selling the bulldog edition of the *Globe and Mail* by name."

George McCullagh with his children George and Ann at a Toronto Maple Leafs baseball game, late 1940s. (CITY OF TORONTO ARCHIVES, FONDS 1257, SERIES 1057, ITEM 3534)

On weekends, Ann rode with her father, but her brothers George and Robert did not. They simply weren't interested. Riding created a special bond between father and daughter, but McCullagh was close to all his children. Photographers from McCullagh's papers took pictures of the children and their father and put them in the newspaper. Robert, the oldest, was born just before his father bought the *Globe*. There were three years between Robert and George. The youngest, Ann, was born in 1937.

While there was a closeness between the parents and children, all three McCullagh kids were packed off to boarding schools. Robert ended up at Trinity College in Port Hope. George was enrolled in Upper Canada College, and Ann went to Havergal College (a place she enjoyed, and where she is still one of its most enthusiastic alumna).

Downtown, McCullagh spent his workday at the *Globe and Mail* headquarters, and long lunch hours at the new downtown hotspot, Winston's. The restaurant had been a diner haunted by newspaper people like McCullagh until it was bought by two Hungarian immigrants, Oscar and Cornelia Berceller, in 1940, tarted up and renamed for Winston Churchill. They set aside a table for McCullagh, who used it most days when he was in Toronto.

McCullagh began to cling to John Bassett more and more, with George Drew filling in when he could find time to escape his political duties. "When George was down in the dumps," an old friend of Bassett's told author Maggie Siggins, "Bassett was the only person who could cheer him up. McCullagh became too attached to John, too dependent on him."[22]

The depressions were awful. Friends would be talking to McCullagh when a seemingly normal sentence would be broken by a long silence. "He wouldn't respond," one of his friends said. "You'd phone his secretary and she would find him out cold on the floor."[23] (Whether McCullagh was actually unconscious or simply refusing to engage is unclear.) Strangely, people at the heart of the British elite seemed to know more about McCullagh's mental health than the leaders of Canada. Likely Lord Beaverbrook heard of McCullagh's problems directly from McCullagh himself, or second-hand through the Bassetts. However the story got to London, McCullagh's mental health wasn't news to people at the very core of British power. Cabinet minister and former newspaper publisher Brendan Bracken, Winston Churchill's most loyal colleague, believed McCullagh suffered terribly, and that the Canadian publisher struggled to have a life worth living. Bracken had seen Churchill's black-dog days when the great prime minister lost all hope, upped his alcohol intake (which was, in normal times, astounding) and threatened suicide. McCullagh could have used a confidante like Bracken.

The owner of the *Globe and Mail* made do with what he had. McCullagh found ways to entice Bassett to the rural estate and made his visits tolerable. The McCullaghs and the Bassetts spent hours watching first-run movies in the estate's private theatre. John Bassett didn't mind the time demands. McCullagh, despite his problems, was still Bassett's hero. But Moira Bassett began to find the visits exhausting.

McCullagh's loneliness and unhappiness started affecting his work habits. He never seemed to be able to focus on the *Telegram*, except when he needed to use it as a weapon. The *Globe and Mail* was his real love. The offices of the two papers were only a few blocks apart, so McCullagh would show up at the *Telegram* from time to time. He'd sit in the newsroom with his feet on a reporter's desk and hold court with the city room staff. Then he'd leave without visiting the business office. When he wasn't on a low, he loved to trade stories with the journalists and talk sports. He was still part-owner of the Maple Leafs hockey team, having bought up more stock in the 1940s to take an unsuccessful run at gaining control of the Leafs and the Gardens. He was still a force at the racetrack: his colt Speedy Irish, for which he paid more than $6,000, placed second in the 1949 King's Plate, behind Epic, owned by E.P. Taylor.[24]

Bill Wright was a less frequent visitor to the city. He'd begun having respiratory problems, likely caused by his heavy smoking. Back in Barrie, Wright became a fixture of the community, which was then a town of about thirty thousand and was not yet a satellite city of Toronto. McCullagh still shielded Wright from the would-be dealmakers who showed up at the door, but Wright was generous to the people he knew in his adopted hometown.

People in Barrie saw him as a man with a knack for learning about other people's problems, and, if possible, solving them with money. Howard Posie came back from the war and couldn't find a house for himself and his family, so Wright gave him one. The Royal Victoria Hospital received the very substantial sum of $200,000 from Wright. He helped pay for a new arena for the Barrie Colts, which was then a Junior-A team, and showed up to most of their games. He didn't mingle with many strangers in Barrie, but fundraisers for local service clubs knew they could count on him when raising money for Christmas baskets for the poor, and for civic projects. He made a 162-acre tract available to the Barrie Flying Club for an airfield. This time, he took a mortgage for part of the value of the land, knowing people who could afford to fly private planes could also be expected to pony up part of the cost of their hobby. When they didn't make the payments, Wright didn't foreclose. Later, when someone praised him for "giving" the land, Wright replied. "I didn't give it. I presented it to them and accepted a mortgage. Now, I'm afraid, they're broke. That's the same as giving, I guess."[25]

Wright kept a cow at his stable, and, at least once, families in need found the richest man in the country on their doorstep with a pail of fresh milk. He liked to be thanked for his generosity, and he saved every note. But he wasn't seen by the people of Barrie as some kind of benevolent angel. In fact, he was rarely seen at all. Most days, he never left the house. When he did go down the hill into Barrie, he'd shoot pool for twenty-five cents a game and collect those quarters when he won.

Wright spent a lot of his time doting on his young nieces. He'd pay for them and a dozen or two of their friends to go to Saturday afternoon matinees at one of the town's theatres. By the time McCullagh bought the *Telegram*, Wright's sister, brother-in-law and their children were among the few people who saw him anymore. His walks around Barrie became less frequent. Comfortable chairs that had been put out on the lawns were moved up to the house because Wright found the walk too strenuous.[26]

Wright's decline must have added to McCullagh's emotional problems. The old man was the father figure in George McCullagh's life, the one man of his generation who always had McCullagh's praise and loyalty. The old prospector's decline left McCullagh alone. He had always needed Wright as a partner, first, as a financial backer for his newspaper deals, and then as someone to give credibility to schemes like the Leadership League. When critics of the *Globe and Mail*'s editorial policies attacked the people behind the curtain, McCullagh could deflect that criticism by calling it an attack on a proprietor—Wright—who had an unblemished record of honesty in the business world and a sterling military career.

* * *

As the new *Telegram* took shape, the newspaper war with the *Star* ramped up, and the political fight over Holy Joe Atkinson's will turned ugly, McCullagh decided it was a good time to tour Europe. He travelled on the *Queen Mary* and dined with fellow passenger Winston Churchill, who was still seething in Opposition after being turned out of power by an ungrateful electorate at the end of the Second World War.

Through the spring of 1949, McCullagh visited Paris, where he signed the hotel registry "George McCullagh, Newspaperman, Toronto,"[27] and then went on to parts of France where construction workers were still repairing war damage. The French economy was a mess. Despite the injection of American money under the Marshall Plan, most people were broke, and commerce was barely alive.

"You can't get over the feeling that something has happened to the Englishman," McCullagh said after he got back to Toronto. "He works hard, very hard at times. He is steady, persevering, but you get the feeling that he takes it perhaps a bit too well. You are afraid that there has disappeared a very essential ingredient of the British character, the capacity to be indignant. If this be a true appraisal, did the war do it, or did scarcity and the doubtful pleasure of austerity drive the Londoner into this unrebellious state?"[28]

Germany, he saw, was in even worse shape. Not only were its major cities shattered, but thousands of people who had been driven out of Pomerania, Silesia and Czechoslovakia, or who had fled the Soviets occupying the eastern part of the country, were still living in camps and tent cities. Some of them even squatted in abandoned Nazi concentration camps. McCullagh wasn't sure Nazism was really dead. He later told the story of a German traffic cop, a refugee from Russian-occupied East Prussia, who, when commended by McCullagh for grinding the swastika from his old military belt, grinned and twisted the buckle to show the Nazi emblem was still there, up against his skin.

After the Western Allied powers and the West German government introduced the Deutschmark in the summer of 1948, the Soviets
blockaded West Berlin. The Americans, with the help of their British
and French allies, were keeping the city alive with an airlift of food and
fuel. The Cold War was getting much, much colder. McCullagh asked
many of his hosts if they thought Europe and America could stop a
Soviet lunge into western Europe.

He believed they probably couldn't. McCullagh, who got along
with most people, saw the Germans were friendly but depressed.
Many of them seemed to want out of Europe, and McCullagh thought
immigrants from that shattered country would fit in well in the
German-settled region around Kitchener, Ontario.[29]

He went to London, where he met Beaverbrook and other important business leaders. Lester Pearson, then working at Canada's High
Commission, took McCullagh to Wembley Stadium for the FA Cup final
between the Wolverhampton Wanderers and Leicester City. There
were 100,000 people in the stadium. The publisher had never seen anything like it, and he became emotional as all the crowd stood on their
feet before the game to sing the hymn "Abide With Me." McCullagh
watched people bow and curtsey to Princess Elizabeth and Philip,
Duke of Edinburgh, though it doesn't seem as if McCullagh got close
enough to meet them.

"They [the soccer players] played vigorously, but, if they collided
with an opponent, which they frequently did, and knocked him to the
ground, they stopped to pick him up," McCullagh said when he got
back to Canada. "When I heard some of the spectators say they were
quite rough, I thought they should come and see how we knock them
down and drag them out in Maple Leaf Gardens."

Still, he found London troubling. The city was poor and broken.
Bomb damage was being slowly repaired, and rationing was as strict as
it had been in the worst years of the war. No one seemed to have any
money. Many of the great country houses, places that McCullagh had

tried to emulate with his Bayview estate, were being torn down by owners who couldn't afford the upkeep and taxes. Obviously, McCullagh thought, socialism wasn't making things any better. But capitalism had somehow failed, too.[30]

After London, McCullagh went out into the countryside to chat up farmers. Whether they were horse people or small-holding farmers was left unclear. Then he headed south to Geneva, where he stopped for a while, and which was untouched by the war, as was Rome. The pope found time for a brief audience.

"Of all of the countries I visited, excepting Germany, England is going through toughest days," McCullagh reported to a joint meeting of the Canadian and Empire Clubs in the Royal York Hotel at the end of May 1949. "In far more grave days during the war—possibly because of the emotional stimulus that comes to one's rescue in these times— the Englishman was more cheery and carefree and even optimistic." Now, McCullagh said, there was some defeatism in the air, though the British tended to hate the Russians more than they feared them.

Despite his doubts about British capitalism, the real problem, McCullagh said, was socialism. The Labour government had brought in "soak the rich" budgets. They had cut the length of the work week. "Man's best hobby is his work," McCullagh asserted. Canadians should take heed of what was happening in Britain and resist the Left's siren songs. "There might be some excuse for England drifting into Socialism after she spent her material and human wealth so lavishly for the defense of all of our freedom. But if political leaders espouse this social doctrine to a young and rich country like ours, it's nothing short of wicked. Security?—Yes, for the aged and ailing, but as a philosophy of life, surely not! The way to combat Socialism and Communism is to amend capitalism and make it work."

As for the defeated Axis powers, the Germans were as arrogant as ever, while the Italians, McCullagh believed, were quite happy to have lost the war. Only Florence, which had suffered terrible battle damage, was having a hard time rebuilding. But, even there, the people seemed cheerful and affectionate.

So how could Canada's business leaders, now assembled, keep Marx at bay? Get rid of the great class gulfs in Canadian society, McCullagh said. Get to know and understand employees. He told the Bay Street crowd that, while dining with Winston and Randolph Churchill, the seventy-four-year-old lion was reminded by his son, "Now, father, don't forget to stand on your dignity." Winston replied, "My boy, I have never known anyone's dignity to become higher by standing on it." It was classic Churchill, a quip that is so good it's hard to believe it was spontaneous. Maybe it was an act cooked up between father and son, a little show for a somewhat interesting and important guest. Maybe McCullagh didn't hear it first-hand. But it made McCullagh's point quite well.[31]

McCullagh seemed quite pleased with the trip, and with his report to the downtown Toronto club crowd who pecked at their lunches in the Royal York Hotel ballroom. He liked his journalism so much that he had the speech printed up, and anyone who called the *Globe and Mail* could get a copy for free. The *Globe and Mail* sent out thirty-six thousand copies.[32] The paper's editors were wise enough to run a promotion for it on the front page. The next day, the *Globe and Mail* printed the whole thing. CFRB recorded it and broadcast the lecture at 10 p.m. that night. McCullagh must have felt important, though most of his analysis turned out to be quite superficial. Then McCullagh published a booklet filled with his observations, which he gave to subscribers of his newspapers and sent to his friends, including Lord Beaverbrook.

He followed up the Royal York speech with a national radio broadcast on the same topic. Later, McCullagh received letters from tens of thousands of listeners across Canada who liked what they heard. With an election just months away, McCullagh was back in the game.

17

DREW
FLAMES OUT

Anyone who closely follows Canadian politics will be able to pick an election that they think was influenced by biased or incompetent journalism. For McCullagh's generation and people who became politically aware around the time of the Second World War, the 1949 federal election stands out. The campaign is all but forgotten now, but, because it seemed that the Liberal era had ended with the recent retirement of Mackenzie King, most people believed this election would be a historic moment, a great generational change. And the flames were fuelled by the leaders of the three newspapers that were locked in a fight to the death in Toronto.

"It was really a reprehensible period in news coverage," John MacFarlane, then a senior *Telegram* editor, told writer Maggie Siggins years later. "McCullagh asked the *Telegram* [not the *Globe and Mail*] to assume a role in the coverage of that election which was warped and distorted and which I, unfortunately, and the *Telegram* as a whole were party to."[1]

King had finally shuffled off, replaced by the bland and distant Louis St. Laurent. The Liberals had been in power for fourteen years straight, and, except for the five years of R.B. Bennett's Tory administration and a few weeks in 1926, had held office since 1922. Any reasonable person was open to the idea that it was time for a change. George Drew was federal Tory leader. He was relatively young, engaging, handsome, and his party's major policies were no different from those of the federal Liberals.

McCullagh turned, again, to radio, even though he had always been let down by this medium. The previous year, when an election seemed likely, he'd paid for a national broadcast in support of Tory leader John Bracken. Now the election was finally underway and George Drew was party leader. So McCullagh paid, yet again, to cut dozens of records to be sent to radio stations across Canada. Like the rest of his broadcasts, they were written for a newspaper editorial page, not for radio audiences.

McCullagh and Drew seemed inseparable, and for both, this was a rendezvous with destiny. McCullagh saw their friendship as more than just a political partnership with social overtones. In a 1944 letter to Drew, McCullagh described how they'd watched out for each other's mental health.

"We have been thrown together in a purpose and with a quite extraordinary community of thought on public questions," McCullagh told his friend. "Whatever has been accomplished we have done together and God knows the going has been none too encouraging. Perhaps we have helped each other more than we have both realized. I can certainly remember many times when my spirits were pretty low and you have taken the optimistic view. In all probability you can recall similar circumstances."[2]

McCullagh could never have this kind of relationship with Hepburn, who handled his own demons by going on benders. Nor could he expect King to help him when he was on one of his lows. King would have listened to him for a while, and then tried to calculate how much time McCullagh had left. People at the newspapers knew about the highs and lows and covered for McCullagh. Bassett, with his upbeat personality, could sometimes cheer McCullagh up. But Drew was the man who took him to fishing camps or on holidays in Barbados. Now, it seemed, Drew was on the threshold of becoming prime minister of Canada.

In this election, the Tories could exploit three Liberal vulnerabilities. Inflation was eating away at wage earners' buying power. There was a shortage of affordable housing for wartime veterans and their baby boomer children. And the government was running big budget surpluses while collecting income taxes at almost wartime rates.

The Tories were up against federal justice minister Louis St. Laurent, King's designated successor. To McCullagh's fury, Toronto *Star* writers worked hard to recraft Laurent's image from an aloof corporate lawyer to that of doting "Uncle Louis" who had a smile and a hug for anyone. The lawyerly image was the real man, but St. Laurent had sense enough to play for the cameras. He wasn't a particularly warm person, he had no real connection to working people, and he was a politician to the core, but that wasn't the message *Star* readers received. The Uncle Louis persona survives to this day, among the few Canadians who have ever heard anything about this rather uninteresting, unimaginative but capable prime minister.[3]

On McCullagh's command, the *Telegram*'s reporting staff tried to create a mirror image of St. Laurent as an aloof machine politician who was more comfortable in the boardroom of a major bank than in a crowd of children. The paper sent reporters to Ottawa and into Quebec to dig up dirt on the new prime minister. St. Laurent might not be "Uncle Louis," but he was also not a crook. The best the *Telegram* could do was rehash old scandals from the King years, stories that voters were sick of hearing.

At the same time, the *Star* tried to make the thwarting of Holy Joe's will an election issue. Any Liberal candidate giving a speech in a boondock like Thessalon or Creemore would get ink in the *Star* if they denounced the McCullagh-Drew conspiracy to destroy Holy Joe's legacy.[4]

The Tories simply couldn't find a reason why voters should throw St. Laurent out of office. Taxes might be high, houses might be hard to find, and inflation might be pushing up prices, but the economy was still booming. Everyone, including Mackenzie King, had expected the Depression to resume after the war, but it was clearly over. It didn't take long for the consensus to form among all the journalists covering the campaign and the editors in Toronto that Drew was losing, and that the gap between the Liberals and Tories was widening.

That's when McCullagh decided the Drew campaign needed a dose of McCullagh. He would take to the airwaves again to support his old friend.

First, McCullagh moaned to his nationwide audience about unfair competition in the newspaper industry. He claimed the *Star* got a special deal from the federal government that made it exempt from sales taxes, a deal worth $108,000 a year to McCullagh's competitor. The *Star Weekly* got this break because it was classified as a magazine. Anyone could see that it was a newspaper. The government, he said, was paying for the *Star*'s support. But not too many Canadians could feel sorry about a multi-millionaire publisher who was raking in fat profits from two major newspapers.

Then there was Holy Joe Atkinson's will, which many Liberals were defending. Listeners might not have been too upset about the profits from Canada's biggest newspaper flowing to a charity that helped the sick, poor and disposed. And McCullagh was angry about the sale of the Canadair aircraft plant to Americans, for far less money than the federal government had invested in it. But the war was over, and many industries were being shaken up.

"Don't be hoodwinked any longer, ladies and gentlemen," he told the listeners of this broadcast:

Ad for a radio speech by George McCullagh in support of his friend Conservative leader George Drew. (*GLOBE AND MAIL*)

You are told Drew can't win. I tell you he can win, and I urge each and every one of you to get out and vote for his candidate. Assure him of the support, adequate for the job, he has promised he will do. From British Columbia, Newfoundland to the Prairies and the Maritimes send Progressive Conservative members to parliament and show these power-drunk ministers that we are capable of asserting our right to govern...

What are the worst things they can say about George Drew? He is too good-looking. He talks too much. He is a stuffed shirt. Look with me into his record and be fair. He has qualities and defects like all the rest of us. I think the record establishes that his qualities far outweigh his defects. George Drew's claims to leadership are many. He has character, courage, and initiative, supplemented by boundless energy, in my opinion. He has a better conception of the glorious future this country can attain than any other man in public life.

Drew was no dictator, McCullagh said. And, he continued, charges made by Drew's enemies that the Tory leader had no feelings for his fellow human beings were flat-out wrong. "Please believe me, to anyone who knows him well, this is a miserable libel," said the publisher of the country's national political newspaper. "He is a very human guy. The single occasion I have seen him in the last three months was last Sunday afternoon. He came with his wife and his two little children for a swim in the pond at my farm. Here is a little story that Mr. Drew probably wouldn't appreciate me telling. He mentioned it was the first time in five weeks that he and his wife had seen their kiddies. They, I assure you, are just as precious to him as your children are to you."[5]

The speech was political poison, broadcast across Canada on eighty-five radio stations.

"I was covering the Drew entourage when I got a telephone call from McCullagh in Belleville," *Telegram* reporter Wes Hicks told writer Maggie Siggins when she was researching her biography of John Bassett. "'Drew's not coming across as a common man in this campaign,' McCullagh fretted. 'Of course not,' I replied. 'He's a big, handsome aristocrat, the least common man I've come across.' 'Well,' said McCullagh, 'I'm going on the air to correct the impression that he's not for the common man. Will you listen and let me know what you think?'

"He was a truly tremendous speaker. He was doing well, going on about Drew's concern for the common man when suddenly he said, 'Why just last week, George and I were sitting around the swimming pool on my estate...I thought, 'Oh, no, he's blown it.'"[6]

So McCullagh took another shot at it. This time, the speech was more about McCullagh than Drew. It was one of the best speeches McCullagh ever gave, and it is an interesting insight into the publisher's psyche. The speech had the usual digs at the CBC and the Toronto *Star*, but it was really a sort of biography. As usual, it started with McCullagh framing himself as a victim and trying to turn the table on his tormentors. At the same time, he wanted to show he was a regular guy. Since snobbery was not one of his faults, the speech seems like one of his most honest efforts.

"I will tell you of political skullduggery, acts so dishonest that you may doubt the truth of my statements," McCullagh confided to the many hundreds of thousand of people who were listening. "I do not make them carelessly. What I reveal to you will be proven, no matter which government is elected... In the thirteen years that I have been a newspaper publisher, I have been called a lot of cute names. These epithets have come from the Communists and the Socialists, from the Liberals and the Tories. I have been called a 'little pipsqueak,' a 'subsidized playboy,' the "boy dictator," and a 'gigolo to a mining millionaire.' A 'cheat,' a 'thief,' a 'liar' are among the terms of endearment that I have seen applied to myself in my own newspapers."

McCullagh said he could take the name-calling. That's the way the political game was played. "Neither do I wish to indicate that I am insensitive to it. I confess, when my children tearfully tell their mother what some of their chums say about their dad, I sometimes wonder whether it is worthwhile." And now C.D. Howe, St. Laurent's most important cabinet minister, was on the hustings saying "the two Georges" were the "most sinister association in Canada."

"Them's tough words!" McCullagh told his listeners. "I'm not perfect, but I'm not that bad."

He even mentioned his father and, for once, bragged about the old man's union work: "My mother came from England as a young girl from a family of nine. My father emigrated from Northern Ireland, one of a family of eight. They were simple, respectable, God-fearing parents. My father was a small earner and carried a union card all his life. My four sisters and I were raised in frugal circumstances."

McCullagh claimed he wasn't a Tory stooge. He'd been brought up as a Liberal. He'd donated and campaigned for the party and "learned the Liberal creed at the feet, so to speak, of the former Prime Minister,

Mr. Mackenzie King." He'd never been to a Conservative convention in his life. But the Liberals had lost their way. They'd allowed the public service to take Parliament's place. Only George Drew could restore democracy.

As for the socialists, they were peddling class prejudice.

> One of the most vicious and the most phony—capitalized by Liberals, socialists and Communists alike—is that entitled 'Soak the Rich.' Let us X-ray these merchants of hate and see how they are deceiving you.
>
> I don't want to return to the poverty of my childhood, nor do I recommend great riches as a goal for any of you. But you know, as I know, that there are good people and bad people in every walk of life. For those privileged snobs who do not assume the responsibilities of their wealth, I have a wholesome contempt, and so do you. You know the class of men—the ones who think because they have had the good fortune to accumulate some money, they are socially better than their fellow-man. But their existence does not justify condemning the rich and big business as monsters. That is a negative appeal, ladies and gentlemen, to the defects in human nature, intended to stir the envy and avarice which we all possess. Don't be deceived by this Socialist pap.[7]

McCullagh's pleadings for an end to class warfare were dramatic and very personal, but they didn't convince the voters to abandon Uncle Louis.

* * *

During that campaign, the *Telegram* became reckless in its pro-Drew coverage. Veteran journalist Norman Campbell wrote most of the pro-Drew stories at the *Telegram*. Peter Dempson was assigned the thankless task of covering the prime minister's campaign. For a while, Dempson did the best he could, sending carefully crafted stories of St. Laurent's bland speeches back to Melinda Street. They were buried on the inside pages, while Campbell's pieces got prime *Tely* real estate. Dempson, a new reporter who seems to have been well-liked, went to the elfin Campbell and asked for advice. The senior reporter reminded Dempson that it was McCullagh who paid him. If anyone booed the prime minister, get that into the lead paragraph. If there were any stumbles in St. Laurent's campaign, make them news.

Dempson began taking his photographer into the highest parts of the arenas where the prime minister spoke so they could shoot the empty seats at the farthest ends of the halls. Every rally has them, and the image of a foreground of empty chairs framing a far-off politician has become a hoary staple of biased journalism. That image was splashed across the front page. And no matter how many people clapped and cheered for St. Laurent, *Telegram* readers only saw words about the cat-calls. The *Star* was, of course, running stories that were mirror images of the *Telegram*'s campaign coverage. But while *Telegram* underestimated St. Laurent's crowds, the *Star* overestimated them.

When St. Laurent and his senior ministers like C.D. Howe spoke, they went after McCullagh as much as Drew. It must have been strange for voters in small-town Canada, far from the newspaper war, to hear about the evils of Canada's most powerful publisher. The prime minister told a crowd in Brockville about the arrogance of "the two Georges," while Howe called them liars for suggesting the Liberals were on the take from aircraft makers.[8]

The weekend before Howe's attack, McCullagh had given a speech in Toronto claiming the Liberals in Ottawa exempted the *Star Weekly* from an 8 percent tax on newsprint. This was proof, McCullagh said, of favouritism. Ignoring five decades of newspaper history, the *Telegram* and *Globe and Mail* owner charged that the *Star*'s loyalty had been purchased with a tax break. In its Saturday paper, which had a much larger circulation than Monday to Friday editions of the *Telegram*, the front-page headline, in end-of-the-world-sized type, screamed: "LIBERALS PAYING OFF THE STAR."

Drew held a rally—the *Globe and Mail* called it a "victory rally"—at Massey Hall on June 23. The place was packed, but it was a small hall. Mackenzie King had often filled the much bigger Maple Leaf Gardens for the same kind of events. Drew stood in front of the thirty-three hundred people in the hall (five hundred more were listening at the nearby Metropolitan Church House, while another fifteen hundred people crowded the sidewalks on Shuter Street) to defend his friendship with George McCullagh. It was no different, Drew said, than St. Laurent's close relationship with the Toronto *Star*.

"If he [McCullagh] had been in the city, I would have been very proud to have him on the platform tonight. If we had more people like George McCullagh prepared to fight for a free press, this country would be a lot better and safer." Cheers went up from the crowd. "I say to Mr. St Laurent that if he deplores friendships, I am sorry he has such a friend as the Toronto Daily Star."

A voice echoed up from the crowd: "That's it! Give it to 'em!"[9]

Whatever gloves were still left on the *Star* and the *Telegram* came off on the afternoon of election day as Torontonians headed to the polling stations. Playing up a supposed connection between Drew, crypto-fascist Quebec premier Maurice Duplessis and reptilian former Montreal mayor Camillien Houde (who'd be interned in 1940 for undermining Canada's war effort), the *Star* ran what's been called the most-mocked banner headline in Canadian history:

KEEP CANADA BRITISH
DESTROY DREW'S HOUDE
GOD SAVE THE KING

It was likely the last time the *Star* advocated for Canadian "Britishness."

George McCullagh was one of the *Telegram*'s many readers who believed Campbell's and Dempson's reporting and got a most unpleasant jolt on election night. The result was a humiliation for George Drew: the Liberals won a massive majority—190 seats out of 262. The *Telegram* came out of the election looking ridiculous. Soon Campbell, Dempson, other members of the Ottawa bureau and the *Telegram*'s senior political editors were summoned to McCullagh's office.

"I want you to know, that no time did I suggest we cover the campaign as we did," McCullagh told his staff. "I never issued any instructions to conduct a pro-Drew or anti-St. Laurent campaign... The prestige of the *Telegram* has been harmed." McCullagh added the obvious: "[I]n the eyes of many readers, we look a little silly. Now that the campaign is over, we're going to dig in and make the *Telegram* the best and fairest newspaper in Toronto. I want all of you, when covering a political meeting or any such event, to be objective."[10]

He waved a copy of *Maclean's* magazine, the most important periodical in the country, which had published a well-researched study into the biased coverage, just to ensure no one missed it. "I want everyone to know that we are not, under any circumstances, going to repeat this performance."

If any of the Parliament Hill reporters laughed, they managed enough control to do it after they left the meeting.[11]

Maybe McCullagh meant it that day. His political reporters and senior political editors might have believed he meant it. But the *Telegram* was locked in a war with the *Star* that was as much a conflict of ideologies as it was a competition for readers and advertisers. Politics was on the front lines of that war, and it was personal.

Drew's political career would stumble on, though he would never win another election.[12] But the two Toronto afternoon papers were the biggest losers. In their scorched earth campaign, they had lost sight of their job and had engaged in a brutal war with each other, using the two major national parties as proxies. Anyone with common sense could see their recklessness.

McCullagh was just forty-four years old when his best friend self-destructed. The publisher, after some serious stumbles in the Hepburn years, was becoming a star of the Conservative Party. He was younger than George Drew and John Diefenbaker. McCullagh had reached an age when the public would stop seeing him as a prodigy and start taking him seriously as a man with both business success and life experience. He'd had so much success as a young man. What would he achieve in the prime of life?

18

DYING AND STAYING VERY DEAD

By 1949, McCullagh's hair had turned steel grey, and he'd lost a lot of weight since the war. He looked older than his forty-four years, partly because of his smoking, partly because he got too much sun, partly because he was working himself to death. He was publishing two very large and different newspapers, one of which was the underdog in a fight for survival against a very powerful and motivated competitor. He was also working hard to help his friend George Drew become prime minister of Canada. He was still involved in the mining industry, sitting on corporate boards, and he also had a stake in Maple Leaf Gardens and a seat on its board. McCullagh was often downtown until late at night, watching the Leafs or the fights—sometimes he could see both at the same time—or just hanging around the *Globe and Mail*'s cafeteria or the *Telegram*'s newsroom. McCullagh was travelling a lot, making long trips to Europe and shorter ones to New York, Washington, Barbados and to fishing resorts in northern Ontario. At the same time, he was a dedicated father.

He was also constantly besieged by political opponents, critical media competitors and, sometimes, labour union organizers. A man with thicker skin might have been able to take that, but McCullagh could not. It was too much.

In 1950, while the Ontario legislature was debating a new labour code, reporters and editors at the *Telegram* were trying to organize a newsroom union. McCullagh fought back, horrified at the idea of sharing some of his power with the Newspaper Guild, which was affiliated with the AFL-CIO. After McCullagh published a *Globe and Mail* editorial denouncing the rather weak labour legislation, McCullagh's old foe, CCF leader Ted Jolliffe, stood up in the legislature to denounce McCullagh.

He said the editorial was "cheap. It is distorted, but that is about what we have come to expect from Dr. C. George McCullagh.[1] And I may add that for Mr. McCullagh, of all people, to impute personal interest in this matter is the strangest touch of all. Because if there is anybody in this country who has a personal interest in this matter it is the same Mr. McCullagh, who has for some months engaged in a union-busting campaign." Jolliffe went on to talk about McCullagh's interests in keeping the unions out of northern Ontario mines, and added, "May I say that there is no statement I have made in this legislature that I would not make outside this House and to Dr. McCullagh's handsome face."[2]

It was a good thing that no one called Jolliffe on the threat, because the Ontario Labour Relations Board investigated the union drive at the *Telegram*, held a hearing on the charges, and found McCullagh hadn't intimidated his employees. The newsroom union organizers had faced tough pressure from people on the *Telegram*'s very conservative news staff, and the campaign had folded.[3]

* * *

The union drive was the beginning of a stream of bad news for McCullagh. In mid-September 1951, Bill Wright fell ill at his house in Barrie. He was seventy-five years old. His First World War records show a catalogue of health problems, from a weak heart to kidney disease, and Wright was such a heavy smoker that he didn't even put down his cigarette when he had his portrait taken in his wartime uniform. (He tried to keep it low and out of sight, but it's there.) He was frail in the last few years of his life, but he was only bedridden for a week when he died. Even on his deathbed, Wright was taking phone calls from his business advisors and dictating letters. He died at 1 a.m. on September 20, 1951.[4]

The *Globe and Mail* obituary, which was carefully vetted by McCullagh, if not written by him, generously called Bill Wright the founder of the paper. The obituary took up most of the front page, with two full pages of stories and pictures inside. A large photograph of the old prospector loomed under the gigantic banner headline. The coverage rivalled that of the death of King George VI five months later.

The funeral was held at the Lloyd and Steckley Funeral Home in Barrie. Organizers asked Rev. S.E. Lewis of Barrie's magnificent old Collier Street United Church to officiate, though Wright didn't want a church funeral. He was buried in Barrie Union Cemetery. The pallbearers were George McCullagh, J. Maitland MacIntosh, Charles Burns, Harry Kimber and Harry Signia (his mining friends and *Globe and Mail* executives from Toronto), and J.H. Rodgers, A.E. Flynn, and J.B. Craig (his friends from Barrie).

Wright's death devastated McCullagh. His own father had died eight years before, but McCullagh had shown very little grief. The mawkish obituaries and praise for Wright extracted from people who almost certainly never knew him show how McCullagh used his power as publisher and owner to cry out through the pages of the *Globe and Mail*.

McCullagh was no longer reliant on Wright's money to finance his newspaper investments. For almost a decade, McCullagh had been the owner of the *Globe and Mail*, and Wright had no financial interest in the *Telegram*. McCullagh's papers were making money, and he wasn't carrying any serious personal debt. This anguish was about the loss of a real friend, a surrogate father, and one of the foundations of McCullagh's life.

Wright and McCullagh were secretive about their finances, but Wright's wealth was put on the public record when the will was probated. After Wright set up a charitable trust for the Hospital for Sick Children in the late 1940s to help smooth the way for McCullagh to buy the *Telegram*, he was worth about $11 million, which had the buying power of at least $100 million in modern dollars. Wright had a hobby for rainy days: rewriting his will. There were about twenty versions at the time of his death. Nothing could change the fact that he had no children. The money would have to go to his sister and nieces, split between fifteen heirs. And, because it was Wright, the will was overly complicated and rather strange. The text said it was designed that way to "ensure that my estate shall be carefully and skilfully managed, conserved and used for the permanent and lasting benefit of each and all of my main beneficiaries."

First, he left nothing to charity. Wright was no Holy Joe Atkinson. He only gave when he was alive. The government's big, unavoidable tax bite took $3 million, and that was charity enough.[5] He was not willing to take any risks with his money, even in death, because "in these changing and uncertain times any one of a number of major disasters beyond my power to foresee or to provide against [the reduction of] the capital and income of my estate to a fraction of its size and value."

Rather than simply dole out the inheritances, Wright set up a trust. Every year, each heir was to get a portion of the interest earned on the $7 million. Those payouts weren't much: just $1,200 a year to adults and $600 to kids, with periodic bonus payouts of $50,000 to adults. The seven adult heirs went to court in 1954 and got a raise, to $1,800 a year, which, even then, was not a lot of money. They were back in court again in 1962, after some eighteen months of preliminary hearings and legal preparation, to make the argument that the dead cannot control their fortunes from the grave. The court upheld the will.

In 1964, what was then called the Ontario Supreme Court upheld the will and gave the heirs a raise. In 1972, they divided up the accumulated interest, a substantial amount of money. The original $7 million was left to generate more interest until the ancient Rule of Perpetuities kicks in. Remember those young nieces Wright liked to play with on his Barrie porch? They, and five other young heirs, must be gone for twenty-one years before *their* heirs get to divide up the estate—the original $7 million, plus the interest that's accumulated since 1972. That should happen in the middle of this century, but it may well be later.[6]

Ed Hargreaves and Wright's sister Frances took over the rest of the house and lived there until both died. Frances was buried beside her brother and the house was sold in 1963.[7] The Wright-Hargreaves mine outlasted Wright by four years. When the vein petered out at 8,172 feet, the mine had produced $157,308,926 worth of gold, calculated at US$20 per ounce until 1933 and US$32 afterward.[8] With today's prices, the value of that gold would be close to $20 billion. The site of the Wright-Hargreaves mine is now used by a Kirkland Lake theatre company for outdoor performances.[9]

The era of the wilderness prospector was coming to an end, and these people, along with their fantastic stories of finding great veins of gold and silver, would be forgotten within a couple of decades. Wright left few footprints in Canada, and none in Barrie except for a hockey trophy and an ugly old house that's a stop on a heritage walking tour. Wright is remembered in the Canadian Mining Hall of Fame, which is not on most tourism maps.

* * *

One day in 1951, McCullagh stopped as he was leaving the *Telegram* building, shook the hands of a reporter and congratulated him on an obituary he had written. "You know, I have always had great respect for reporters. You never know which reporter is going to have the last word to say about you."[10]

Despite Pierre Berton's assertion just two years before that McCullagh's story was just half-told, McCullagh's health was broken. The decline, already noticeable during the 1949 election campaign, accelerated when Bill Wright died. McCullagh had travelled to Barrie six weeks after Wright's death for a meeting of the board of directors of the Wright-Hargreaves mine, but that was just about the last work McCullagh ever did. Wright's death broke him, and as the months passed, his physical and mental health sank deeper. The loss of his psychiatrist, Dr. Robert Foster Kennedy, who dropped dead in Bellevue Hospital that January, may also have left him feeling vulnerable. Very few psychiatrists subscribed to Dr. Foster's views that the brain was little more than a machine that could be reset with electroshock treatments. How was McCullagh going to find someone to replace him?

McCullagh rarely went into his newsrooms after the November 1951 provincial election that was held a few weeks after Wright died. By February 1952, he had stopped going into work at all. "He just burned out, just physically burned out," his daughter Ann, who was fifteen in 1952, said.[11] Harry Kimber, who knew every nook and cranny of the operation, took over the day-to-day work of publishing the *Globe and Mail* while John Bassett ran the *Telegram*.[12] Then, in the winter and spring, McCullagh had two mild heart attacks.

By the summer of 1952, friends noticed McCullagh was starting to perk up a bit. He stayed at home in Thornhill on the first weekend of August—the Civic Holiday weekend in Ontario—while Phyllis and the children were away at a lodge. He was supposed to join them that Wednesday. Instead, he decided to die while the children and Phyllis were away.

McCullagh's body was found in the pond near his Bayview house. He was just forty-seven years old. He died in the afternoon of Tuesday, August 5. The newspapers said he died of a heart attack. It would be decades before author Maggie Siggins and former *Globe and Mail* editor Richard Doyle revealed that McCullagh had killed himself. Siggins, in her biography of John Bassett, said there were rumours that he did it directly, with a gun, or had fallen off the wagon and drowned himself in the estate's pond (often described as a pool). The "pool" is always a fixture of accounts of McCullagh's death, though it is very unlikely that booze was involved.

Doyle, who wrote about the suicide in his book *Hurly-Burly*, which was an account of his time at the *Globe and Mail*, doesn't give any description of McCullagh's supposed suicide, although he would certainly have heard the details. He was on the *Globe and Mail* staff when McCullagh died, and just over a decade later, he would become the paper's editor-in-chief. In *Hurly-Burly*, Doyle says it was common knowledge among *Globe and Mail* executives that McCullagh had killed himself after suffering months of depression, insomnia and physical pain, and that his death, while a shock, was not a huge surprise to the people who were running the newspaper.

The stigma of suicide kept all the news media from telling the truth about McCullagh's death. And even if they'd wanted to break that news, McCullagh's power protected his reputation, even in death. Anyone who wanted to tell the truth would have to disprove the coroner's claim that McCullagh died of a heart attack. And McCullagh didn't carry any life insurance, so there wouldn't be a claim from the family that could be challenged in court.

* * *

Senior managers at the *Globe and Mail* were among the first people to learn of McCullagh's death. Top editors were told at about 5 p.m., and they kept it a secret as long as they could. Ed Phelan, the managing editor, called Richard Doyle into his office at 6:30 p.m. and told him the publisher was dead. "I don't want you to say anything about this. His kids are at camp or some place and they haven't been told. If we spread it about, it will wind up on the radio and that must not happen. At the same time, we have to get ready. We won't go in without the story. Hold the first five pages open. No ads at all, nothing until I give you the word."¹³

All big newspapers keep prewritten obituaries of prominent people, but a discreet check of *Globe and Mail* files for McCullagh's turned up nothing. McCullagh also had the bad timing of being found dead when the paper was right on deadline. Eventually, word arrived from family members that Phyllis and the children had been told. Now, pages of news copy for what had been the front page and the major news pages were scrapped, and stories, including a fresh obituary, were written by shocked and grieving journalists while impatient press operators waited to fire up their machines. Many of the paper's best editors and writers were on holiday, and they had to hurry back from their cottages and camps to spend the night writing stories while dealing with their own strong emotions and worry for the future. It's not clear what McCullagh's senior employees and his family were told about the cause of death, but journalists heard strange details about it. In one version, the coroner who said McCullagh died of a heart attack in his bed was accused of lying. A chauffer had carried the big man from the pond to his bedroom.

Whatever the cause of McCullagh's death, and what his friends and employees knew of its circumstances, their shock was real.

The main story ran under the headline "GEORGE McCULLAGH DIES," with the sub-headline, "Belief in Democracy Publisher's Beacon." A second story, running under the big photograph of the publisher, was labelled, "His Loss Felt Across Canada." Inside, there were photos of McCullagh travelling to England in 1936 with Bill Wright and the elder John Bassett, the man who had opened Fleet Street doors to McCullagh. A large picture showed McCullagh accepting the King's Plate trophy from George VI.

"George McCullagh was the most human of men. If the love of fellow men is the hallmark of leadership, this was the secret of his great success. He found personality an absorbing interest, and he was an incredibly acute judge of motives," Dalgleish wrote in the *Globe and Mail* editorial. The editor was either quite heartbroken, or good at faking it.

"George McCullagh was a masterful character. He held strong views, he was emotionally vibrant and he had the quality, rare but instantly recognizable, of influencing men's minds and actions. He himself was a brilliant success. He admired success in others and the talents which achieved it...During his lifetime, Mr. McCullagh was the subject of innumerable legends, many of which were entirely without foundation. But just as his vigorous personality and meteoric career created stories, so he loved to tell them. He had the wit and mingled gaiety and sadness of his Irish forebears. Few men in Canada were better raconteurs."[14]

Ken Taggart wrote the *Globe and Mail* obituary: "To those who knew him only slightly or by reputation, he was a complex, two-fisted mystery man with whom none could argue, who dominated those around him, who could be dissuaded from no course upon which he had decided. To those who worked for him, he was a disciplinarian who could be forgiving, a colleague who was known by his first name by most of his staff, a battler who grinned when given an argument, a debater of open mind who would readily capitulate and accept correction when proved wrong."[15]

Bruce West, who worked for the *Globe* when McCullagh bought the paper, described his boss, whose death he'd heard about just ten minutes before he began writing the piece, as "a two-fisted Canadian."

But, West went on to say, "he was also the most tender-hearted and sentimental person who ever lived. Ask the staffer who lost his mother about the letter from his publisher. Ask the staffer who thought his wife wasn't going to get well and was dumbfounded to have the publisher come into his office and order him to take her to one of Canada's highest-priced specialists. He also ordered him not to worry about the fee."[16] Bobbie Rosenfeld told her readers how McCullagh took out his chequebook when he learned her brother needed expensive treatment in the United States. The grief was real, and it was obvious. Readers could almost hear the sobs in the *Globe and Mail* and *Telegram* newsrooms.

Years later, Ralph Hyman, a reporter who'd been there through the whole show, told CBC journalist Larry Zolf, "George McCullagh was the last publisher who cared more about what went into the newspaper than anything else."[17]

Journalists of the time, especially those with direct experience fighting the black dog or nursing friends through bouts of depression, saw McCullagh's death coming, and some believed it was a mercy. Brendan Bracken, founder of the *Financial Times*, was Winston Churchill's alter ego through the war, and had carried Churchill through many bouts of severe emotional illness. He wrote to Lord Beaverbrook the day after McCullagh died: "I suppose it is right to use the platitude 'it is better for him that he is dead' about George McCullagh. The world must be a terrible place for a man with melancholia akin to madness."[18]

* * *

Despite the years of acrimony between McCullagh and Toronto *Star* managers, and the ongoing newspaper war between the *Star* and the *Telegram*, the *Star*'s obituary writer was generous, and he added touches of humour that captured the spirit of the man. George McCullagh "worked hard and played hard." There were "Horatio Alger aspects to his life story and he never failed to make it known to the biographers who interviewed him for magazine stories. The story is told that when he bought the old Toronto Globe, the article regarding his succession to the publisher's office was sent back to the reporter responsible with instructions to 'work in more of the Alger stuff.' I matter how one might disagree with his policies, his story was indeed one of the outstanding examples of Horatio Algerism in Canada's history."[19]

The publishing schedules of the *Globe and Mail* and the *Star* and *Telegram* prevented the afternoon papers from scooping McCullagh's favourite paper on the founder's obituary, but *Star* subscribers got thousands of words of description and praise about the man who'd so desperately wanted to destroy the newspaper they were reading.

The *Globe and Mail* ran an entire page of praise for McCullagh from editorials printed in fifteen small newspapers across Canada.[20]

Premier Leslie Frost paid tribute to McCullagh as a "courageous man" who "gave everything in the causes he espoused." Bishop R.J. Renison said Mr. McCullagh "was one of my greatest friends. I knew him when he was just a boy, delivering papers, and I regarded him as one of the most gifted boys I ever met."

George Drew, who was still leading the federal Tories, called his friend "a truly great Canadian. Few men have given more unselfish public service. He had the courage to express his deep convictions and on many occasions gave leadership on questions of the utmost national importance." David Croll, who McCullagh had driven out of Hepburn's cabinet during the Oshawa strike and was now a Liberal member of Parliament, managed to find kind words: "We sold newspapers together. I knew George McCullagh from the days when we were just young chaps. In later years, we did not always agree, but he was a fair man who never forgot his own humble origin. He was a friend to the returned man and he was a friend to all minorities. To die at the height of a career is indeed tragic."

Ted Jolliffe, leader of the CCF in the Ontario legislature, was just as kind: "He really believed, as he often told me, in presenting the news fairly and took pride in seeing his papers give space to newsworthy stories, whether for or against his own views. He was a hard fighter but he did not allow his own sometimes extreme opinions to obscure his sincere appreciation of a good news page."

His business and media pals Conn Smythe, John Bassett, Roy Thomson (whose son would buy the *Globe and Mail* in 1980), *New*

York Times publisher Arthur Hays Sulzberger, financial editor Wellington Jeffers, and Bob Farquharson, who had assigned McCullagh his first story as a *Globe* reporter and had risen to managing editor of the *Globe and Mail* before leaving to run *Saturday Night*, all had good things to say about him.

Probably the saddest tribute came from Lou Grossman, president of the Toronto Newsboys' Association: "We newsies always knew him as George, never as Mr. McCullagh. He knew us all and was never too busy or too big to speak to us on the corner and joke with us. He knew many of us by our first names. He was a regular fellow, and one of the boys. We felt he was a newsie himself."[21]

Only the left-wing *Canadian Forum* had the nerve to take him on. There was a lot of truth in its assessment of the man, which came out a month after McCullagh died: "In practice the McCullagh philosophy had elements of feudalism, not met with in public life since the passing of the American tycoons of the last century... He exercised a benevolent paternalism over his newspaper world and will perhaps be best remembered for personal kindness than for any great impetus he gave to the national future."[22]

Maybe it was expected that powerful people and journalists would praise their dead colleague for a day or two. It's normal now that a famous person gets a full blast of positive publicity when they die. Then a few friends and maybe some colleagues might show up for a funeral. McCullagh got much more of a send-off. People lined Bloor Street to pay their respects at the funeral home where McCullagh was laid out. There were so many of them that the police had to close the street. The same thing happened at the funeral, which was presided over by Bishop Renison. It was a huge show of public support for a man who had reached so many people through the pages of his newspaper and over the radio. But there were also people who knew McCullagh through the worlds of horse racing and sports. There were newspaper sellers, politicians, merchants, industrialists, competing publishers, and ordinary people who somehow had connected with this extraordinary man.

* * *

Six weeks after McCullagh's death, his will was published. The estate was valued at $4,625,000, with death duties of $2,141,000.[23] Tax experts told the *Star* that probate values, for tax purposes, tend to be on the low side. The will allowed the Toronto *Telegram*'s directors to run the paper for twenty-one years so they could choose the best time to sell it. When he bought the *Tely*, McCullagh denied he had used any of Wright's money. "I am on the hook for the *Tely* and it is my responsibility to get off that hook." The will showed he was telling the truth: he was paying off the *Telegram* financing loan at $300,000 a year. The *Globe and Mail* was not mentioned by name in the will, and there was no valuation of McCullagh's financial interest in it.

Phyllis McCullagh got use of the family home, a yearly income of $7,500, plus one-quarter of the income of the estate until her death or remarriage. She very quickly sold the Thornhill property to Dr. Edward Earle Shouldice, who turned it into one of the world's pre-eminent hernia clinics. McCullagh's house is still there, but has been renovated and added to. Some of the landscaping of the grounds has been left the way it was when McCullagh died.

One-quarter of the remaining cash was divided among McCullagh's four sisters, and the rest of McCullagh's assets were held in trust for his children.

John Bassett, backed by department store owner John David Eaton, quickly bought the *Telegram* and controlled the city's first private television station, which went on the air a month after McCullagh died. A short story announcing the new TV station ran on the same Toronto *Star* front page that had carried the news of McCullagh's death. It's too bad McCullagh missed out on the television age. He would have enjoyed TV and might have been good at it.

Phyllis McCullagh sold the *Globe and Mail* in 1955 to the Webster family of Montreal. It was their first investment in the newspaper business, and they were the people who removed McCullagh's name from the newspaper's masthead. Ten years later, the paper was sold to FP Publications, which published the *Financial Post*, the *Winnipeg Free Press* and the *Montreal Star*. In 1980, the paper passed into the hands of the Thomson family, and is now owned by Woodbridge, the family's holding company, which also owns Thomson Reuters.

The William H. Wright Building survived until 1974, when it was torn down and the site developed for First Canadian Place. In 1963, the *Telegram* moved from its sixty-four-year-old headquarters at Bay and Melinda Streets to a modern new building at 444 Front Street West (near Spadina Avenue). The *Globe and Mail* took over that building after the *Telegram* folded in 1971. It was torn down and high-rise condominiums were built on the site in 2017. Except for the Thornhill house, there's little physical evidence left of McCullagh's life. The scenes of his triumphs—the Wright Building, most of the racetracks, Maple Leaf Gardens as he knew it—are gone, as is the version of Toronto where he evolved from a kid just in from nowhere to a man with a serious chance of running the country.

* * *

If George McCullagh had been a happy, healthy man, he could have lived into the 1980s or even later, seeing the rise of big television networks and national newspaper chains. In a normal lifespan, he would have lived through the entire Cold War, the Swinging Sixties, the reaction of the 1970s. He would have been sixty-three when Pierre Trudeau became prime minister of Canada. His afternoon paper, the *Telegram*, folded in 1971, the year McCullagh would have turned sixty-six. In a sense, McCullagh had just half of a life, but he put much more into it, and got more out of life, than most people. His children adored him. Daughter Ann remembered him at her 1958 wedding to Lyman Hogarth by having a boy's choir sing George's favourite songs, and the buffet table was centred with a golden replica of her father's King's Plate trophy filled with yellow flowers.

But Phyllis never forgave him—either for dying or, if the rumours were true, killing himself. In 1966, she married George Drew, whose wife had died the year before. For a time, she allowed McCullagh's papers to be used by historians such as John Saywell of York University, when Saywell was writing a biography of Mitch Hepburn. But sometime after Drew's death in 1973, Phyllis burned the papers so they could never be used for a biography, an act that has thwarted writers ever since. Mrs. McCullagh's daughter Ann told me her mother hated her husband because intellectually she couldn't keep up with him. "That's why she destroyed his papers and tried to erase his memory. She was a very bitter woman."[24] At the time of her death in 1981, Phyllis was trapped in a court battle with George Drew's children, who believed she was recklessly spending their inheritance.

* * *

What are George McCullagh's legacies? First, and most important, there's the *Globe and Mail*. It has changed hands three times since McCullagh's death, and its founder is long-forgotten in the newsroom and the executive suite. Still, from its design to its editorial point of view, the paper shows some of the fingerprints of its founder. The *Globe and Mail* is smaller than it used to be, and much more focused on lifestyle and business, but that seems to be a reasonable adaption to the modern marketplace. More disturbingly, its arts and political coverage have markedly declined in this century. Comparisons between McCullagh's version of the *Globe and Mail* and today's can only be done with the realization that the media world of the mid-twentieth century is barely in the same universe as the modern publishing environment.

The *Globe and Mail* continues to be the best newspaper in the country, but it's had to adapt to two brutal realities: newspaper readership in Canada has declined since the early 1980s, and most Canadians expect to get free news online. Great newspapers like the *New York Times* have been able to adapt to the challenges of the internet. It remains to be seen if the owners of the *Globe and Mail* will make the investment in journalistic and managerial talent that would result in a paper that people find interesting and indispensable.

The *Telegram* is gone, but journalists who were hired by McCullagh kept the newspaper war going for almost two decades, and some of them were among the founders and Day Oners of the *Toronto Sun*. Despite the many ownership changes at the *Sun*, its news columns and editorial page still have echoes of the voices of those old *Telegram* hands.

Then there are the National Newspaper Awards, which were in their third year when McCullagh died. He had started the annual competition, and even now the awards serve to remind cynics that there is still some life in the Canadian newspaper business.

As the decades passed, McCullagh was remembered by family, friends and old-timers in the newspaper industry until they, too, were gone. In 1953, a portrait of McCullagh was unveiled in the editorial boardroom of the *Globe and Mail*. Two years later, it was taken down and put into storage.

ACKNOWLEDGEMENTS

I worked on this book for more than a dozen years, off and on, so I am bound to miss some people who deserve thanking. In rough chronological order, I'd like to thank fellow faculty members at Concordia University in Montreal, where I made my first presentation on McCullagh. The late Ross Perigoe was particularly supportive of this project, even after I left Concordia to return to writing.

I was able to interview Ann McCullagh Hogarth, George McCullagh's daughter, several times. She is likeable, smart and blunt, like her father. Her stories about growing up in Thornhill were delightful, and I am grateful for them.

The staff at Library and Archives Canada, the Library of Parliament, the Toronto Reference Library, City of Toronto Archives, CBC's audio archives, the Department of National Defence's History and Heritage section, and the archives of the Parliament of the United Kingdom were especially helpful.

I am indebted to several historians. Among them are the late Paul Quilty, who wrote his master's thesis on the Loyal Orange Lodge in Ontario; Prof. John Saywell, who supervised Quilty's thesis and wrote a fact-filled biography of Mitchell Hepburn (and was the last historian to see McCullagh's papers before they were destroyed); and Dr. Jeff Keshen, president of the University of Regina, who supervised my PhD thesis and so reviewed my earlier work on George Drew, George McCullagh and the King government's attempt to cover up the Hong Kong disaster of 1941. Military historian Dr. James McKillip has been my friend since we met in grade ten, and his advice is consistently good. George Kampouris, a paleontologist friend, listened to many of my McCullagh stories and I almost talked him into a prospecting trip to northern Ontario. It still might happen. I'd also like to thank all the authors who wrote the books and articles that contained information about McCullagh, and the people and places of his time. Because of the shortage of primary source material, I mined a lot of other people's work for a fact here, an anecdote there, and scene-setting material. Among them are the late Sen. Richard Doyle, Adam Levine, Maggie Siggins, Pierre Berton, and David Hayes.

Dan Wells, owner and publisher of Biblioasis, green-lit this book in 2019 and has been patient. He runs the best mid-sized press in Canada, and he does it well. Janice Zawerbny edited this book in its early stages, before leaving for another company. Her work on structure and tone gave the book its voice. Copyeditor Linda Pruessen is a true saint who should be rewarded in this life, rather than having to wait. She has saved me from so many sins.

My family have always been supportive, and I am grateful to all of them. My wife, Marion, our three children and our grandson make it easier to struggle with the ups and downs of being an author in Canada. In that regard, I would like to thank Ken Whyte, Doug Hunter, Ken McGoogan and Charlotte Gray for fighting the good fight, our struggle to convince Canadians that our stories—researched literary non-fiction—are worth reading, and worth telling.

NOTES

INTRODUCTION

1   Robert Fulford, "George McCullagh," *Globe and Mail*, April 15, 1998. Posted on RobertFulford.com and available at https://web.archive.org/web/19990824022838/http://www.robertfulford.com/McCullagh.html/

CHAPTER 1: **THE HUSTLER**

1   There have been several Great Depressions. In the nineteenth century, the period from 1873 to 1896 was called the Great Depression. Hopefully, the 1929–40 Great Depression will hang onto the title indefinitely.

2   To be fair, there are lots of sulphur springs in southern Ontario. In some places, well water from deep underground smells like rotten eggs and tastes awful. It's a natural consequence of the local geology. The rocks were formed from old sea beds.

3   I am playing a little fast and loose here. The Irish Catholics who lived in the Lucan area were usually Liberal voters, but switched to the Tories when a local Conservative fixer ran a Catholic for the Tories in 1878. The Donnellys stayed loyal to the Liberals, adding to their alienation from the local community. But Canadian voters, including those around London, were willing to be wooed by both major parties. This was a factor in Liberal premier Oliver Mowat's sabotage of the subsequent trials of the Donnelly killers. Had the trials been moved from London to another part of Ontario, the killers of the Donnellys would certainly have been convicted and some would have hanged. As for McCullagh's potential customers, even die-hard Tories bought the *Globe* if it contained news they could use. For farmers, that might be up-to-date crop prices. For lawyers, it would be the paper's coverage of Ontario Court of Appeal decisions (which the *Globe and Mail* had the poor sense to drop at the end of the twentieth century).

4   Hydro power is something we take for granted, but the entire system could have ended up wired by a hodge-podge of gouging little companies. The people who made sure it didn't happen are owed a great debt. Sir Adam Beck has a statue on Toronto's University Avenue and is commemorated with a plaque in front of his yellow-brick London house. For a good description of how Ontario's power system became its great industrial advantage, see E.B. Biggar, *Hydro-Electric Development in Ontario* (Toronto: Ryerson Press, 1920).

5   The author is indebted to Jennifer Grainger, whose book *Early London: A Photographic History from the Orr Collection, 1826–1914* (Windsor, ON: Biblioasis, 2016), was a goldmine of information about the look and feel of early twentieth-century London, Ontario.

6   Mackenzie King was likely the luckiest politician in Canadian history. Almost all his opponents were nonentities and strange people. The first one, Arthur Meighen, was an unpleasant man who managed to blow a string of fabulous political opportunities. In 1926, he had King on the ropes over a kickback scandal, but people were repelled by Meighen's nasty politicking. When King seemed like bad luck, it often turned out to be good luck: King was turned out of office in 1930 just before the Depression bit hard. The man who beat him, R.B. Bennett, ended up being blamed for the Depression, and King just had to wait for the voters to vent their rage. Next came a string of leaders who most history professors and political junkies would never be able to name on a bet: Robert Manion, John Bracken, and Richard Hanson. And no one would remember George Drew if he had not been premier of Ontario before moving to Ottawa to be crushed. The Tories wouldn't find a solid leader until John Diefenbaker took control of the party, and that was after King (and George McCullagh) were off the stage. For an almost cruel discussion of King's string of opponents, see Frank Underhill, *In Search of Canadian Liberalism* (Toronto: Macmillan, 1960), 117.

7   Allen Bartley, *The Ku Klux Klan in Canada: A Century of Promoting Racism and Hate in the Peaceable Kingdom* (Halifax: Formac, 2020), 40–41. Klan rallies were held in Delaware, near the edge of London, but the movement had support throughout southwestern Ontario, outside the Irish Catholic areas, with crosses being burned in Dresden and Wallaceburg in 1925, (see Bartley, *The Ku Klux Klan*, ch. 3).

8   Croll mentioned his time selling newspapers with McCullagh in the *Globe and Mail*'s obituary material of George McCullagh.

9   Pierre Berton, "The Amazing Career of George McCullagh," *Maclean's*, January 15, 1949.

CHAPTER 2: NEWSIES AND GOLD

1   The siege lasted from November 1899 to February 1900. Keep in mind that South Africa is in the Southern Hemisphere.

2   Peter Newman, *Flame of Power: The Story of Canada's Greatest Businessmen* (Toronto: Longmans Green & Co., 1959), 118.

3   Right theory, wrong treasure: Geologists had been perplexed for years by people finding loose diamonds in North American glacial gravel, but they'd been unable to find the kimberlite pipes that are diamond ore. Chuck Fipke and Stewart Blusson realized this relatively soft rock was scraped into low-lying Canadian Shield land by glaciers and filled with water.

4   Brown is said to have sold her own rather poor gold prospects for more than $40,000, and Oakes gave her a small piece of his Lake Shore Mine. She ended up a very wealthy woman, buying real estate in the region. See Joan Walker, "The Unsquelchable Roza Brown," *Maclean's*, December 2, 1964.

5   Accounts of this differ slightly. Wright said he was there when Oakes went through the ice. George Tough gave an interview to *Gold* magazine in 1935, which is quoted in Charlotte Gray's book *Murdered Midas: A Millionaire, His Gold Mine, and a Strange Death on an Island Paradise* (Toronto: HarperCollins, 2019), saying Wright showed up later that night, when Oakes had been warmed up with a pot of coffee. I like Wright's version better.

6   Newman, *Flame of Power*, 121.

7   I talk a lot about the lottery of penny stocks that attracted amateur investors like June bugs to fly zappers. The smart money went into bonds. During the Depression, solid gold mining companies like Hudson Bay Mining and Smelting issued five-year 6 percent convertible debentures at par. In a time of deflation and rock-bottom interest rates, these were a fantastic investment. Even some of the smaller mine companies made good on bond issues that not only protected their investors' capital, but also paid decent returns. See J. Graeme Watson, "Mining Financing in Canada," in *Canadian Investment and Foreign Exchange*, ed. J.F. Parkinson (Toronto: University of Toronto Press, 1940), ch. XIX.

8   Obituary of William Wright, *Star* (Toronto), September 20, 1951, 1 and 3.

9   Michael Barnes, *Fortune in the Ground: Cobalt, Porcupine and Kirkland Lake* (Erin: Boston Mills Press, 1986), 175. There is also a picture of Wright in an army uniform.

10 Gray, *Murdered Midas*, 47.

11 By the 1990s, the big chartered banks would take over the Canadian retail stock trade.

12 Christopher Armstrong, *Blue Skies and Boiler Rooms: Buying and Selling Securities in Canada, 1870–1940* (Toronto, University of Toronto Press, 1997), 29.

13 Geoffrey Bocca, *The Life and Death of Harry Oakes* (London, Weidenfeld and Nicolson, 1958), 57.

14 "War Horse Facts," Brooke, n.d., https://www.thebrooke.org/get-involved/every-horse -remembered/war-horse-facts?gclid=CjwKCAiAy9jyBRA6EiwAeclQhOjGazO9xbDA GuoTutbb4pCUFuHlyRKumWphf2qsHjGMsFi7VLS6NBoCXjgQAvD_BwE.

15 Wright's service file is available from the Directorate of History and Heritage, Department of National Defence. The author wishes to thank Dr. James D. McKillip for providing this file.

16 Like many old Anglo-Canadian pretensions, the naming of houses is a forgotten part of an almost-lost culture. The author has no idea where Wright came up with this odd name. The house, at 55 Peel Street, is now a nursing home. It has a checkered past, likely being built with money stolen from the Simcoe County municipal government. The thief later paid back the money with the profits of a South American mine (Heritage Barrie, "Grand Home Tours," n.d., https://www.barrie.ca/Culture/Heritage/Documents/ Walking-Tours/Grand_Homes_Walking-Tour.pdf).

17 "Nat Dyment's Nephew Trained Brookdale Horses," *Sault Star*, January 16, 1973, 14; "Barrie Lumber King Led Horse Racing Dynasty," Simcoe.com, August 16, 2018.

18 Obituary of William Wright, *Star* (Toronto). The Westminster was rather downscale, and is long gone. It was on the west side of Jarvis Street, about a block south of Gerrard Street, which is now the edge of the Ryerson University campus.

19 Ross Harkness, *J.E. Atkinson of the Star* (Toronto: University of Toronto Press, 1963), 6.

20 Diaries of William Lyon Mackenzie King, Library and Archives Canada (LAC), October 23, 1935; available in a searchable format at www.collectionscanada.gc.ca/king/023011 -1020-e,html (henceforth referred to as "King diaries"). Joe Atkinson was staying at Laurier House at the time, helping King pick his cabinet.

21 King diaries, July 22, 1939.

22 King diaries, October 19, 1935. Atkinson did make some recommendations about King's 1935 cabinet. Atkinson opposed the appointment

23 King also wanted money to help cover the cost of buying and restoring William Lyon Mackenzie's house in downtown Toronto. Holy Joe drew the line at his $1,000 donation for the statue and would not give more money for the house. King put his ancient friend, Sir William Mulock, to work fundraising for the house project. Mackenzie House, at 82 Bond Street, is still a museum dedicated to the leader of the Rebellion of 1837.

24 "Wife Spanking" (editorial), *Star* (Toronto), March 1, 1938.

25 Harkness, *J.E. Atkinson*, 151. See also King diaries, December 23, 1927. Robert Borden's Union government had offered Atkinson a knighthood during the First World War, but he turned it down (King diaries, February 17, 1928).

26 Herbert Cranston, *Ink on My Fingers* (Toronto: Ryerson Press, 1953), 68.

27 Cranston, *Ink on My Fingers*, 72.

28 Cranston, *Ink on My Fingers*, 75–76.

29 Cranston, *Ink on My Fingers*, 84–85. Cranston died in 1952 after almost thirty years of owning the *Midland Free Press*, the best weekly in Canada. In 1933, Cranston's career at the *Star* was murdered in one of the many little office knife fights that has made the Toronto *Star* a notorious place to work since the beginning.

CHAPTER 3: GEORGE McCULLAGH'S TORONTO

1 Edith Firth, ed., *The Town of York*, vol. 2 (Toronto: Champlain Society, 2013), ix.

2 The author met Lefty in 1984, interviewing him for a *Globe and Mail* story that was part of the paper's coverage of the 1984 Los Angeles Olympics. Coincidentally, it was the first Olympics in decades in which Canadian boxers were contenders, though none won gold. Welterweight Bert Schneider won a gold medal at the 1920 games, and Canada's fifty-two-year gold medal drought was ended by super-heavyweight fighter Lennox Lewis in 1988.

3 McCullagh's personality was described at length in an editorial that ran in the *Globe and Mail* on August 6, 1952, the day after his death. The writer was obviously someone who knew him well. Oakley Dalgleish is the most likely candidate.

4 The tour was documented with short articles in the *Globe*. See, for example, "Gananoque Effects Big Local Branch of 'Just Kids' Club," *Globe*, May 12, 1928, and "Cobourg Citizens Call Mass Meeting for Safety Club," *Globe*, May 15, 1928.

5 "George C. McCullagh Joins Harley, Milner," *Globe*, June 11, 1929.

6 The author's father worked for the firm in the early 1950s, when it was Ross, Knowles. The successor company, Pitfield Mackay Ross, merged with Dominion Securities in 1984. Four years later, RBC Securities took over the company.

7 "Company Prefers Booklet on Gold," *Star* (Toronto), September 11, 1936, 17.

8 That's supposed to be about $18,000,000 in today's dollars, but McCullagh made this money at a time when almost everyone else was broke. The figures also don't translate well in terms of real estate and other assets. An ordinary house in Toronto cost about $1,000 in the Depression. The same house would sell now for at least a thousand times that amount. In 1930, a person with $1 million was seriously rich. See CIP Inflation Calculator,https://www.in2013dollars.com/us/inflation/1930?amount=1000000#:~:text=%241%2C000%2C000%20in%201930%20is%20equivalent,cumulative%20price%20increase%20of%201%2C621.58%25.

9 Allister Grosart interview with Peter Stursberg, summer 1979. LAC, Peter Stursberg Fonds, Reference No. R5637-0-0-E, MG31-D78, Vol. 34.

10 Armstrong, *Blue Skies and Boiler Rooms*, 283

11 Armstrong, *Blue Skies and Boiler Rooms*, 234–35

12 Armstrong, *Blue Skies and Boiler Rooms*, 27. In 1912, this silver mine went out of business (see "Temiskaming and Hudson's Bay Mining Company–Closed Down," *Porcupine Advance*, July 26, 1912, http://news.ourontario.ca/timmins/2667943/data). But dreams never die: a prospector searching near the old Hudson Bay mine recently found a diamond deposit (see "Junior Miner Finds Diamond While Looking for Silver, Cobalt," *Northern Ontario Business*, August 20, 2018, https://www.northernontariobusiness.com/industry-news/mining/junior-miner-finds-diamond-while-looking-for-silver-cobalt-1031318).

13 Neil McKenty, *Mitchell Hepburn* (Toronto: McClelland and Stewart, 1967), 34.

14 Roy Greenaway, *The News Game* (Toronto: Clarke Irwin, 1966), 177–79.

CHAPTER 4: OWNING A PREMIER

1 In this century, it would be the backdrop for the terrifying *It* movies.

2 Both were related to writer Farley Mowat: Oliver Mowat Biggar was a cousin, Premier Oliver Mowat was a great-great uncle.

3 King had written a sharply anti-Asian report for the Laurier government after white rioters went on a rampage in Vancouver and burned down much of the city's Chinatown. King, like many other "progressives" of the time, believed the Chinese were the cause of the country's miniscule drug problem. See Emily Murphy's *The Black Candle* (Toronto: Thomas Allen, 1921).

4 This mine is spelled "Hyslop" in the correspondence between McCullagh and Hepburn. The mine, near Matheson, Ontario, ran as an open-pit operation for several decades. See McKenty, *Mitchell Hepburn*, 93.

5 The paper would be saved by J. Herbert Cranston. It closed in 2013, having survived for 117 years.

6 McKenty, *Mitchell Hepburn*, 55.

7 For these old political stories to make any sense at all, the reader should imagine an Ontario with less than one-third its modern population. Almost everything in Toronto past Lawrence Avenue, Leaside and the Humber River is farmland, with a sprinkling of small towns around it, and middling-sized cities like Hamilton and Kitchener off in the distance. Ottawa extends from old Vanier (called Eastview then) to Westboro, and as far inland as the new Glebe suburb and parts of Old Ottawa South. London was confined to the area between Oxford Street and a strip on the south side of the Thames. Thunder Bay was still two warring little towns, Fort William and Port Arthur. Basically, anything in Ontario that isn't obviously old was built after this period. Half of the people lived on farms, many of the rest lived in small towns, and Ontarians had a much better grasp of what was happening outside their communities. Hepburn's Midland speech would not have received much coverage in today's media because there is no serious newspaper in Midland and provincial political coverage in media is sparse. Mitch would have to tweet the speech himself. If transported in time, he probably would quickly amass loud, bizarre and obnoxious social media followers.

8 Greenaway, *The News Game*. 28

9 Greenaway, *The News Game*, 25

10 King diaries, October 23, 1935.

11 The building, in Rosedale, became a military hospital during the Second World War. It was demolished in 1961, and the site is now a park.

12 McKenty, *Mitchell Hepburn*, 62.

13 While men's ability to calculate length is often questionable and sometimes even absurd, the list takes up about a third of the very long story published in the Toronto

Star the day after the funeral. "Many Mourn Loss of Percy Parker," *Star* (Toronto) April 23, 1936, 35.

14 "Envies University-Educated Men Says 31-Year-Old U.of T. Governor," *Star* (Toronto) September 29, 1936, 3.

15 Martin Friedland, *The University of Toronto: A History* (Toronto: University of Toronto Press, 2002), 325.

16 Friedland, *University of Toronto*, 318.

17 Friedland, *University of Toronto*, 324.

18 The *Ottawa Journal* called this admission "journalistic nudity." See David Hayes, *Power and Influence: The Globe and Mail and the News Revolution* (Toronto: Key Porter, 1992), 55.

19 Donald Cameron Masters, *Henry John Cody: An Outstanding Life* (Toronto: Dundurn Press, 1995), 211.

20 Kenneth C. Dewar, *Frank Underhill and the Politics of Ideas* (Montreal: McGill-Queen's University Press, 2015), 98.

21 "Name C.G. McCullagh to University Board," Toronto *Daily Star*, December 29, 1936, 6.

CHAPTER 5: MEETING MR. WRIGHT

1 In the three years that McCullagh worked in the newsroom, he'd never had a bylined article. These were rare in the 1920s: Ernest Hemingway, at the Toronto *Star* a few years earlier, rarely had them, either.

2 For an examination of this transition, see Minko Sotiron, *From Politics to Profit: The Commercialization of Canadian Newspapers, 1890–1920* (Montreal, McGill-Queen's University Press, 1997).

3 Richard Doyle, *Hurly-Burly: My Time at the Globe and Mail* (Toronto: Macmillan, 1990), 75.

4 Canadian knighthoods would soon be endangered under the new Mackenzie King government, but during the Bennett years, a remarkable number of rich Canadians were knighted, including King's friend Lyman Duff, the chief justice of the Supreme Court of Canada. Bennett retired to England, where he was made a viscount.

5 Alexander Brady, *Canada* (London: Ernst Benn,1932), 143–44.

6 Oakes' murder in the Bahamas in 1943 remains one of the great unsolved mysteries of Canadian finance, and is still the subject of considerable speculation. Geoffrey Bocca (*Life & Death of Harry Oakes* [London: Weidenfeld and Nicolson, 1958], 71), makes the claim that Wright was one of the few Canadian magnates who would defend Oakes.

7 Berton, "The Amazing Career of George McCullagh."

8 Berton, "The Amazing Career of George McCullagh."

9 Berton, "The Amazing Career of George McCullagh."

10 "Make Canada More Secure Is Aim of Globe Publisher," Toronto *Daily Star*, November 3, 1936, 40.

11 McCullagh wasn't the only person kicking the tires of the *Globe*. The Southam family, which owned papers in Montreal, Ottawa, Hamilton, Winnipeg, Calgary, Edmonton and Vancouver, has been fishing for the *Globe* since 1930. The company would also try, and fail, to buy the *Globe and Mail* in 1955. Had it succeeded, the future of Canadian newspapers would have been radically different. After several sales, the core of the Southam corporation evolved into PostMedia. Charles Bruce, *News and the Southams* (Toronto: Macmillan, 1968), 376.

12 "William Wright Buys the Globe," *Daily Star* (Toronto), October 15, 1936.

13 King diaries, January 6, 1937.

14 King diaries, January 6, 1937.

15 "The Globe and Mail Board of Directors To Be Recognized Leaders, To Aid Canadian Betterment," *Globe*, November 4, 1936, 3.

16 *Star* (Toronto), October 15, 1936.

17 Doyle, *Hurly-Burly*, 75.

18 "The Globe Board of Directors to Board of Directors To Be Recognized Leaders, To Aid Canadian Betterment," *Globe*, November 4, 1936.

19 "W.W. Wright Buys the Globe, C.G. McCullagh President," Toronto *Daily Star*, October 19, 1936.

20 That would change by the end of the century.

21 The time sequence can be confusing to people who are used to wide-open Sundays. In the 1930s, none of the Toronto newspapers published on Sunday. Reporters collected material through the weekend for editions that were published late Sunday night (the *Globe* and the *Mail and Empire*) and Monday starting around noon (the *Star* and the *Telegram*).

22 Pierre Berton, *My Times: Living with History 1947–1995* (Toronto: Random House, 1996), 42.

23 Floyd Chalmers, *Both Sides of the Street: One Man's Life in Business and the Arts in Canada* (Toronto: Macmillan, 1983), 77.

24 King to McCullagh, Mackenzie King papers (King papers hereafter), November 13, 1936, LAC C-3689, No. 189288..

25 King to McCullagh, King papers, November 13, 1936. The blurb "Honoring 'The Little Rebel'" appeared on the *Globe* editorial page on November 12, 1936.

26 McCullagh to King, King papers, November 17, 1936. The back-and-forth continued for a few weeks, with both men fawning over each other and offering to help carry their new friend's onerous burdens.

27 Doyle, *Hurly-Burly*, 35.

28 Hayes, *Power and Influence*, 44.

29 Grosart later worked on George Drew's federal campaign. See Peter Stursdberg interview with Allister Grosart, 1979, Peter Stursberg fonds, LAC MG 31 D 78 Vol. 34.

30 Judith Robinson, "Labor's Moment," *Globe*, November 12, 1936, 4.

CHAPTER 6: **THE GLOBE AND MAIL**

1 Profit and Loss Statement of the Newspaper Section of the *Mail and Empire* for Month of September 1936. George Drew papers, LAC RG 150, Accession 1992-93/166, Box 2665, file no. 953.

2 Berton, *My Times*, 43.

3 Quoted in Hayes, *Power and Influence*, 52.

4 Maggie Siggins, *Bassett: John Bassett's Forty Years in Publishing, Business and Sports* (Toronto: Lorimer, 1979), 20.

5 "Menace to Protestantism and to Clean, Honest Politics," *Kincardine News*, reprinted on the editorial page of the Toronto *Telegram*, November 30, 1936.

6 Editorial, Toronto *Telegram*, November 30, 1936.

7 Tabloids were the exception to this rule. Papers like the *Toronto Sun*, which is a morning tabloid, slowly filled their news hole in the early evening, then mapped out their front page near midnight—after sports events were finished—for press runs in the early morning. Changes could be made until 1 a.m., and, in an emergency, the *Sun* would replate its front page during its press run. In the end, most of its pages were filled with institutional news and short features that were not time-sensitive.

8 Message to Readers, quoted in Hayes, *Power and Influence*, 53.

9 Quoted in Hayes, *Power and Influence*, 53.

10 "Wealth May Buy Newspapers, It Cannot Buy Public Opinion," Toronto *Telegram*, November 30, 1936.

11 Doyle, *Hurly-Burly*, 18.

12 There are several good descriptions of this amazing building, which stood on the northwest corner of King and Bay Streets. David Hayes, in *Power and Influence*, and Richard Doyle, in *Hurly-Burly*, described this news shrine in detail. It was also featured in the *Globe and Mail*'s own columns as it was being built and when it was opened, and is mentioned in just about every profile of McCullagh that's been written. The building was torn down to build First Canadian Place. This seems, to this author, to have been a bad trade.

13 Doyle, *Hurly-Burly*, 17.

14 Doyle, *Hurly-Burly*, 17.

15 Twenty-five thousand people came through the newsroom that day. "See The Globe and Mail's New Home," *Globe and Mail*, May 9, 1938.

16 "London Pays High Honor to Publisher," *London Free Press*, November 12, 1936.

17 Doyle, *Hurly-Burly*, 19.

18 Doyle, *Hurly-Burly*, 18. Washroom description is from Pierre Berton's January 1949 *Maclean's* piece.

19 Jamie Bradburn, "Historicist: Citizen McCullagh," *Torontoist*, October 3, 2009.

20 Hayes, *Power and Influence*, 55.

21 Quoted in Berton, "The Amazing Career of George McCullagh."

22 Siggins, *Bassett*, 11.

23 Siggins, *Bassett*, 11.

24 Maggie Siggins, in her 1979 book *Bassett*, has several descriptions of MacFarlane and the discipline he brought to the *Telegram* newsroom. I worked under MacFarlane at the *Toronto Sun* years later. In the late 1970s, when MacFarlane was in his early sixties, he seemed much older and had little interaction with staffers. Each day, he wrote a memo nitpicking writing and spelling errors in the paper. To me, he seemed like a somewhat broken, embittered man, kept around by former *Telegram* employees like Doug Creighton and Peter Worthington for old time's sake. No one of my generation knew about his spectacular past, and I regret not trying harder to get to know him.

25 These anecdotes of Bassett's early days in journalism are from Siggins, *Bassett*, 32–34.

26 Doyle, *Hurly-Burly*, 23.

27 "Wallace to Leave Globe and Mail," *Star* (Toronto), December 16, 1938, 1.

28 Doyle, *Hurly-Burly*, 21.

29 Berton, "The Amazing Career of George McCullagh," 9.

30 See Robert John Renison, *One Day at a Time: The Autobiography of Robert John Renison* (Toronto: Kingswood House, 1957).

31 "Mr. Rowe Gets an Answer" *Globe and Mail*, September 6, 1937.

32 Even in the 1970s and early 1980s, drunken politicians were a common sight. The author, while working for a Toronto newspaper, found a former governor general leaning in a downtown doorway, almost incoherent, and a few weeks later came across a former premier of Ontario staggering down the street, blind drunk. Both times, he sent them home in cabs. In contrast, while working for nearly twenty-five years on Parliament Hill, beginning in the early 1990s, I never saw a senior politician drunk in public. It would have been career suicide in Ottawa in those years, and few in the media would have called a cab.

CHAPTER 7: **POWER AND POLITICS**

1   Profit and Loss Statement of the Newspaper Section of the *Mail and Empire* for Month of September 1936. George Drew papers, LAC RG 150, Accession 1992-93/166, Box 2665, file no. 953.

2   McCullagh to King, King papers, December 5, 1936, Vol. 220, No. 189290

3   McCullagh to King, King papers, December 5, 1936, Vol. 220, No. 189296. In the 1930s, provincial wings of the federal parties were still, at least nominally, parts of the same organizations. This would end under Hepburn. Provincial parties may share the same labels as their federal counterparts, but they make their own policies, and ask for federal campaign support only when they believe it will do them some good.

4   At about the same time, Ian Mackenzie, the Liberal cabinet minister who had organized McCullagh's victory celebrations in Toronto and London, was writing to King: "I think you will agree that the situation now existing will be of great value to yourself and your Government" (Mackenzie to King, King papers, December 5, Vol. 220, No. 189306).

5   McCullagh to King, King papers, December 5, Vol. 220, No. 189297.

6   King diaries, November 19, 1936.

7   Berton, "The Amazing Career of George McCullagh," 9.

8   Siggins, *Bassett*, 44.

9   Berton, *My Times*, 42.

10 Berton, *My Times*, 42.

11 Hayes, *Power and Influence*, 55.

12 Coincidentally, these kinds of social programs had been introduced in Germany under the Kaiser long before the Canadian government came around to seeing their benefits.

13 Siggins, *Bassett*, 34. Whatever Bassett felt about this man and his ideas, the debate did nothing to soften Bassett's views on unions, and he would later use labour problems as an excuse to shut down the Toronto *Telegram*. In fact, he'd been given very sweet offers for the *Telegram*'s real estate and circulation list. It turned out that the *Telegram*, which folded in 1971 as Canada was headed into a recession, was worth more dead than alive.

14 Saywell, *Just Call Me Mitch: The Life of Mitchell F. Hepburn* (Toronto: University of Toronto Press, 1991), 271.

15 Saywell, Just Call Me Mitch, 271..

16 See Saywell, *Just Call Me Mitch*, ch. 9.

17 Saywell, *Just Call Me Mitch*, 282.

18 Saywell, *Just Call Me Mitch*, 282.

19 "Mr. Hepburn's Duty Is Clear," *Globe and Mail*, March 23, 1937.

20 Frank Radford Crawley (producer), "Ottawa On The River," YouTube video, National Film Board, 1941, 17:35, https://www.youtube.com/watch?v=Vegh2_B2oLo&t=870s.

21 For this section, I've drawn on Peter Meehan, "The East Hastings By-Election of 1936 and the Ontario Separate School Tax Question," *Historical Studies* 68 (2002): 105–32.

22 The value of the St. Lawrence Seaway, which opened a generation after the Depression, is debatable. After an initial uptick in shipping trade, it has turned out to be a financial disappointment. Its locks can't handle big container vessels and tankers. Most port infrastructure has been torn down in Toronto and small towns on the Great Lakes with the overall decline in shipping. Meanwhile, species introduced through its canals and locks, and from bilge pumped from ocean-going freighters, have caused serious damage to the Great Lakes ecosystem and devastated its fisheries.

23 Saywell, *Just Call Me Mitch*, 287.

24 King diaries, January 6, 1937.

25 King diaries, January 7, 1937.

26 Saywell, *Call Me Mitch*, 282–83.
27 The Hislop property, in South Porcupine, did produce gold, and it still draws prospector interest. See https://www.rscmme.com/report/Kirkland_Lake_Gold_Ltd_Hislop_Mine _20-2-2018. The quote is from Doyle, *Hurly-Burly*, 21. A shorter version was used by McKenty.
28 See "Measuring Worth," https://www.measuringworth.com/calculators/uscompare/ relativevalue.php.
29 McCullagh made the Bahamas part of his travel circuit, visiting the country again in August 1937 when Wright's friend Harry Oakes was living there. His vagueness in his letter to King might reflect a reluctance to tell the prime minister he was visiting the notorious tax fugitive, who was despised by King.
30 Since 1900, only Mitch Hepburn and Dalton McGuinty have won back-to-back Liberal majorities in Ontario provincial politics.
31 King diary, March 4, 1937.
32 King diary, March 25, 1937.

CHAPTER 8: SONS OF MITCHES

1 Sam Gindin, *The Canadian Auto Workers: The Birth and Transformation of a Union* (Toronto: James Lorimer, 1995), 23.
2 Siggins, *Bassett*, 37.
3 See "The Globe and Mail Communist Scare," *Lindsay Warder*, reprinted in Toronto *Star*, May 6, 1937, 4.
4 Saywell, *Just Call Me Mitch*, 304–5.
5 The reader may be confused by by my use of "communist" and "Communist." The Communist Party was illegal in the United States and its members met in secret or tried to conceal their political activities using political parties that did not have "Communist" in their name. During the time covered in this chapter, Tim Buck identifiend himself as a member of the Communist Party and so gets the upper-case treatment.
6 Saywell, *Just Call Me Mitch*, 93.
7 These generalizations are, hopefully, true for English Canada. The situation in Quebec was quite different. Its union movement, during the first half of the century, was similar to that of pre-war Europe, where company and stooge unions were a normal occurrence, especially in fascist countries. The Federation of Catholic Workers of Canada was one such empty union. For a brief description of the cleavages in the Canadian labour movement, see G.P. deT Glazebrook, *A History of Canadian External Relations* (Toronto: Oxford University Press), 328–32.
8 Harkness, *J.E. Atkinson*, 236.
9 In the latter role, Mackenzie was one of the chief cheerleaders for the internment of Japanese-Canadian civilians in early 1942.
10 "Outcome Not in Doubt Now" (editorial), *Globe and Mail*, April 15, 1937.
11 "'Maintenance of Law and Order is Only interest,' says Rogers," *Star* (Toronto), April 15, 1937.
12 "'Maintenance of Law and Order.'"
13 Saywell, *Just Call Me Mitch*, 320.
14 The OPP was founded at the turn of the century to police the Cobalt-area mining camps and later expanded into other parts of northern and central Ontario, north of the Canadian Shield. Hepburn's recruitment of special constables for the Oshawa strike effectively brought the OPP south of the French River and Lake Nippissing. It would still be another thirteen years before the OPP became the official police force across the

province, outside communities that had their own police forces. But in the public mind, the OPP's genesis was in Oshawa.

15   Doyle, *Hurly-Burly*, 23.

16   Saywell, *Just Call Me Mitch*, 236.

17   Quoted in Doyle, *Hurly-Burly*, 22.

18   Briand J. Young, "George McCullagh and the Leadership League," quoted in Saywell, *Just Call Me Mitch*, 583, note 21.

19   See Saywell, *Call Me Mitch*, 323.

20   "Says 'Hepburn Hussars' worse than Iron Heel," *Star* (Toronto), April 15, 1937, 1.

21   "Ladies and gentlemen, and comrades in the greatest of all the wars the world has ever known," he said at the rally, where organizers had given front-row seats to First World War veterans, many in early middle age. Bland had an interesting take on that four-year slaughter, calling it "the war of emancipation and deliverance of the working man." It was a not particularly accurate take on the war, at least on the Western Front ("Trials of Oshawa Derided by Dr. Bland in Union Meet," *Star* (Toronto), April 15, 1937, 12).

22   "Trials of Oshawa Derided by Dr. Bland in Union Meet," *Star* (Toronto), April 15, 1937, 12.

23   "Says 'Hepburn Hussars' worse than Iron Heel," *Star* (Toronto), April 15, 1937, 1. Joe Atkinson pushed for the union of the Methodist, Presbyterian and Congregationalist churches into the United Church, and made sure the *Star* gave a lot of ink to its clergy. And, in 1937, the political views of ministers of big city churches were still news.

24   King diary, April 13, 1937.

25   "GM Strikers Demand Hepburn Withdraw from Peace Efforts," *Star* (Toronto), April 15, 1937, 1.

26   "GM Strikers Demand Hepburn Withdraw."

27   "GM Strikers Demand Hepburn Withdraw."

28   Cranston, *Ink on My Fingers*, 72.

29   The following year, an all-party committee at Queen's Park held hearings on the Hydro contracts and found there was no corruption. "No Suggestion of Hydro Graft says Conant," *Globe and Mail*, June 18, 1938, 1.

30   "Premier Reveals Atkinson Threats Over CIO Issue Dismissal," *Globe and Mail*, June 16, 1938, 1; "M'Cullagh's Price for Favour is Charge," Toronto *Daily Star,* June 9, 1938. 1.

31   "M'Cullagh's Price for Favour is Charge," Toronto *Daily Star,* June 9, 1938. 1.

32   McKenty, *Mitchell Hepburn*, 112.

33   McKenty, *Mitchell Hepburn*, 112.

34   Letter from J.G. Munro, Secretary of the Sudbury Mine and Smelter Workers' Union, No. 239, to Hugh Thompson, UAW Strike Committee, Oshawa. Archives of Labor and University Affairs, Wayne State University (no file no.). Reproduced in Gindin, *Canadian Auto Workers*, 59.

35   McKenty, *Mitchell Hepburn*, 112–13

36   Gindin, *Canadian Auto Workers*, 63.

37   In the end, McCullagh was right, at least for a while: union membership at Oshawa's GM plant collapsed, and didn't revive until the Second World War. Halfway though the war, as inflation crept up and labour shortages gave workers more bargaining power, the UAW signed its first collective agreement enshrining wage and seniority rights. See Gindin, *Canadian Auto Workers*. 65.

38   "Dismissal M'Cullagh's Price for Favor, Is Charge," *Star* (Toronto), June 3, 1938, 1. Croll stuck around the Ontario legislature until 1940, sitting as a Liberal backbencher. He ran for Ontario Liberal leader in 1943 but lost to Harry Nixon. Croll was elected to the House of Commons, but Mackenzie King would never put a Jew in his cabinet. Both Roebuck

and Croll were appointed to the Senate by Mackenzie King, and had long, distinguished careers in the Upper House.

39 Doyle, *Hurly-Burly*, 23.

CHAPTER 9: **THE COUP**

1   Don Nerbas, "Howard Robinson and the 'British Method': A Case Study of Britishness in Canada during the 1930s and 1940s," *Journal of the Canadian Historical Association*, 20, no. 1 (2009): 139–60. Beatty pushed for a bailout of the CPR, and the merger of the CPR and Canadian National Railways under the CPR, which would allow Beatty to cherry-pick the railway routes that were the most profitable. See Don Nerbas, *The Politics of Capital: The Crisis and Transformation of Canada's Big Bourgeoisie, 1917–1947* (PhD thesis, University of New Brunswick, 2010), https://central.bac-lac.gc.ca/.item?id=NR87674&op=pdf&app=Library).

2   Saywell, *Just Call Me Mitch*, 586, note 48.

3   "Spectacular Developments Rumored at Queen," *Star* (Toronto) May 5, 1937, 1.

4   Not all media felt the same way as the Toronto *Star* and the *Lindsay Warder*. The Toronto *Telegram* thought a coalition might somehow put an end to "class warfare." See McKenty, *Mitchell Hepburn*, 123.

5   McKenty, *Mitchell Hepburn*, 121.

6   Rowe interview with Peter Stursberg, 1978, Stursberg fonds, LAC MG31 D-78 Vol. 37.

7   In fact, for the rest of his life, Rowe would deny he'd ever bought into the idea at all. Again, see interview with Peter Stursberg, 1978, LAC MG31 D-78 Vol. 37. Rowe died in 1984, after decades in the House of Commons, a short stint as interim leader of the federal Progressive Conservatives, and a term as Ontario's lieutenant-governor.

8   McKenty, *Mitchell Hepburn*, 124-25.

9   The Tory leadership campaign was especially ugly. Drew claimed his party was full of "antagonistic forces" that needed to be purged. "There have been paid canvassers working with the idea of destroying me personally. These hired henchmen of the mysterious have claimed that I have used worlds reflecting on the French Canadians. These hired hammer men say that I am opposed to the C.N.R. and that I said so in an article. I can only say, and I know my French-Canadian friends will believe me, that never have I used any words that may be construed as a reflection on their race, religion or political beliefs. I have never written any article about the railroads, either the C.N.R or C.P.R." The "political assassins" were "spreading malicious gossip that my wife and I are no longer living together. My answer to that is that it is not true and that no one has found greater happiness in married life than I have." ("Drew Says Mud Slingers Paid to Kill His Chances," the *Star* (Toronto), November 19, 1938. Drew cut out this article and kept it until he died.)

10 King diary, January 6, 1938.

11 "Spectacular Developments Rumored at Queen's Park," *Star* (Toronto), June 15, 1937, 1.

12 McCullagh's paper gave space on its front page to five long articles that Drew wrote of this trip. Drew was an astute observer of the Soviet Union but admired what he saw in Mussolini's Italy and in Nazi Germany. See Kirk Niergarth, "'No Sense of Reality': George A. Drew's Anti-Communist Tour of the USSR and the Campaign for Coalition Government in Ontario, 1937," *Ontario History* 107, no. 2 (Fall 2015).

13 "Spectacular Move Seen in Rumors," *Star* (Toronto), June 15, 1937, 4.

14 The rumours likely started because of McCullagh's friendships with Lord Beaverbrook, who owned the *Evening Standard*, and Brendan Bracken, founder of the *Financial Times*.

15 "British Seeking Press Control Here Is Fear," *Star* (Toronto), June 15, 1937, 1.

16 "Spectacular Move Seen in Rumors." King must have believed Gardiner, since the Prairie politician stayed on through King's years in office, always in the agriculture portfolio. Gardiner ran for Liberal leader in 1948, after King retired, but lost to Louis St. Laurent. He might best be remembered now by Canadian history buffs as the villain in the 2006 CBC mini-series *Prairie Giant: The Tommy Douglas Story*, where he was portrayed as a racist, a drunk, and a strike-breaker. He was none of those things, and the CBC, under pressure from people of all political stripes in Saskatchewan, suppressed further showings of the docu-drama and apologized.

17 King diary, July 6 and 7, 1937. Nathanson also promised to send a team to Laurier House to install a private movie theatre, and had his Ottawa theatres send over first-run films for King and his guests to watch. All this was, of course, free. Politicians got away with that kind of thing in 1937. Nathanson was probably unaware of King's appalling prejudice against Jews.

18 "Labor Asks 'Further Action' in Globe and Mail Dispute," *Star* (Toronto), August 20, 1937, 5.

19 "Labor Asks 'Further Action.'"

20 "Labor Drops Effort to Re-instate Writer," *Star* (Toronto), September 13, 1937, 29.

21 "Politicians Who Trifle Are Condemned," *Globe and Mail*, October 4, 1937, 1.

22 "Horse Show Wins Dividend," *Globe and Mail*, October 4, 1937, 25.

23 "—Who? Condemned Publisher of the Globe and Mail Denounces Betrayal of Trust," Drew papers, LAC RG 150, Accession 1992-93/166, Box 2665 (this collection hereafter cited as "Drew papers).

24 "The Principle Involved," *Globe and Mail*, October 5, 1937, 6.

25 "The Principle Involved."

26 "Rowe Asks Attitude of Globe and Mail on Liquor Control," *Globe and Mail*, August 30, 1937, 1.

27 McKenty, *Mitch Hepburn*, 134

CHAPTER 10: **RADIO KILLED THE NEWSPAPER STAR**

1 Brian Young, "C. George McCullagh and the Leadership League," *Canadian Historical Review* 47, no. 3 (September 1966). 209, fn. 31

2 Editorial, *Globe and Mail*, December 13, 1938.

3 King diaries, January 6 and 25, 1938.

4 Lorne T. Morgan, "The Origins and Development of Fascism," in H.A. Innis, ed., *Essays in Political Economy* (Toronto: University of Toronto Press, 1938), 167.

5 Rowe was never tarnished by that fact, and came out of the Depression as a respected Tory elder statesman. He was appointed lieutenant-governor for a five-year term in 1963. In all his time as provincial Tory leader, he had never been able to win a seat in the legislature. He did, however, serve in the House of Commons after he lost the October 1937 election, winning a by-election.

6 For a very good explanation of Alberta Social Credit's war on the province's newspapers, see M.E. Nicholls, *(CP): The Story of Canadian Press* (Toronto: Ryerson Press, 1948), ch. 38.

7 See Roger Bird, ed., *Documents of Canadian Broadcasting* (Ottawa: Carleton University Press, 1988), 133–44 (Document 19).

8 Sandy Stewart, *A Picture History of Radio in Canada* (Toronto: Gage, 1975), 17–25.

9 See Bird, *Documents of Canadian Broadcasting*, 196–99 (Document 24).

10 *Social Justice* magazine survived until American's entry into the Second World War, and then was suppressed under the Espionage Act. Wartime laws and the Church hierarchy

forced Father Coughlin off the air for good during the war, and he lived quietly in Royal Oak until his death in 1977.

11 Alberta's oil boom would come much later. There had been oil and gas discoveries near Calgary in 1914, a short period of speculation afterwards that mostly ended in tears, and renewed interest in Alberta oil potential in the early 1930s. The Turner Valley oil field was well-known by 1936, but investment capital had dried up to the point that the oil business became a very marginal part of the provincial economy and created few jobs. The big surge in production came after the Second World War.

12 Though maybe I am being a bit hard on Social Credit, as governments freely wrote cheques to people during the recent pandemic. Social Credit's monetary policies seem utterly cerebral compared to right-wing politicians who now claim Bitcoin and other electronic currencies should supplant money issued by sovereign states.

13 The "Canadian Dainty" accent is almost extinct. It was an affected mid-Atlantic speech pattern that was popular with the country's financial and political elite, especially those centred in Toronto. It was ubiquitous among University of Toronto students, graduates and faculty. Raymond Massey, the actor, and his brother Vincent, who became governor general, affected this accent, as did actor Christopher Plummer, who morphed it into a Received Pronunciation English accent when he needed to. Actor Donald Sutherland is one of the few prominent people who still use it, though its careful diction can be picked up in the speech patterns of Justin Trudeau. This accent was one of the strongest delineators of class in Canada before the 1970s.

14 Saywell, *Just Call Me Mitch*, 366.

15 King diary, November 3, 1937. Later that month, when the talkative governor general visited Toronto, McCullagh told Tweedsmuir he'd had enough of Hepburn and would use his paper to drive the premier out of office (King diaries, November 29, 1937).

16 King diaries, July 30, 1938.

17 Drew was campaigning while his wife was pregnant. In January 1938, she gave birth to a baby boy. McCullagh, supposedly in the thrall of Drew's political opponent Mitch Hepburn, sent flowers. See Drew to McCullagh, January 22, 1938, Drew papers.

18 George McCullagh to George Drew, January 20, 1938, Drew papers.

19 King's obsession and paranoia with this visit show through in his diary entries of late October, 1938. McCullagh met with several members of King's cabinet, and the *Globe and Mail* publisher was one of the VIPs invited to a dinner at Rideau Hall by Lord Tweedsmuir (the novelist John Buchan), who became a collector of McCullagh gossip.

20 "Uck, Communist, Assails George McCullagh," *Globe and Mail*, January 17, 1939, 5.

21 "Sir Edward Beatty Urges Help for Salvation Army," *Globe and Mail*, December 8, 1938.

22 "Murray Cites CBC Policy," *Globe and Mail*, January 16, 1939.

23 "Letters Show How Ottawa Invoked Ban," *Globe and Mail*, January 17, 1939.

24 Ibid.

25 Editorial, *Globe and Mail*, January 6, 1939.

26 Permission had been refused and "The Board of Governors has instructed that no permissions for new commitments on non-basic networks shall be granted until at least after the board has received the representations of private stations at the next board meeting expected at the missile of March." ("McCullagh-CBC Feud Eclipses Radio Address Hitting Canada's Politics," Toronto *Telegram*, January 16, 1939, 1.)

27 See *Star* (Toronto), January 28, 1939, 20.

28 *Globe and Mail*, January 16, 1939. All five speeches were reprinted as booklets by the *Globe and Mail*. They are fairly scarce, but Library and Archives Canada has a complete set.

29 Irving Abella and Harold Troper chronicle the King government's abandonment of European Jews to the Nazis in their book *None Is Too Many: Canada and the Jews of Europe* (Toronto: Lester & Orpen Dennys, 1982). Closer to home, King bought up much of the land around his cottage in the Gatineau Hills to "prevent Jews or other undesirable people from getting in." (Allan Levine, quoting the King diaries, in *King: William Lyon Mackenzie King: A Life Guided by the Hand of Destiny* [Vancouver: Douglas and McIntyre, 2012], 169.)

30 Levine, *King*, 405.

31 Harkness, *J.E. Atkinson*, 292–93; Kirk Niergarth, "'No Sense of Reality.'" Niergarth is critical of Drew, but the fact remains that his take on Stalin, and on the Potemkin villages shown to high-status visitors to the Soviet Union, was much more astute than much of the journalism of the time.

32 King diaries, January 17, 1939.

33 Bartley, *The Ku Klux Klan*, 179.

34 Abella and Troper, *None Is Too Many*, 41.

35 Abella and Troper, *None Is Too Many*, 61.

36 Doyle, *Hurly-Burly*, at page 25, outs the ghost writers.

37 "Is a Citizen's Right to Hire a Hall Gone?" *Globe and Mail*, January 14, 1939. 1

38 Editorial, *Globe and Mail*, January 26, 1939.

39 "Urges Canadians Abolish Provincial Governments as Misfits and Luxuries," Toronto *Telegram*, January 23, 1939.

40 "MP Is Critical of M'Cullagh," *Globe and Mail*, January 18, 1939.

41 "Women Enjoined to Wield Influence for Political Good," *Globe and Mail*, February 6, 1939.

42 "The Leadership League" (McCullagh radio speech), *Globe and Mail*, February 13, 1939, 1. This was one of the five speeches later published by the *Globe and Mail* as a booklet.

43 Siggins and Young both describe this scene.

44 For those who can't wait, Baldwin became one of the Second World War press censors who would sometimes vex McCullagh.

45 Siggins, *Bassett*, 44.

46 Leadership League Page, *Globe and Mail*, February 27, 1939.

47 "Count Your Problems," *Globe and Mail*, February 23, 1939, 7.

48 *Globe and Mail*, February 16, 1939, 7.

49 Ibid.

50 Siggins, *Bassett*, 44.

51 Young, "C. George McCullagh and the Leadership League," 216.

52 *Globe and Mail*, March 7, 1939, 7.

53 For a description of Bassett's role in the Leadership League, see Siggins, *Bassett*, 37–45.

54 *Globe and Mail*, March 7, 1939, 7.

55 William Raynor, *1939: Canada on the Doorstep* (Toronto: Dundurn, 2011), 62–63.

56 "Ballots, Ballots, More Ballots," *Globe and Mail*, February 22, 1939.

57 *Star* (Toronto), February 3, 1936.

58 The nasty editorial comments are from Young, "The Leadership League," 218.

59 King diaries, February 27, 1939. It's not clear what Tweedsmuir meant by "young men"— whether he was talking about Bassett and McCullagh, or was referring to the young thugs who had been a key part of the movements that propelled Mussolini and Hitler into power.

60 King diaries, March 8, 1939.

61 Young, "The Leadership League," 214.

62 "A New Day in Sight," *Globe and Mail*, February 2, 1939.

63 Siggins, *Bassett*, 45.

64 Drew's clippings are part of the collection of his papers kept by Library and Archives Canada (MG 32 C3).

65 Banting did not live through the Second World War. He was killed in a plane crash in early 1941. By then, Banting had spent years working on biological weapons, research on protecting pilots flying at high altitude from suffering blackouts, and even had a finger in early atomic bomb research. His ideas on the use of gas in the Second World War are not as far-fetched as they might seem. Millions of people were gassed in Nazi Germany's death camps. The Japanese used gas in battle in China. There is a good book to be written on why Hitler—who was temporarily blinded by gas in the First World War—never unleashed his country's massive gas stocks, even when it became obvious Germany would lose the war. For a description of Banting's military work in the last years of his life, see John Bryden, *Deadly Allies: Canada's Secret War 1937–1947* (Toronto: McClelland and Stewart, 1990), especially ch. 2.

66 There will always be controversy over the death of Manfred von Richthofen. My own take: he may have been killed by ground fire as some historians claim, but Brown had him beat. The Canadian pilot was just above and behind him, and forced von Richthofen close to the ground. Whether Brown fired the kill shot is immaterial.

67 Douglas Fetherling, *The Rise of Canadian Newspapers* (Toronto: Oxford University Press, 1990), 116.

68 Siggins, *Bassett*, 69.

69 In 1942, McCullagh volunteered to restructure the hospital to make it more efficient. The hospital was closed in 2003, though some of its best programs were picked up by other downtown hospitals.

70 This was likely the celebration banquet at the National Club where McCullagh gloated over his purchase of the *Globe*.

71 "Leadership League Is Handed to People," *Globe and Mail*, March 16, 1939.

72 "Leadership League Is Handed to People."

73 King diaries, April 4, 1939.

74 "Publisher, CBC Settle Dispute," *Globe and Mail*, April 5, 1939.

CHAPTER 11: ARCHWORTH

1 Doyle, *Hurly-Burly*, 39.

2 "Torqui Wins Feature Stake at Sutton Show," *Globe and Mail*, August 10, 1937.

3 Social Notices, *Star* (Toronto), October 5, 1938, 26.

4 *Star* (Toronto) May 21, 1938, 3; *Star* (Toronto), October, 13, 1938, 14.

5 "Horse Dies in Jumping Ring 'Tried Too Hard,' Says Rider," *Star* (Toronto) September 10, 1938, 9.

6 Archworth was the foal of Wright's horses Worthmore and Archipelago.

7 "Several Bargains at Woodbine Sales," *Star* (Toronto), October 6, 1938, 12.

8 "Archworth," Canadian Horse Racing Hall of Fame, n.d., https://www.canadianhorse racinghalloffame.com/2014/05/29/archworth/.

9 "Along Turf Row," *Star* (Toronto), September 21, 1938, 23.

10 The race still exists. Now called the Cup and Saucer Stakes, it is run at Woodbine. The Long Branch racetrack closed in 1955.

11 Douglas Eppes, "Hoof Beats," *Globe and Mail*, June 2, 1938, 24.

12 Several people told a version of this quip. I got it from Ann McCullagh Hogarth, who didn't hear it herself, but was told by her father.

13 King George VI and Queen Elizabeth established a royal visit tradition, charming the Old Woodbine crowd at the 1939 Plate, won by Archworth, owned by C. George McCullagh, trained by Mark Cowell and ridden by Denny Birley. (See picture at "History of Queen's Plate," https://woodbine.com/queensplate/history-of-queens-plate; Hall of Fame, https://www.canadianhorseracinghalloffame.com/2014/05/29/archworth/.)

14 Allan Levine, *King*, 296 and King diaries, May 22, 1939. The stress of the royal visit seems to have fired up King's ever-present paranoia. Along with his suspicion that the King's Plate was fixed, King became convinced that Alan (Tommy) Lascelles, who organized George VI's tour of Canada, was conspiring with George Drew to keep King off the royal train.

15 "Mr. McCullagh Bereaved," *Globe and Mail*, May 26, 1939.

16 Meighen papers, LAC, Reference R14423-0-6-E.

17 Archworth was scheduled to race on May 27 in a handicap race against Bunty Lawless. Both owners cancelled the race, McCullagh because he was in mourning, and Bunty Lawless owner Willie Morrissey because he believed the handicappers assigned too much weight to his horse ("Plate Victor Withdrawn," *Globe and Mail*, May 27, 1939). A week later, McCullagh was competing at the Toronto Horse Show, with En Route winning "Best Horse" in a coin toss ("Horse Ties for Two Prizes, Loses Both on Coin Toss," *Globe and Mail*, June 5, 1939).

18 "Archworth," Canadian Horse Racing Hall of Fame.

19 Archworth was inducted into the Canadian Horseracing Hall of Fame in 2014.

CHAPTER 12: **GEORGE MCCULLAGH AT WAR**

1 "CG McCullagh sails today on the Mauretania," *New York Times*, July 29, 1939.

2 Doyle, *Hurly-Burly*, 28.

3 "McCullagh of the Globe had phoned to say he wished to speak to me over the phone. I sent word through secretary that I had to rest and would be glad to have any message sent through him. I am going to adopt a policy of not attempting to talk with anyone over the phone unless I ring them myself...So far as McCullagh is concerned, it is all part of the gang business that he and others associated with him have in hand. They see now that I have spiked the National Government thing for a while, and want to horn in in some other way. I have no lessons in leadership to learn from McCullagh" (King diaries, September 13, 1939). Less than a week later, King was on the phone to McCullagh to solicit the publisher's help in dumping Ian Mackenzie from his job as defence minister. Mackenzie had been the go-between for McCullagh and King during the Oshawa strike (King diaries, September 19, 1939).

4 King diaries September 20, 1939.

5 Likely King realized he couldn't lose two ministers. Power was a major Quebec politician with a large network of friends and relatives in key Liberal positions in Ottawa and Quebec City. Despite his problems with alcohol, Power turned out to be a very capable minister. His grandson, Lawrence Cannon, ran as a Conservative and was an able minister in the government of Stephen Harper before being appointed ambassador to France.

6 King diaries, September 20, 1939.

7 King diaries, September 20, 1939.

8 King diaries, October 16, 1939.

9 Quebec's French-language media was another matter. *Le Devoir* and other major publications opposed the war from the start. Many, such as *L'Action Catholique*, were pro-Mussolini and silent on Hitler.

10 King diaries, October 24, 1939.

11 King diaries, November 19, 1939.

12 "German Aim of Conquest No New Idea," *Globe and Mail*, November 20, 1939.

13 For details of the second speech, see "Plea Voiced to Wipe Out Isms' Threat," *Globe and Mail*, November 27, 1939. For what happened at the Belgian embassy dinner, see King papers, vol. 270, 229229; King diaries, Nov. 3, 1939.

14 McCullagh may have served some time as a weekend soldier in the militia, but had never achieved high rank.

15 Warren Baldwin, "Civil Servants Back Reform Cry," *Globe and Mail*, February 23, 1939, 7. Baldwin went back to work for the *Globe and Mail* on Parliament Hill after the war. It is unlikely McCullagh had any inkling of how Baldwin and his colleagues saw him.

16 Brockington turned out to be a poor choice. In 1942, the system was revamped, renamed the Wartime Information Board, and John Grierson took over. He was later run out of the job for alleged communist leanings. Canada's wartime propaganda system is ripe for a good publicly accessible study.

17 King diaries, September 15, 1939.

18 The Allies did virtually nothing to save Poland, which was, itself, a quasi-fascist dictatorship. They also stayed silent when the Soviet Union committed the same offence as Nazi Germany. Sixteen days after Hitler invaded, the Soviets seized eastern Poland. Admittedly, much of that territory had been taken from Russia in an ugly, now-forgotten campaign near the end of the Russian Civil War. Many Poles did manage to escape and fight for the Allies. Polish fliers were an important part of the RAF's order of battle during the Battle of Britain. After the war, when the Soviets occupied all of Poland, a large number of Polish veterans, many of whom had spent the war under the command of the British, fighting in western Europe, immigrated to Canada.

19 "Freedom Works Both Ways," *Globe and Mail*, November 21, 1939, 6.

20 Drew to McCullagh, November 22, 1939, Drew papers.

21 Robinson was one of the first women to win a National Newspaper Award. She was fired from the *Globe and Mail* in 1941, supposedly because of a witty comeback she made during an editorial board meeting. McCullagh told the writers he could easily talk Franklin Roosevelt into bringing the US into the war, to which Robinson answered "on whose side?" The story was told by Robert Fulford in "George McCullagh," *Globe and Mail*, April 15, 1998, 7.

22 Memorandum, Perry, December 8, 1939, LAC RG2, Privy Council Office (Records of the Directorate of Censorship), Vol. 5968, File: *The Globe and Mail*.

23 "Newspapers and the War," *Globe and Mail*, December 11, 1939, 6.

24 "Sensible Censorship Wanted," *Globe and Mail*, December 12, 1939, 6.

25 "Press Censorship in Capable Hands," *Globe and Mail*, December 13, 1939, 6.

26 The leafleteers were prosecuted by Gerald Fauteux, who later founded the University of Ottawa law school and was appointed to the Supreme Court of Canada.

27 Doyle, *Hurly-Burly*, 34–35.

28 King diaries, December 5, 1939.

29 Doyle, *Hurly-Burly*, 29.

30 "Honor is Paid To Publisher," *Globe and Mail*, December 18, 1939.

31 "Fear People Not Aroused to Top Pitch," *Globe and Mail*, January 11, 1940, 1.

32 "Drew Asks House To Sound Demand For Ottawa Action," *Globe and Mail*, January 17, 1940, 1.

33 King diaries, January 22, 1940.

34 King diaries, January 23, 1940.

35 Bruce Papers (Queen's University archives), January 31, 1940, quoted in Young, "The Leadership League," 225.

36 "Democracy Under Test," *Globe and Mail*, January 30, 1940, 6.

37 "Call Off the Censors," *Globe and Mail*, January 31, 1940, 6.

38 Final Report of the Directorate of Censorship. LAC RG2, Privy Council Office (Records of the Directorate of Censorship), Vol. 5941, (NF).

39 "Drew Holds Free Speech Threatened," *Globe and Mail*, March 1, 1940, 1.

40 Now part of the City of Toronto, in the former borough of Etobicoke.

41 "Drew Charges Censoring Here Just Like Nazis," *Globe and Mail*, March 2, 1940, 1.

42 "Manion Says Censorship of Radio Talks Carried to 'Ridiculous Heights'," *Globe and Mail*, March 2, 1940, 4.

43 "Manion Calls Vote For King Liberty Peril," *Globe and Mail*, March 4, 1.

44 "Climaxing Censorship Comedy," *Globe and Mail*, March 6, 1940, 13.

45 "Curb on Speech Is Embittering to Roy Brown," *Globe and Mail*, March 12, 1940, 1. Brown ran unsuccessfully as a Liberal in the 1943 provincial election. See *Globe and Mail*, July 22, 1943, 6.

46 Levine, *King*, 308. King's timing was, as usual, impeccable. A few months after the Canadian election, Britain's major parties agreed to continue the Depression-era National Government under Winston Churchill. The 1940 Canadian election was held before the German blitzkrieg through Norway, Denmark, the Netherlands, Belgium and France. The Tories might have done much better if the election had been held in the fall of 1940.

47 King diaries, March 14, 1940.

48 King diaries, March 15, 1940.

49 "Boland Will Also Oppose Bruce at Convention," *Star* (Toronto), February 26, 1940, 2.

50 Blackmore, a financial expert, joined the *Globe and Mail* after the war and rose to be its business editor before leaving to teach at Waterloo Lutheran (Wilfrid Laurier) University. Toronto TV watchers might remember him for financial advice spots on CFTO in the 1980s. He died in 2002. His obituary ran in the *Globe and Mail* on May 9, 2002.

51 King diaries, June 15, 1940. King spent this terrifying month at Kingsmere, trying not to crack under the stress. As the Nazis polished their boots for their march into Paris, King was writing to King George VI to demand a change in the order of precedence for cabinet ministers attending public events. King wanted this done before the arrival of the Earl of Athlone, who was replacing Tweedsmuir, who had recently died. King appointed Ralston, the finance minister, to fill Roger's spot, partly on the recommendation of Joseph Atkinson. See King diaries, June 13, 1940.

52 In fact, the election was held in 1943.

53 King diaries, March 8, 1941.

54 "Flying Officer George McCullagh Now Improving," *Globe and Mail*, February 28, 1. On May 30, 1941, the *Globe and Mail*, in a tiny story headlined "George McCullagh Posted to Reserves," reported that McCullagh's military career was effectively over.

55 The series ran June 21–30, 1941.

56 Deborah Lindsay, ed., *Ottawa at War: The Grant Dexter Memoranda* (Winnipeg: Manitoba Record Society, 1994), 186–87.

57 The author owns Gen. Charles Foulkes' set of *In Defence of Canada*, James Eayers' Governor General Award–winning four-volume study of twentieth-century Canadian military policy. Foulkes was the kind of man who marked up his books. In a chapter about government spending in the Depression, Foulkes wrote, "No navy = no commitment," which was a fair summary of King's policy. It's also a clear statement of how the generals saw King. Foulkes led the second Canadian infantry division in the Normandy campaign, organized the transfer of the Canadians in Italy to the Low Countries, and accepted the German surrender in the Netherlands on May 5, 1944.

58 Dexter memo, September 16, 1941, quoted in Lindsay, *Ottawa at War*.

59 Lindsay, *Ottawa at War*, 196.

60 Lindsay, *Ottawa at War*, 200.

61 King diaries, November 7, 1941.

62 "Guard of Honor by RCAF Contributes Military Dignity to Thornhill Garden Party," *Globe and Mail*, June 12, 1941.

63 Stalin may have put out peace feelers by then. If Soviet records of these overtures exist— a big if—they'd make the basis of a great book. Certainly, Stalin was ready to deal after Stalingrad, and Hitler, if he hadn't been a deluded sociopath, would have been smart to take him up on it. See "British Book Says German and Soviet Officieals Met in '43 to Discuss Peace," *New York Times*, January 4, 1971, https://www.nytimes.com/1971/01/04/archives/british-book-says-german-and-soviet-officials-met-in-43-to-discuss.html.

CHAPTER 13: **WARS WITHIN A WAR**

1 Doyle, *Hurly-Burly*, 40.

2 Quoted in Doyle, *Hurly-Burly*, 45.

3 Harkness, *J.E. Atkinson*, 335.

4 Greenaway, *The News Game*, 189

5 The details of the libel and the trial, along with the private apology, are from Harkness, *J.E. Atkinson*, 335–36.

6 Canada, Parliament, *House of Commons Debates (Hansard)*, March 12, 1942, 1539, and March 22, 1942 1570–71.

7 King diaries, July 8 and July 17, 1942, quoted in Saywell, *Call Me Mitch*, 486.

8 Dexter memo, January 20, 1942, quoted in Lindsay, *Ottawa at War*.

9 Dexter memo, January 20, 1942, quoted in Lindsay, *Ottawa at War*.

10 The relationship between King and Churchill was complicated, but it's clear that King saw Churchill as a loose cannon, while Churchill believed King was a nonentity without the killer instinct needed by a wartime leader. For example, when Churchill gave his "some chicken, some neck" speech to the Canadian House of Commons just six days after the fall of Hong Kong, King made it clear that he believed the speech—which received rave reviews in the English-speaking world—was too aggressive. See Lord Moran's diary entry, quoted in David Dilkes, *The Great Dominion: Winston Churchill in Canada, 1900–1954* (Toronto: Thomas Allen, 2005), 216. Churchill seems to have been appalled at the presence Vichy France's ambassador Rene Ristelhueber in the diplomat's gallery. During the speech, Churchill looked up at Ristelhueber to heap scorn on him and his government. King knew Quebec's media and political elites had a soft spot for Vichy. King also knew his government was on shaky ground with the collaborationist regime, as the Free French had just seized St. Pierre and Miquelon from Vichy using the giant monitor submarine *Surcouf*, which had been moored in Halifax. There is a chapter in my book *Fog of War* (Douglas & McIntyre, 2012) on Canada's strange relationship with Vichy.

11 Dexter memo, January 12, 1941, quoted in Lindsay, *Ottawa at War*.

12 James Eayers, *In Defence of Canada: From the Great War to the Great Depression* (Toronto: University of Toronto Press, 1964), 120.

13 Floyd S. Chalmers, *A Gentleman of the Press* (Toronto: Doubleday, 1963), 298. The story was a sensation around the world, was translated into thirty languages, and was issued as a pamphlet by the League of Nations.

14 The Royal Commission on the Canadian Expeditionary Force to the Crown Colony of Hong Kong, 1942.

15 Most scholarly work on the Hong Kong expedition concludes that Canadian troops were ill-trained and poorly equipped. See for example, Brereton Greenhouse, *"C" Force to Hong Kong: A Canadian Catastrophe* (Toronto: Dundurn, 1997) and Tony Banham, *Not the Slightest Chance: The Defence of Hong Kong, 1941* (Vancouver: UBC Press, 2003).

16 Hanson was officially the leader of the Opposition in the House of Commons, but if, by some miracle, King had called a federal election, Meighen would have been the leader in that campaign and would have become prime minister if the Tories had won.

17 King diaries, July 1, 1942.

18 Lindsay, *Ottawa at War*, 307. The Dexter memos are the best analysis of the King years written by someone close to power. Dexter wrote to his editor or the owner of the *Winnipeg Free Press* almost every day, sharing his observations and gossip from deep inside the Ottawa bubble. He kept carbon copies of these memos, which were later donated to Queen's University. Unfortunately, Queen's history department has no scholars who are interested in them, and few other historians take the time to use them.

19 King diaries, July 1, 1942.

20 Ruling, B.B. Perry, Toronto, July 16, 1942. LAC RG2, Privy Council Office (Records of the Directorate of Censorship), Vol. 5960, File: Drew Letter.

21 Memorandum, B.B. Perry, Toronto, July 16, 1942. LAC RG2, Privy Council Office (Records of the Directorate of Censorship), Vol. 5960, File: Drew Letter.

22 Memorandum, Bert Perry, July 16, 1942. LAC RG2, Privy Council Office (Records of the Directorate of Censorship), Vol. 5960, File: Drew Letter.

23 Ruling, Ottawa, Eggleston, July 17, 1942. LAC RG2, Privy Council Office (Records of the Directorate of Censorship), Vol. 5960, File: Drew Letter.

24 Memorandum, Halifax (Jefferson), July 17 1942. LAC RG2, Privy Council Office (Records of the Directorate of Censorship), Vol. 5960, File: Drew Letter.

25 Memorandum, B.B. Perry, July 21, 1942. LAC RG2, Privy Council Office (Records of the Directorate of Censorship), Vol. 5960, File: Drew Letter.

26 Dexter believed the Drew campaign over Hong Kong actually helped save King's government from the internal fight over conscription and the level of Canadian participation in the war. All the factions in cabinet and the senior ranks of the military came together in defence of the Hong Kong deployment, since there was good reason why all of them would wear it. As well, King was willing to sacrifice the West Coast Japanese-Canadians over the issue of Hong Kong, especially because of the anger generated by reports of Japanese mistreatment and murder of Canadian and allied POWs (Lindsay, *Ottawa at War*, 241).

27 All these editorial comments are from "Gagging Process of Censorship Draws Protests Across Canada," *Globe and Mail*, July 24, 1942, 6.

28 Ibid.

29 Dexter memo, June 12, 1942, quoted in Lindsay, *Ottawa at War*, 241.

30 King diaries, November 9, 1942.

31 King diaries, November 14, 1942 (miswritten as 1943).

32 King diaries, December 29, 1940.

33 Sifton received most of the Grant Dexter memos. Dafoe got the rest.

34 In fact, Bracken wanted the leadership offered to him so he could accept it on his own terms, the same way he had accepted the premiership of Manitoba from the United Farmers of Manitoba in 1922 when it elected a majority without a leader. (This also happened to the United Farmers of Ontario, who offered their leadership to E.C. Drury after their leaderless party's surprise victory in 1919.). The Tory leadership was a curse in 1942, not a gift, and Bracken knew he had to make serious changes in both policy

and organization if it was to be a contender. In the end, he failed at both. (J.W. Dafoe to Dexter, November 28, 1942, quoted in Lindsay, *Ottawa at War*).

35 Lindsay, *Ottawa at War*, 393.
36 McCullagh likely didn't know that Gen. Andrew McNaughton didn't want to break up the Canadian First Army, which was training in England, and wanted to lead it in the invasion of France. Despite the general's lobbying, Canadian troops were taken from England and sent to Sicily in July 1943, and later to Italy, before being reunited with their comrades in northern Europe in the last months of the war. By then, McNaughton was long gone.
37 "Geo. M'Cullagh Is In London; Sees Changes," *Globe and Mail*, March 8, 1943; "Publisher Sees Troops Aiding British-U.S. Ties," *Globe and Mail*, April 23, 1943.
38 McCullagh to Drew, May 14, 1943, Drew papers.
39 "George McCullagh Calls on President Roosevelt," *Globe and Mail*, May 7, 1943.
40 "R. Foster Kennedy"(obituary), *Neurology*, July 1, 1952.
41 Jamie Bradburn, "Historicist: Citizen McCullagh."
42 Hayes, *Power and Influence*.
43 Siggins, *Bassett*, 67, and Hayes, *Power and Influence*, 55.
44 Robinson and Dalgleish closed their weekly paper when the war ended. She wrote several books, was a regular freelancer for well-paying magazines, and joined the *Telegram* as its Ottawa columnist in 1953. She was the first woman to win a National Newspaper Award for political reporting. Robinson died of cancer at Glenora, in Prince Edward County, in 1961, at the age of sixty-four.
45 "George H. McCullagh, Father of Publisher," *New York Times*, September 25, 1943.
46 Drew to McCullagh, February 17, 1943; McDonald to Drew, March 1, 1943, Drew papers.
47 Memo, Stevenson to McCullagh, July 22, 1943, Drew papers.
48 Memo, Stevenson to McCullagh, July 27, 1943, Drew papers.
49 Interestingly, provincial premierships have never been a stepping stone to national power in Canada. Only one Canadian premier or former premier has become prime minister of Canada. Charles Tupper was given the Tory leadership and asked by the governor general to form a government in the spring of 1896. Voters got rid of him as fast as they could, turning him out of office in sixty-eight days. This is still the record for shortest occupancy of the job. This contrasts with the United States, where state governors frequently win the presidency.
50 Ironically, the former chair of the CBC when it was McCullagh's pre-war whipping boy.
51 Drew to McCullagh, November. 30, 1943, Drew papers; Saywell, *Call Me Mitch*, 522.
52 "Publisher Was Asked to Aid Rig Convention," *Globe and Mail*, July 30, 1943.
53 They didn't.
54 Listeners in 1943 would have heard a dog whistle here that most modern readers would miss. Quebec's Francophones were also Roman Catholics, who were objects of suspicion by the vast majority of McCullagh's listeners. Their religion was considered by the vast majority of English and Scots-Irish Canadians to be much more abhorrent and treasonous than their "race."
55 "Ontario Needs 'Unbreakable Bulwark' Against Ottawa Bureaucracy: McCullagh," *Globe and Mail*, July 4, 1943, 8.
56 King diaries, July 4, 1943.
57 "Vancouver MP Claims Drew Is Visionary," *Globe and Mail*, August 3, 1943. Mr. McGeer would have done well on social media.
58 King diaries, August 11, 1943.
59 Greenaway, *The News Game*, 184–85.

60 For the story of how Canada's hockey stars and team owners adapted to the Second World War and tried to serve their country while keeping the game alive for the benefit of civilian morale and their own careers, see Douglas Hunter, *War Games: Conn Smythe and Hockey's Fighting Men* (Toronto: Viking, 1996).

61 Editorial, *Globe and Mail*, November 28, 1943.

62 The records of this correspondence are kept by the archives of the House of Lords. See GB-061 BBK/A/240.

63 Drew to McCullagh, from Montreal, November 30 1943, Drew papers.

64 Censorship records, RG2, Privy Council Office (Records of the Directorate of Censorship), December 15, 1943.

CHAPTER 14: SENDING ZOMBIES TO WAR

1 "Honesty of Purpose Newspaper's Best Asset, Says George McCullagh," *Globe and Mail*, March 6, 1944.

2 Very roughly speaking, support for conscription was generational as well as regional. Young men like McCullagh who had not seen action in the First World War were among its most vocal proponents. Men of King and Atkinson's generation tended to oppose it, or at least be less enthusiastic. This would be the opposite of the last time the draft was an issue in North America, in the United States during the Vietnam War.

3 At least the Leafs won a game. The Canadiens swept the Chicago Black Hawks in the 1944 final. Toronto hockey fans are among the saddest, most dog-loyal in the world, but this time, "next year" actually came through, with the Leafs winning the Stanley Cup in 1945 in an exciting series against the Detroit Red Wings that went to seven games.

4 Free French and Polish units were also all-volunteer. The French, who had no government other than the collaborationist Vichy regime, and the Polish government in exile were in no position to draft anyone to fight on the side of the Allies at this point.

5 Dexter memo, September 24, 1944, in Lindsay, *Ottawa at War*. The generals believed Germany would be knocked out when Allied troops got across its borders, and were convinced the war would be over by February at the latest. This makes the Zombie issue rather moot, since the transfer of any more than a token force from Canada, along with their equipment, to the fighting front would take weeks. The use of Zombies in the Pacific theatre was not even on the table. Angus L. Macdonald, the minister in charge of the navy, believed the US didn't seriously want Canada's troops for island fighting, and they had not let the Australians go north of New Guinea. Canada expected to divert its navy, and add to it, in what was expected to be a dragged-out campaign. See Dexter memo, September 25, 1944, in Lindsay, *Ottawa at War*.

6 Chorley Park was a monstrosity that was almost in the same league as Casa Loma. Built in Rosedale just before the First World War, it was a giant mansion in the style of a Loire chateau. It cost more than $200,000 to build and $25,000 a year to maintain. Hepburn closed the place in 1937. It was briefly owned by the Hospital for Sick Children, which couldn't find a use for it. During the Second World War, it served as a hospital and as the warehouse for Red Cross packages that were shipped overseas to Canadian soldiers held as POWs. In 1960, after a long controversy about its potential uses, the mansion was torn down. The site is now a park.

7 Terry Copp, *Cinderella Army: The Canadians in Europe, 1944–1945* (Toronto: University of Toronto Press, 2006), 178–79.

8 *Globe and Mail*, October 28, 1944.

9 It would not be the last time that a letter-writer would have deep, complex feelings, backed with citations, about a publication he insisted he could no longer read. Drew papers.
10 Drew to McCullagh, November 15, 1944, Drew papers.
11 King diaries, October 25, 1944
12 King diaries, November 29, 1944
13 Atkinson seems to have changed his mind on conscription for military and political reasons. After McNaughton's loss in North Grey, Atkinson became convinced the federal Liberals would be crushed in Ontario in the upcoming election unless King changed course on conscription. See King diaries, February 10, 1945. King smoothed the waters with Atkinson by giving the *Star* publisher a powerful role in planning social policy platforms for the 1945 election, and setting aside military land at the foot of Yonge Street that was used to build a new *Star* headquarters after both men were dead. King realized Atkinson would have supported the CCF if it were not for the personal relationship they had. See King diaries, January 19, 1944, April 12, 1944, and December 24, 1946.
14 Copp, *Cinderella Army*, 179.
15 *Star* (Toronto), May 19, 1945, 28.
16 "MacLeod Attacks Drew's Policies," *Globe and Mail*, May 17, 1945.
17 George McCullagh Political Broadcast, CBC, May 31, 1945. Courtesy CBC Archive.
18 Greenaway, *The News Game*, 186.
19 Ibid.
20 See J.T. Morley, *Secular Socialists: The CCF In Ontario, A Biography* (Montreal, McGill-Queen's University Press, 1984), 50–51.
21 The case was not reported in law journals, and newspaper reports didn't dive into the issue of costs, so they left out an important part of the story. The fourteen unsuccessful plaintiffs could have been on the hook for part of the legal bills of the newspaper and the exterminator. It gets much more complicated for the two "successful" plaintiffs. The defendants may have had to pay costs to them, but only if there had never been a substantial offer to settle. Cost awards rarely cover the actual bill of the lawyers, and calculation of them vexes everyone in the legal profession. The point of all this is that someone involved may have had to write a hefty cheque. Litigation is a poker game, and a one-penny verdict is not always what it seems. For coverage of the case, see "Parley Held in Libel Action," *Globe and Mail*, December 19, 1944; "Judge Studies Move to Oust Libel Action," *Globe and Mail*, December 20, 1944; "Hear Counsel as Libel Action Nearing Close," *Globe and Mail*, January 9, 1946; "1-Cent Damages Awarded Two in Libel Suit," *Globe and Mail*, January 10, 1945. It took almost a year for the Ontario Court of Appeal to hear the case.
22 Drew to McCullagh, March 16, 1945, Drew papers.
23 King diaries, June 6, 1945.
24 King diaries, June 8, 1945
25 Lindsay, *Ottawa at War*, 502.
26 King diaries, May 8, 1947.

CHAPTER 15: **THE GREAT TORONTO NEWSPAPER WAR**

1 There was a letter in-between that is not in the Drew archival material.
2 Drew to McCullagh, February 12, 1948, Drew papers, Hong Kong file.
3 Drew to McCullagh, February 19, 1948, Drew papers, Hong Kong file.
4 This may or may not have been true. More likely, it was just one of those fortuitous events that worked out well for everyone involved except Stalin.

5 In fact, under pressure from draftees and their families, the Americans had been shipping troops home as fast as they could, while ten million Soviet troops, members of the armies that crushed Hitler, were camped behind the new Iron Curtain.

6 Telegram, Drew to McCullagh, August 2, 1947.

7 "Nine Honorary Degrees Conferred at University of Toronto,"*Globe and Mail*, Nov. 22, 1947. Cody, who had been president of the university when McCullagh was appointed to the board of governors, and chancellor after 1946, opposed McCullagh's honorary degree. It was granted after his retirement (Donald Campbell Masters, *Henry John Cody: An Outstanding Life* [Toronto: Dundurn, 1995], 287).

8 Ian Sclander, "The Beaver Comes Home," *Maclean's* January 15, 1948.

9 Drew to McCullagh, February 9, 1948, Drew papers, Hong Kong file.

10 King eventually served 7,815 days.

11 Robertson had lost two children to scarlet fever. The deaths devastated him and his wife, and they devoted the rest of their lives, and almost all their fortune, to raising money for children's charities. The Robertsons were also backers of public health initiatives, like milk pasteurization.

12 Berton, "The Amazing Career of George McCullagh," 8.

13 Cooke's name may be familiar to readers from his later ownership of major sports franchises in Canada and the United States, including the Washington Redskins, the Los Angeles Lakers and the Los Angeles Kings.

14 "Rumor Wm. H. Wright to Pay $7 million for Telegram," *Star* (Toronto), July 31, 1947, 4.

15 "Employees Make Offer on Telegram," *Star* (Toronto), October 29, 1948.

16 Southam had papers in Montreal, Ottawa, Hamilton, Winnipeg, Calgary, Edmonton and Vancouver. The only other papers in that league were the independent *Halifax Herald*, the *Montreal Star*, the *Ottawa Journal*, the *Kingston Whig Standard*, the *London Free Press*, the *Winnipeg Free Press* and the *Vancouver Province*.

17 Siggins, *Bassett*, 65.

18 Toronto *Telegram*, December 1, 1948.

19 The *Record* would later be purchased by Conrad Black, maintaining its tradition of ownership by rich young men on the make. It was, in its heyday, one of the best newspapers in Canada, attracting talent because of its location in a gorgeous part of Canada that's within an easy drive of Montreal.

20 Siggins, *Bassett*, 18

21 Val Sears, *Hello Sweetheart, Get Me Rewrite: The Last of the Great Newspaper Wars* (Toronto: Key Porter, 1988), 18–19, After McCullagh's time, the *Telegram* would move into a flashy building west of the downtown, at 444 Front Street West. That building would, after 1970, be the headquarters of the *Globe and Mail*. The *Telegram*'s owners kept the old Melinda Street building and loaned it to the founders of the *Toronto Sun*. The building may have been antiquated, but it did sit on the most expensive real estate in Canada. The new building is also gone, demolished in 2015 to make space for a condominium project.

22 John Bassett interview with Peter Stursberg, 1975, Stursberg fonds, LAC MG 31 D78 Vol. 13.

23 Sears, *Hello Sweetheart*, 19.

24 Sears, *Hello Sweetheart*, 25.

25 Lytle was the grandfather of Toronto journalist Christie Blatchford.

26 The fight must have happened in the previous year's season, when Juzda was a Ranger. There seems to have been no hard feelings, because Juzda was signed to play for the Leafs starting in the 1947/48 season. He won two Stanley Cups with the Leafs, in 1949 and 1951. He retired in 1952 and died in 2008.

27 The entire rebuttal to Lytle is from Jim Coleman (column), *Globe and Mail*, June 7, 1948, 16. There's a quip that journalism is the chosen profession of the smartest people of the working class. This was not the case with Coleman, whose father, Dalton, was president of the Canadian Pacific Railway. In his youth, the senior Coleman was a journalist, and fostered his son's determination to become a sportswriter. Jim Coleman had a seventy-year career in the newspaper business.

28 Berton, *My Times*, 42. Unfortunately, we'll likely never know whether the date led to anything interesting, or if they just divided up the money, skipped dinner and went home alone, with each other, or with someone else..

29 "Fellow Newsman," *Globe and Mail*, August 6, 1952.

30 Doyle, *Hurly-Burly*, 40; Robert Fulford, *Best Seat in the House: Memoirs of a Lucky Man* (Toronto: Harper Collins, 1998), 42. Rosenfeld's name was stripped from the National Newspaper Award for sportswriting in 2022 because of racially insensitive columns she wrote at the *Globe and Mail*.

31 Sears, *Hello Sweetheart*, 22

32 Siggins, *Bassett*, 73.

33 See Siggins, *Bassett*, 68, for a description of Bert Buckland and his role in McCullagh's newspapers.

34 "Canada: ONTARIO: Big Business," *Time*, December 6, 1948.

35 Toronto *Telegram*, December 10, 1948.

36 Toronto *Star*, December 11, 1949. The *Telegram* and *Star* slagging match is described in Siggins, *Bassett*, 66.

37 Berton, *My Times*, 42. Many Canadian publishers were unimpressed with *Time*'s assault on the Canadian market, and, eventually, the government responded by setting new rules for foreign magazines that are sold in Canada. Eventually, the Canadian magazine industry settled for direct subsidies and the federal government lifted the restrictions on US imports. If you want to know how well that's worked out, visit your local magazine stand.

38 "Canada: ONTARIO: Big Business," *Time*.

39 The paper boys incident comes from Harkness, *J.E. Atkinson*, 354.

40 Berton, *My Times*, 9.

41 Walker-Stursberg interviews, July 1979, Stursberg fonds, LAC MG 31 D7 Vol. 38. The material about the apartment in New York comes from a letter from McCullagh in the Beaverbrook papers held by the Parliamentary Archives of the United Kingdom, GB-061, BBK-A and BBK-H.

42 Berton biographer A.B. McKillop specifically credits the McCullagh piece for the honing of Berton's investigative skills and Berton's realization that he could research a biography without the participation of, or even in the teeth of opposition from, the subject of the piece. See A.B. McKillop, *Pierre Berton: A Biography* (Toronto: McClelland and Stewart, 2008), 243–44.

CHAPTER 16: **FIGHTING HOLY JOE'S GHOST**

1 King diaries, May 10, 1948.

2 King diaries, May 11, 1948.

3 King says in his May 10, 1948, diary entry that he remembered meeting Atkinson to talk about the plan but was shocked to learn, after Atkinson's death, of the magnitude of the foundation bequest. In fact, Atkinson spelled out the entire plan in a long meeting with King on April 19, 1943, when he told King that the *Star* would be left to a foundation. That enterprise would use the *Star*'s profits to fund charities.

4 Harkness, *J.E. Atkinson,* 350.

5 Harkness, *J.E. Atkinson,* 355

6 Quoted in Harkness, *J.E. Atkinson,* 355.

7 Despite Boyd's dangerous line of work and his frequent trips to prison, he lived to be an old man, dying in 2002 at the age of eighty-seven.

8 Harkness, *J.E. Atkinson,* 360.

9 Tory had quarterbacked the deal for the *Telegram.* When the claim about Tory was made in the legislature on April 6, 1949, provincial treasurer Leslie Frost equivocated (*Star* (Toronto), April 6, 1949). Tory flat-out denied he had any hand in the drafting of the bill or the cabinet discussions beforehand (*Globe and Mail,* April 7, 1949).

10 *Globe and Mail,* March 28, 1949.

11 *Globe and Mail* (front page editorial), March 21, 1949.

12 Harkness, *J.E. Atkinson,* 357.

13 *Star* (Toronto), March 30, 1949.

14 *Star* (Toronto), April 6, 1949.

15 Quoted in Harkness, *J.E. Atkinson,* 357.

16 Roy Greenaway, *The News Game,* 186.

17 Frost never seriously tried to enforce the Charitable Gifts Act. In early 1958, the trustees bought the paper. They issued voting stock to themselves and sold non-voting stock to outside investors and employees. In the end, the foundation received about $20 million, a great fortune in mid-twentieth-century dollars. It has used the money for many good works in Canada. The trustees took an oath in the Ontario Supreme Court that the paper would always adhere to Atkinson's social and economic values. That share structure survived until 2020, when the paper was sold to two Toronto private equity investors and its shares were delisted. The new owners promised to maintain the Atkinson Principles. Interestingly, during the so-called WE Charity Scandal of 2020, *Toronto Star* journalists had no corporate memory of their own newspaper being used as a fundraiser in Atkinson's social enterprise charity, or that the *Telegram* had been one for years.

18 Siggins, *Bassett,* 54.

19 Although McCullagh had a reserve rank in the air force and had trained as an officer cadet, it doesn't appear that he got his pilot's licence. The Grummand Mallard was flown by a professional pilot on McCullagh's staff. It was an expensive plane, with a list price of about US$150,000. The plane was popular with people like McCullagh, who liked to fly into wilderness areas to fish, and with rich Englishmen who used them to get to their Caribbean retreats. The plane somewhat resembles a military PBY flying boat. The presidents of General Motors and Freuhauf Trailers owned Mallards, as did the Aga Khan and King Farouk of Egypt, an impressive sales record for a plane that was only sold for five years. In commercial use, the plane could hold eighteen passengers and two flight crew members. Like other flying boats, the Mallard was deceptively safe-looking, but could stall easily if a pilot miscalculated the wind direction on takeoff or landing.

20 It seems the man was never without a cigarette. He's holding one in a studio portrait taken just after the First World War and used in the *Saturday Night* article. He seems to be making a small effort to hide it, but it's there.

21 Interview with Ann McCullagh Hogarth by telephone, February 13, 2012.

22 Siggins, *Bassett,* 73.

23 Siggins, *Bassett,* 74.

24 Conn Smythe built the Gardens and had created the team as we know it—except for the fact that, back then, it won—but never had enough money to get full control. Ownership

was split with the original owners of the St. Pats and the Campbell family. Smythe doesn't seem to have held a grudge over McCullagh's attempt to get control.

25 William Wright obituary, *Star* (Toronto), September 20, 1951.

26 Ken Taggart, George McCullagh obituary, *Globe and Mail*, August 6, 1952.

27 "Fellow Newsman," *Globe and Mail*, August 6, 1952.

28 "Lights of London Fail to Brighten Public Spirit," *Globe and Mail*, April 21, 1949.

29 Most of the German immigrants to that part of Ontario had arrived in the nineteenth century, but German was still the first or second language of many of the people who lived in Kitchener, Waterloo County, and parts of neighbouring Pert and Oxford. Germans who did settle in Ontario after the war tended to spread out across the country. Some former POWs even went back to northern Ontario, having, for some reason, taken a shine to that part of Canada.

30 Radio speech, September 6, 1949. The text was reprinted in the *Globe and Mail* the next day.

31 Radio speech, September 6, 1949.

32 "McCullagh Goes on Air to Answer Mud-Slingers," *Globe and Mail*, June 23, 1939.

CHAPTER 17: **DREW FLAMES OUT**

1 Siggins, *Bassett*, 70.

2 Siggins, *Bassett*, 70–71.

3 Jean Chrétien, a lawyer of similar instincts and interests, and of the same kind of limited policy imagination, knew enough to mimic St. Laurent's common-man schtick, and kept a bust of St. Laurent outside his parliamentary office on the third floor of the Centre Block of the Parliament Buildings.

4 *Toronto Star*, June 23, 1949.

5 The full text of the radio speech was printed in the June 26, 1949, editions of the *Telegram* and the *Globe and Mail*, starting on p. 1.

6 Siggins, *Bassett*, 72.

7 "Liberals Allowing Star To Avoid $108,000 Tax Free CBC Time, too, in Special Privileges, McCullagh Discloses," *Globe and Mail*, June 25, 1949, 1.

8 See, for example, "2 Georges Campaign Against Aircraft Trade," *Globe and Mail*, June 11, 1945, and "St. Laurent's Utterances on Sinister Friendships Unworthy of His Office," *Globe and Mail*, June 23, 1939.

9 "Drew Victory Reception Overflows Massey Hall," *Globe and Mail*, June 24, 1949.

10 Robert Lewis, *Power, Prime Ministers and the Press: The Battle for Truth on Parliament Hill* (Toronto: Dundurn: 2018), 130–31. Lewis was drawing heavily on Peter Dempson's *Assignment Ottawa: Seventeen Years in the Press Gallery* (Toronto: General Publishers, 1968). For an excellent analysis of the ugly *Star-Telegram* election fight, see Sidney Katz, "How Toronto's Evening Papers Slanted Election News," *Maclean's*, August 15, 1949.

11 Dempson's *Assignment Ottawa*, quoted in Lewis, *Power, Prime Ministers and the Press*, 129–30.

12 He finally gave up all hopes of a comeback during the Diefenbaker years, when he was given the very cushy job of Canadian High Commissioner to Great Britain.

CHAPTER 18: **DYING AND STAYING VERY DEAD**

1 McCullagh had been awarded an honorary doctorate from the University of Toronto the previous fall.

2 "Jolliffe Claims Publisher Guilty of Union Busting," *Globe and Mail*, April 7, 1950.

3   "Board Vindicates Publisher, Intimidation Charge Fails," *Globe and Mail*, June 23, 1950. The guild was certified in the *Telegram* newsroom when John Bassett took over the paper in the fall of 1952. The *Globe and Mail* was unionized in 1955, when the paper was sold to the Webster family of Montreal.

4   "Globe and Mail Founder, Pioneer, Philanthropist, Veteran of Two Wars. William Wright Dies," *Globe and Mail*, September 21, 1951.

5   Unavoidable until 1972, when Ontario became one of the very few jurisdictions in the developed world to get rid of its inheritance tax. The province does charge for probate, but the cost is nowhere near the taxes paid on the Wright estate.

6   Toni Williams, "The Long Wait of Bill Wright's Heirs: 80 Hit the Jackpot in 2041," *Maclean's*, May 5, 1962. Since many of the heirs of Bill Wright were alive and well in 1962, and the author almost certainly had no way of foretelling the date of their deaths, the 2041 date is pure speculation. Nor could she have any idea of the reproductive rate of Wright's heirs, so there may be eighty heirs when the money is finally divided. Or there maybe one lucky winner. Or none, which means another big payday for the lawyers.

7   Barnes, *Fortunes in the Ground*, 175.

8   Barnes, *Fortunes in the Ground*, 221.

9   As of 2020, they have their own Facebook page under "Wright-Hargreaves."

10 Siggins, *Bassett*, 73.

11 Interview with Ann McCullagh Hogarth, June 9, 2020.

12 Kimber, who'd also been part of a conspiracy of major publishers to break the newspaper unions, got the job for real when McCullagh died and held it until the paper was sold in 1955. He died in 1966. Bruce West wrote a moving column about Kimber at the time of his death. See "A Man's Monument," *Globe and Mail*, February 7, 1966. He wrote a similar piece in 1952 when McCullagh died, which is discussed below.

13 Doyle, *Hurly-Burly*, 83.

14 Editorial, *Globe and Mail*, August 6, 1952.

15 "George McCullagh Dies: Belief in Democracy Publisher's Beacon," *Globe and Mail*, August 6, 1952, 1.

16 "Fellow Newsman," *Globe and Mail*, August 6, 1952.

17 York University Archives, Larry Zolf Fonds, Collection 0110, "Conversations With Canadians," Call Number: 1995-013/018.

18 Richard Cockett, ed, *My Dear Max: The Letters of Brendan Bracken to Lord Beaverbrook, 1925–1958* (London: Historians Press 1990), 132.

19 "C. George McCullagh Telegram AND Globe Publisher, Dies at 47," Toronto *Star*, August 6, 1942, 1.

20 Sadly, all but three of these papers are now out of business.

21 All the quotes from prominent Canadians and from the newsboys are from "Tributes Flow in For George McCullagh," *Globe and* Mail, August 6, 1952. For an interesting account of the newsboys and their association, see Ellen Scheinberg, "Paper Pushers," in John Lorinc et al, eds., *The Ward: The Life and Loss of Toronto's First Immigrant Neighbourhood* (Toronto: Coach House Press, 2015), 215.

22 Quoted in Siggins, *Bassett*, 55.

23 *Star* (Toronto), September 20, 1952, 7.

24 Interview with Ann McCullagh Hogarth, February 13, 2012.

INDEX